MW01590867

The Proper Tax Base

Series on International Taxation

VOLUME 39

Founding Editors

Richard Doernberg, Kees van Raad and Klaus Vogel †

Senior Editor

Professor Dr Kees van Raad,
International Tax Center, University of Leiden

Managing Editors

Professor Ruth Mason,
University of Connecticut School of Law
Professor Dr Ekkehard Reimer,
University of Heidelberg

The titles published in this series are listed at the end of this volume.

The Proper Tax Base

Structural Fairness from an International
and Comparative Perspective—Essays
in Honor of Paul McDaniel

Edited by

Yariv Brauner

Martin James McMahon, Jr.

Wolters Kluwer
Law & Business

Published by:
Kluwer Law International
PO Box 316
2400 AH Alphen aan den Rijn
The Netherlands
Website: www.kluwerlaw.com

Sold and distributed in North, Central and South America by:
Aspen Publishers, Inc.
7201 McKinney Circle
Frederick, MD 21704
United States of America
Email: customer.service@aspenpublishers.com

Sold and distributed in all other countries by:
Turpin Distribution Services Ltd.
Stratton Business Park
Pegasus Drive, Biggleswade
Bedfordshire SG18 8TQ
United Kingdom
Email: kluwerlaw@turpin-distribution.com

Printed on acid-free paper.

ISBN 978-90-411-3286-4

© 2012 Kluwer Law International BV, The Netherlands

Printed and Bound by CPI Group (UK) Ltd, Croydon, CR0 4YY.

Summary of Contents

Summary of Contents

Table of Contents

Table of Contents

Preface

Paul McDaniel was a dedicated tax scholar with an intellectual interest and in-depth mastery covering a wide range of tax issues. He was most well-known for his work with Stanley Surrey in developing tax expenditure analysis[1] and later as a leading international tax scholar and teacher, but he also wrote on many other diverse topics, ranging from domestic budget issues,[2] charitable contribution deductions,[3] estate and gift tax issues[4] to tax policy choices in support of developing countries,[5] the interaction of trade and tax laws,[6] and taxation and human rights.[7]

In all of his works, Paul McDaniel sought, first and foremost, academic integrity and rigorous analysis. More importantly, in everything he did in life he advocated above all else fairness to everyone. It is symbolic therefore that this book that

---

1. See, e.g., "The Tax Expenditure Concept in the International Context," *Maandblad Belasting-beschouwingen*, 47e Jaargang no. 2–3, p. 115 (February, March 1978), S. Surrey & P. McDaniel, "The Tax Expenditure Concept and the Legislative Process," in *The Economics of Taxation*, ed. H. Aaron & M. Boskin 123 (Washington, D.C.: The Brookings Institution, 1980); S. Surrey & P. McDaniel, *Tax Expenditures* (Cambridge, Mass.: Harvard University Press, 1985).
2. See, e.g., "Tax Expenditures as Tools of Government Action" in *Beyond Privatization: The Tools of Government Action*, ed. L. Salamon (Washington, D.C.: The Urban Institute Press, 1989); S. Surrey & P. McDaniel, "Tax Expenditures: How to Identify Them; How to Control Them," *Tax Notes* 15(1982): 595.
3. See, e.g., "The Charitable Contribution Deduction (Revisited)," *Southern Methodist University Law. Review* 59 (2006): 773.
4. See, e.g., "Estate Planning Problems Created by Oil and Gas Interests," *Oklahoma. Law. Review.* 15 (1962): 381.
5. See "The U.S. Tax Treatment of Income Earned in Developing Countries," *George Washington. International Law. Review* 35 (2003): 265.
6. See, e.g., "Trade and Taxation," *Brooklyn Journal of International Law* 26 (2001): 1621.
7. See, e.g., "Taxation and Human Rights (North America)" in *Taxation and Human Rights, Proceedings of a Seminar held in Brussels in 1987* during the 41st Congress of the International Fiscal Association (Deventer: Kluwer Law and Taxation Publishers, 1988) 7.

started as a celebratory project in his honor, and unfortunately became a memorial composition, focuses on the quest for the "fair" tax base.

Part I is devoted to Paul McDaniel's most notable, and most voluminous, body of work—the analysis of tax expenditures and their exposure in the federal budget process, including the invention of the tax expenditures budget.

The book begins with Paul's last scholarly work: "The Staff of the Joint Committee on Taxation Revision of Tax Expenditure Classification Methodology: What is to be Made of a Change That Makes No Changes?," published posthumously by the Canadian Tax Foundation in 2011.[8] In this chapter, Paul McDaniel continued his lifelong pursuit of transparence in the Federal budget process through a normative and balanced tax expenditure budget construction. The chapter criticizes the attempt by the Staff of the Joint Committee on Taxation to revise the tax expenditure budget analytical model in a manner that was viewed by Paul McDaniel as unprincipled, lacking true progress, and potentially detrimental to the original goals of the original project.

Chapter 2, "Taxing Tax Expenditures," written by Martin J. McMahon, Jr. follows naturally, recounting the history of the development of tax expenditure analysis and its enshrinement in the U.S.' federal budget process and explaining the core values of tax expenditure analysis. The chapter examines the proposition that tax expenditure subsidies should be taxed in the same manner that direct subsidies would be taxed under a Schantz-Haig-Simons normative income tax. It concludes, however, that taxing tax expenditures may not be administratively feasible in all cases. The chapter further criticizes recent calls for extensive revisions to tax expenditure analyses methodology, arguing that most, if not all of the failures of the income tax system as it exists today, derive from the failure of the political process to appreciate and apply the wisdom of tax expenditures analysis as developed by Stanley Surrey and Paul McDaniel.

Chapter 3, "The Tax Expenditure Concept Globally," written by Miranda Stewart, is devoted to another facet of Paul McDaniel's work on tax expenditures, highlighting his leadership in the comparative analysis of tax expenditures. Since the 1980s, many developed countries have established comprehensive tax expenditure reporting, and the current state of play is evidenced by a 2010 Organisation for Economic Co-operation and Development (OECD) report. Some developing countries also carry out tax expenditure reporting, a measure that is recommended by the International Monetary Fund (IMF) in its Code for Fiscal Transparency of 2007 and by the World Bank. However, in spite of this expansion of use of the concept, many developing countries do not report tax expenditures, and many issues remain for those countries that do report them. This chapter surveys the global use of tax expenditure analysis and reporting, and focuses in particular on the increase in tax expenditure reporting in developing countries. It discusses tax expenditure reporting in Chile, South Africa, and India and considers the purpose and value of tax expenditure reporting for governments and civil society, the

---

8. In L. Philipps, N. Brooks & J. Li (eds.), *Tax Expenditures: State of the Art* (Toronto: Canadian Tax Foundation, 2011): 3:6–3:13.

associated difficulties, and the issues and challenges that must be overcome to achieve meaningful tax expenditure reporting.

Chapter 4, "Tax Reform and Tax Expenditures in Australia," written by Richard J. Vann, considers the strengths and weaknesses of the tax expenditure concept as a tool for tax reform. It does that while Australia completes a substantial review of its tax system called Australia's Future Tax System (AFTS), and although not as fiscally pressed as many other countries, is proceeding with some substantial changes to the tax system and is contemplating others. Tax expenditure analysis makes little or no appearance in the AFTS report on these fundamental issues regarding the tax system, although the underlying idea of taxing income from different sources in the same manner is influential at various points. The chapter critiques some of the conclusions of the report, using insights from tax expenditures analysis, to portray a realistic view of a potential tax reform in Australia. It further argues that despite the utility of modern welfare economics in formulating tax reform proposals, the simplified slogans used in its name are less justifiable bases for tax reform, and hence expresses preference for a tax expenditure analysis as a practical platform for tax law reform.

Chapter 5, "Tax Reform Paul McDaniel Style: The Repeal of the Grantor Trust Rules," written by Laura E. Cunningham and Noël B. Cunningham, analyzes a more specific tax reform proposal, this time in the United States. In this chapter also critically examines tax reform methodology, expressing appreciation of Paul McDaniel's contribution to the study of tax law reform. The chapter focuses on the so-called grantor trust rules, which once were an important structural provision of the U.S. federal income tax, that were designed to prevent wealthy, high tax-bracket taxpayers from retaining control of their assets while shifting the income from those assets to lower tax-bracket trusts. Given the sharp reduction in maximum tax rates, and the flattening of the rate brackets applicable to trusts, the grantor trust rules no longer play a useful role. The chapter asserts that they are being used, however, to avoid transfer taxes on enormous amounts of wealth. It concludes that they are clearly not tax expenditures, they are structural provisions of the Internal Revenue Code that must stand up to scrutiny on equity grounds, which they clearly cannot do. They are therefore ripe for repeal in a Paul McDaniel style tax reform.

Part II focuses on Paul McDaniel's quest for a fair tax base in the context of a substantive tax reform. Paul McDaniel has covered various angles of tax reform in the United States, and participated in several discourses, some of which contributed to actual reforms of the U.S. federal income tax laws. This part covers three fundamental issues related to these discourses.

Chapter 6, "Horizontal Equity Revisited," written by James Repetti and Diane Ring, contributes to a discourse in which Paul McDaniel and James Repetti participated in the early 1990s regarding the utility of the notion of "horizontal equity" in the tax reform analysis.[9] This contribution followed the original debate

---

9. See "Horizontal Equity and Vertical Equity: The Musgrave/Kaplow Exchange," *Florida. Tax Review* 1 (1993): 607.

between economists Robert Musgrave and Louis Kaplow. Musgrave argued that while horizontal equity is met by satisfaction of the various criteria for vertical equity, this equivalency does not mean that it is derived from it; he concluded that that horizontal equity is a stronger primary rule. Kaplow, on the other hand, argued that horizontal equity simply is not a useful tool for tax policy analysis because it has no normative content and no significance apart from vertical equity. In this chapter, following the above-mentioned former contribution by McDaniel and Repetti, argues for a different perspective and formulates the role of horizontal equity in tax reform in the context of distributive justice, where, Repetti and Ring argues, it makes an important contribution, although only in that context.

Chapter 7, "What is this Thing Called Source?," written by Lawrence Lokken, explores the international tax norm concept of "income source." which divides tax bases between competing jurisdictions. Source rules, although evolving to be fairly universal in design and even in substance, pose challenges in contemporary international tax practice because they represent explicit legal compromises and simplified formulae that clearly diverge from the underlying economic activity to which they apply. This is particularly problematic when the current U.S. international tax regime is heavily based on a pseudo-economic rhetoric. This chapter proposes that the U.S. statutory source rules and their practical application could be improved by a statement of an overall conception underlying these rules. The chapter further provides such a conception. It explains why neither the ability to pay principle nor the benefit principle, standing alone, can be the basis for these rules. Rather, it suggests, combining them—apportioning a taxpayer's ability to pay among the competing jurisdictions in a way that reflects the relevant benefits they receive from such jurisdictions.

Chapter 8, "Formula Based Transfer Pricing," written by Yariv Brauner, argues that the current debate over the reform of the taxation of cross-border business income between supporters of formulary taxation and those of the existing system masks, and hence interferes with, the more urgent, yet lesser in scope, reform of the current international transfer pricing regime. The chapter supports reforming the international tax rules applying to cross-border business income to apply formulary apportionment,[10] and demonstrates that the majority of the arguments against such a reform do not apply, or are significantly weaker, in light of the collapse of the current arm's length based international transfer pricing regime. The chapter further discusses design premises and concerns for U.S.' policy makers when they approach this reform.

Part III is a tribute to Paul McDaniel's deep interest and knowledge of the tax laws of countries other than the United States, and his particular interest in the development of international tax law in Europe.

Chapter 9, "The EU proposed CCCTB—Some tax treaty issues," written by Kees van Raad, examines the tax treaty implications of one of the most important

---

10. Paul McDaniel had also been a strong advocate of formulary international tax reform. See, e.g., "Formulary Taxation in the North American Free Trade Zone," *Tax Law Review* 49 (1994): 691.

recent developments in European tax law—the proposal to adopt a European wide common consolidated corporate tax base (CCCTB), with a view to significantly mitigating administrative and compliance costs for multinational enterprises that operate in Europe. The chapter exposes some of the challenges that the proposal, which is based on formulary apportionment, poses to taxpayers in cases where tax treaties, which typically are based on the arm's length principle to allocate income between related parties that are taxpayers in two different jurisdictions, apply. The chapter concludes that creativity on the side of the European Union and flexibility on the side of non-Member States are required to overcome these difficulties. In support of the proposal, the chapter reiterates that it is important that these cross-border issues are solved because their solution will control whether CCCTB has a future.

Chapter 10, "Shared Legal Orders: Some Thoughts about the Influence of EU Case Law on International Tax Law Rules of the EU Member States," written by Irene J.J. Burgers, asks how the case law of the European Court of Justice (ECJ) affects the international tax laws of the Member States. The chapter focuses on the application of the exemption method and the transfer pricing rules. It asserts that at first sight EU Treaty and international tax laws clash in that the EU Treaty prohibits different tax treatment of cross-border situations whereas international tax law treats resident and nonresident taxpayers differently. Yet, both legal regimes may learn from each other. The chapter elaborates on several lessons that these legal regimes may adopt from each other.

Chapter 11, "Intra-Group Loans—a Swedish Perspective," written by Bertil Wiman, focuses on the application of the Swedish arm's length pricing principle in a recent domestic case, which recognized that the group relationship might, for various reasons, warrant an "arm's length" price that differs from an "arm's length" price between unrelated companies, and discusses whether that decision is applicable to cross-border transactions under Chapter 14, section 19 of the Swedish Income Tax Act (ITA) and the 1995 OECD Transfer Pricing Guidelines for Multinational Enterprises and Tax Administrations. The chapter concludes that domestic Swedish case should be narrowly applied only to loans between related Swedish parties. It should not be applied to cross-border loans, because the Swedish arm's length provision governs, and the wording of that provision, interpreted in light of the discussion in the OECD Transfer Pricing Guidelines, does not support considering the group relationship as a factor in determining an "arm's length" price.

Chapter 12, "European VAT and Jurisdiction to Tax," written by Antonio Vázquez del Rey, focuses on the European Value Added Tax, the world's most popular version of a consumption tax, and the one that is effectively harmonized by EU law, in contrast to the income tax that is not harmonized under EU law. The chapter explains the features of VAT that result in taxing end-user consumption indirectly, through production or sales taxes levied on the producer or the supplier of goods or services, which successively shift the tax burden of taxation forward to the customer, ultimately to be borne by final consumer. The EU VAT thus is first and foremost a general tax on consumption. Under the VAT, the territoriality principle implies that only those taxable events that take place within the territory of the State are subject to taxation. A key determination is therefore the place of supply, which can be particularly challenging when more than one tax jurisdiction is involved, e.g., where goods are produced in one State but consumed in another. If both States assert place-of-supply status double taxation can result. In order to determine which jurisdiction is entitled to apply the VAT to the transaction, the literature has traditionally relied on the principles of origin and destination. The "destination principle" implies that goods are taxed where they are actually consumed, regardless of the jurisdiction where they have been produced or manufactured. From this derives taxation upon imported goods, while exported goods benefit from a tax refund. By contrast, the "origin principle" implies that goods are taxed in the jurisdiction where they have been produced, regardless of the place where they are to be consumed. As a result, imports are not subject to tax while exports remain taxed, i.e., the exporter does not benefit from a tax refund. The primary characterization of VAT as a tax on consumption justifies that, when dealing with international trade, the legal structure greatly relies on the destination principle. The chapter rigorously explores the meaning of this principles and its importance in the context of jurisdiction to tax.

Martin J. McMahon, Jr. and Yariv Brauner
Gainesville, Florida, USA
2011.

Part I

Tax Expenditures

Chapter 1

The Staff of the Joint Committee on Taxation Revision of Tax Expenditure Classification Methodology: What Is To Be Made of a Change That Makes No Changes?*

Paul R. McDaniel**

In May 2008, the staff of the Joint Committee on Taxation (the "JCT" staff) issued a report, *A Reconsideration of Tax Expenditure Analysis*, that proposed a new two-part methodology to determine whether any particular provision of the Internal Revenue Code would be classified as a tax expenditure. According to the JCT staff, the existing tax expenditure analysis, which was based primarily on deviations from the Schanz-Haig-Simons definition of income and had been in use since 1968, did not "advance either of the two goals that inspired its original proponents: clarifying the aggregate size and application of government expenditures, and

---

* Reproduced with the permission of the Canadian Tax Foundation from, Paul R. McDaniel, "The Staff of the Joint Committee on Taxation Revision of Tax Expenditure Classification Methodology: What Is To Be Made of a Change That Makes No Changes?," in *Tax Expenditures: State of the Art*, ed. Lisa Philipps, Neil Brooks & Jinyan Li (Toronto: Canadian Tax Foundation, 2011), 3:1–3:13.

** (Deceased.) James J. Freeland Eminent Scholar in Taxation and Professor of Law Emeritus, University of Florida Levin College of Law.

Yariv Brauner & Martin James McMahon, Jr. (eds), *The Proper Tax Base: Structural Fairness from an International and Comparative Perspective—Essays in Honour of Paul McDaniel*, pp. 3–15.
© 2012 Kluwer Law International BV, The Netherlands.

improving the Internal Revenue Code." This chapter reviews the structure of historic tax expenditure analysis and its role in legislative policy making. It concludes that the rationale of the JCT staff for adopting a new methodology did not justify the change, and that the methodology recommended by the JCT staff in its 2008 report is inferior to the historic methodology used to identify tax expenditures, particularly in light of the fact that the "new" methodology resulted only in the elimination of two items from the list of tax expenditures.

1.1   INTRODUCTION

In May 2008, the Staff of the Joint Committee on Taxation (the JCT staff) issued the report, *A Reconsideration of Tax Expenditure Analysis*.[1] The report was occasioned by the perceived deficiencies of the existing tax expenditure analysis (utilized since 1968), which, according to the JCT staff, did not "advance either of the two goals that inspired its original proponents: clarifying the aggregate size and application of government expenditures, and improving the Internal Revenue Code."[2] Accordingly, the JCT staff proposed a new two-part methodology for classifying a particular Code[3] provision as a tax expenditure.

On October 31, 2008, the JCT staff issued its annual *Estimates of Federal Tax Expenditures for Fiscal Years 2008–2012*,[4] employing the classification methodology discussed in its earlier report.

In this chapter, I analyze and critique the approach adopted by the JCT staff. There are four main sections. In the first section, I detail the methodology historically used to classify Code provisions either as part of the normal structure of an income tax or as a tax expenditure. The second section sets forth the new methodology adopted by the JCT staff. In the third section, the reasons given for the JCT staff changes are critiqued and found wanting. The fourth section presents my conclusions.

1.2   METHODOLOGY HISTORICALLY USED TO CLASSIFY CODE PROVISIONS

A tax system has six essential elements:

   (1) definition of the tax base;
   (2) establishment of generally applicable tax rates;

---

1. United States, Staff of the Joint Committee on Taxation, *A Reconsideration of Tax Expenditure Analysis*, JCX-37-08 (Washington, DC: US Government Printing Office, May 12, 2008) (herein referred to as "the JCT Staff Report").
2. *Ibid.*, 1.
3. Internal Revenue Code of 1986, as amended (herein referred to as "the Code").
4. United States, Staff of the Joint Committee on Taxation, *Estimates of Federal Tax Expenditures for Fiscal Years 2008–2012*, JCS-2-08 (Washington, DC: US Government Printing Office, Oct. 31, 2008) (herein referred to as "the 2008 tax expenditure estimates").

(3) definition of the taxable unit;
(4) establishment of accounting rules, including the taxable period, to be applied;
(5) adoption of an international tax system; and
(6) adoption of necessary administrative procedures.

Tax expenditures can be introduced in any of these basic elements. But, obviously, different criteria for classification of provisions as tax expenditures must be employed since no single normative criterion is applicable to all the basic elements. The discussion in this section identifies the criteria that historically have been used for the classification task.

1.2.1   THE TAX BASE

The starting point for classifying provisions in the Code that determine the individual tax base generally, but not exclusively, has been the Schanz-Haig-Simons (S-H-S) definition: income is "the algebraic sum of (1) the market value of rights exercised in consumption and (2) the change in the value of the store of property rights between the beginning and the end of the period in question."[5] To put it more simply, income equals the increase in net worth plus consumption during the relevant period of time. The corporate tax base generally has been derived from accounting standards, since S-H-S has not been applied to corporate income.[6]

Although S-H-S is the starting point for classification of tax base Code provisions applicable to individuals, it has never been used exclusively or rigidly in that process. From the outset, certain provisions that technically might fall within the S-H-S definition have been excluded from tax expenditure accounts. Notable among such items is the realization requirement.[7] But, until the JCT staff report, S-H-S appeared to be a useful tool in identifying tax expenditures in the individual tax base provisions of the Code.

1.2.2   TAX RATES

S-H-S has nothing to say about the tax rate structure. Nonetheless, tax expenditure reports have identified deviations from the generally applicable rate structure as tax expenditures. Tax expenditure analysis does not posit any particular rate structure as normative. Once policy makers have decided upon such a structure,

---

5. H. Simons, *Personal Income Taxation* (Chicago: University of Chicago Press, 1938), 50.
6. See United States, Staff of the Joint Committee on Taxation, *Estimates of Federal Tax Expenditures for Fiscal Years 2007–2011*, JCS-3-07 (Washington, DC: US Government Printing Office, Sep. 24, 2007), 7.
7. Issues in dealing with the tax base are discussed more extensively in S. Surrey & P. McDaniel, *Tax Expenditures* (Cambridge, MA: Harvard University Press, 1985), 186–188.

deviations from that structure for particular types of income—for example, the special 15% top rate for capital gains and dividends—should be classified as tax expenditures.[8]

1.2.3 THE TAXABLE UNIT

Tax expenditure analysis does not dictate answers to the question of what is to constitute a given taxable unit. Thus, for example, questions involving whether married couples should file jointly, how to treat corporations and their share-holders, how to treat partnerships and their partners, and how to treat trusts and their grantors and beneficiaries, all must be resolved by the policy makers in Congress and the administration. No tax expenditure is created as long as the policy settled upon is applied consistently. If exceptions to the basic policy are adopted, tax expenditures may be created.[9]

1.2.4 ACCOUNTING RULES

The S-H-S definition requires adoption of an accounting period but does not specify what that period should be. Following common accounting practices, the standard of one year is generally adopted. Rules are also required to allocate items of income and deduction to the proper year. Here, resort generally has been made to financial reporting practices and procedures. This approach was made explicit in 1968 Treasury tax expenditure analysis. That analysis stated that it would use "widely accepted . . . standards of business accounting" in its classification of particular tax accounting rules in the Code.[10] Deviations from basic accounting rules can create tax expenditures—for example, the cash method of accounting permitted for agricultural businesses.

1.2.5 INTERNATIONAL TAX SYSTEM

A country may adopt any of three international tax systems: worldwide taxation with foreign tax credit ("WWT" with "FTC"), exemption of foreign-source income, or deduction for foreign taxes paid. The first system generally is based

---

8. *Ibid.*, 191–192.
9. For example, the personal exemptions granted for minor children and students have not been classified as tax expenditures, apparently on the basis that this treatment was appropriate in the taxable unit context. But a number of countries provide direct children's allowance payments and do not grant income tax exemptions. That fact casts some doubt on the U.S. classification of exemptions for minors and students.
10. See the 2008 tax expenditure estimates, *supra* note 4, at 3. Tax and financial accounting rules are not always the same, given the differing objectives of the two systems. But those divergences do not, in and of themselves, create tax expenditures or tax penalties.

on capital export neutrality, the second on capital import neutrality, and the third on competitive (non-) neutrality. No tax expenditure results from the adoption of any one of the systems.[11] The basic U.S. system, adopted in the early 1920s, has been the first system (WWT with FTC). That being the case, special rules that have deviated from that principle have been classified as tax expenditures. The most notable tax expenditure was created by the ability of a U.S. multinational to defer U.S. tax on foreign-source income earned by its foreign subsidiaries until that income is repatriated to the United States. Elaborate rules govern when deferral is permitted. The deferral privilege, from the perspective of the WWT with FTC system, constitutes a tax expenditure in the form of an interest-free loan from the U.S. government to the qualifying U.S. multinational. Other examples include the ill-fated export subsidies held to be invalid by World Trade Organization panels.[12]

1.2.6   Tax Administration

The rules providing administrative guidance by and for the Internal Revenue Service, taxpayers, and tax advisers generally do not involve the creation of tax expenditures. Nonetheless, if special rules are adopted in the Code tax administration provisions, tax expenditure classification may be appropriate.[13]

With this brief review of the conceptual standards that generally have been followed in the United States since adoption of the 1974 Budget Reform Act, I now turn to the changes in classification methodology proposed by the JCT staff report and applied in the 2008 tax expenditure estimates.

1.3   METHODOLOGY ADOPTED BY JCT STAFF

For a variety of reasons, the validity of which will be addressed in the next section, the JCT staff report (issued, as noted above, in May 2008) proposed a changed methodology for presenting the annual report on tax expenditures. The JCT staff proposed to divide tax expenditures into two new categories: tax subsidies and tax-induced structural distortions (TISD).

1.3.1   Tax Subsidies

A tax subsidy is a provision that is "deliberately inconsistent with an identifiable general rule" of the Code and that collects less revenue than does the general

---

11. See Surrey and McDaniel, *supra* note 7, at 192–193.
12. See P. McDaniel, "Trade Agreements and Income Taxation: Interactions, Conflicts, and Resolutions," *Tax Law Review* 57 (2004): 275–300, for a discussion of these cases.
13. See Surrey and McDaniel, *supra* note 7, at 193–94.

rule.[14] This approach is similar to and based on the so-called reference tax approach developed by economist Seymour Fiekowsky when he was in the U.S. Treasury Office of Tax Analysis,[15] and included in "Special Analysis G" of the fiscal 1983 budget.[16]

The JCT staff did not adopt a second leg of Fiekowsky's methodology, namely, the requirement that the provision under consideration could be replaced by a direct spending program. In the JCT staff's view, this second test would result in unnecessary and ultimately "fruitless debates" about whether a hypothetical direct spending program could in fact replicate the tax subsidy.[17]

The JCT staff subdivided the tax subsidies category into three subcategories: tax transfers, social spending, and business synthetic spending.

Tax transfers include payments made to program beneficiaries even if they have no positive tax liability—that is, refundable tax credits. Examples include the refundable element of the earned income credit and the child tax credit.[18]

The social spending subcategory includes tax subsidies that are intended to subsidize particular activities or to provide incentives for specialized activities. Examples include itemized deductions for interest, medical and dental expenses, and property taxes for owner-occupied housing.[19]

The business synthetic spending subcategory, as its name implies, encompasses tax subsidies "intended to subsidize or induce behavior directly related to the production of business or investment income."[20]

The JCT staff report then lists examples of items included in the tax subsidies category, some of them surprising. For example, the last-in first-out (LIFO) method of accounting is considered a tax expenditure. No explanation is provided as to why this method should be classified as a tax expenditure.

1.3.2   TAX-INDUCED STRUCTURAL DISTORTIONS

The second broad category used for classification purposes is the TISD methodology. The JCT staff report defines the term "as structural elements of the Internal Revenue Code . . . that materially affect economic decisions in a manner that imposes substantial efficiency costs."[21] The deferral of tax on unrepatriated earnings of a foreign subsidiary is an example of a TISD. Surprisingly, the deductibility

---

14. JCT staff report, *supra* note 1, at 39.
15. See S. Fiekowsky, "The Relation of Tax Expenditures to the Distribution of the "Fiscal Burden," *Canadian Taxation* 4 (1980): 211–219, at 214.
16. See "Special Analysis G," in United States, Office of Management and Budget, *Budget of the United States Government: Fiscal Year 1983* (Washington, DC: US Government Printing Office, 1982).
17. JCT staff report, *supra* note 1, at 40.
18. *Ibid.*, 44.
19. *Ibid.*, 44–45.
20. *Ibid.*, 45.
21. *Ibid.*, 41.

of interest coupled with the nondeductibility of dividends is another TISD example.

The JCT staff report proposed to use efficiency as the only criterion to be employed in applying TISD. The report argues that efficiency is a more neutral concept than the traditional standards of equity and simplicity. It argues that the most important issues relate to the taxation of business and investment income, areas in which efficiency is (perhaps) the most important issue.

1.3.3   THE 2008 TAX EXPENDITURE ESTIMATES

As noted above, the JCT staff published its annual estimates of tax expenditures in October 2008, employing the classification system outlined in the preceding section. The report contains six tables. In this chapter, I will focus on the first three. The first table, entitled "Tax Transfers," consists entirely of refundable tax credits, for both individuals and corporations.[22] The report notes as to tax transfers: "These are Tax Subsidies that effectively operate as hybrid tax/spending programs; each is essentially a direct spending program that uses Code concepts to determine eligibility for the refunded tax system infrastructure to deliver funds."[23]

The second table presents tax expenditure estimates for processes determined to be "Social Spending."[24] The standard employed to classify a tax expenditure provision as social spending was not set forth in either the May report or the October estimates.

The third table lists the tax expenditures determined by the JCT staff to be "Business Synthetic Spending."[25] As the title implies, the tax expenditures in this table overwhelmingly benefit corporations.[26]

One of the striking things that comes through in the 2008 tax expenditure estimates is that there is so little change in the listing of tax expenditures. When one compares the 2007–2011 tax expenditure estimates with the 2008 estimates, one finds that, with two exceptions, all items listed as tax expenditures under the prior

---

22. See the 2008 tax expenditure estimates, *supra* note 4, at 50. The two largest tax expenditures in the tables are the earned income credit and the child tax credit.
23. *Ibid.*, 48.
24. *Ibid.*, 51–59. Examples of certain social spending tax expenditures are discussed *ibid.*, at 12–18.
25. *Ibid.*, 60–68 and 19–24.
26. The TISD category discussed above includes tax expenditures (and tax penalties) in both the tax subsidies and the business synthetic spending categories and is not set forth in a separate table. See the 2008 tax expenditure estimates, *ibid.*, 25–34.

    The final three tables will not be discussed in detail in this paper. Table 4 lists two tax expenditure provisions that are no longer so classified: deferral of tax for certain foreign-source income of U.S. corporations and the excess of certain depreciation rules over the alternative depreciation system in the alternative minimum tax (AMT) provisions (*ibid.*, at 69). These exceptions will be discussed in the third part of the paper. Table 5 provides data on the distribution of selected tax expenditures by income classes (*ibid.*, at 70). Table 6 provides distributional data with respect to the home mortgage interest deduction and the phase-outs of the standard deductions and personal exemptions (*ibid.*, at 71–76).

"normal structure" approach are also listed as tax expenditures under the new classification approach.[27] I will return to this curiosity in the following section.

1.4   CRITIQUE OF THE REASONS FOR THE JCT
           STAFF'S CHANGES

The JCT staff report argues that the traditional approach of tax expenditure analysis has been undercut for several reasons. According to the JCT staff, these include the following: (1) Critics have argued that the concept of a "normal" tax system is inadequate to support tax expenditure analysis that "cannot be defended from criticism as a series of ultimately idiosyncratic or pragmatic choices."[28] Tax expenditure analysis has been "[d]riven off track by seemingly endless debates about what should or should not be included in the 'normal' tax base."[29] (2) The "normal" tax concepts are seen by some critics as a tool to achieve tax reform; that is, tax expenditure analysis is driven by a tax reform agenda.[30]

The JCT staff report was less concerned about the correctness of these criticisms than the fact that the criticisms exist. The report argued, therefore, that the normal tax structure approach needed to be replaced with a methodology seen to be more neutral and more principled.[31]

The first of the changes was to replace the normal tax structure approach with a reference tax approach. As noted earlier, the reference tax approach was first developed by Fiekowsky.[32] Under the Fiekowsky methodology, two questions are asked. First, is a provision an exception to a general rule contained in the Code? And second, can the special provision be replaced by a direct spending program that is reasonably administrable? The JCT staff report adopts the first but not the second aspect of Fiekowsky's reference tax methodology.

There are several points that can be raised by the adoption of the modified reference tax approach. The first is that it is a recognition by the JCT staff that some normative standard has to be employed. This standard is used in providing the expenditure estimates for the largest single category developed by the JCT staff, the social spending estimates (a subcategory of tax subsidies).[33] The JCT staff thus concluded that the reference tax approach was preferable to the normal tax approach, even though, as we shall see, the new approach produced results nearly identical to those under the normal tax approach.

But is the reference tax approach preferable to the normal tax structure methodology? There are a number of problems with the reference tax approach that

---

27. Obviously, the 2007 estimates, *supra* note 6, did not include the many tax expenditures adopted in 2008 and 2009.
28. JCT staff report, *supra* note 1, at 7.
29. *Ibid.*, 8. See also *ibid.*, 29–33.
30. *Ibid.*, 34–38.
31. *Ibid.*, 37.
32. See *supra* note 15.
33. See the 2008 tax expenditure estimates, *supra* note 4, at 51–59.

make a claim for its superiority less than convincing. First, as recognized in the JCT staff report, many tax expenditures cannot readily be classified as exceptions to some general rule. Indeed, as one examines the social spending list in the 2008 tax expenditure estimates, one is struck by the large number of tax expenditures provided by means of tax credits—for example, the host of education tax credits. What general rule are these credits exceptions to? The classification of such tax credits is relatively straightforward under the normal tax structure approach, but is considerably less clear (may one say, "arbitrary"?) under the reference tax methodology. This problem flows from the need to identify exactly which provisions in the Code are reference tax provisions. Interestingly, when the reference tax approach was first introduced in the 1983 budget documents, the Office of Management and Budget provided the same list of the basic elements of an income tax system as were set forth in the first section of this chapter. No guidance was given as to how to identify tax expenditures in these elements,[34] nor is any provided by the JCT staff report or by the 2008 tax expenditure estimates.

So what is to be made of a change that makes no changes? As noted above, all but two of the 2007 tax expenditures are included in the 2008 tax expenditure estimates. This is not the result one would have expected from the extended discussion of the criticisms that some commentators have leveled at the normal tax expenditure methodology. Moreover, the replacement of the S-H-S approach, which has a rich intellectual history, with a methodology that has no historical or intellectual underpinnings seems hardly a step forward. The one positive aspect of the JCT staff report is that it does identify those Code provisions that are tax expenditures. In my view, the pre-2008 JCT tax expenditure estimates had the correct classification standard.[35]

I turn now to the second major classification approach by the JCT staff, TISD. Recall that the provisions placed in this category are "structural elements . . . that materially affect economic decisions in a manner that imposes substantial efficiency costs."[36] The first problem with this characterization is that it is internally inconsistent. At least in normal usage, a Code provision cannot be both a structural provision and at the same time a tax expenditure. Tax expenditures are not part of the structure of the income tax; they are spending programs implemented through the tax system that are identifiable as such precisely because they are inconsistent with the structure of an income tax.

There is, however, a more fundamental problem with this classification methodology: neither the 2008 tax expenditure estimates nor the JCT staff report

---

34. For a more detailed critique of the reference tax methodology, see Surrey and McDaniel, *supra* note 7, at 194–96.
35. It is beyond the scope of this paper to provide an analysis of why the S-H-S approach to tax base issues is the superior methodology. My views are contained in Surrey and McDaniel, *supra* note 7, at 186–94. For an excellent current analysis of why S-H-S is a preferable and, indeed, necessary tool in tax expenditure analysis, see J.C. Fleming, Jr. & R. Peroni, "Reinvigorating Tax Expenditure Analysis and Its International Dimension," *Virginia Tax Review* 27 (2008): 439–562.
36. JCT staff report, *supra* note 1, at 41.

contains anything that tells us what criteria the staff used to identify the Code provisions placed in this category. It is true that all but two of the 2007 tax expenditure items appear in the 2008 tax expenditure estimates. But there is no discussion of why this is so. As Fleming and Peroni point out, it is essential that an objective standard be utilized to identify tax expenditure provisions.[37]

The problem is that without such an expressly stated classification standard, one has no idea why a particular provision constitutes a tax expenditure and other provisions do not. Presumably, the efficiency analysis employed by the JCT staff would not be applied to Code section 162(a) (trade or business expense), but why not?

The JCT staff report emphasizes that these provisions will be analyzed solely on the basis of an efficiency construct. Efficiency, however, is at best an analytic construct; it is not a classification tool. As McMahon has pointed out, efficiency is not an objective in and of itself, but rather a means to encourage economic growth.[38]

Moreover, there are several notions of "efficiency," as discussed by economist Jane Gravelle.[39] As Gravelle points out, any of the uses of the term require a model or models to implement, and these models include critical assumptions that may or may not conform to reality.[40] This is not to say that efficiency analysis has no role to play in evaluating tax expenditures. But these analyses in our context have to assume that they are dealing with tax expenditures to begin with. As noted above, no clue is provided as to why particular provisions are classified as tax expenditures and therefore are subject to efficiency analysis. It appears that the JCT standard for classification of a provision is the TISD list and is based on "We know when we see it." Perhaps these tax expenditures were ones left over from the 2007 estimates that were not included in the social spending table.

I turn now to the second objection to traditional tax expenditure analysis that the JCT staff report chose to single out. This objection is that some see the normal tax construct as a tool to achieve tax reform by eliminating existing (and not adopting new) tax expenditure programs.[41] It is certainly true that Surrey's *Pathways to Tax Reform*[42] explicitly set forth such an agenda: tax expenditure analysis should result in the repeal of tax expenditures or transfer to a direct spending program.

What is not reflected in criticism of this initial Surrey view is how much it changed by the time *Tax Expenditures* was published in 1985.[43] In the

---

37. See *supra* note 35, at 154–65.
38. See M. McMahon, Jr., "The Matthew Effect and Federal Taxation," *Boston College Law Review* 45 (2004): 993–1128, at 1074, citing Liam Murphy and Thomas Nagel, *The Myth of Ownership: Taxes and Justice* (New York: Oxford University Press, 2002), 69.
39. J. Gravelle, *The Economic Effects of Taxing Capital Income* (Cambridge, MA: MIT Press, 1994), 29–32.
40. *Ibid.*, 32–43.
41. *Supra* note 30.
42. S. Surrey, *Pathways to Tax Reform: The Concept of Tax Expenditure* (Cambridge, MA: Harvard University Press, 1973).
43. Surrey and McDaniel, *supra* note 7.

chapter dealing with the relation between tax expenditures and tax reform, we stated: "A tax expenditure is a spending program and must be analyzed in spending terms. To attempt to discuss the program as if it were a normative tax provision is to disregard this fact."[44]

And further: "In the final analysis, there appear to be no inherent differences between tax expenditures and direct expenditures, in terms of either tax policy or budget policy. A refundable taxable credit and a direct grant program can produce identical results in terms of beneficiaries, distribution of benefits, and desired objectives. The same is true of direct loans and repayable, interest bearing [deferral tax expenditures]."[45]

I took the matter a step further in an article published later in 1985: The term "tax reform"—and the analytic and political arguments that accompany it—has continued to be applied to efforts to repeal or eliminate tax expenditures. Yet, since the introduction of the tax expenditure concept in 1969, we have had the ability to realize that action with respect to tax expenditures does not involve "tax" reform at all; it involves "spending" reform. As in the case of effective tax rate analysis, tax reform as a concept can properly be applied to the structural components of a tax system—the appropriate rates of tax, definition of the taxable unit, adjustments in accounting rules, etc. But, the concept of "tax reform" has no more relevance to efforts to repeal spending programs run through the tax system than it does to efforts to repeal direct spending programs. The failure to accept this fact has, I believe, contributed significantly to the failure of "tax reform" efforts; the arguments for tax reform are simply not relevant responses to asserted needs for spending programs.[46]

In examining the tax expenditure literature since 1985, I have found only one article that discusses the relation of tax expenditures and tax reform. That discussion, by Toder,[47] is generally consistent with the view outlined above.

The foregoing does not mean that tax policy is irrelevant to tax expenditures. But the role of tax policy is not to seek repeal or modification of tax expenditures— those are spending program issues. Rather, the role of tax policy is to see that the tax expenditures are treated properly for income determination purposes. Thus, if a given tax expenditure is the functional equivalent of a direct spending program and the benefits of that direct spending program would be included, either directly or indirectly, in gross income, then the tax expenditure also should be included. The direct approach is followed in Code section 87 (the alcohol and biodiesel fuels credit). Another direct approach may be to reduce the basis of assets related to a given tax expenditure. The indirect method of income inclusion is found in Code section 280C, where the deduction of specified tax expenditures is required

44. *Ibid.*, 81.
45. *Ibid.*, 116–117.
46. P. McDaniel, "Identification of the 'Tax' in 'Effective Tax Rates,' 'Tax Reform' and 'Tax Equity'," *National Tax Journal* 38 (1985): 273–279, at 277.
47. E. Toder, "Tax Expenditures and Tax Reform: Issues and Analysis," in *Proceedings of the Ninety-Eighth Annual Conference on Taxation* (Washington, DC: National Tax Association, 2006), 472–479.

to be reduced by an allowable credit for the same expenditures. The result of this reduction is identical to including the credit in gross income.

Where a provision defers income inclusion, it is the equivalent of a direct government loan program. Since few, if any, direct government loan programs are interest-free, a tax expenditure loan program should also bear interest. This procedure is followed in the treatment of so-called interest charge DISCs[48] and deferred distributions from foreign trusts.[49]

There is thus a role for tax policy analysis by the JCT staff in dealing with tax expenditures. The JCT staff report made no reference to this role.[50]

A brief word should be added about the two provisions that were included in the 2007 estimates but excluded from the 2008 estimates: tax deferral for foreign-source income earned by controlled foreign corporations; and depreciation of rental housing, other buildings, and equipment in excess of the alternative depreciation system contained in the alternative minimum tax (AMT).

The reason for the removal of the foreign-source income deferral in the 2008 tax expenditure estimates is not explained. Indeed, the discussion of deferral would lead one to believe that it is a tax expenditure, as has been previously been the case.[51] The distorting effects of the deferral are well known: It is a benefit to U.S. multinationals only if their subsidiaries derive their income in a jurisdiction with a lower tax rate than that of the U.S. Economist Martin Sullivan has conducted a series of studies that show that an increasing percentage of offshore assets and profits of U.S. multinationals are located in countries with tax rates below 20%.[52]

It is possible that the JCT staff position on deferral arguably could be justified by the U.S. treatment of corporations and their shareholders as separate taxpayers. (If this is the reason, the change arguably could have been made under the normal tax approach.) In my view, the principle of capital export neutrality, as reflected in the worldwide taxation of U.S. corporations with a credit allowed for foreign income taxes, is a much more powerful principle in the international context. Fleming and Peroni convincingly demonstrate that deferral of income earned by U.S. controlled foreign corporations is a tax subsidy, and a poorly designed one at that.[53]

---

48. I.R.C. § 995(f).
49. I.R.C. § 668.
50. This is not to say that the report has no value. Using spending program tests, detailed analyses are provided for the earned income credit, individual retirement accounts, and the research and experimentation tax credit. See *supra* note 1, at 60 and 68–77.

    There are important budget issues involved in the use of tax expenditures, but these issues presumably should be dealt with by the Congressional Budget Office and the Congressional Budget Committee. See E. Kleinbard, "The Congress Within the Congress: How Tax Expenditures Distort Our Budget and Our Political Processes," *Ohio Northern University Law Review* 36 (2010): 1–30, for a critical analysis of these issues.
51. See the 2008 tax expenditure estimates, *supra* note 4, at 33–34.
52. See, e.g., M. Sullivan, "U.S. Multinationals Shifting Profits Out of the United States" *Tax Notes* 118 (2008): 1078–1082.
53. Fleming and Peroni, *supra* note 35, at 528–41.

One can be more sympathetic to the removal of the excess of depreciation for buildings and equipment over AMT depreciation. It was never clear why AMT depreciation was the appropriate standard to begin with. I think most would agree that in a normal tax system, economic depreciation should be the standard employed. But this is a difficult standard to apply. As Gravelle has observed, "[d]epreciation is easy to assess in theory, but difficult in practice."[54]

1.5   CONCLUSIONS

In examining the JCT staff report and the 2008 tax expenditure estimates, I reach the following conclusions:

(1) In identifying social spending tax expenditures, the JCT staff correctly recognized the need for an external standard to be applied in classifying provisions as tax expenditures. The reference tax standard that it adopted, however, was not the correct one. That standard has little to support it in either tax or economic analysis and lacks any real substantive context. Indeed, identification of the relevant reference Code provision may be a more uncertain endeavor than using S-H-S for the individual tax base. Taking that approach, the JCT staff will almost surely fail in its effort to tamp down debate about tax expenditure analysis. It certainly will not satisfy proponents of using S-H-S as a principal tool in the classification process. Lastly, the approach seems unlikely to satisfy those commentators who argue that there is no normative standard at all on which tax expenditure analysis can be based.

(2) The JCT staff report also fails to note that those who support the publication of tax expenditures have long since ceased to identify repeal of tax expenditures with tax reform. Spending reform and analysis are the appropriate tools for dealing with tax expenditures.

(3) There is a role, albeit unfortunately ignored by the 2008 JCT staff reports, for traditional tax policy analysis in dealing with tax expenditures. That role is to determine the correct income tax treatment of the subsidies run through the tax system, just as is done for direct spending programs.

(4) Finally, the fact that virtually all the tax expenditures listed in the 2007 tax expenditure estimates are included in the 2008 estimates leads one to question what the whole exercise was about. Changing the titles of tables under which tax expenditure estimates are presented does not seem to be an important exercise for the JCT staff to engage in. It is to be hoped (and recommended) that in preparing future tax expenditure estimates, the JCT staff will return to the traditional normal tax structure classification system.

---

54. Gravelle, *supra* note 39, at 96. Also see Gravelle's extended discussion of the difficulties encountered in properly determining economic depreciation, *ibid.*, 99–104.

Chapter 2
Taxing Tax Expenditures?

Martin J. McMahon, Jr.[*]

2.1 INTRODUCTION

Stanley Surrey introduced tax expenditure analysis to U.S. tax and budget policy in the late 1960s.[1] After elaborating the concept in the early 1970s,[2] he teamed with Paul McDaniel in subsequent years to further refine the purpose and methodology of tax expenditure analysis.[3] Surrey's final words on tax expenditure analysis were published posthumously in 1985, but Paul McDaniel continued to present and defend their vision of tax expenditure analysis for another twenty-five years.

---

[*] Stephen C. O'Connell Professor of Law, University of Florida Levin College of Law. I thank Cliff Fleming, Jim Repetti, and Gregg Polsky for very helpful comments on prior drafts, and my research assistant, Diane Dick, for assistance in researching and editing. All remaining errors are my own.

1. S. Surrey, Excerpts from remarks before The Money Marketeers on *The U.S. Income Tax System—The Need for a Full Accounting*, Nov. 15, 1967, in United States Department of the Treasury, *Annual Report of the Secretary of the Treasury on the State of the Finances for the Fiscal Year Ended June 30, 1968* (Washington, D.C.: Government Printing Office, 1969) at 322.
2. See S. Surrey, *Pathways to Tax Reform* (1973) (*Pathways*).
3. See, e.g., S. Surrey & P. McDaniel, "The Tax Expenditure Concept: Current Developments and Emerging Issues," *Boston College Law Review* 20 (1979): 225 (Emerging Issues); S. Surrey & P. McDaniel, "The Tax Expenditure Concept and the Budget Reform Act of 1974," *Boston College Industrial & Commercial Law Review* 17 (1976): 679 (Tax Expenditure Concept).

Yariv Brauner & Martin James McMahon, Jr. (eds), *The Proper Tax Base: Structural Fairness from an International and Comparative Perspective—Essays in Honour of Paul McDaniel*, pp. 17–45.
© 2012 Kluwer Law International BV, The Netherlands.

Tax expenditure analysis was enshrined into law by The Congressional Budget and Impoundment Control Act of 1974,[4] which requires the President's annual budget submission to Congress to contain a list of tax expenditures, which the Treasury Department prepares. In addition, since 1972 the Staff of the Joint Committee on Taxation has produced its own tax expenditure list annually.

Decades later, there remains no better explanation of the core of tax expenditure analysis than appeared in the opening pages of Surrey and McDaniel's classic 1985 book, *Tax Expenditures*:[5]

> The tax expenditure concept posits that an income tax is composed of two distinct elements. The first element consists of structural provisions necessary to implement a normal income tax, such as the definition of net income, the specification of accounting rules, the determination of the entities subject to tax, the determination of the rate schedule and exemption levels, and the application of the tax to international transactions. These provisions compose the revenue-raising aspects of the tax. The second element consists of the special preferences found in every income tax. These provisions, often called tax incentives or tax subsidies, are departures from the normal tax structure and are designed to favor a particular industry, activity, or class of persons. They take many forms, such as permanent exclusions from income, deductions, deferrals of tax liabilities, credits against tax, or special rates. Whatever their form, these departures from the normative tax structure represent government spending for favored activities or groups, effected through the tax system rather than through direct grants, loans, or other forms of government assistance.[6]

The reference to a "normal income tax" means an income tax based on the Schanz-Haig-Simons normative concept of the definition of income.[7] Since the Schanz-Haig-Simons definition of income does not address issues such as accounting methods, taxable unit, exemptions levels or inflation adjustments, those issues also must be addressed in designing a "normal income tax."

The following section of this chapter considers the question of whether tax expenditure analysis deals with a "tax reform" issue or a "spending reform" issue. Section 3 briefly discusses criticisms of tax expenditure analysis. Section 4

---

4. Pub L. No. 93–344, § 601, 88 Stat. 297, 323.
5. S. Surrey & P. McDaniel, *Tax Expenditures* (Cambridge: Harvard University Press, 1985). (*Tax Expenditures*).
6. Surrey & McDaniel, *Tax Expenditures, supra* note 5, at 3. A substantially similar description also appears in Surrey, *Pathways*, at 6. Credits, particularly refundable credits (apart from the few structural credits, such as the credit for taxes withheld and the foreign tax credit), stand out most clearly as spending provisions. See Surrey & P. McDaniel, *Tax Expenditure Concept, supra* note 3, at 225, 266–72 (1979).
7. Surrey & McDaniel, *Tax Expenditures, supra* note 5, at 4. The Schanz-Haig-Simons definition of income means the sum of all consumption and all increase in asset values during a taxable period. H. Simons, *Personal Income Taxation: The Definition of Income as a Problem of Fiscal Policy* (Chicago: University of Chicago Press, 1938), 50. Surrey and McDaniel point out that tax expenditure analysis can apply to any kind of tax and not just an income tax. Surrey & McDaniel, *Tax Expenditures, supra* note 5, at 3–4.

examines the possibility of including in gross income the value of the benefit received through tax expenditures on the ground that tax expenditures are the functional equivalent of cash grants from the government. It posits that the failure to tax expenditures is essentially another tax expenditure. Finally, section 5 reviews recent proposals not only to curb the enactment of new tax expenditures, but to dramatically scale back existing tax expenditures.

2.2   "TAX REFORM" VERSUS "SPENDING REFORM"

As originally conceived, tax expenditure analysis was designed to lead to better budget management by controlling spending in the form of targeted tax relief and was simultaneously viewed as "tax reform." Surrey's first book on the concept, published in 1973, was entitled *Pathways to Tax Reform*. In that book, Surrey described tax expenditures as provisions that "weaken[] the fairness and structure of the income tax."[8] In the concluding chapter of *Pathways to Tax Reform*, Surrey wrote as follows:

> Federal tax reform must cope with the tax expenditure structure that has grown up within the income tax system. . . . [The preferred course of action] is to survey the entire list of tax expenditures to see which can be dropped without any substitute federal financial assistance, which can be replaced by direct programs of financial assistance and what are the contours of those direct programs, and which should be retained as representing the best available vehicles for providing desired financial assistance.[9]

But other passages in *Pathways to Tax Reform* presage what Surrey's answer would have been. For example, in discussing the deduction allowed for medical expenses by section 213 of the Internal Revenue Code, Surrey wrote "I dislike the end consequences of . . . using a tax deduction and hence the tax system" to subsidize family medical expenses.[10] By "end consequences," Surrey was referring to the "upside down effect" of providing subsidies through tax deductions, which invariably results in a greater subsidy to taxpayers in higher marginal income tax brackets than to taxpayers in lower marginal income tax brackets, and persons with insufficient gross income to generate a tax liability before taking into account such deductions receiving no subsidy. It is fair to conclude that *Pathways to Tax Reform* set forth an agenda that would have eliminated all tax expenditures from the Internal Revenue Code and transferred to direct spending programs those subsidies that Congress desired to retain.

Twelve years later, however, Surrey's follow-up book, coauthored with Paul McDaniel, was titled simply *Tax Expenditures*.[11] The differing title reflects a shift

---

8. Surrey, *Pathways, supra* note 2, at 5.
9. *Ibid.*, 247.
10. *Ibid.*, 22.
11. *Ibid.*, 3.

in focus by the architects of tax expenditure analysis that has not been fully appreciated by both its critics and advocates alike. In the first chapter of *Tax Expenditures*, Surrey and McDaniel make an important point about their evolving view of tax expenditure analysis:

> The classification of an item as a tax expenditure does not in itself make that item either a desirable or undesirable provision; nor does it indicate whether the inclusion of the item in the tax system is good or bad fiscal policy. The classification of an item as a tax expenditure is purely informative, just as the presence of an item in the direct budget of a government is informative; it is simply a way of announcing that the item is not part of the normative tax structure. This being so, it is appropriate to ask whether the presence of those items in the tax system is desirable or undesirable, given existing budget policy, tax policy, and other relevant criteria.[12]

This excerpt reveals that from Surrey and McDaniel's perspective tax expenditures are not "loopholes"—avoidance techniques devised by tax practitioners that circumvent congressional intent—but rather preferences consciously enacted by Congress. Moreover, Surrey and McDaniel's analytical model is based on the rubric that the beneficiary of one of these tax preferences actually has paid the tax due under the normative tax structure apart from the tax preference and in turn then is paid by the government the amount of the preferential benefit—hence the term "tax expenditures"—although the two countervailing payments are netted in practice.[13]

In Chapter 3 of *Tax Expenditures*, Surrey and McDaniel wrote as follows: "A tax expenditure is a spending program and must therefore be analyzed in spending terms. To attempt to discuss the program as if it were a normative tax provision is to disregard this fact."[14]

Recognizing that most tax expenditures represent financial assistance that "the legislators really do want to provide," Surrey and McDaniel conclude that "tax reformers" bent on simply eliminating tax expenditures on the ground that they "offend traditional notions of horizontal and vertical tax equity" will fail.[15] They conclude that "[t]ax reform seems likely to succeed only if it is accompanied by a substitute direct spending program or a properly structured tax assistance program."[16] Nevertheless, they also conclude that "many existing tax expenditures represent unneeded government assistance and should yield to tax reform efforts with no substitution of another program."[17] Elimination of tax expenditures in the latter category can be accompanied by general rate reduction.[18]

---

12. *Ibid.*, 5–6.
13. Surrey & McDaniel, *Tax Expenditures, supra* note 5, at 25.
14. *Ibid.*, 81.
15. *Ibid.*, 89.
16. *Ibid.*
17. *Ibid.*, 90.
18. *Ibid.*, 98.

According to this analytical rubric, most "tax reform" proposals, which generally are aimed at eliminating or curbing tax expenditures, actually are spending control proposals.[19] This being so, for spending decisions to be made rationally, criteria are necessary to "determine the choice between tax and direct expenditures, and an analysis of the possible consequences of each choice."[20] Stated somewhat differently, "[a] government's decision to provide assistance through the tax system ... is really a fiscal policy decision disguised as a tax policy decision. Accordingly the approach and analysis applied should be similar to those used in direct budget spending decisions."[21]

In an article published the same year that *Tax Expenditures* was published, Paul McDaniel even more explicitly explained the metamorphosis of tax expenditure analysis:

> The term "tax reform"—and the analytic and political arguments that accompany it—has continued to be applied to efforts to repeal or eliminate tax expenditures. Yet, since the introduction of the tax expenditure concept in 1969, we have had the ability to realize that action with respect to tax expenditures does not involve "tax" reform at all; it involves "spending" reform. As in the case of effective tax rate analysis, tax reform as a concept can properly be applied to the structural components of a tax system—the appropriate rates of tax, definition of the taxable unit, adjustments in accounting rules, etc. But, the concept of "tax reform" has no more relevance to efforts to repeal spending programs run through the tax system than it does to efforts to repeal direct spending programs. The failure to accept this fact has, I believe, contributed significantly to the failure of "tax reform" efforts; the arguments for tax reform are simply not relevant responses to asserted needs for spending programs.[22]

Referring to the above passage twenty-five years later, McDaniel said as follows:

> The above does not mean that tax policy is irrelevant to tax expenditures. But, the role of tax policy is not to seek repeal or modification of tax expenditures, those are spending program issues. Rather the role of tax policy is to see that the tax expenditures are treated properly for income determination purposes. Thus, if a given tax expenditure is the functional equivalent of a direct spending program and the benefits of that direct spending program would be included, either directly or indirectly, in gross income then the tax expenditure should be also.[23]

---

19. *Ibid.,* 26.
20. *Ibid.,* 27.
21. *Ibid.,* 70.
22. P. McDaniel, "Identification of the 'Tax' in 'Effective Tax Rates,' 'Tax Reform,' and 'Tax Equity'," *National Tax Journal.* 38 (1985), 273, 277.
23. P. McDaniel, "The Staff of the Joint Committee on Taxation Revision of Tax Expenditure Classification Methodology: What Is to Be Made of a Change That Makes No Changes?," in *Tax Expenditure Analysis: The State of the Art,* ed. L. Philipps, N. Brooks & J. Li (Toronto: Canadian Tax Foundation, 2011), 3:6 (Change That Makes No Changes).

This is a little understood facet of tax expenditure analysis, even though it is reflected at times in provisions of the Code that deal with tax expenditures, as will be explored further in Part 4.

2.3   THE FAILURE OF CRITICISM OF TAX
        EXPENDITURE ANALYSIS

Over the years, there have been many critics of tax expenditure analysis. Some of their criticisms, such as the assertion that tax expenditure analysis posit that "lurking behind the concept of the tax expenditure is a more sinister premise. . . . It is the subtle disposition to think of all income as virtual state property, and forbearance to tax away every last penny of it as itself a tax expenditure,"[24] are so silly as to hardly need refutation. Nevertheless, arguments of this sort have been ably refuted.[25]

Probably the most vigorous truly intellectual criticism of tax expenditure analysis has been that the "normative tax base" is beyond definition, and that the provisions that are labeled "tax expenditures" in Surrey and McDaniel's model are actually reflections of social and economic values regarding the proper tax base.[26] The Staff of the Joint Committee on Taxation concluded in a 2008 report that "[T]he proponents of traditional tax expenditure analysis have failed to respond convincingly to the criticisms of the "normal" tax as underspecified,"[27] because "there no longer is a near-universal consensus view as to the ideal tax system."[28] However, the report of the Staff of the Joint Committee on Taxation failed adequately to consider the powerful refutation of this criticism reflected in the scholarly literature. Indeed, Paul McDaniel's final scholarly publication concisely demonstrated the weaknesses of the report of the Staff of the Joint Committee on Taxation.[29] Professors J. Clifton Fleming and Robert Peroni also have very successfully refuted these criticisms and the critique of these criticisms in the Report of the Staff or the Joint Committee,[30] exposing in great detail the political and ideological currents that motivate such attacks.

---

24. C. Fried, "Whose Money Is It?," *Washington Post*, Jan. 1, 1995, at C7, quoted in J.C. Fleming, Jr. & R. Peroni, "Reinvigorating Tax Expenditure Analysis and Its International Dimensions," *Virginia Tax Review* 27 (2008): 437, 491 "Reinvigorating Tax Expenditure Analysis").
25. Fleming & Peroni, "Reinvigorating Tax Expenditure Analysis," *supra* note 24, at 491–93.
26. See, e.g., B. Bittker, "Accounting for Federal 'Tax Subsidies' in the National Budget," *National Tax Journal* 22 (1969): 244; D. Kahn & J. Lehman, "Tax Expenditure Budgets: A Critical View," *Tax Notes* 54 (Mar. 30, 1992), 1661, 1662–1663; M. McIntyre, "A Solution to the Problem of Defining Tax Expenditures," *University of California at Davis Law Review* 14 (1980): 79.
27. Staff of the Joint Committee on Taxation, 110th Cong., *A Reconsideration of Tax Expenditure Analysis* 35 (Joint Comm. Print 2008) (JCT Staff, *Reconsideration*).
28. JCT Staff, *Reconsideration, supra* note 27, at 36.
29. McDaniel, "Change That Makes No Changes?," *supra* note 23, at 3:6–3:11.
30. Fleming & Peroni, "Reinvigorating Tax Expenditure Analysis," *supra* note 24, at. 437; J.C. Fleming & R. Peroni, "Can Tax Expenditure Analysis Be Divorced From a Normative Tax Base?: A Critique of the 'New Paradigm' and Its Denouement," *Virginia Tax Review* 30 (2010): 135.

I believe that these criticisms of tax expenditure analysis stem from a fundamental misunderstanding of the essence of Surrey and McDaniel's model. The critics have substituted a notion that tax expenditure analysis is premised on the principle that the actual income tax base ought to be identical to the normative income tax base postulated by Surrey and McDaniel for Surrey and McDaniel's principle that tax expenditure analysis is merely a tool to identify whether or not the wisdom of any particular provision in the Internal Revenue Code ought to be evaluated using criteria of tax policy or criteria applicable to, and possibly the process that applied to, spending decisions.[31] Many other modern commentators recognize this difference.[32] To be sure, Surrey and McDaniel suspected that many, perhaps most, tax expenditures would fail to pass muster as desirable and effective spending programs and thus would be eliminated.[33] But any such personal judgment about the efficacy of certain provisions was separate and distinct from the analytical model.

In 2008, the Staff of the Joint Committee on Taxation issued the report, *A Reconsideration of Tax Expenditure Analysis.*[34] The report concluded that the method of tax expenditure analysis premised upon a normative income tax baseline, and which had been used by the government since 1968, failed to achieve its goals of "clarifying the aggregate size and application of government expenditures, and improving the Internal Revenue Code."[35] The Staff of the Joint Committee proposed to replace the traditional methodology for classifying provisions as tax expenditures with a new two-part method under which any provision that provided a "tax subsidy" or produced a "tax-induced structural distortion" would be classified as a tax expenditure. Under this system, a "tax subsidy" provision is the one that is "deliberately inconsistent with an identifiable general rule" in the Code and which collects less revenue than would result from application of the general rule.[36] "Tax-induced structural distortions" are "structural elements of the Internal Revenue Code . . . that materially affect economic decisions in a manner that imposes substantial efficiency costs."[37] The Staff of the Joint Committee

---

31. See, e.g., D. Shaviro, "Rethinking Tax Expenditures and Fiscal Language," *Tax Law Review* 57 (2004): 187, 201–202.
32. L. Burman, "Is the Tax Expenditure Concept Still Relevant?," *National Tax Journal* 56 (2003): 613, 614 (The purpose of the tax expenditure estimates is to subject spending programs administered through the tax code to the same Congressional scrutiny and control as direct expenditures.).
33. See, e.g., Surrey, *Pathways, supra* note 2, at 134–49; Surrey & McDaniel, *Tax Expenditures, supra* note 4, at 71–97.
34. JCT Staff, *Reconsideration, supra* note 27, at 27.
35. *Ibid.,* 35.
36. This approach is similar, but not identical to, the so-called "reference tax" approach developed by economist Seymour Fiekowsky when he was in the United States Treasury Department Office of Tax Analysis, see S. Fiekowsky, "The Relation of Tax Expenditures to the Distribution of the "Fiscal Burden," *Canadian Taxation* 2 (1980): 211, 214, and was included in Special Analysis G of the fiscal 1983 budget. Office of Management and Budget, The Budget of the United States Government, Fiscal Year 1983—Special Analysis G (1982).
37. JCT Staff, *Reconsideration, supra* note 27, at 41.

then published its 2008 Tax Expenditure Estimates employing this new methodology, and, somewhat amazingly, the only real change was the deletion of two tax expenditures from prior years: tax deferral for foreign income earned by controlled foreign corporations, and depreciation of rental housing, other buildings, and equipment in excess of the alternative depreciation system contained in the alternative minimum tax.[38] In response to the 2008 tax expenditure analysis, Paul McDaniel marveled, "So what is to be made of a change that makes no changes?"[39] In a fairly rapid about face, however, in 2010, the Staff of the Joint Committee abandoned the approach it adopted in 2008 and re-embraced the traditional normative income tax baseline.[40]

What is to explain this lurching dance by the Staff of the Joint Committee? A believer in coincidence might attribute it to the arrival and departure of a fairly short-term chief of staff. Under the Surrey and McDaniel analytical model, there is nothing that is per se pejorative in classifying a provision as a tax expenditure. On the other hand, labeling a provision as a departure from normal rules or as inefficient sets the stage for opponents to attack the very existence of the provision. A departure from normal rules violates the tax equity criterion of horizontal equity, and a provision that is inefficient violates the tax policy criterion of minimizing interference with economic decision-making. Viewed as tax provision, it becomes even more indefensible. Simultaneously, however, it might provide extra emphasis to the uninitiated on the "disguised spending" nature of tax expenditures, at least those that were relabeled "tax subsidies." Evidence of such a goal lies in the statements and writings of Kleinbard, the chief of staff of the Joint Committee on Taxation, following his departure. In a published speech shortly after his departure, he criticized the proliferation of tax expenditures that "distort not only tax policy, but also our whole concept of the size and activities of the federal government,"[41] and called for "containing tax expenditures" that "are being systematically overused in ways that materially distort policy decisions, budget presentations, and government resource allocations,"[42] by moving their consideration into the jurisdictions of the various substantive congressional committees so that they would compete for funding with direct spending provisions. Kleinbard subsequently expanded on his original critique, and the tenor of his publications, standing together, much resemble the original agenda of Stanley Surrey in *Pathways to Tax Reform*.[43]

---

38. See Staff of Joint Committee on Taxation, 110th Cong., *Estimates of Federal Tax Expenditures for Fiscal Years 2009–2013* (Joint Comm. Print 2008).
39. McDaniel, "Change That Makes No Changes?," *supra* note 23, at 3:6.
40. See Staff of Joint Committee on Taxation, 111th Cong., *Estimates of Federal Tax Expenditures for Fiscal Years 2009–2013* (Joint Comm. Print 2010) (JCT Staff 2010 Estimates).
41. E. Kleinbard, "How Tax Expenditures Distort Our Budget and Our Political Process," *Tax Notes* 123 (May 18, 2009) 925, 925.
42. *Ibid.*, 936.
43. See *ibid.*; E. Kleinbard, "Tax Expenditure Framework Legislation," 63 *National Tax Journal* 353 (2010) (Framework Legislation).

2.4   TAXING TAX EXPENDITURES

2.4.1   Determining Which Tax Expenditure Subsidies
           Should Be Taxed

Under the McDaniel formulation of tax expenditure analysis, from a strict tax policy perspective, as opposed to a spending policy perspective, the only relevant question about tax expenditure provisions is determining how to properly tax the recipients of the benefits of the expenditure.[44] In addition to causing the same types of inefficiencies as direct subsidies, when federal taxation and federal spending are taken together,[45] the failure to tax expenditures undermines overall progressivity, in a subtle, nontransparent manner, because such exclusion disproportionately benefits high-income taxpayers. In essence, the failure to tax expenditures is another tax expenditure.

Taxing tax expenditures does not necessarily mean, however, that all tax expenditures should result in additional income tax consequences. If tax expenditures are treated in the same manner as direct spending benefits are treated under the income tax, the question of the proper income tax treatment of the tax expenditure turns on how direct spending would be treated under a normative income tax. However, this is not necessarily a simple question to answer.

Generally speaking, most tax expenditures can be sorted into three broad categories: (1) fiscal assistance to state and local governments, (2) subsidies to stimulate businesses or investment activities, some available only to individuals, some of which are available only to corporations, and some of which are available without regard to whether the activity is conducted directly by an individual or by a business entity, and (3) subsidies to promote social welfare. The first category includes, and is limited to, the section 103 exemption of interest on state and local bonds, which is intended to allow state and local governments to issue bonds at less than the prevailing rate of interest. The second category includes such tax expenditures as preferential rates for capital gains and dividends, accelerated depreciation and expensing for certain investments in business assets, and the exclusion of the inside build-up in whole life insurance policies. The third category includes such tax expenditures as the earned income tax credit, the section 24 child credit, deductions for charitable contributions,[46] most exclusions of employer-provided fringe benefits (particularly the exclusion of employer

---

44. See McDaniel, "Change That Makes No Changes?," *supra* note 23.
45. For the notion that progressivity is best measured not simply by examining the tax system, but by considering the progressivity of government spending, see E. Steuerle, "And Equal (Tax) Justice for All," *Tax Notes* 86 (Jan. 10, 2000): 269.
46. Note, however, that McDaniel has advanced a very good argument that the charitable contribution deduction for cash contributions and for property to the extent of the donor's basis in the property, is not a tax expenditure; the tax expenditure lies in the exclusion from gross income by the ultimate beneficiaries of the contribution—the individuals who are benefitted by the charitable organization's activities. P. McDaniel, "The Charitable Contribution Deduction (Revisited)," *Southern Methodist University Law Review* 59 (2006): 773.

provided health care and insurance), and the exclusion for Medicare, social security and public assistance benefits. To be sure, some tax expenditures are difficult to classify under this taxonomy. For instance, deferral of taxes on earnings in qualified retirement funds might be viewed as either a subsidy to investment and business activities, designed to increase savings and thus investment (which would fall into the second category), or as method of increasing retirement income over what it otherwise would have been (which falls into the third category).

Only those tax expenditures that fall into a category other than the first category—fiscal assistance to state and local governments—need to be examined for the purpose of determining the proper tax treatment of the federal governmental subsidy. The exemption from federal income taxation of the income of state and local governments derived from their governmental functions (or operating public utilities)[47] is not a tax expenditure, but is part of a normative income tax system.[48] It is true that the figurative "bucket" for delivering the tax expenditure subsidy to state and local governments is a leaky bucket, because of the "trickle up" effect that results from the interest rate on such bonds being significantly higher than the after-tax rate of return on taxable bonds for top-bracket investors. This occurs because the supply of bonds exceeds the demand for bonds by top-bracket taxpayers. Because not all such bonds are purchased by top-bracket taxpayers, state and local governments therefore must offer higher rates of interest to attract investments by lower-bracket taxpayers. As a result, the top-bracket taxpayers, who would have been content with a lower interest rate, receive a windfall equal to the excess of the interest rate offered on the bonds than the lower rate for which they would have settled.[49] Thus, only part of the subsidy is actually delivered to state and local governments, and high bracket taxpayers receive a windfall. Arguably, this windfall ought to be included in gross and taxed in the same manner as other windfalls,[50] but doing so likely would be unadministrable, as it would be difficult, if not impossible, to calculate annually the dollar value of the windfall to particular taxpayers.

Tax expenditure benefits that fall into the second category—subsidies to businesses or investment activities—at first blush clearly ought to be taxed under normative income tax principles. Direct governmental subsidies to business are

---

47. I.R.C. § 115.

48. Surrey, *Pathways, supra* note 2, at 209–22 (the tax system provides assistance to state and local governments through the exemption for interest on state and local bonds and the deduction for state and local taxes; revenue sharing, which was then in effect is viewed as direct spending, without any discussion of the failure to tax it as a tax expenditure); see also B. Bittker & L. Lokken, *Federal Taxation of Income, Estates and Gifts,* 3rd ed. (New York: Warren, Gorham & Lamont, 1999), para. 1.2.8 (discussing the potential constitutional basis for the exclusion for income of state and local governments derived from performing their governmental functions).

49. See B. Bittker, "Equity, Efficiency, and Income Tax Theory: Do Misallocations Drive Out Inequities," *San Diego Law Review* 16. (1979): 735; S. Maguire, Cong. Research Service, *Tax-Exempt Bonds: A Description of State and Local Government Debt* (2008), 3–4.

50. See Commissioner v. Glenshaw Glass Co., 348 U.S. 426 (1955).

generally includable in gross income,[51] even though no section of the Internal Revenue Code expressly so provides. However, many of those tax expenditure subsidies might be excludable by corporate taxpayer under section 118, as non-shareholder contributions to capital,[52] unless section 118 itself were to be viewed as a tax expenditure provision, which it currently is not, at least officially. However, as unclear as the application of the exclusion for nonshareholder contributions to capital might be, under the most recent Supreme Court articulation of the definition,[53] and in light of the principle that general business subsidies, even if earmarked for a particular purpose and received by a corporation, are includable in gross income (and thus not excludable under section 118),[54] treating tax expenditures as excludable nonshareholder contributions to the capital of a corporation should be considered to be an extraordinary stretch.

Analysis of whether tax expenditure benefits that fall into the third category—social welfare payments—should be taxed is even more complex. In general, either the Code or administrative practice excludes social welfare benefits that are intended to alleviate poverty or financial hardship, such as Medicaid,

---

51. See, e.g., Standley v. Commissioner, 99 T.C. 259 (1992), *aff'd by order*, 24 F.3d 249 (9th Cir.1994) (payments from the Department of Agriculture under the Dairy Herd Termination Program to dairy farmers who sold cattle for slaughter at less than their fair market value for dairy purposes were taxable); Graff v. Commissioner, 74 T.C. 743 (1980), *aff'd*, 673 F.2d 784 (5th Cir.1982) (mortgage interest reduction payments made on behalf of the owner of low-income rental housing under § 236 of the National Housing Act were held to be taxable income to the property owner).

52. See "Tax Expenditure Concept," *supra* note 3, at 273.

53. In United States v. Chicago, Burlington & Quincy Railroad Co., 412 U.S. 401 (1973), the taxpayer, which operated a railroad, entered into contracts with a number of states under which the states funded the construction of highway undercrossings and overcrossings, crossing signals, signs, and floodlights. The railroad agreed to maintain the improvements once installed. The Supreme Court articulated the test for determining whether a receipt is a contribution to capital as follows:

> We can distill from [Detroit Edison Co. v. Commissioner, 319 U.S. 98 (1943), and Brown Shoe Co. v. Commissioner, 339 U.S. 583 (1950)] some of the characteristics of a non-shareholder contribution to capital under the Internal Revenue Codes. It certainly must become a permanent part of the transferee's working capital structure. It may not be compensation, such as a direct payment for a specific, quantifiable service provided for the transferor by the transferee. It must be bargained for. The asset transferred foreseeably must result in benefit to the transferee in an amount commensurate with its value. And the asset ordinarily, if not always, will be employed in or contribute to the production of additional income and its value assured in that respect. 412 U.S. at 413.

Note also that the contributions to capital exclusion should not be available to individuals or members of partnerships and limited liability companies. I.R.S. Gen. Couns. Mem. 38944 (Dec. 27, 1982) (§ 118(a) applies only to corporations; it does not apply to partnerships). But see K. Blanchard, "The Taxability of Capital Subsidies and Other Targeted Incentives," *Tax Notes* 85 (Nov. 8, 1999): 781.

54. See Baboquivari Cattle Co. v. Commissioner, 135 F.2d 114 (9th Cir. 1943) (amounts received by a corporation under the Soil and Water Conservation Act in consideration of making certain conservation improvements and following certain conservation practices were includable in the gross income of a corporation).

Supplemental Nutrition Assistance Program (SNAP) benefits (formerly known as food stamps), public housing assistance, etc. In contrast those benefits that are substitutes for wages, such as unemployment compensation,[55] are includable in gross income. Although in theory all benefits generally should be included in the recipient's income,[56] where the benefits are based upon need, little if any tax is likely to be paid on these amounts and the exclusion therefore might be defensible on administrative grounds. An exclusion based on administrative convenience generally is not considered to be a tax expenditure. Nevertheless, the current view is that the exclusion from gross income of cash public assistance benefits (which include Supplemental Security Income benefits and Temporary Assistance for Needy Families benefits) constitutes a tax expenditure.[57]

Focusing solely on public assistance benefits for the needy, from this perspective we come to what appears to be the somewhat anomalous conclusion that social welfare benefits paid to people whose market income is considered to be insufficient to meet their basic needs—and who due to exemptions and the standard deduction, along with the EITC would not otherwise face a tax liability—ought to be required to include social welfare benefits in gross income. As a result they possibly could face an obligation to pay federal income taxes in an amount equal to some portion of those social welfare payments, if the social welfare payments are viewed as the marginal income that results in crossing the threshold into a tax liability.

One response to the argument that such an outcome would be anomalous would be to draw an analogy to unemployment compensation. Since 1987, pursuant to section 85, unemployment compensation generally has been fully includable in gross income. Prior to 1987, unemployment compensation was includable only if the sum of the taxpayer's adjusted gross income and unemployment benefits exceeded specified levels. The rule was changed to require 100% inclusion of unemployment compensation on the theory that unemployment benefits "essentially are wage replacement payments [that] should be treated for tax purposes in the same manner as wages."[58] Congress reasoned that "repeal of the prior-law

---

55. I.R.C. § 85.

56. Surrey & McDaniel, *Tax Expenditures, supra* note 3, at 203. There might be some division of opinion among theorists regarding whether means-tested social welfare payments normatively ought to be considered to be income. See J. Foreman, "The Income Tax Treatment of Social Welfare Benefits," *University of Michigan Journal of Law Reform* 26 (1993): 785, 799–805 (discussing the various viewpoints). The argument that such benefits are not normatively income appears to be based on the notion that they do not provided discretionary spending power. Under the Surrey & McDaniel view, however, "disposable income" is not the proper normative measure of income. "Emerging Issues," *supra* note 3, at 260, n. 88.

57. See JCT Staff 2010 Estimates, *supra* note 40, at 7. See also Senate Committee on the Budget, Tax Expenditures: Compendium of Background Material on Individual Provisions, prepared by Congressional Research Service, 102d Cong., 2d Sess. 473 (S. Print 102–119, 1992) (while no specific rationale has been advanced for this exclusion [of social welfare payments], the reasoning may be that the Congress did not intend to tax with one hand what it gives with the other).

58. Staff of Joint Committee on Taxation, 99th Cong., *General Explanation of the Tax Reform Act of 1986* (Joint Comm. Print 1987), 29.

partial exclusion contributes to more equal tax treatment of individuals with the same economic income," and further concluded that "if wage replacement payments are given more favorable tax treatment than wages, some individuals may be discouraged from returning to work."[59]

It might be reasonable to conclude that social welfare benefits to the needy are a form of wage replacement, since the social welfare payments would not have been received if the recipient had earned adequate wages (or had investment income) to cover basic human needs. Any exclusion should result only from the application of personal exemptions and the standard deduction, and possibly the EITC, which despite its inclusion in the tax expenditure budget[60] might be viewed as the third leg of the normative structure for determining the threshold of taxability. On the other hand, if most recipients of social welfare benefits never would cross the threshold of income subject to positive tax rates, the administrative burdens of requiring so many more individuals to determine whether or not they were required to file a tax return might not be worth the elegant theoretical purity of the suggestion.

2.4.2   DETERMINING HOW TO TAX TAXABLE EXPENDITURE SUBSIDIES

The tax expenditures that are the easiest to tax as if they were benefits received from direct spending programs are credits based upon an amount incurred as an ordinary and necessary business expense that is deductible in calculating taxable income.[61] Generally speaking, such tax expenditures can be included in the income tax base simply by disallowing any deduction in an amount equal to the credit with respect to the expenditure that gave rise to the credit. Current law does exactly this with certain business tax credits relating to wage payments, including, among others, the section 45A Indian employment credit, the section 45P credit or differential wages paid by an employer to employees who are reservists who have been called to active duty, the section 51A work opportunity credit, and the section 1396 empowerment zone employment credit.[62] Similar rules apply to expenses for which credits are claimed under section 41 for increased research expenses,[63] section 45C for testing certain clinical drugs,[64] and section 43 for enhanced oil recovery,[65] among others.

A more direct manner of taxing a business subsidy is simply to include the amount of the credit in gross income. This is the rule with respect to the section 40 alcohol fuels credit and the section 40A biodiesel fuels credit.[66] In most instances,

---

59. *Ibid.*, 29.
60. See JCT Staff 2010 Estimates, *supra* note 40, at 21.
61. See "Tax Expenditure Concept," *supra* note 40, at 272.
62. I.R.C. § 280C(a).
63. I.R.C. § 280C(c).
64. I.R.C. § 280C(b).
65. I.R.C. § 43(d)(1).
66. I.R.C. § 87.

the method chosen to tax the tax expenditure does not matter; the results will be identical if the taxpayer's operations are profitable and the credit does not exceed the tax otherwise due. However, if the taxpayer is in a net operating loss situation, the results will differ; results also will differ if the amount of the credit is limited by the amount of tax otherwise due, since business credits are generally not refundable.[67]

If, however, the credit is allowed for an expenditure that must be capitalized, the counterpart of denial of a deduction is a reduction in basis, which thereby reduces future cost recovery allowances. This is required with respect to a number of credits, including, for example, the section 45D new markets credit,[68] and the section 45F credit for employer provided child care if claimed with respect to depreciable property, such as facilities and equipment.[69] Reduction of basis is not, however, the equivalent of currently including the credit in income. Although a reduction in basis eventually results in an increase in taxable income in an amount equal to that which would have been included in gross income under an inclusion model, reduction of basis in lieu of current inclusion in gross income effects a deferral of taxation of the tax expenditure. Thus, there is in essence an interest free loan from the government, which is another tax expenditure that remains buried and untaxed, unless an additional remedial tax consequence is required.

Surrey and McDaniel have observed that the denial of a deduction or a reduction in basis in an amount equal to a credit is a "technique for achieving the equivalent of a taxable tax credit [that] evidences clever work by tax technicians," but one that "does not represent a sufficient response to the broader issue of the proper income tax treatment of the subsidies made available through tax expenditures."[70] Tax expenditures in the form of a deduction present a more difficult problem. A tax expenditure in the form of a deduction can represent either a permanent exclusion from the tax base or an interest free loan through deferral of tax liability attributable to accelerating the deduction. Almost all deduction-based tax expenditures fall into the latter category because they represent either (1) current deductions for capital expenditures that otherwise would have been depreciable or amortizable, such as the limited deduction for equipment purchases under section 179 or expensing the cost of drilling oil and gas wells under section 263(c), or (2) an allowance of amortization or depreciation deductions at a rate more rapid than the decline in economic value of the asset with respect to which the amortization or depreciation is allowed, such as accelerated depreciation under section 168.[71]

From tax a policy perspective, these timing-preference tax expenditures that result in an interest free loan from the government to the taxpayer should result in

---

67. There are problems raised by limitations on the application of credits against alternative minimum tax liability.
68. I.R.C. § 45D(h).
69. I.R.C. § 45F(f)(1).
70. "Tax Expenditure Concept," *supra* note 3, at 274.
71. See JCT Staff 2010 Estimates, *supra* note 40, at 21 (depreciation).

realization of gross income equal to the value of the benefit, i.e., the value of the interest foregone by the fisc. Determining the value of the benefit is, however, a Herculean task. As Paul McDaniel pointed out in his final scholarly publication, economic depreciation is a theoretical concept that is nearly impossible practically to determine.[72] Furthermore, even if economic depreciation were determinable, because the retirement date of depreciable assets and their salvage value are both indeterminate in any particular tax year before their retirement, the value of the tax benefit as computed for any particular tax year would, of necessity, be merely tentative, and adjustments, which should give rise to real interest payments, frequently would be necessary in future years.

The complexity would be completely unadministrable, but at least as far as deferral tax expenditures for business taxpayers are concerned the issue might be a tempest in a teapot. Arguably, the benefit of deferral realized from tax expenditures to business taxpayers could be excluded on the grounds of administrative convenience—an exclusion that is not itself a tax expenditure. For a deferral tax expenditure, there are two deemed circular cash flows. The first is the amount of tax deferred, which is the loan principal that is later repaid when deferral ends. The second deemed circular cash flow, which is where the subsidy arises, is a deemed interest payment from the taxpayer to the government that is rebated. If the interest is deductible, the section 163 deduction for the deemed interest should offset the inclusion in gross income of the rebated interest.[73] However, there are a variety of limitations on the deductibility of business interest, some of which are application specific, such as section 263A(f) requiring capitalization of construction period interest, and others of which are taxpayer-activity specific, such as the section 469 passive activity loss rules. Simply ignoring the interest subsidy on the theory that the gross income inclusion and interest deduction cancel out would sidestep these rules, but the complexity of dovetailing these rules with rules requiring inclusion and, if otherwise allowable, an interest deduction, would be beyond comprehension.

On the other hand, the deferral can be viewed as a simple deferral of taxes due, rather than as a business related loan. Section 163(h) and the Treasury Regulations deny any deduction for interest paid on taxes by a taxpayer other than a corporation,[74] even if the taxes arise from business income,[75] and by analogy,

---

72. McDaniel, "Change That Makes No Changes?," *supra* note 23, at 3:8 (citing J. Gravelle, *The Economic Effects of Taxing Capital Income* (Cambridge, MA: MIT Press, 1994) at 96, for the proposition that "Depreciation is easy to assess in theory, but difficult in practice."); P. McDaniel & S. Surrey, "Tax Expenditures: How to Identify Them: How to Control Them," *Tax Notes* 15 (1982): 595.
73. To be sure, a deferral tax expenditure results in an after-tax internal rate of return for the advantaged investment that exceeds 1- (before-tax IRR × tax rate). See P. McDaniel, et. al., *Federal Income Taxation, Cases and Materials*, 6th ed. (New York: Foundation Press, 2008), at 499–501. However, that enhanced after-tax internal rate of return is the result of financial leverage from the loan on which no interest is due.
74. Temp. Reg. § 1.163-9T(b)(2).
75. See, e.g., Robinson v. Commissioner, 119 T.C. 44 (2002), and cases cited therein.

there should be no interest deduction for the deferred taxes "loaned" to the taxpayer. As a result, the interest rebate includable in gross income would not be offset by a deduction. Simple application of the existing rules, however, would treat corporations, which can deduct interest on taxes, differently than all other business taxpayers. Thus the proper resolution turns on whether the rule applicable to corporations, allowing a deduction for interest paid on income taxes, or the rule applicable to taxpayers other than corporations, disallowing a deduction for interest paid on income taxes, is theoretically correct. That question is beyond the scope of this chapter.[76]

Tax expenditures that result from deviations in the determination of gross income come in the form or either (1) exclusions, which are permanent, or (2) nonrecognition, which, at least in theory, results "merely" in deferral.[77] The most common exclusions are for (1) interest on state and local bonds, (2) a wide range of employer provided fringe benefits, (3) earnings on certain educational savings funds, (4) a wide range of social welfare receipts such as public assistance benefits and most social security benefits, (5) many veterans' benefits, (6) most gain recognized on the sale by an individual of a principal residence, and (7) accrued gains upon death (coupled with a tax-free basis step-up for the successor in interest). Except for the exclusion of state and local bond interest, which applies to both individuals and corporations, almost of the exclusions apply only to individuals. On the gross income side, various nonrecognition rules apply to both individuals and corporations. Among the more salient nonrecognition rules are section 1031 like-kind exchanges and tax-free corporate reorganizations, which include properly structured mergers and acquisitions. In addition, individuals are accorded deferral on investment income earned with respect to qualified retirement plans savings and the inside build-up in certain whole life insurance and annuity policies.

Taxing the "subsidy" in tax expenditure exclusions would require including in gross income the amount of tax forgone as a result of the exclusion. If absolute accuracy is desired, a short-cut, such as allowing an exclusion for only, for example, 85% of the receipt, and including the remainder of the receipt in gross income, will not work because such a rule would fail to take into account the graduated rate schedule for individuals. Furthermore, the taxable subsidy to an individual would have to be calculated in a manner that reflects the fact that an exclusion might result in portions of the preference item being excluded at different rates. Thus, the calculation would be inordinately complex, and

---

76. Boris Bittker argued that under the Haig-Simons definition of income, federal income tax payments should not be treated as consumption expenditures and thus should be deductible. See B. Bittker, "Income Tax Deductions, Credits, and Subsidies for Personal Expenditures" *Journal of Law and Economics* 16 (1973): 193, 201. However, federal income taxes are not deductible under current law, and it is the framework of current law that is relevant.

77. For an individual taxpayer, deferral through nonrecognition and the attendant substituted basis rules can turn into an exclusion though the § 1014 tax-free step-up in basis at death, which is itself a listed tax expenditure. For corporations, deferral can extend forever and after taking into account the time value of money, deferral for a long enough period, even if well short of forever, is as good as an exclusion.

compliance would be burdensome for many lower income taxpayers, who have positive income tax liabilities and who benefit from tax expenditure exclusions. Those calculations would also be very difficult for the tax return preparers to whom the taxpayers who benefit from such tax expenditures turn for help.

Unless the approach described above, in which the benefit of deferral would be ignored in taxing tax expenditures, is adopted on the grounds that a deemed interest payment and the taxable subsidy in the form of a deemed rebate of the interest cancel out, taxing gross income deferral tax expenditures, such as section 1031 like-kind exchange treatment, would be even more complicated. Since deferral is the equivalent of an interest-free loan from the government to the taxpayer, theoretically the amount of gross income subject to tax would be the amount of foregone interest. To avoid taxpayer-by-taxpayer determinations of the appropriate interest rate, interest might be computed at some multiple of the applicable federal rate—the rate at which the U.S. Treasury borrows—for an obligation of a term comparable to the deferral period. (Alternatively, as suggested by Surrey and McDaniel, the Treasury might charge express interest each year on the tax savings produced by the deferral.[78]) Deferral from nonrecognition generally is for an indefinite term, it might be for one year, or it might be for fifty years (or more), or for any period in between. It might appear that the "loan" could be viewed as a demand loan, with the foregone interest determined as if the loan were a short term loan. But this solution would vastly understate the value of long-term deferral, and a retrospective adjustment, although possible,[79] would be very complex. The loan might better be viewed as a long term loan, with a prepayment option. The result under such a view is even more complex than under the demand loan analogy, because the full amount of the foregone interest would be includable in the taxpayer's income in the year of the investment, but the full amount of the forgone interest is indeterminate.

Indeed, the six-hundred pound gorilla in the room with respect to gross income deferral tax expenditures is the treatment of qualified deferred compensation and Individual Retirement Accounts. The Staff of the Joint Committee on Taxation estimates the cost of these exclusions for the five-year period between 2009 and 2013 to be nearly $600 billion.[80] It would be theoretically possible to tax the value of the deferral (or to impose express interest on the deferred taxes). Furthermore, in this case, the deemed interest payment would not necessarily offset the deemed annual subsidy because section 163(d) would limit, and defer, the interest deduction—in most cases deferring almost all of the interest deduction until payout, and even then requiring a complex calculation of the portion of each distribution from the plan that represented investment income accrued within the plan, against which deferred interest would be deductible, and how much represented distributions of initial contributions of deferred wages (or other compensation).

---

78. Surrey & McDaniel, *Tax Expenditures, supra* note 5, at 93.
79. See Treas. Reg. § 1.460-6 (dealing with the percentage-of-completion look-back method for reporting income from long-term contracts).
80. See JCT Staff 2010 Estimates, *supra* note 40, at. 43, Table 1.

However, only a die-hard tax policy purist would fail to consider such a solution to be oxymoronic. Thus, taxing that tax expenditure is simply a political nonstarter.

A third category of tax expenditures is preferential rates, such as the preferential rate accorded to individuals' long-term capital gains and, from 2001 through 2012, qualified dividends received by individuals. Measuring the tax expenditure benefit from these tax expenditures will depend on the manner in which the special rate is provided. Under current law the benefit of the fixed ceiling on the tax rate applied to long-term capital gains varies among taxpayers in different marginal tax brackets for ordinary income differently than it would if the preferential rate were a uniform fraction of the taxpayer's normal marginal rate. If rate preferences are provided through arbitrary maximum rates, rather than through a parallel but uniformly proportionately lower rate schedule for each income tax bracket, the benefits of the preferential rates are not proportionate for taxpayers in the different tax brackets. For example, for taxpayers who normally are subject to the 25% marginal tax bracket, a 15% rate for capital gains is a 40% rate reduction, while the benefit of a 15% rate to taxpayers otherwise subject to the 35% marginal tax bracket is approximately a 57% reduction from the rates applicable to ordinary income. By according capital gains a preference through maximum rates, rather than by a parallel but uniformly proportionately lower rate schedule for each income tax bracket, the rate reduction generally inures disproportionately to taxpayers in the higher tax brackets.

If the tax benefit of the rate preference is to be taxed, the amount includable in gross income should be the difference between the amount of tax the taxpayer would have owed absent the rate preference and the amount of tax that the taxpayer owes as a result of the rate preference (before taking into account the tax on the tax expenditure subsidy). Note that according a rate preference to the additional tax would itself be an additional tax expenditure subsidy, thereby generating another round of computations, and so we head down the rabbit hole.[81]

By this point, it should be clear that taxing the subsidies provided through tax expenditures would entail introduction of additional complexities into the already mind-numbing complexity of the Internal Revenue Code. As Surrey and McDaniel pointed out in 1979, "normative structure dedications, such as for wages or costs of producing income, should not be complicated and distorted to achieve what can be done directly and simply."[82] If the prospect of such added complexity is not daunting enough, there is a further reason not to attempt to tax expenditure subsidies. As discussed in the following section, we really do not know exactly who to tax.

2.4.3   TAXING TAX EXPENDITURES IS UNADMINISTRABLE

Up to this point we have been assuming that a tax expenditure subsidy actually benefits only, and fully, the taxpayer to whom it is accorded by the provisions of

---

81. See L. Carroll, *Alice's Adventures in Wonderland* (Philadelphia: Henry Altemus, 1897), 1.
82. Surrey & McDaniel, "Tax Expenditure Concept," *supra* note 3, at 274.

the Internal Revenue Code. That may be true with respect to certain tax expenditures, for example, the section 32 child credit, but it is not all clear and in some cases clearly not the case, with respect to tax expenditures that can be obtained only by engaging in a market transaction with a third party. In the case of these tax expenditure subsidies, which constitute the overwhelming bulk of all tax expenditures, the benefit nominally conferred on a taxpayer by the statute may be shifted, in whole or in part, to the counter-party to the taxpayer's transaction through market forces. One example of such a situation, which has already been discussed, is the effect of the exclusion for interest on state and local bonds, which permits state and local governments to issue bonds at lower than market interest rates, thereby shifting the benefit of the tax preference from the bond holder to the to the bond issuer. In that case, the nominal recipient of the tax expenditure benefit—for example, in the case of tax exempt bonds, the investor—bears an "implicit tax."

There are numerous other examples of tax expenditures the benefits of which are shifted by market forces, price or yield changes to a person other than the taxpayer who nominally benefits from the preference. Owners of whole life insurance policies receive a lower yield on the inside build-up than they would receive if the build-up were currently taxed, thereby shifting some of the benefit of the tax preference to the insurance company issuing the policy.[83] The home mortgage interest deduction very well might result in home mortgage interest rates and the price of homes being higher than they otherwise would be, thereby shifting some of the benefit to home mortgage lenders and the owners of existing housing stock and home builders.[84] The credits for higher education tuition payments have may have resulted in greater increases in college tuition than otherwise would have occurred, thereby shifting some of the benefit to colleges and universities.[85] Even the benefit of the section 24 child care credit arguably might be shifted, at least in part, to employers in the form of the ability to pay

---

83. The tax-preferred treatment of the inside build-up leads to an increased demand for whole life insurance, United States Treasury Department, Tax Reform for Fairness, Simplicity, and Economic Growth, Vol. 2 (1984): 259–262 thereby driving up the price (unless the supply is perfectly elastic), which results in a lower yield, see M. Scholes, et. al., *Taxes and Business Strategy, A Planning Approach,* 4th ed. (Englewood Cliffs, N.J.: Prentice Hall, 2008): 124. But see, M. Knoll, "Of Fruit and Trees: The Relationship Between Income and Wealth Taxes," *Tax Law Review* 53 (2000): 587, 601, n 61 (life insurance might bear relatively low implicit taxes because investors' access to the funds is limited).

84. See, e.g., P. Jackson, Cong. Research Service, *Fundamental Tax Reform: Options for the Mortgage Interest Deduction* (2005): 21 (if the home mortgage interest deduction were repealed, mortgage interest rates would fall in response to the lower demand for mortgage debt); M. White & L. White, "The Tax Subsidy to Owner-Occupied Housing: Who Benefits?," *Journal of Public Economics* 3 (1977), 111–126 (the value of the mortgage interest deduction is capitalized into housing prices).

85. See B. Long, "The Impact of Federal Tax Credits for Higher Education Expenses," in *College Choices: The Economics of Which College, When College, and How to Pay For It,* ed. C. Hoxby (University of Chicago Press and the National Bureau of Economic Research, 2004), NBER Working Paper 9553 (March 2003), http://www.nber.org/papers/w955; S. Dynarski, "The Behavioral and Distributional Implications of Aid for College," *American Economic Review* 92 (May 2002): 279.

lower wages to recipients of the credit while leaving the employees' net-after tax income either unchanged or increased by less than the credit.[86] These are just a few examples of the various "demand subsidies" delivered through tax expenditures the benefits of which are to some extent or another capitalized into the market price for the item for which the tax expenditure is provided.[87] However, there is an inherent difficulty in pursuing this analysis. "Data on and understanding of real-world effects may be lacking or too indirect to trace."[88] Thus, we really do not know exactly who to tax on the benefit derived from any particular tax expenditure.

2.5   REVENUE ENHANCEMENT, SPENDING REFORM, AND TAX REFORM—CURBING TAX EXPENDITURES

2.5.1   TAX EXPENDITURES ARE BOTH INEFFICIENT AND INEQUITABLE

Because some significant portion, but almost certainly not all, of the benefit of many, but not all, tax expenditures obtained by engaging in market transactions with third parties is capitalized into market prices, these types of tax expenditures are doomed to give rise to both inefficiency, i.e., create economic distortions, and inequity.[89] The home mortgage interest deduction can serve as a quintessential example of the lose-lose nature of tax expenditure subsidies. From an efficiency perspective, investment capital is diverted from other uses into an increased stock of owner occupied homes.[90]

Similar problems arise with any demand-based subsidy, however provided. In the context of analyzing subsidies for low income housing, the Staff of the Joint Committee on Taxation has described the phenomenon as follows: "[I]f market supply does not respond to the increase in demand which the subsidy creates, the benefit of the subsidy would flow to landlords in the form of higher rents. Even if, as a result of the subsidy, recipients can successfully buy more or better housing, some of the benefit of the subsidy will not be spent on housing because demand

---

86. D.C. Johnston, "Is the Child-Care Credit Parent Friendly?," *Tax Notes* 129 (Nov. 8, 2010): 735.
87. Note that the benefit of some tax preferences is not subject to capitalization into the market price. Only tax expenditures that are asset specific, as opposed to taxpayer specific, are subject to tax capitalization. If an asset bears no tax preference generally, but is tax preferred if owned by a particular taxpayer, for example, bonds owned by an IRA or another tax-exempt pension fund pension fund, then the market price (or yield) of the asset cannot be affected by the tax preference. See C.E. Steuerle, *Taxes, Loans, and Inflation* (Washington, D.C.: The Brookings Institution, 1985): 59–60.
88. Surrey & McDaniel, *Tax Expenditures, supra* note 5, at 88.
89. *Ibid.*, 86. See also United States Treasury Department, *Tax Reform for Fairness, Simplicity and Economic Growth*, Vol 1 (1984), at 14–15, 37–42 (proposing repeal or limitation of many tax expenditures to enhance both market efficiency and equity).
90. See, e.g., United States Congressional Budget Office, *The Tax Treatment of Home Ownership: Issues and Options* (September 1981): 27; Staff of the Joint Committee on Taxation, 102nd Cong., *Overview of Entitlement Programs* (Joint Comm. Print 1992), at 1044, n. 29.

subsidies are rarely fully efficient (this is because money is fungible and can be spent on many types of consumption)."[91]

The same principles hold true with respect to any good or service for which a tax expenditure subsidy, whether as a credit, an accelerated deduction, or as a deduction for a personal living expense, is provided to the buyer.

The inequity problem of the home mortgage interest deduction arises from two sources. The first source of inequity lies in the partial capitalization of the tax expenditure. When a tax expenditure is only partially capitalized, because demand at the highest tax brackets for the item receiving the tax preference is insufficient to clear the market, the change in the market price shifts the entire benefit from the taxpayer nominally granted the tax preference to the counter-party only at tax brackets below the highest tax bracket. As a result the higher-tax bracket, i.e., higher income, taxpayers receive windfall.[92]

The second source of inequity is the "upside down effect" previously discussed. For example, to the extent that the benefit of the home mortgage interest deduction is not captured by home sellers and lenders, through higher home prices and higher interest rates, the benefits of the deduction accrue primarily to upper income taxpayers, primarily the top one-quarter.[93] As stated by one leading fiscal economist, "[w]ith respect to any conceivable policy objective, the pattern of tax benefits seems to be capricious and without rationale."[94] Surrey and McDaniel note that "[i]t is safe to say that Congress would never approve a direct program to encourage home ownership that specifically stated that it provide no benefits to . . . 85 percent of homeowners . . . and that the benefits would increase as a home-owner's income grew, so that the richest people reaped the maximum benefits."[95]

2.5.2   Tax Expenditures Are of Questionable Efficacy

Despite the double whammy of inefficiency and inequity, there has been little or no examination by the government regarding the effectiveness of tax expenditure subsidies,[96] despite Surrey and McDaniel's entreaty for such examination. However, studies by those outside of government frequently demonstrate that tax expenditure subsidies often fail to achieve their policy goals. For example,

91. Staff of the Joint Committee on Taxation, 102nd Cong., *Description and Analysis of Tax Provisions Expiring in 1992*, at 73 (1992).
92. Surrey & McDaniel, *Tax Expenditures, supra* note 5 at 86.
93. *Ibid.*, 77–78. According to estimates by the Staff of the Joint Committee on Taxation, almost 75% of the benefit of the home mortgage interest deduction goes to taxpayers with incomes of $100,000 of more, and of that approximately 32% of the benefit goes to taxpayers with incomes of $200,000 of more. See JCT Staff 2010 Estimates, *supra* note 40 at 54, Table 3.
94. H. Aaron, "Income Taxes and Housing," *American Economic Review* 60 (1970), 589, 803.
95. Surrey &McDaniel, *Tax Expenditures, supra* note 5, at 78.
96. Report of the President's Advisory Panel on Federal Tax Reform, *Simple, Fair, and Pro Growth: Proposals to Fix America's Tax System* (2005), 27; United States General Accounting Office, *Tax Policy: Tax Expenditures Deserve More Scrutiny* (June 1994).

experts conclude that the deduction for home mortgage interest "is unlikely to influence the homeownership rate," but does lead to over-consumption of owner-occupied housing by those who were already inclined to own homes.[97] As noted previously, the credits for higher education tuition payments have resulted in greater increases in college tuition than otherwise would have occurred, thereby shifting some of the benefit to colleges and universities. In addition, the monetization of tax expenditures through tax shelter transactions, in which passive investors, rather than actual business operators, reap the benefits of the subsidy when it is possible to do so, adds a pure "wasteful spending" element to the mix.[98] A similar analysis applies to a great many other tax expenditure subsidies. Thus, in reality, there are already three strikes against most tax expenditures.

2.5.3   THE CASE FOR CURBING TAX EXPENDITURES

There are additional distortions caused by tax expenditures. Edward Kleinbard, former Chief of Staff of the Joint Committee on Taxation, has vigorously advocated the elimination of many, if not most of the tax expenditures provided in the Code because tax expenditures corrupt the political process.[99] He reasons as follows:

> By excluding tax expenditures from the reach of most budget framework processes, Congress privileges tax expenditures over explicit spending. In doing so, Congress largely ignores the social costs of using tax subsidies to distort private sector allocations of goods and services, and the deadweight loss of higher taxes used to pay for these subsidies . . . . And at the same time, Congress both operates through and capitalizes on the prism of fiscal illusion.[100]

Because these spending programs are operated through the tax Code, they "effectively fall between the budget cracks."[101] Kleinbard echoes, and quotes, a similar analysis by Paul McDaniel over twenty years ago:

> Nonetheless, the budget process [i.e., the tax expenditure budget] has not proved an effective device by which to review, control, and coordinate tax expenditures with direct spending. The review of tax expenditures has been left to ad hoc actions by tax writing committees. Tax expenditures are largely

---

97. E. Glaeser & J. Shapiro, "The Benefits of the Home Mortgage Interest Deduction," *Tax Policy and the Economy* 17 (2003): 37, at 40, 76–80; see also W. Gale, J. Gruber & S. Stephens-Davidowitz, "Encouraging Homeownership Through the Tax Code," *Tax Notes* 115 (2007): 1171, at 1179 (the home mortgage interest deduction "has little if any positive effect on homeownership").
98. See, e.g., Surrey & McDaniel, "Tax Expenditure Concept," *supra* note 3, at 256–57.
99. E. Kleinbard, "How Tax Expenditures Distort Our Budget and Our Political Process," *Tax Notes* 123 (May 18, 2009): 925; see also Kleinbard, "Framework Legislation," *supra* note 43.
100. Kleinbard, "Framework Legislation," *supra* note 43, at 354.
101. *Ibid.*, 359.

uncontrolled by the budget process because no effective limits are imposed on them. The tax writing committees are not given directions by the budget resolution as to the level of tax expenditures for a given fiscal year. Instead, the committees are given an overall revenue figure that they are to meet. But they can meet this revenue target by increasing or reducing rates, personal exemptions, or the standard deduction for non-itemizers. Finally, there is virtually no coordination between tax expenditures and actions by the authorization-appropriations committees in the same budget area.[102]

But Kleinbard also evidences a belief that tax expenditures, particularly those that were labeled tax subsidies in the 2008 Report of the Staff of the Joint Committee on Taxation, simply ought not to exist in any form, whether as tax preferences or as outright spending.

Many tax expenditures, particularly those that are designed as business incentives, thus distort market prices and behavior through legislative fiat. Think how difficult it would be to enact into law a new tax expenditure benefitting one industry, if only the sponsor were required to describe his proposal as a "government economic five-year plan" rather than "targeted tax relief." Tax expenditure analysis is a way of demonstrating to policymakers the fundamental equivalence of "targeted tax relief" with a "tax and spend" big government.

Second, the introduction of [tax expenditures] in a revenue neutral fashion [by increasing rates] has another profound economic effect, which is that the tax rate imposed on the incomes of all [other] producers not adroit enough to have lobbied for their own targeted tax relief has increased. Here again economists have something really important to say: all taxes, no matter how beautifully implemented, impose "deadweight losses." "Deadweight loss" means that some transactions that are rational in a world without taxes become unaffordable in a world with those taxes, and therefore simply do not take place, and society as a whole becomes less wealthy. Because of deadweight loss (the transactions that remain unconsummated) . . . the cost to the private sector of paying taxes is greater than the value of those taxes transferred to the public sector (and in turn recycled back to individuals). . . .

What all this means is that, by virtue of granting "revenue neutral targeted tax relief," the . . . government may raise the same aggregate revenues as it did previously, but in doing so is imposing disproportionately more deadweight loss on the remaining taxable . . . private sector. Government revenues may stay constant, but the country as a whole is poorer by virtue of the incentive. This result is one of the great ironies of many tax expenditures, particularly those that fall into the category of business incentives—once the incentive's

---

102. *Ibid.*, quoting P. McDaniel, "Tax Expenditures as Tools of Government Action," in *Beyond Privatization: The Tools of Government Action*, ed., L. Salamon (Washington, D.C.: Urban Institute Press, 1989) 167, 178.

impact on tax burdens for others is considered, it impoverishes the country even more than it enriches the beneficiaries of the legislative largesse.[103]

In this respect, Kleinbard's position is quite similar to that of Surrey and McDaniel twenty-five years ago, when they concluded as follows.

[M]any tax expenditure incentives or corresponding direct programs may have little justification. Certainly most existing studies on the efficiency of tax expenditure incentives indicates a low response in relation to the funds involved.[104]

Kleinbard goes on to explain that the same deadweight loss problem arises when tax expenditures are not offset by rate increases, that is to say that targeted tax relief through tax expenditures always produces a deadweight loss that leaves the country poorer.[105]

Tax expenditures also exacerbate the deficit. There is little doubt that the U.S. government is facing a dire fiscal crisis due to revenue shortfalls. An August 2010 Congressional Budget Office (CBO) report summarizes the picture as follows.

In the CBO's current-law projections, once the economy has recovered the federal budget deficit amounts to between 2.5 percent and 3.0 percent of [gross domestic product] from 2014 to 2020. Projected deficits total $6.2 trillion for the 10 years starting 2011, raising federal debt held by the public to more than 69 percent of GDP by 2020, almost double the 36 percent of GDP observed at the end of 2007.[106]

The CBO report goes on to explain the import of these long-term projections as follows.

Although running deficits during or shortly after a recession generally hastens economic recovery, persistent deficits and ever-growing debt would have several negative consequences for the United States. National saving and investment would be lower than they would be otherwise, reducing output, wages, and incomes in the long run. If the payment of interest on the extra debt was financed by imposing higher marginal tax rates, those higher rates would discourage work and saving and further reduce output. Alternatively, policy-makers could choose to offset rising interest costs, at least in part, with reductions in benefits and services. Moreover, growing debt would increasingly restrict policymakers' ability to use fiscal policy to respond to unexpected challenges, such as economic downturns or international crises.

---

103. E. Kleinbard, "The Congress Within the Congress; How Tax Expenditures Distort Our Budget and Political Process," *Ohio Northern University Law Review* 36 (2010) 1, 8–9 (Congress Within the Congress).
104. Surrey & McDaniel, *Tax Expenditures, supra*, note 5, at 87.
105. Kleinbard, "Congress Within the Congress," *supra* note 103, at 10.
106. United States Congressional Budget Office, *The Budget and Economic Outlook: An Update*, available at http://www.cbo.gov/ftpdocs/117xx/doc11705/08-18-Update.pdf.

Unless policymakers restrain the growth of spending substantially, raise revenues significantly above their average percentage of GDP of the past 40 years, or adopt some combination of those two approaches, persistent budget deficits will cause federal debt to rise to unsupportable levels.[107]

Some expert analysts have predicted that continuation of the current patterns of taxing and spending likely will lead to "catastrophic budget failure ... with a significant probability of hyperinflation."[108]

This analysis makes it clear that the United States inevitably faces the choice of either raising taxes, cutting spending, or effecting some combination of the two, as politically unpalatable as those actions might be. However, the CBO also casts a damper on the idea of raising large amounts of revenue through generally higher marginal tax rates. Thus, unless the United States were to adopt a broad-based consumption tax, such as a value added tax (VAT) to supplement the income tax, on the revenue side the most readily apparent remedy to the fiscal crisis is base broadening.

Professor Calvin Johnson focuses on the need for revenues for the federal government as well a on the economic distortions that flow from tax expenditures.[109] He points out that federal spending over the next decade is projected by the Congressional Budget Office to be 150% of projected revenues. Because continuing deficits of that magnitude are not sustainable, he concludes that significantly increased tax revenues are inevitable. Johnson treats tax expenditures as "loopholes" and reasons as follows:

A tax does the least damage if it is as broad as possible, neutral, and unavoidable. A broader tax base means the lowest feasible tax rates, at whatever the level of revenue. The tax should be neutral across all investments so that it is the pretax demand, not the tax loopholes, that determines the allocation of capital.[110]

Johnson lists "loopholes," the closing of which he views as important revenue raisers. Although not all of the items on Johnson's list of "loopholes" are included in the tax expenditure budgets prepared by either OMB or the Staff of the Joint Committee on Taxation, and not every tax expenditure is on his list of "loopholes," many of the items are listed as tax expenditures. In the end, Johnson concludes, "[m]aking taxation more comprehensive and neutral will improve both the fairness and efficiency of the tax system."[111] Johnson's point should be very well taken, because some estimates show that the forgone revenues from tax expenditures exceed the total amount of personal income taxes

---

107. *Ibid.*, 27.
108. L. Burman, J. Rohaly, J. Rosenberg & D. Lim, "Catastrophic Budget Failure," *National Tax Journal* 63 (2010): 563, 581.
109. C. Johnson, "How to Raise $1 Trillion Without a VAT or a Rate Hike," *Tax Notes* 128 (Jul. 5, 2010): 101.
110. *Ibid.*, 102.
111. *Ibid.*, 107.

collected.[112] Furthermore, other studies indicate that federal taxes would need to be raised by almost 40% "to reduce—not eliminate, just reduce—the deficit to 3 percent of our GDP, the 2015 goal the Obama administration set in its 2011 budget," and "[t]hat tax boost would mean the lowest income tax rate would jump from 10 to nearly 14 percent, and the top rate from 35 to 48 percent."[113]

Johnson conflates tax expenditure analysis and tax reform, much the way Surrey originally did, and that very well may be the modern trend, at least as far as labeling is concerned. A 2010 Congressional Research Service Report concluded as follows:

> Tax expenditures account for a large proportion of the resources the federal government uses to achieve various national goals. In 2009, it was estimated that tax expenditures amounted to about $1 trillion and accounted for about a quarter of total expenditures. When combined with outlays for mandatory spending programs and net interest payments, almost three-quarters of total expenditures are for permanent programs that many claim are more or less on "autopilot." The proportion of total expenditures subject to annual review by the Appropriations Committees in the appropriations process has been declining over the past two decades. Given the long-term fiscal imbalances, part of the solution will likely involve tax reform and the limitation or outright elimination of some tax expenditures. Tax expenditure analysis can be a useful tool for policymakers considering tax reform proposals.[114]

This conclusion is not really any different than that which was reached by Surrey and McDaniel twenty-five years ago. In discussing tax expenditures in the context of tax reform in *Tax Expenditures*, they noted that many tax expenditures "are spending assistance that the legislators really do want to provide,"[115] and that the underlying desire for the expenditure often doomed to failure efforts to repeal them without substituting a direct spending alternative. Nevertheless, they went on to conclude that "many existing tax expenditures represent unneeded government assistance and should yield to tax reform efforts with no substitution of another program."[116]

Curbing tax expenditures thus appears to be a win-win solution to a number of vexing budgetary and administrative problems. First, from a tax administration

---

112. Committee for a Responsible Federal Budget, "Lets Get Specific: Tax Expenditures," October 2010, http://crfb.org/sites/default/files/Lets_Get_Specific_-_Tax_Expenditures_2.pdf, at 2 (last visited Oct. 15, 2010).

113. R. Altshuler, D. Lim & R. Williams, "Desperately Seeking Revenue" (Tax Policy Center, 2010), http://www.taxpolicycenter.org/UploadedPDF/412018_seeking_revenue.pdf (last visited Oct. 15, 2010).

114. T. Hungeford, Congressional Research Service, *Tax Expenditures and the Federal Budget* (2010), 17. See also Report of the President's Advisory Panel on Federal Tax Reform, *Simple, Fair, and Pro Growth: Proposals to Fix America's Tax System* (2005), 37–327 (generally treating repeal or modification (including expansion) of tax expenditures as tax reform rather than as spending reform).

115. Surrey & McDaniel, *Tax Expenditures, supra* note 5, at. 89.

116. *Ibid.*, 90.

perspective, the Internal Revenue Code is simplified every time a tax expenditure provision is repealed. The greater the number of tax expenditures repealed, the greater the corresponding simplification.[117] The transaction costs of business planning, as well as tax planning and compliance, can be significantly reduced. However, curbing tax expenditures will not be an easy political task. In recent years, Congress has shown an increasing affinity for new tax expenditures. In the first decade of the twenty-first century Congress added over thirty new tax expenditure credits to the Internal Revenue Code,[118] not to mention a variety of preferential deductions.[119]

Second, as noted by Surrey and McDaniel and recently reemphasized by Kleinbard, spending decisions can be approached more rationally if subsidies are provided through direct spending programs, with proposals evaluated by the congressional committees with appropriate jurisdiction, rather than by the House Ways and Means and the Senate Finance Committees.[120] This change, if effected, should result in better targeted spending and better coordinated eligibility.

Third, and most importantly, each and every tax expenditure repealed (or reduced) will result in less spending whenever the repealed (or reduced) tax subsidy is not replaced, or is only partially replaced, by new or increased direct spending. This is the heart of the reasoning underlying tax expenditure analysis as Surrey and McDaniel observed in 1985.

> Whether the objective is control of the aggregate level of federal spending or a balanced budget, failure to include tax expenditures fully in the budget process means that only 75 percent of total federal spending will be considered. As long as this practice persists, federal spending will be under no meaningful control.[121]

It seems clear in 2011, twenty-five years after Surrey and McDaniel's warning, that once tax expenditures are taken into account federal spending is spiraling further out of control. According to the Congressional Budget Office, the federal budget deficit was slightly less than $1.3 trillion in fiscal year 2010, which was approximately $125 billion less than the deficit in fiscal year 2010, and was equal to 8.9% of gross domestic product (GDP), down from 10.0% in 2009.[122] Relative to the

---

117. See *ibid.*, 26. Of course, where tax expenditures are replaced by direct spending programs, those direct spending programs will be complex—likely more complex than was the tax expenditure that they would replace—and the beneficiaries of the spending programs, their lawyers (other than tax lawyers) and the agencies administering the direct spending program will face greater complexity. *Ibid.*, at 93–94.
118. See B. Bittker, M. McMahon, Jr. & L. Zelenak, *Federal Income Taxation of Individuals*, 3rd ed. (New York: Warren, Gorham & Lamont, 2002), paras. 20.16–20.33, 27.09A–27.11E.
119. *Ibid.*, paras. 14.08, 14.11[8]–[10], 14.13.
120. Surrey & McDaniel, *Tax Expenditures, supra* note 5, at 106–107; Kleinbard, "Framework Legislation," *supra* note 43, at 359.
121. Surrey & McDaniel, *Tax Expenditures, supra* note 5, at 37.
122. Congressional Budget Office, Monthly Budget Review, Fiscal Year 2010 (Oct. 7, 2010), http://www.cbo.gov/ftpdocs/119xx/doc11936/SeptemberMBR.pdf (last visited Oct. 15, 2010).

size of the economy, the 2010 deficit was the second-highest shortfall (second only to that which occurred in 2009) since 1945.[123]

The deficit problem briefly described above adds further dimension and context to the tax expenditure quagmire. In 1985, Surrey and McDaniel observed that "tax expenditures keep tax rates high,"[124] and that net savings from tax expenditure repeal could be used to reduce marginal rates.[125] Today, however, the situation is different. In light of CBO data, in the second decade of twenty-first century, tax expenditure analysis urgently must be applied to eliminate as many tax expenditures as possible, without quibbling over whether the elimination of tax expenditures constitutes "spending reform" or "tax reform." This action is necessary to reduce the structural budget deficit. Nevertheless, when approaching repeal of tax expenditures, it is important to keep in mind the warning of Surrey and McDaniel that "[t]ax reform thus really becomes spending reform and requires the analytical tools used in evaluating spending programs."[126] To the extent repealed tax expenditures are replaced by direct spending programs, the budget deficit would not be narrowed. But even if some sort of direct spending program replaces some repealed tax expenditures, one might hope that the inefficiencies of tax expenditures, which so often reward taxpayers for engaging in a behavior in which they would have engaged without any incentive from the government, might be eliminated by more narrowly focused, and funded, direct spending programs.[127]

2.6   CONCLUSION

Today, tax expenditure analysis is second nature to all accomplished tax policy analysts, regardless of whether the particular analyst labels the repeal or modification of any particular tax expenditure as "spending reform" (or control) or as "tax reform." It is easy to forget that tax expenditure analysis was not always such an ingrained aspect of tax discourse. Decades of work by Paul McDaniel and Stanley Surrey advanced what was once an obscure notion to the forefront of tax and budget analysis. Although the two primary works regarding tax expenditure analysis, *Pathways to Tax Reform*, in 1973, and *Tax Expenditures*, in 1985, tended to focus tax expenditure analysis on the spending side of the budget, the political process, exemplified by the base broadening in the Tax Reform Act of 1986,[128] has more often viewed the tax expenditure budget as a list of potential tax reform issues. So too have most tax scholars who have recently focused attention

---

123. *Ibid.*
124. Surrey & McDaniel, *Tax Expenditures, supra* note 5, at 102.
125. *Ibid.*, 26.
126. *Ibid.*, 91.
127. *Ibid.*, 82–83.
128. Pub. L. No. 99–514, 100 Stat. 2085. See also United States Treasury Department, *Tax Reform for Fairness, Simplicity and Economic Growth* Vol. 1 (1984), 14–15, 37–42.

on tax expenditures. But all should bear in mind that with only a few exceptions, all of the income base broadening that has occurred over the past thirty years builds on the shoulders of the pioneers of tax expenditure analysis, Paul McDaniel and Stanley Surrey, and most, if not all of the failures of the income tax system as it exists today, derive from the failure of the political process to appreciate and apply the wisdom in their classic 1985 book, *Tax Expenditures*.

Chapter 3

The Tax Expenditure Concept Globally

*Miranda Stewart**

Paul McDaniel was a leader in comparative analysis of tax expenditures.[1] Since the 1980s, many developed countries have established comprehensive tax expenditure reporting, and the current state of play is evidenced by the recent OECD (2010) report. Some developing countries also carry out tax expenditure reporting and it is recommended by the IMF (Code for Fiscal Transparency, 2007) and World Bank. However, in spite of this expansion in use of the concept, many developing countries do not report tax expenditures and many issues remain for those countries that do report. This chapter surveys the use of tax expenditure analysis and reporting globally, and in particular the increase in tax expenditure reporting in

* Professor of Law, Co-Director of Taxation Studies, Law School, University of Melbourne, Australia. I am fortunate to have been taught and mentored by Professor McDaniel as a student and acting assistant professor at NYU School of Law between 1997 and 2000, and during a visit to the University of Florida Levin College of Law in 2007. It was always a rich learning experience, and a great privilege and pleasure, to work with Paul. The research in this chapter draws on Mark Burton and Miranda Stewart, *Promoting Budget Transparency through Tax Expenditure Management* (March 2011), a report prepared for the International Budget Partnership (www.internationalbudget.org), and published at SSRN of Melbourne Legal Studies Research Paper No. 544 (June 13, 2011), available from www.ssrn.edu. I am grateful for the funding provided by the IBP and for their valuable experience in budget transparency work in developing countries.
1. P. McDaniel & S. Surrey (eds.), *International Aspects of Tax Expenditures: A Comparative Study* (1985).

Yariv Brauner & Martin James McMahon, Jr. (eds), *The Proper Tax Base: Structural Fairness from an International and Comparative Perspective—Essays in Honour of Paul McDaniel*, pp. 47–85.
© 2012 Kluwer Law International BV, The Netherlands.

developing countries. This chapter discusses tax expenditure reporting in Chile, South Africa and India and considers the purpose and value of tax expenditure reporting for governments and civil society; the associated difficulties; and the issues and challenges that must be overcome to achieve meaningful tax expenditure reporting.

3.1   INTRODUCTION

"The purpose of a tax expenditure list is to give useful information about the extent to which government is intervening in the economic and social life of a country by running spending programs through its tax system."[2]

In 1985, Paul McDaniel and Stanley Surrey published the classic *International Aspects of Tax Expenditures: A Comparative Study*, which brought together scholars from the U.S., Canada, U.K., Sweden, the Netherlands and France to analyze and compare the definition and concept of tax expenditures in their different income tax, value added tax and wealth tax systems. Since the 1980s, many developed countries have established comprehensive tax expenditure reporting and tax expenditure analysis and reporting has continued to spread globally. An increasing number of "emerging" and "developing" countries now carry out tax expenditure reporting and it is recommended by the OECD, the IMF and the World Bank.

These global trends in increasing and more widespread tax expenditure reporting and the development of international norms about practice and implementation form part of a larger story about the emergence and spread in the last decade of "soft law" or norms that promote budget transparency.[3] Since the late 1990s, budget transparency has attracted increasing attention from international institutions, governments, and nongovernment actors concerned with budgets and fiscal policy reform. In this context, tax expenditure reporting has become both more widespread and more consistent across countries. Even so, it remains the case that many countries, in particular low income developing countries, still do not report tax expenditures (more generally, many of these countries still have very poor fiscal transparency). Challenges also remain for countries that do report tax expenditures.

Section 3.2 of this chapter surveys global trends in tax expenditure reporting and discusses the way in which tax expenditure reporting has been adopted as an element of the overall goals of budget transparency of international institutions, including the International Monetary Fund (IMF) and the Organisation for Economic Cooperation and Development (OECD). Section 3.3 turns to examine the experience of tax expenditure reporting in three "emerging" countries: South Africa, Chile and India. In all three countries, tax expenditure reporting has

---

2. *Ibid.*, 6.
3. This is discussed in depth in L. Philipps & M. Stewart, "Fiscal Transparency: Global Norms, Domestic Law, and the Politics of Budgets," *Brooklyn Journal of International Law* 34 (2009):797.

been embraced, to some extent, by both governments and civil society groups, as an element of budget transparency. Section 3.4 discusses the purpose and value of tax expenditure reporting for budget processes, governments and civil society organizations; and examines some of the issues and challenges that must be overcome to achieve meaningful tax expenditure reporting. A key element of this analysis is to be clear about the purpose of such reporting—and here, the chapter returns to the original goals of McDaniel and Surrey. Section 3.5 concludes.

3.2   GLOBAL TRENDS IN TAX EXPENDITURE REPORTING

Tax expenditure reporting began in the late 1960s on opposite sides of the Atlantic Ocean. In Germany, the Treasury has since 1967 published a report on tax subsidies and preferences.[4] In the United States, the first tax expenditure report was prepared by the U.S. Treasury in 1968.[5] In 1974, the U.S. budget law required the U.S. Treasury to report all federal tax expenditures annually in the budget.[6]

During the 1970s, scholarly interest in tax expenditures began to increase in a number of countries, largely as a result of the leadership in this field by McDaniel and Surrey including their discussion of the concept in various publications.[7] In 1976, Stanley Surrey and Emil Sunley of the United States brought together at the International Fiscal Association Israel IFA Congress, tax experts from 19 different countries to examine the use of tax incentives as an instrument for achievement of governmental goals.[8] At that time, only the governments of United States, Germany and Japan—using a concept of "special taxation measures" which was not comprehensive—reported tax expenditures.[9] However, the increased scholarly attention at this time occurred parallel to, and also stimulated, increased Treasury interest in many countries and in subsequent years, tax expenditure reporting began

---

4. Law to Promote Economic Stability and Growth of 1967, Germany ("Gesetz zur Forderung der Stabilitat und des Wachstums der Wirtschaft," see I. Mussener, Germany National Report, in S. Surrey & E. Sunley (eds.), *Tax Incentives as an Instrument for Achievement of Governmental Goals*, Cahiers de Droit Fiscal International, Vol LXIa (Jerusalem, Israel, 1976), p. 195.
5. 1968 Annual Report of the Secretary of the Treasury (US).
6. The Congressional Budget and Impoundment Control Act 1974 Pub. L. No. 93–344 Sec 601, 88 Stat. 297, 323; see US Office of Management and Budget, *Analytical Perspectives, Budget of the US Government, Fiscal Year 2011*, Chapter 17 (Washington DC: Government Printing Office, 2010), available at www.gpoaccess.gov/usbudget/fy11/pdf/spec.pdf.
7. S. Surrey (1973) *Pathways to Tax Reform*; S. Surrey & P. McDaniel, "The Tax Expenditure Concept: Current Developments and Emerging Issues," *Boston College Law Review* 20 (1979): 225; S. Surrey& P. McDaniel, "Tax Expenditures and the Budget Reform Act of 1974," *Boston College Industrial. & Commercial Law Review* 17 (1976): 679' P McDaniel, "The Impact of the Tax Expenditure Concept on Tax Reform" in W Neil Brooks (ed.) *The Quest for Tax Reform: The Royal Commission on Taxation Twenty Years Later* (Toronto: Carswell, 1988), 387–396.
8. S. Surrey & E. Sunley (eds.), *Tax Incentives as an Instrument for Achievement of Governmental Goals*, Cahiers de Droit Fiscal International, Vol LXIa (Jerusalem, Israel, 1976).
9. Torao Aoki, Japan National Report, in Surrey & Sunley (eds.), *ibid.*, 423.

to be adopted by a number of other countries, including Austria in 1978, Canada and France in 1979, Spain in 1979 and Australia in 1982.

Today, almost all OECD member country governments conduct some form of tax expenditure reporting. The OECD surveyed comparative country experience in 1984, 1996 and again in 2010. In 2001, the OECD published a detailed statement of *Best Practices for Budget Transparency* in which it describes the budget as "[t]he single most important policy document of governments, where policy objectives are reconciled and implemented in concrete terms."[10] In 2010, the OECD reported in detail on the process, content and issues relating to tax expenditure reporting in Canada, France, Germany, Japan, Korea, The Netherlands, Spain, Sweden, the U.K. and the U.S.[11] The concept is being reinvigorated, in budgetary and academic debates in some of these countries, including the United States.[12] In the United States, nongovernment organizations are paying significant attention to tax expenditures in an attempt to push for tax reform.[13] New Zealand originally started reporting tax expenditures in 1984 and stopped a few years later; however, in 2010 it began again to report tax expenditures.[14] The summary comparison of tax expenditures as a percentage of GDP in selected countries is extracted below in Table 3.1.

The IMF has also developed standards and codes on budget transparency and now assesses country practices using a process of fiscal Reports on Standards and Codes (ROSCs).[15] The IMF *Code and Manual for Fiscal Transparency* published in 2007 recommends that tax expenditures be reported in budget documents.[16] The *Manual* states:

> An important difference compared with expenditure programs is that tax expenditures do not require formal annual approval by the legislature (though some may be subject to sunset clauses); they remain in effect as long as the tax

---

10. OECD, *Best Practices for Budget Transparency* (2001) 1(3) OECD J. ON BUDGETING 1 [hereinafter *OECD Best Practices*]; see also prior reports in OECD (1984), *Tax Expenditures: A Review of Issues and Country Practices*, OECD, Paris; OECD (1996), *Tax Expenditures: Recent Experiences*, OECD, Paris.

11. OECD (2010) *Tax Expenditures in OECD Countries*, OECD: Paris http://www.oecd.org/document/37/0,3343,en_2649_34119_44961317_1_1_1_1,00.html.

12. See the history in McMahon, Chapter 2 in this volume; for a thoughtful discussion of tax expenditure analysis as an element in budget transparency and decision-making about government spending (its main purpose, as suggested in this chapter), see E. Kleinbard, "Tax Expenditure Framework Legislation," *National Tax Journal* 63 (2010): 353.

13. Participants include the Urban Institute and Brookings Institution Tax Policy Center, e.g., Burman, Leonard E, Eric Toder and Christopher Geissler, "How big are Total Individual Tax Expenditures and Who Benefits from Them?" (2008) *Tax Policy Center Discussion Paper* Number 31 (December), available from http://www.taxpolicycenter.org/; and the Center on Budget and Policy Priorities at http://www.cbpp.org/.

14. New Zealand, 2010 Tax Expenditure Statement, Budget 2010, http://purl.oclc.org/nzt/b-1296 p. 1.

15. International Monetary Fund (IMF) (2007) *Code* and *Manual on Fiscal Transparency*, *IMF*: Washington DC http://www.imf.org/external/np/pp/2007/eng/051507m.pdf; see *IMF Fact Sheet* at http://www.imf.org/external/np/exr/facts/fiscal.htm which reports that at December 2010, 93 countries had posted fiscal ROSCS on the IMF public website.

16. IMF, *ibid.*, Code § 3.1.3.

Table 3.1. Tax Expenditures in Selected OECD Countries

International comparison of tax expenditures (% of GDP)[†]
Latest actual year available

Purpose of tax expenditure. Income tax*	Canada (2004)	Germany (2006)	Korea (2006)	Netherlands (2006)	Spain (2009)	United Kingdom (2006)	United States (2008)
General tax relief	0.00	0.00	0.05	0.00	0.00	0.00	0.00
Low-income non-work related	0.02	0.00	0.03	0.00	0.04	0.09	0.11
Retirement	1.68	0.00	0.02	0.06	0.17	2.32	1.02
Work related	0.39	0.03	0.03	0.06	0.01	0.15	0.07
Education	0.12	0.00	0.12	0.06	0.00	0.00	0.13
Health	0.27	0.00	0.29	0.00	0.00	0.00	1.05
Housing	0.20	0.18	0.05	0.05	0.41	1.20	1.05
General business incentives	0.41	0.00	0.68	0.48	0.52	0.77	0.41
Research & development	0.24	0.00	0.15	0.07	0.03	0.04	0.09
Specific industry relief	0.05	0.01	0.18	0.18	0.04	0.11	0.23
Intergovernmental relations	1.55	0.03	0.00	0.00	0.00	0.00	0.63
Charity	0.21	0.00	0.13	0.09	0.02	0.09	0.33
Other	0.02	0.00	0.02	0.01	0.17	0.12	0.09
Total	5.16	0.26	1.75	1.06	1.41	4.90	5.21
Capital income taxation							
Accelerated depreciation	0.00	0.00	0.00	0.00	0.00	1.40	0.35
Interest	0.00	0.00	0.00	0.00	0.00	0.02	0.01
Dividends	0.27	0.04	0.00	0.00	0.00	0.00	0.02
Capital gains	0.35	0.00	0.00	0.00	0.16	1.65	0.33
Subtotal	0.62	0.04	0.00	0.00	0.16	3.07	0.70
Total	5.77	0.29	1.75	1.06	1.57	7.97	5.91
Make work pay provisions	0.01	0.00	0.01	0.04	0.74	0.35	0.06
Total	5.78	0.29	1.76	1.10	2.31	8.32	5.97

51

Table 3.1. (cont'd)

	Canada (2004)	Germany (2006)	Korea (2006)	Netherlands (2006)	Spain (2009)	United Kingdom (2006)	United States (2008)
Non-income tax related	1.16	0.45	0.72	0.90	2.25	4.47	0.00
Total	6.94	0.74	2.48	2.00	4.55	12.79	5.97
Structural items	3.22	0.00	0.03	0.00	0.28	4.24	0.20
Income tax expenditures by type*							
Credits	1.44	0.00	0.02	0.06	0.34	1.52	0.34
Deductions, exemptions & exclusions	2.64	0.28	1.70	0.80	1.61	4.92	4.63
Deferrals	1.50	0.00	0.00	0.05	0.00	1.47	0.80
Reduced rates	0.21	0.01	0.04	0.19	0.36	0.41	0.20

' For everiy country except for Canada and Spain, fiscal years rather than calendar years are used. For the United Kingdom, fiscal year 2006–07 is used (from April 6, 2006 to April 5, 2007).
* classification of income tax expenditures by purpose and by type is to some degree arbitrary.

Source: OECD (2010) Tax Expenditures in OECD Countries, OECD: Paris http://www.oecd.org/document/37/0,3343,en_2649_34119_44961317_1_1_1_1,00.html.

law is unchanged, and are therefore not subject to the same regular degree of scrutiny as actual expenditure. A proliferation of tax expenditures can therefore result in a serious loss of transparency.[17]

Consequently, the IMF recommends that the government budget or other fiscal papers should include a statement of the main central government tax expenditures. The statement should set out the public policy purpose of each provision, its duration, and the intended beneficiaries. Fiscal estimates of the revenue foregone from major tax expenditures should be provided and compared with the estimated results of previous tax expenditures compared with their policy purposes. This helps in assessing the effectiveness of tax expenditures compared to expenditure provisions. IMF Fiscal ROSCs for 94 countries are publicly available at www.imf.org and many of these discuss whether tax expenditures are reported, and if so how, in the subject country. The IMF has sought to encourage tax expenditure reporting in a number of Eastern European countries, if this would suit the overall budget and tax situation of the country.[18]

---

17. IMF, Manual *supra* note 15, para. [187].
18. For example, see Fiscal ROSC (2009) for Estonia, p. 10; Fiscal ROSC (2005) for Bulgaria, p. 26; Fiscal ROSC (2003) for Albania, paras. 19, 44, available from www.imf.org. Of these three countries, only Estonia has taken some steps towards establishing a tax expenditure report.

One reason suggested by the IMF (and others) for reporting tax expenditures is that they appear to cause significant losses of revenue, compared to the tax base in a particular country.[19] In Korea, tax expenditures across all taxes comprise 2.52% of GDP and more than 14% of all tax revenues collected.[20] In the U.K. and Canada, tax expenditures are estimated respectively 46% and 64% of total tax and nontax revenues of the central government.[21] In Chile, tax expenditures comprise 20.95% of government spending.[22] More generally, a research study of tax systems in Central America found that the tax base of many countries is narrow and there are many exemptions. In Guatemala, it was found that: ""tax expenditures," i.e., exemptions, exonerations, deductions, and other special privileges . . . were equal in value, in terms of foregone revenues, to the entire total of tax receipts."[23] A recent study of tax systems in Africa also indicates that many tax exemptions and other tax expenditures exist, "representing a staggering opportunity cost . . . in terms of revenue forgone. These typically favor the wealthy and should be greatly reduced or preferably abolished."[24] In particular, this is the case in indirect tax or tariff systems, as demonstrated by the experience in India (see Table 3.2). This is of great importance for countries which rely predominantly on such indirect taxes and tariffs for government revenue, including many low income countries. It has been estimated that in 2006 in Burundi, 60% of imports were exempted partly or fully from paying tax or duties, which amounted to a loss in tax revenue equivalent to 10.7% of GDP and 65.5% of revenues, while in 2006/7 in Tanzania, tax exemption amounted to 32% of total revenue and 5% of GDP.[25]

Another reason for tax expenditure reporting is that legislatures need to know about different kinds of "off-budget" spending, including tax expenditures, as the IMF recently explained:

> Tax expenditures can be another form of off-budget spending. Tax expenditures are exemptions and other tax concessions that fall outside the usual benchmarks for taxes. They are adopted to provide a benefit to a specific activity or class of taxpayer. Although there is a debate on how to measure tax expenditures, given their quasi-budgetary nature, parliament needs to be informed as to their amplitude, so as to exercise control over their size.[26]

---

19. IMF, Manual, *supra* note 15, para. [187]. See also Zhicheng Li Swift, *Managing the Effects of Tax Expenditures on National Budgets* (World Bank, Working Paper No. 3927, 2006).
20. OECD, *supra* note 11, Table II.9, p. 188; Table II.10, p. 190.
21. OECD, *supra* note 11, Canada: Table II.2, p. 176; U.K.: Table II.22, p. 206.
22. http://siteresources.worldbank.org/DATASTATISTICS/Resources/GDP.pdf.
23. M. Gallagher, "Assessing Tax Systems Using a Benchmarking Methodology," *Discussion Paper prepared for USAID*, available from www.fiscalreform.net, p. 7.
24. North-South Institute (2010), *Enhanced revenue mobilization in sub-Saharan Africa: constraints and opportunities*, OECD GLOBAL FORUM ON DEVELOPMENT 2010, Domestic Resource Mobilization for Development: the Taxation Challenge Session II Panel on "How can DRM through taxation help reduce poverty and inequality?," Roy Culpeper. All papers available at http://www.nsi-ins.ca/english/events/WiltonPark.asp, p. 1.
25. *Ibid.*
26. IMF, *Manual on the Role of the Legislature in the Budget Process* (April 2010), 13.

Table 3.2.   *Fiscal Significance of Tax Expenditures*

Country	Estimated Fiscal Significance of Tax Expenditures	Sources
Canada	Central government tax expenditures comprise 10.16% of GDP and 64.96% of central government total tax and non-tax receipts.	2004: OECD (2010), Table II.1, p. 173 and Table II.2, p. 176.
Chile	Central government income tax expenditures comprise 3.5% of GDP and 20.95% of direct central government expenditures.	2010: Chile, National Budget 2011, Table VII.4 (see further Table 4.4 below).
Germany	Central government tax expenditures comprise 0.74% of GDP, 8.81% of direct central government expenditure and 8.48% of central government total tax revenue.	2006: OECD (2010) Table II.5, p. 182 and Table II.6, p. 184.
India	The government estimates that corporate tax expenditures comprise 30% of total corporate tax revenues collected, while excise tax expenditures comprise 164% of total excise revenue collected (see further Table 4.1 below).	2009–10: India Ministry of Finance, Statement of Revenue Foregone 2010–11, Budget annex 12, Table 12, p. 33
Korea	Central government tax expenditures comprise 2.52% of GDP and 14.52% of central government total tax and non-tax receipts.	2006: OECD (2010) Table II.9, p. 188, Table II.10, p. 190.
South Africa	Central government tax expenditures comprise 3.4% of GDP and 12.5% of total tax revenue collected.	2008–09: South Africa National Budget 2011, Budget Review p. 64.
United Kingdom	Central government tax expenditures comprise 17.03% of GDP and 46.84% of total tax receipts.	2006–07: OECD (2010) Table II.21, p. 204, Table II.22, p. 206

A third reason is one of designing a "good" or effective tax system. The IMF describes tax expenditures as, in general, being a "second best" policy relative to direct spending, and it is suggested that identifying tax expenditures may assist in removing them from the tax system. If a government decides to introduce a new tax expenditure (exemption, credit or deduction), this should be done as part of the normal budget cycle, alongside regular budget spending, to help the parliament scrutinize the proposal and decide if it is the best policy.[27]

The World Bank in the past was a strong advocate of tax incentives for industrial development. However, it has now moved towards the IMF view of a broad tax base and low rates, and has begun to take a strong interest in governance.[28] In this context, it emphasizes good budget practices, suggesting that, like other government lending and other items of fiscal policy, tax expenditures "should be transparent and included in the budget."[29] The World Bank is currently developing a Public Expenditure Diagnostic Toolkit which includes several questions about tax expenditures.[30] One question that the Toolkit asks is "how significant are tax expenditures as a percentage of total budgeted expenditure?" (Qu 2.5.11). It also asks "do the estimates of new public policy proposals cover tax expenditures?" (Qu 2.6.4d). The Toolkit proposes a set of questions that would assist a civil society organization to track who knows about different kinds of off-budget fiscal operations, including off-budget funds, physical assets of the government, financial assets, and tax expenditures. Table 3.3 extracts key questions from the World Bank diagnostic table and modifies them to target tax expenditures. If these questions cannot be answered by participants or observers of budget processes, it is clear that increased reporting is required of tax expenditures.

Nongovernment organizations have also begun to examine the use of tax expenditure reporting as part of a civil society-grounded project to increase budget transparency. The goal of these organizations is, in part, to refocus budget transparency norms so as to advance a fiscal politics that emphasizes the values of distributive justice, participation and democratic legitimacy. Globally, some nongovernment organizations have made efforts at the international level to encourage and assess budget transparency in different countries.[31] The International Budget Partnership (IBP), a spin-off of the well-regarded U.S. Centre on Budget and Policy Priorities (Washington DC), is the most prominent of these "budget"

---

27. *Ibid.*
28. M. Stewart, "Global Trajectories of Tax Reform: The Discourse of Tax Reform in Developing and Transition Countries," Harvard International Law Journal 44 (2003): 139; M. Stewart & S. Jogarajan, "The International Monetary Fund and Tax Reform," British Tax Review 2. (2004): 146.
29. A. Shah (ed.) (2007) *Budgeting and Budgetary Institutions* (World Bank, Washington DC, available from http://siteresources.worldbank.org/PSGLP/Resources/BudgetingandBudgetaryInstitutions.pdf, p. 80.
30. See http://web.worldbank.org/WBSITE/EXTERNAL/TOPICS/EXTPUBLICSECTORAND GOVERNANCE/EXTPUBLICFINANCE/EXTTPA/0,contentMDK:20237087~menuPK: 2090883~pagePK:148956~piPK:216618~theSitPK:390367~isCURL:Y,00.html.
31. The concept of "transparency" has a venerable history, arising out of the fight against corruption: see Transparency International: The Global Coalition Against Corruption, www.transparency.org.

Table 3.3. *Who Knows What About Tax Expenditures*

	Tax Expenditures	*Action taken*
Who keeps account of tax expenditures?	(specify agency)	If yes, what action is taken? How is accounting carried out?
Who manages financial control of tax expenditures?	(specify agency)	
To which government agency are tax expenditures reported?	(specify agency)	How is report done? What is content of report?
Who audits tax expenditure reporting and management?	(specify audit agency)	How is audit managed?
Are tax expenditures reported to Cabinet?	(Yes/No)	How is report done? What is content of report?
Are tax expenditures reported to Parliament?	(Yes/No)	How is report done? What is content of report?
Are tax expenditures reported to the public?	(Yes/No)	How is report done? What is content of report?
Are tax expenditures reviewed by the media and/or civil society organizations/NGO's?	(Yes/No)	How is review done? How does government hear views about tax expenditures?

Source: World Bank, http://web.worldbank.org/WBSITE/EXTERNAL/TOPICS/EXTPUBLICSECTOR
ANDGOVERNANCE/EXTPUBLICFINANCE/EXTTPA/0,,contentMDK:20237087~menuPK:
2090883~pagePK:148956~piPK:216618~theSitePK:390367~isCURL:Y,00.html *(with variations by author).*

NGOs.[32] The rationale for an NGO focus on budget transparency is expressed as follows:

> In the context of widespread poverty in the developing world, citizens and civil society organizations are increasingly focusing on the budget and its effects on the distribution of resources, leading them to demand more and better budget information.[33]

---

32. The IBP mission is set out and all its publications are available at www.internationalbudget.org.
33. IDASA (Alta Fölscher et al), *Transparency And Participation In The Budget Process—South Africa: A Country Report* (IDASA) (December 2000), p. 3.

The IBP and other civil society organizations have observed what has been happening in the international institutions and developed countries, and have also taken the lead in researching fiscal transparency, developing their own standards of transparency, sometimes modified from those of other organizations.[34] In the late 1990s, the IBP worked with the Institute for Democracy in South Africa (IDASA) to formulate an alternative budget transparency questionnaire for use in South Africa and other African countries.[35] The IBP and IDASA have lauded the IMF Code as "an important advance in efforts to promote fiscal transparency," while also asserting that "it is limited, particularly when it is examined from the perspective of promoting participation in the budget decision-making process."[36] The IBP also helped to initiate a comparative study of budget transparency in five Latin American countries, designed and carried out by civil society groups and academics.[37]

The IBP prepares an ambitious biannual Open Budget Index (OBI) survey, the third of which was reported in 2010 (the OBI commenced in 2006). The OBI examines budget practices in a large number of countries through a detailed questionnaire applied every two years by local, independent academic or civil society researchers to assess performance in each country. The 2010 OBI surveyed 94 countries. It is obviously incomplete; as well as missing many countries with poor transparency, it also excludes a number of OECD countries with reasonably good budget practices, including Australia, Canada, Denmark and Japan, presumably because no civil society organization or academic has taken it upon themselves to carry out the survey. Nonetheless, next to the IMF published Fiscal ROSCs, it is the most comprehensive survey of government budget practices globally, and importantly does this from a civil society perspective. Tax expenditure reporting is addressed in the 2010 OBI, which reveals that out of 94 countries surveyed, only 36 are identified as carrying out any tax expenditure reporting.[38] Where countries do report tax expenditures, the report ranges from a minimal or partial identification and basic costing of tax expenditures, to a detailed description and analysis of tax expenditures, the benchmark tax system, and revenue foregone over a period of years. The level of detail will depend on resource and data constraints of governments. The view is taken here that even a minimal tax expenditure report that identifies costs and explains the most important tax expenditures, is better than no report at all.

---

34. M. Petrie, "Promoting Fiscal Transparency: The Complementary Roles of the IMF, Financial Markets, and Civil Society" 6–14 (Int'l Monetary Fund, Working Paper No. 03/199, 2003), available at http://www.imf.org/external/pubs/ft/wp/2003/wp03199.pdf.
35. IDASA, *supra* note 33.
36. *Ibid.*, p. 6, n. 4.
37. IBP, *Index of Budget Transparency in Five Latin American Countries: Argentina, Brazil, Chile, Mexico and Peru*, Jan. 10, 2002, http://internationalbudget.org/resources/LAbudtrans.pdf.
38. A summary analysis of these and other countries that carry out tax expenditure reporting is in Appendix 1 to Mark Burton and Miranda Stewart, *Promoting Budget Transparency through Tax Expenditure Management: A Report on Country Experience for Civil Society Advocates* (May 2011).

3.3 COUNTRY CASE STUDIES

This part moves from the general survey above to examine the experience and processes of tax expenditure management in three emerging countries: India, Chile and South Africa. The purpose is to show how tax expenditure reporting has developed over time, and the differences and similarities in approach, in each country. These countries are particularly interesting because in all of them, tax expenditure reporting has grown in the context of an activist-led push for increased transparency in the budget.

3.3.1 INDIA

India has a very significant, growing economy and is also the world's largest democracy (population 1.18 billion). India faces considerable pressure upon its resources and political processes combined with the opportunities and risks of significant economic growth. In this context, India has been relatively successful in establishing a robust and transparent approach to fiscal measures, at least at the federal (Union) level of government, which includes reporting on tax expenditures. However, it is important to note that under India's federal system of government, significant taxing and spending powers apply at provincial levels as well as the federal level. In particular, provinces are responsible for levying a Value Added Tax (VAT), whilst the national government imposes personal income and corporate taxes. Tax expenditure analysis at this point is almost exclusively carried out at the federal level.

Tax expenditure analysis in India dates back to the early 1980s.[39] Today, the Indian government publishes annually in its budget papers the *Statement of Revenue Foregone under the Central Tax System*. The current approach to reporting tax expenditures was proposed under the authority of the Fiscal Responsibility and Budget Management Act (2003)[40] (FRBMA) passed by the federal Parliament (Lok Sabha) and the accompanying Fiscal Responsibility and Budget Management Rules (2004). The Act was enacted as part of a widespread fiscal reform designed to tackle the growing budget deficit at that time. It requires statements of fiscal and economic strategy, and the medium-term economic framework, to be put before the legislature each year, including the monitoring of all taxes and expenditures. Under section 6, the central government "shall take suitable measures to ensure greater transparency in its fiscal operations in the public interest and minimize secrecy."

---

39. An early analysis was by A. Gupta, "Management of Tax Expenditures: A Study of the Indian Case" (Working Paper No. 446, Indian Institute of Management, Ahmedabad, 1982). See L Philipps, "Tax Expenditure Analysis in the Global South: Transplanting Fiscal Policy" in Brauner & Stewart (eds.), *Tax Law and Development* (Edward Elgar, 2012 *forthcoming)* for a detailed history of tax expenditure reporting in India.
40. Fiscal Responsibility and Budget Management Act, No. 39 of 2003, Gazette of India (2003).

A key driver for enactment of the FRMBA was to try to constrain the fiscal deficit at the federal level, in part because of international credit pressures. However, the push for greater budget openness in India started with grass roots civil society organizations tracking misuse of funds by local governments.[41] The IMF also promoted reform of Indian budget practices. In its 2001 fiscal ROSC on India, it commented that the country had "achieved a reasonably high level of fiscal transparency," but that "[e]nacting the Fiscal Responsibility and Budget Management Bill would be a major step forward given the emphasis it places on achieving a high standard of fiscal transparency."[42]

The Indian federal Minister for Finance first presented the *Statement of Revenue Foregone* in the 2006–2007 Union Budget.[43] The contents of this annual Statement are regularly reviewed by the Ministry of Finance and the Standing Committee on Finance. The Indian government also established a Task Force to report on reforms to improve revenue collections. The *Statement of Revenue Foregone 2011–12* states:

> The main objective of any tax system is to raise revenues to fund Government expenditures. The amount of revenue raised is determined to a large extent by tax bases and tax rates. It is also a function of a range of measures—special tax rates, exemption, deductions, rebates, deferrals and credits—that affect the level and distribution of tax. These measures are sometimes called "tax preferences." They have an impact on Government revenue (ie they have a cost) and reflect the policy choices of the Government.[44]

The *Statement on Revenue Foregone* defines these "tax preferences" or tax expenditures as follows:

> Tax preferences may be viewed as subsidy payments to preferred taxpayer such implicit payments are referred to as "tax expenditures" and it is often argued that they should appear as expenditure items in the Budget. In this context, the basic issue is not one of tax policy but one of efficiency and transparency—programme planning requires that the policy objectives be addressed explicitly; and programme budgeting calls for the inclusion of such outlays under their respective programme headings. Tax expenditures are spending programmes embedded in the tax statute.[45]

---

41. IBP, Access to Budget Information Empowers Citizens in India, http://openbudgetindex.org/files/IndiaStoryEnglish.pdf (last visited Apr. 8, 2009). Civil society activists include the Center for Budget & Governance Accountability, see, e.g., its Civil Society People's Charter on Union Budget 2008–09: People's Budget Initiative (Nov. 16, 2007), available at http://www.cbgaindia.org/press_releases.php?id=7.

42. IMF, *India: Report on the Observance of Standards and Codes*, para. 29, Country Report No. 04/96 (April 2004), available at http://www.imf.org/external/np/rosc/ind/fiscal.htm.

43. The 2011–12 *Statement of Revenue Foregone*, published in both Hindi and English, is at http://www.indiabudget.nic.in/ub2009–10/statrevfor.htm.

44. *Ibid.*, 1.

45. 2010–11 *Statement of Revenue Foregone, supra* note 33, annex 12, 1.

The Consultative Committee to the Indian Ministry of Finance defines tax expenditures further as reducing the amount of taxes to be paid by certain individuals or entities producing foregone tax revenues. In this sense, the fiscal effects of tax expenditure are just like those of direct government expenditure or grants.[46]

It has been noted that the prevalence of tax exemptions in India, as revealed in its *Statement of Revenue Foregone*, means that there are substantial variations in the effective tax rate paid in different industries and sectors.[47] The proliferation of tax exemptions and other incentives may distort investment decisions and allocative efficiencies of the Indian economy.[48] However, while it acknowledges the revenue foregone and economic costs of tax expenditures, the Indian Government has made a policy decision to maintain many tax incentives in the tax law. It explains:

> Government realizes that a number of tax incentives increase the deadweight costs, distort resource allocations and stunt productivity. On the other hand, keeping the need to promote the social and regional development goals of the Government and the need to provide special incentives to targeted groups, tax expenditures may still be justified and on that count some exemptions may be required to be retained for a longer period than others.[49]

The Indian Task Force on Fiscal Reform considers that tax expenditures can be justified when they are more cost effective than a direct expenditure program, are appropriately targeted to pursue government policy, avoid economic disruptions, do not unduly compromise the vertical and horizontal equity principles of taxation, do not unnecessarily complicate the tax structure, and correct market failures.[50]

As is the case in most other countries, the Indian government uses the revenue foregone method of estimating the cost of individual tax expenditures in their present state, in the current year and the future year. There is no forecast of revenue foregone from proposed future tax expenditures. Since 2009–2010, the revenue foregone is estimated by indicating the potential revenue gain that would be realized by removing the relevant tax expenditure, but assuming that the underlying tax base would not be affected by removal of the measure. The cost of each tax concession is determined independently assuming that other tax provisions remain unchanged. It is noted, however:

> (a) As the behavior of economic agents, overall economic activity or other Government policies could change along with the elimination of the specific tax preferences, the revenue implications could be different to that extent.

---

46. Ministry of Finance, "A Note on Tax Expenditures," 4th Meeting of the Consultative Committee (2007).
47. H. Poirson, "*The Tax System in India: Could Reform Spur Growth?*," IMF Working Paper 06/93, 2006.
48. *Ibid.*, at 15.
49. 2009–10 Union Budget, *Statement of Revenue Foregone under the Central Tax System*, 14.
50. *Ibid.*, 3.

(b) Many of the tax concessions do, however, interact with each other. There-fore, the interactive impact of tax incentives could turn out to be different from the revenue foregone calculated by adding up the estimates and projections for each provision.[51]

The Ministry of Finance also estimates the effective tax rate of various types of corporate tax payer, compared to the nominal tax rate for companies of 30%. It estimates total revenue foregone from tax expenditures in relation to corporate income tax, personal income tax, excise duty and customs duty, relative to the tax collections for these taxes. This is presented in Table 3.4.

Table 3.4.   Indian Total Revenue Foregone from Tax Expenditures, Estimates 2009–2010

(Crore rupees)[52](a)

	Revenue foregone in 2009–10	*Actual tax collection in 2009–10*	*% relevant tax collection 2009–10 (author calculation, rounded)*	*Revenue foregone in 2010–11*	*Estimated tax collection in 2010–11*
Corporate income tax	72881	244725	30%	88263	296377
Personal income tax	45142	132832	34%	50658	149066
Excise duty	169121	102858	164%	198291	133300
Customs duty	195288	85847	227%	174418	131800

(a) 1 Crore = 10 million

Source: 2010–11 Statement of Revenue Foregone, Budget annex 12, Table 12, p. 33.

The main direct tax expenditures in India include:

- exemptions for income and exemptions from long-term capital gains;
- incentives for regional/industrial development to encourage industrial growth;
- incentives for foreign exchange earnings/export of goods and services;
- exemptions for promotion of charitable, religious organizations and other nonprofit organizations;
- incentives for promotion of scientific research and development;
- exemption for income of funds on the basis of their being pass-through entities;

---

51. 2010–11 *Statement of Revenue Foregone, supra* note 33, annex 12.
52. A crore (abbreviated cr) is a unit in the Indian numbering system equal to ten million (10,000,000), or 100 lakh. It is widely used in India, Bangladesh, Nepal, and Pakistan. Large money amounts in India are often written in the form "23 cr," that is, 23,00,00,000 rupees (230,000,000 or 230 million in Western notation).

– exemptions for promotion of welfare of armed services personnel; and
– accelerated depreciation for capital investment.

The *2011–12 Statement of Revenue Foregone* identifies and estimates the revenue cost of 39 major tax expenditures of corporate taxpayers. The aggregate cost of corporate tax expenditures is estimated for the 2009–10 year to be 72,881 Crore rupees and projected estimate for the 2010–11 year is 88,263 Crore rupees. Some examples are extracted in Table 3.5. The largest corporate tax expenditure is accelerated depreciation.

Table 3.5. Examples of Indian Corporate Tax Expenditure Estimates

Item No.	Nature of Incentive	Revenue foregone Crore rupees (a) 2009–10	Projected revenue foregone Crore rupees (a) 2010–11
3	Deduction of export profits of units located in Special Economic Zones (sections 10A and 10AA)	4233	5126
8	Accelerated Depreciation (section 32)	29,308	35,494
11	Deduction on account of donations to charitable trusts and institutions (section 80G)	554	671
17	Deduction of profits of undertakings engaged in providing telecommunications services (section 80-IA)	3,510	4,251
18	Deduction of profits of undertakings engaged in generation, transmission and distribution of power (section 80-IA)	7,236	8,763
22	Deduction of profits of industrial undertakings located in Jammu and Kashmir (section 80-IB)	217	263
28	Deduction of profits of industrial undertakings derived from housing projects (section 80-IB)	986	1,194
36	Deduction of profits of undertakings set-up in Himachal Pradesh (section 80-IC)	2,127	2,576
38	Deduction in respect of employment of new workmen (section 80JJAA)	29	35

(a) 1 Crore = 10 million

Source: Indian Ministry of Finance, 2011–12 Statement of Revenue Foregone, Table 5, p. 22.

Table 3.5 provides a lot of useful information about corporate tax expenditures, even though the revenue foregone estimates must be treated with caution. It reveals the relative revenue cost of different tax preferences or tax breaks; in particular, it reveals the largest tax expenditures, such as accelerated depreciation. This may indicate that this tax provision benefits the widest number of businesses, but also that larger capital investments by large businesses are likely to benefit most from this tax expenditure. It identifies the brief title and legislative section under which the tax expenditure is provided. It does not, however, contain a summary explanation of what the tax expenditure does. It reveals that many Indian tax expenditures relate to targeted concessions for special economic zones, or particular geographic areas that the central government targets to assist in economic development. It also reveals that particular industrial sectors, such as telecommunications, power or mining, benefit from large tax expenditures. The *Statement* also provides further information about the benefit derived from particular industries from tax expenditures, through a lower effective tax rate. For example, information technology agencies have only a 15% effective tax rate and software development agencies have only an 18% effective tax rate.[53]

The *Statement* also estimates major tax expenditures for individuals. Some examples are extracted in Table 3.6. The estimates are based on a sample of 353 million individual tax returns. The total estimated revenue foregone from major individual tax expenditures is 40,297 Crore in 2009–10.

Table 3.6.   Examples of Indian Individual Tax Expenditure Estimates

Item No.	Nature of Incentive	Revenue foregone Crore rupees (a) 2009–10	Projected revenue foregone Crore rupees (a) 2010–11
1	Deduction on account of certain investments and payments (section 80C)	33,348	37,424
2	Deduction on account of contribution to certain pension funds (section 80CCC)	227	255
4	Deduction on account of health insurance premium (section 80D)	1,080	1,212
5	Deduction on account of expenditure for medical treatment of a dependent who is disabled (section 80DD)	107	120

---

53. 2010–11 *Statement of Revenue Foregone, supra* note 34, annex 12.

Table 3.6.   (cont'd)

Item No.	Nature of Incentive	Revenue foregone Crore rupees (a) 2009–10	Projected revenue foregone Crore rupees (a) 2010–11
9	Deduction on account of rent paid for housing accommodation	74	83
11	Deduction on account of contributions given to political parties (section 80GGC)	170	191
13	Deduction of profits of undertakings engaged in development of Special Economic Zones in pursuance to SEZ Act, 2005 (section 80-IAB)	215	241
21	Higher exemption limit for senior citizens	1376	1544
22	Higher exemption limit for women	2272	2550

(a) 1 Crore = 10 million

Source: Indian Ministry of Finance, 2011–12 Statement of Revenue Foregone, Table 7, p. 22.

The tax expenditure in Item 1 of Table 3.6 is by far the largest single individual tax expenditure. The description of this tax expenditure is not very informative, but in a Note to the Table, the *Statement* provides that this covers "investments in various savings instruments, repayment of principal of housing loan and payment of tuition fees for children."

In respect of indirect taxes, the bulk of tax expenditures are area-based exemptions (specific regional and export-oriented tax incentives). Other indirect tax subsidies relate to health and family welfare, defense and strategic sector, goods for educational and R&D/exhibitions, supplies to UN projects and diplomatic concessions, export promotion, power generation, and environmental protection. Excise tax expenditures include area based exemptions, health and family welfare, defense and strategic sector, goods for educational and R&D, supplies to UN projects and diplomatic concessions, export promotion, items of mass consumption, power generation and environmental protection. Customs duty exemptions include inputs and intermediates for the IT sector, research and educational material, computer literacy, sports, export promotion related exemptions, defense, security related imports, machinery, equipment, parts for specified public transport projects, petroleum exploration, R&D etc and exemptions for goods imported by United Nations, International organizations, diplomatic missions.

In 2005, the central Indian government did a substantial reform of tax expenditures in customs duties. The Minister for Finance stated:

> Exemptions have revenue implications. But they do serve a number of objectives by ensuring that the imported goods are not only available but also at lesser cost. Exemptions also serve to stimulate domestic economic activity by creating a level-playing field. However, it is also true that exemptions once granted tend to continue even if the objective has since been met and even if alternative and more transparent mechanism is available for achieving the desired objective.[54]

The *Statement of Revenue Foregone* reveals that exemptions in customs and excise significantly exceed the tax base (see Table 3.4). As customs reform takes place gradually in India, primarily to reduce tariffs, this affects estimates of tax expenditures. For example, the government took advantage of a decision to reduce overall rates of duty, to review a number of exemptions in the 2005 Budget. As a result, 34 exemptions were removed from the customs duties law. The revenue foregone from customs tax expenditures reduces as the overall customs rates reduces.

3.3.2   CHILE

In Chile, there is a Constitutional reporting obligation for tax expenditures, as is the case in several other Latin American "civil law" countries. The Constitution requires that all the fiscal benefits affecting State taxes be stated in the Budget Law every year:

> Article 19 of the Constitution of the Republic of Chile
>
> The Constitution guarantees every person:
>
> 22. No arbitrary discrimination by the State and its Agencies in economic matters. Only by virtue of law, and provided it does not produce such discrimination, may particular direct or indirect benefits in favour of some sector, activity or geographical zone be authorized, or special levies that affect one or another established. In the case of tax expenditures or indirect benefits, the assessment of the cost of such expenditures shall be annually included in the Budget Law.[55]

---

54. cited in Standing Committee on Finance (2005–06) Fourteenth Lok Sabha, Ministry of Finance, *Widening the Tax Base and Evasion of Tax*, 33rd Report (February 2006), 18 para. 29.
55. Constitution of the Republic of Chile, Art. 19.22 http://www.leychile.cl/Navegar?idNorma= 242302 [Unofficial translation by research assistant, Manuel Cardenas]: La Constitución asegura a todas las personas:

    > Para 22.- La no discriminación arbitraria en el trato que deben dar el Estado y sus organismos en materia económica. Sólo en virtud de una ley, y siempre que no signifique tal

In keeping with this mandate and in line with the recommendations of the IMF and the OECD, the Chilean Tax Administration (SII) conducts an annual estimate of tax expenditures. Interestingly, as noted by the IMF Fiscal ROSC for Chile of 2003, this reporting only began in 2001 and its legal basis in the Constitution was only made clear after the Fiscal ROSC.[56] The annual tax expenditure report is included in the *Report on the Public Finances* which accompanies the submission of the budget every year. The *Report* for 2011 (issued October 2010) presents the estimate made by the Chilean Tax Administration for 2009 tax expense relating to income tax and VAT and a projection for 2010 and 2011.

The *Report* defines tax expenditures as a transfer of public resources that is achieved by reducing tax obligations with respect to a benchmark tax, rather than by a direct expenditure.[57] For income tax (of individuals and enterprises), methodologically, the assessment of each tax expenditure is conducted independently; that is assuming that the other tax reliefs remain unchanged. First, revenue foregone from each individual tax expenditure is estimated based on a simulation that redoes every taxpayer's income tax return declaration, adding to its taxable base the exempt income or deduction, or reversing the effect of a deferral of income. Second, based on the aggregated data of the tax returns, the basic data about cost of tax expenditure is obtained directly from the aggregated declarations or the tax revenue estimate and then adjustments are made to simulate the repeal of the tax relief. The final totals incorporate the combined effect that is equivalent to the simultaneous repeal of the tax reliefs.

In estimating the revenue foregone from tax reliefs in the VAT, the method incorporates a supposed change in behavior by taxpayers: the repeal of a tax relief produces less income available to taxpayers, thereby also decreases their consumption subject to VAT (under the assumption that the total gross disbursement of the agents remains constant). Thus, the assessment calculates the VAT that would not be collected in the event of the repeal of each tax relief. To estimate most of the exemptions, a 1996 model of nondeductible VAT based on the Input-Output Matrix (MIP) of the Central Bank of Chile, is used. This model operates based on the intersectoral sales and purchases associated to the 75 products comprising the MIP. The tax expenditure of each exemption is estimated recalculating the nondeductible VAT of the model and then extending the result to the universe of the tax collection.

Table 3.7 presents the revenue foregone projection for 2011, differentiating tax expenditures by type of tax and type of tax relief. It shows that for income tax,

---

discriminación, se podrán autorizar determinados beneficios directos o indirectos en favor de algún sector, actividad o zona geográfica, o establecer gravámenes especiales que afecten a uno u otras. En el caso de las franquicias o beneficios indirectos, la estimación del costo de éstos deberá incluirse anualmente en la Ley de Presupuestos;....

56. The IMF Fiscal ROSC for Chile (2005) notes that the *Report* itself now states that reporting on tax expenditures is a Constitutional requirement: http://www.imf.org/external/pubs/ft/scr/2005/cr05262.pdf para. 7.
57. Relying on an OECD (2004) definition.

Table 3.7.   Total 2010 Tax Expenditures for Chile

	Millions of $ 2011	% GDP
Income Tax	4.069.010	3.5%
Special Regimes	179.215	0.15%
Exemptions	230.933	0.20%
Deductions	346.560	0.30%
Credits	277.382	0.24%
Tax deferrals	3.034.232	0.61%
Reduced rates	689	0.00%
VAT	889.641	0.77%
Exemptions and untaxed	469.133	0.40%
Credits	420.509	0.36%
Tax deferrals	0	0.00%
TOTAL	4.958.652	4.27%

Source: Table VII.4, Chile 2011 Budget.

the revenue forgone from tax expenditures represents 3.5% of GDP, and this revenue is foregone mainly as a result of the preferential treatment in the form of tax deferrals. The next most important tax expenditures in terms of revenue foregone are deductions from the tax base, tax credits and exemptions and untaxed items. The tax expenditures related to VAT are estimated at 0.77% of GDP, and arise from exemptions, untaxed items and tax credits.

Table 3.8 shows the tax expenditure estimates for 2011, aggregated by sector or objective that each provision seeks to benefit. It shows that 63.92% of the tax expenditures come from preferences that aim to stimulate saving and investment. In second place are incentives to the real estate sector, which account for 9.96% of total tax expenditures, followed by health with 6.92% and education with 5.56%.

Table 3.8.   2011 Tax Expenditures for Chile by Sector

Sector/Objective	Millions of $2011	% PIB	% TOTAL
Savings & Investment	3.169.671	2.73%	63.92%
Real Estate	493.911	0.43%	9.96%
Health	343.289	0.30%	6.92%
Education	275.571	0.24%	5.56%
Promotion of MSEs	227.717	0.20%	4.59%
Sectors Remaining	212.089	0.18%	4.28%
Regional	86.410	0.07%	1.74%
Combined effects unallocated	62.762	0.05%	1.27%

Table 3.8.   (cont'd)

Sector/Objective	Millions of $2011	%PIB	%TOTAL
Transportation	62.154	0.05%	1.25%
Insurance	22.025	0.02%	0.44%
Exporters	3.053	0.00%	0.06%
TOTAL	4.958.652	4.27%	100.00%

Source: Table VII.5 Chile 2011 Budget.

Table 3.9 shows Chile's estimated tax expenditures for the period 2009 to 2011, aggregated by type of tax. It shows that tax expenditures are concentrated mainly in the Personal Income Tax, reaching 2.33% of GDP in the estimate for 2011. The next most costly are in the Income Tax of Enterprises, with 1.17% of GDP and, finally, the tax expenditures related to VAT, estimated at 0.77% of the GDP. It also shows that as time has passed we have seen a significant decrease in tax expense related to the Personal Income Tax, which in 2010 reached 3.72% of the GDP and an increase of the tax expenditure of enterprises, which in 2010 reached 0.93% of the GDP. These changes are explained mainly by the increase of the enterprise income tax rate from 17% to 20% in this time. This reduces the difference between the enterprise income tax rate and the personal income tax rate, causing a decrease of the tax expenditure from the deferral of business income taxation. On the other hand, this explains the increase of tax expenditures related to exemptions, deductions, and deferral of enterprises.

Table 3.9.   Chile estimated tax expenditures 2009–2011

	2009		2010		2011	
	Mill. USD	%GDP	Million USD	%GDP	Million USD	%GDP
(I) Income Tax	6.901	4.22%	9.375	4.65%	8.272	3.50%
A) Enterprises	1.722	1.05%	1.881	0.93%	2.771	1.17%
B) Persons	5.179	3.16%	7.494	3.72%	5.501	2.33%
(II) VAT	1.415	0.86%	1.543	0.77%	1.809	0.77%
TOTAL	8.316	5.08%	10.918	5.42%	10.081	4.27%

Source: Table VII.6 Chile 2011 Budget.

3.3.3   SOUTH AFRICA

South Africa's transition to democracy in establishment of the new state in 1994 brought with it substantial efforts to establish fiscal transparency in the budget process.[58] Its significant efforts are shown by South Africa's overall ranking of first place in the OBI 2010. South Africa has also been ranked highly, indeed above the U.K., in its compliance with OECD *Best Practices* on fiscal transparency.[59] As a leader in the region, South Africa has also influenced the activities of some other countries to conduct fiscal reform and increase budget transparency in recent years. South' Africa has a substantial and informative budget website, including guides to the national budget in Afrikaans, English, Tswana, Xhosa, and Zulu.[60] The Treasury website states: "The Constitution of the Republic (Chapter 13) mandates the National Treasury to ensure transparency, accountability and sound financial controls in the management of public finances."[61]

The high level of fiscal transparency in South Africa was a response both to civil society action and to external influence. The Budget Information Service of IDASA with the IBP produced a report on transparency and participation in South Africa's budget process, released in October 1999 and revised in 2000.[62] Around the same time, South Africa introduced a medium-term expenditure framework for the budget.[63] One of the reasons for the relatively successful implementation of the medium term expenditure framework in South Africa was its link to connection with the local activist push for fiscal transparency.[64]

In 1994, the first *Katz Commission* report into tax reform in South Africa argued that tax expenditure analysis would be useful, but the Commission was unable to quantify the cost of tax incentives "due to the lack of useful and accurate data and a serious manpower shortage in revenue offices."[65] The *Katz Commission* concluded however that the revenue cost of tax expenditures seemed to be substantial, and the inability to cost tax expenditures was "a most unfortunate development which must be changed if South Africa is to develop a rational tax policy."[66] In 2002, the IMF fiscal ROSC for South Africa made a recommendation to introduce a tax expenditure report. South Africa subsequently gave an

---

58. African Fiscal Transparency, South Africa, http://www.internationalbudget.org/resources/SAFRICA.pdf.
59. F. Bastida & B. Benito, "Central Government Budget Practices and Transparency: An International Comparison," Public Administration Review 85 (2007): 667, 680, 684–685.
60. National Treasury, Republic of South Africa, www.treasury.gov.za.
61. National Treasury, Republic of South Africa, The Role of the National Treasury, http://www.finance.gov.za/nt/info.aspx.
62. IDASA, *supra* note 33, at 3. The South African report is said to have influenced research in other countries in Eastern Europe, Africa, and Latin America. *Ibid.,* 4.
63. See Foreword, *in* Nat''l Treasury Dep''t, Republic Of S. Afr., Medium Term Budget Policy Statement (1997), available at http://www.treasury.gov.za/documents/mtbps/1997/all.pdf.
64. Philipps & Stewart, *supra* note 3.
65. Interim Report of the Commission of Inquiry into Certain Aspects of the Tax Structure of South Africa (1994) (The first Katz Commission report), para. 13.5.2; see Republic of South Africa, National Budget 2011, Budget Review Annexure C, 179ff, http://www.treasury.gov.za/documents/national%20budget/2011/review/Annexure%20c.pdf.
66. Interim Report, *ibid*.

undertaking to introduce a basic tax expenditure statement in its budget. In 2003, the government identified some major tax expenditures in its annual Budget Review, with intended further development towards a comprehensive quantitative statement on revenues foregone.[67] A list of tax expenditures was also included in the 2006 Budget.

In the 2011 *Budget Review* paper, the objectives of a Tax Expenditure Statement are stated as being to increase fiscal transparency and accountability; create comparability between direct and indirect government expenditures; and assist in the design of tax policy by promoting and informing public debate. The 2011 *Budget Review* contains for the first time a tax expenditure statement, including a table of aggregate tax expenditures. The Ministry notes that tax expenditures, conservatively estimated, amounted to 3.4% of GDP and 12.5% of total tax revenue collected for the 2008/2009 year.[68]

Tax expenditures have been generally defined as any tax preference, including exemptions that exclude income from the tax base or allowances that are deductible from gross income or a reduction in a rate of tax or tax deferrals that delay the payment of tax.[69] The much longer definition of tax expenditure in the *2011 Budget Review* reflects research by the Ministry of Finance into definitions adopted elsewhere in the world:[70]

> Tax expenditures are indirect government expenditures that are not reported in the normal budget process. They are tax provisions that reduce the amount of tax revenue that could otherwise have been collected. Tax expenditures can be defined as deviations from the benchmark of a current standard tax legislative framework. A benchmark is a reference point against which the nature and extent of a concession can be identified—it is the standard taxation treatment that should apply to similar taxpayers or types of economic activities. Tax expenditures deviate from this benchmark of a good tax system that adheres to the basic principles of neutrality and equity. A less robust but more practical approach is to define tax expenditures merely as a deviation from the basic tax structure, without reference to an ideal benchmark. For example, the U.S. Treasury's definition of a tax expenditure states that a tax expenditure must: (a) be special in that it applies to a narrow class of transactions or taxpayers; and (b) have a general provision and a specific provision that provides an exemption.

---

67. South African Budget Review 2003, Summary of Tax Proposals, Annexure C, p. 228.
68. See Republic of South Africa, National Budget 2011, *Budget Review* p. 64 and Annexure C, 179ff; available at: http://www.treasury.gov.za/documents/national%20budget/2011/review/Annexure%20c.pdf.
69. South African Budget Review 2005, Summary of Tax Proposals, Annexure C, p. 213.
70. Republic of South Africa, *National Budget 2011*, Annexure C, p. 179, available at: http://www.treasury.gov.za/documents/national%20budget/2011/review/Annexure%20c.pdf.

Up until 2009, tax expenditures were listed individually under the categories of personal income, corporate, estate duties and VAT. The policy rationale for each exemption is listed alongside each one, enabling considerable transparency in the reporting process. The *2011 Statement* states that it applies the revenue foregone method, but does not set out how this is estimated. However, where the 2011 *Statement* is more ambitious is in its presentation of time series data for four years regarding tax exemptions (three prior financial years and the current financial year). It does not forecast future revenue foregone nor contain any provisions on future or proposed tax expenditures.

Table 3.10 sets out some specific tax expenditures in the personal income tax, corporate income tax and VAT.

Table 3.10.   South Africa Tax Expenditure Estimates 2011

Table C1 Tax expenditure estimates–R million

Personal income tax	*2005/06*	*2006/07*	*2007/08*	*2008/09*
Pension and retirement annuity[1]	12 722	13 538	15 464	18 349
-pension contributions employees	*4711*	*4911*	*5 495*	*6 567*
-pension contributions employers	*5298*	*5 523*	*6180*	*7386*
-retirement annuity	*2 713*	*3 105*	*3 790*	*4 397*
Medical	9 155	12 541	5 753	6 742
-medical contributions & deductions				
employees	*3 521*	*4 939*	*5 753*	*6 742*
- medical contributions—employers[2]	*5 634*	*7 902*	*n/a*	*n/a*
Interest exemptions	1 290	1 715	2 283	3 033
Secondary rebate (65 years and older)	739	739	769	828
Donations	141	178	230	282
Capital gains tax (annual exclusion)	74	98	121	69
Total: Personal income tax	24 122	29 109	24 620	29 303

Corporate income tax				
Small business corporation tax savings	178	627	747	675
Research and development (R &D)	183	313	286	219
Learnership allowances	179	221	324	193
Strategic Industrial policy[3]	513	281	228	61
Flim incentive	186	194	319	n/a
Urban development zones (UDZ)	28	65	90	85
Total: Corporate income tax	1 267	1 701	1 995	1 233

Table 3.10.   (cont'd)

Value-added tax Zero-rated supplies				
19 Basic Food, items[4]	10 036	11 376	13 107	13 907
Petrol[5]	6 837	7 763	9 176	10 524
Diesel[5]	586	736	948	1 249
Paraffin[5]	430	454	516	520
Municipal property rates	-	2 618	3 008	3 774
Reduced rates for "commercial" accommodation	80	85	95	113
Subtotal: zero-rated supplies	17 969	23 032	26 849	30 086
Exempt supplies (Public transport & education)	604	682	785	832

Source: Republic of South Africa, National Budget 2011, *Budget Review* Annexure C, p. 181, Table 12, http://www.treasury.gov.za/documents/national%20budget/2011/review/Annexure%20c.pdf.

Personal income tax expenditures in South Africa include:

- deductibility of donations to public benefit organizations
- exemptions of scholarships, war and disability pensions
- reduced capital gains tax rate
- exemption on interest income
- deductions for contributions to pension funds and superannuation schemes
- exemptions for certain foreign dividends.

The justification of these tax expenditures is set out in the *Review*. For example, the rationale for the tax preference for contributions to pension funds is to provide long-term budget relief for retiring employees.

Corporate income tax expenditures listed in the 2006 *Review* include tax deductions for mining exactions, exemptions for body corporate, deduction of insurance premiums, allowances for strategic industrial projects, film rebate subsidies, deductions for research and development capital expenditure, accelerated depreciation for research and development buildings. Other corporate tax expenditures listed in 2011 (see Table 3.10) include incentives for films; special development zones; and research and development. Most of the policy rationales for corporate income tax expenditures refer to stimulating industrial investment in particular areas or sectors, for example to encourage film production in South Africa, aid small business development, encourage research and development, or create employment and encouraging investment in general.[71]

---

71. South African Budget Review 2005, Annexure B, Table C.6, p. 215.

However, the *Statement 2011* acknowledges that this most recent analysis misses some important tax expenditures, most importantly accelerated depreciation of business assets (especially mining assets). This is noted as being a potentially significant tax expenditure item.[72] It is stated that at present, data is not available to estimate this tax expenditure.

The VAT law in South Africa exempts certain services and goods from taxation. These are listed as including financial services, road and rail transport, education services and the supply of after school care or crèche. The reasons behind such exemptions are reported as being provided for administrative as well as relief-based purposes.[73]

3.4 PURPOSE AND CHALLENGES OF TAX EXPENDITURE REPORTING

In their 1985 comparative study, McDaniel and Surrey identified issues and challenges in tax expenditure reporting, but concluded at that time, that it was possible to come to a cross-country agreement about the basic elements of a benchmark and approach to tax expenditures. In this regard, it is interesting to compare the experience of India, Chile and South Africa, which all began tax expenditure reporting in the last decade. The brief survey of each country's tax expenditure reporting process and content in the previous section indicates that there are, indeed, substantial similarities in approach of the different countries to tax expenditure reporting, as well as in the types of tax expenditures that exist in each country. This has been a result of policy learning and the development of international budget norms that can be traced to the work of McDaniel and Surrey nearly 3 decades ago. Further, it is clear that as a result, each country's tax expenditure reports have been successful in providing some information about spending through the tax system. At the same time, there are some significant differences between country approaches and each country report also has limitations which must be acknowledged.

The Indian *Statement of Revenue Foregone* contains significant useful information and data analysis of the direct and indirect tax systems levied by the central government. It has been published annually to the legislature and the broader public as part of the annual Budget papers and this greatly enhances budget transparency. However, the *Statement* does not explicitly define the benchmark tax system for all of the taxes that it analyzes. An explicit explanation of the benchmark would assist in tax policy analysis of the tax expenditures. Ideally, the *Statement* would be expanded in the future to deal with estimates over a period of 3 to 5 years, enabling comparison of importance of different tax expenditures over time. The *Statement* should identify in more detail each tax expenditure provision, and what it does (not merely by title and section reference). It should also set out

---

72. See Republic of South Africa, National Budget 2011, *Budget Review* Annexure C, p. 182, http://www.treasury.gov.za/documents/national%20budget/2011/review/Annexure%20c.pdf.
73. South African Budget Review 2005, Annexure B, Table C.8, p. 216.

the tax expenditure as a percentage of GDP and of total tax collection. Finally, the *Statement* deals only with central government tax expenditures. However, as noted, India is a highly decentralized federation, and many of the States provide significant tax incentives and exemptions. It is important to identify the provincial tax expenditures in those taxes.[74] Unlike the reports of many other countries, the Indian *Statement* is accompanied by government statements that explain or justify the policy behind particular tax expenditures, and India also attempts a distributional analysis of the impact of some of its tax expenditures.

Chile has a well-established tax expenditure reporting process which provides useful overall estimates and comparisons across a period of years. It differs from India and South Africa in the strong Constitutional requirement for equality of treatment in economic revenues and expenditures and reporting of any incentives or preferences by region and other characteristics, which provides a very clear legal mandate for tax expenditure reporting. The Chilean tax expenditure report is especially useful in its breakdown of tax expenditures by industry sector. The report is publicly available on the web with other budget papers annually and provides an overall analysis of tax expenditures across three years, which enables a comparison over time. However, it does not provide details of each tax law provision that establishes the exemption or other tax incentive, and its revenue cost and nor does it contain a detailed policy justification of tax expenditures.

The Chilean government could improve its ongoing management of tax expenditures (this could apply to most countries that report tax expenditures). For example, in respect of new tax expenditures, the law is subject to evaluation and justification only in the discussion of the Bill which creates the tax expenditure, and not on an ongoing basis. There do not appear to be any restrictions on new or existing tax expenditures.

As explained in the previous section, South Africa ranks very highly in terms of budget transparency, including in respect of its tax expenditure report. It defines tax expenditures (and the benchmark) in detail. The country government has been explicit about the resources needed for it to prepare a proper tax expenditure report, and has explained that it will gradually expand the report, including for the first time in 2011 a tax expenditure statement in the *Budget Review*, across a 4 year time period but does not forecast revenue foregone in future. The statement includes a policy justification for the tax expenditures, however the most recent statement misses some important tax expenditures, in particular accelerated depreciation, primarily for data requirements.

3.4.1   PURPOSE

The goal stated by McDaniel and Surrey to give "useful information" about the governments "spending programs through its tax system" remains the fundamental

---

74. As far as the author has been able to determine, no provincial Indian government reports tax expenditures.

purpose of tax expenditure reporting (see quote at the beginning of this chapter). The other goals of tax expenditure reporting, including development of good tax policy and reducing revenue loss, are less significant than this fundamental goal. This is partly because they may be considered as "sub-goals" of the overall political goal, and partly because tax expenditure reporting cannot, itself, hope to achieve the ambitions sometimes set for it, of improving tax policy formation or raising revenues.

As indicated in Table 3.2 above, total tax expenditures in a country may be very large in terms of revenue foregone, or of total government expenditure. However, comparing the fiscal significance of tax expenditures is of limited analytic value because of the wide variety in data, definitions and tax system: a comparison merely begs the question of how tax expenditures are identified and measured. The aggregate estimated size of tax expenditures in particular will vary significantly depending on the definition of the benchmark. More fundamentally, recent experience, including in the US, suggests that setting out the massive revenue foregone as a result of key tax expenditures may not have sufficient political weight to generate real tax reform.

So what is the role for tax expenditure reporting in the budget, especially in emerging or developing countries? It is suggested here that tax expenditure reporting and management has primary value as an element of budget transparency for democratic debate. Budgeting is a political and technical process for organizing government fiscal activities.[75] Prudence in fiscal management—in some common-sense way, matching expenditures to revenues—is the essence of budgeting. Just as budgeting has a long tradition, the basic principle of fiscal transparency, under which governmental fiscal activities should be subject to public scrutiny, is not new. In many developing countries, the "organic finance laws" are based on administrative practices that became entrenched during colonial times.[76] Tax expenditure analysis, however, is relatively new—and post-colonial—and so needs to be explicitly incorporated into the budget process.

The political value of enhancing public information and debate is at the heart of tax expenditure reporting, as tax expenditure reporting exposes all forms of government spending to the same level of scrutiny in the budget process by the legislature and the public. This assists in informed decision-making by the legislature and facilitates public understanding and advocacy. Tax expenditure reporting may also enhance a government's fiscal management. If major tax expenditures are not properly identified and reported, the Treasury may overestimate revenues in the budget. This leads to an inaccurate budget and may mean that

---

75. A. Wildavsky, "A Budget for All Seasons? Why the Traditional Budget Lasts," 38 Public Administration Review (1978): 501, 502.

76. M. Stevens, "Institutional and Incentive Issues in Public Financial Management Reform in Poor Countries" (World Bank, Working Paper No. 35106, 2004): 5, available at http://www.wds.worldbank.org/external/default/WDSContentServer/WDSP/IB/2006/027/000090341_20060207162350/Rendered/PDF/351060Institutional0issues.pdf.

sharp expenditure cuts have to be made late by the government when it is executing the budget.[77]

The public debate that may be generated by tax expenditure reporting also promotes public consideration of how the government should act to achieve its various policy goals (e.g., through public ownership of resources, regulation, direct spending, taxation or tax expenditures). Tax expenditure analysis is no different from public policy analysis more generally as it entails consideration of the best means of achieving a government's objectives.

As already suggested, tax expenditure reporting is likely to have a lesser role to play in fundamental tax reform, or in contributing to theory about the definition of the tax base. However, tax expenditure reporting may promote analysis of tax policy principles and potential improvements to the tax system for a particular community. This is because the very process of discussion of how to define tax expenditures and set the tax benchmark can promote closer consideration of a community's aspirations for its taxation system. The benchmark comprises a statement of what the country ought to tax, in an ideal world. Tax expenditure advocacy is one avenue by which civil society organizations can make arguments about what should be taxed and about the existing fairness and effectiveness of the tax system.

More specifically in the context of developing countries, tax expenditure reporting could be used strategically to build domestic political support for base-broadening tax reforms, in particular the repeal of special tax incentives. Many scholars and institutions have criticized developing countries' use of investment tax incentives, pointing out their negative effects on corporate tax revenue and on the efficiency and fairness of tax systems, as well as a process of tax competition.[78] Promoting more transparency at the country level with respect to the cost and distributive impact of tax expenditures could help to resolve this impasse by enabling a country's own citizens to challenge incentives that shift the burden of taxation onto local firms and individuals without achieving any clear benefits.[79]

3.4.2   TAX EXPENDITURE MANAGEMENT AS AN EFFECTIVE ELEMENT
             OF THE BUDGET PROCESS

The purpose of the tax expenditure report is central in determining what information should be provided in it and how it should be monitored, managed and

---

77. See Shah, *supra* note 29, at 242.
78. For the debate on tax incentives and harmful tax competition, see, among other sources, M. Keen & A. Simone, "Tax Policy in Developing Countries: Some Lessons from the 1990s and Some Challenges Ahead," in *Helping Countries Develop: The Role of Fiscal Policy*, ed. S. Gupta, B. Clements & G. Inchauste (Washington, D.C.: International Monetary Fund, 2004): 32; R. Avi-Yonah, "The OECD Harmful Tax Competition Report: "A Retrospective After a Decade," *Brooklyn. Journal of International Law* 34 (2009): 783; Y. Margalioth, "Tax Competition, Foreign Direct Investments and Growth: Using the Tax System to Promote Developing Countries," *Virginia. Tax Review* 23 (2003) 161, 192–194.
79. Philipps and Stewart, *supra* note 3.

evaluated. A government may wish to estimate the overall revenue cost of a policy that is delivered through tax expenditures in order to decide whether the use of the tax system is appropriate, or to comply with demands for "transparency" from international financial institutions. Civil society organizations are more likely to be interested in a broad range of information about tax expenditures for both business and individuals, including the distributional impact of a tax expenditure (who benefits most or who does not benefit at all) and whether particular tax expenditures are effective in achieving public policy goals such as encouraging investment or enhancing saving.

However, merely reporting tax expenditures does not fully enable critical scrutiny of tax expenditures by civil society or government. Active tax expenditure management, of which reporting and costing are two important elements, entails operation of a framework for identifying, measuring and critically assessing the merits of tax expenditures, before they are legislated and on an ongoing basis over time. For example, in addition to its annual published tax expenditure report, a government could periodically examine the cost and justification for its main tax expenditures in detail, with the goal of determining its distributional impact, if the cost is increasing or decreasing over time, whether there continues to be a good policy justification for the tax expenditure compared to other policy goals and instruments. For each tax expenditure, the report should be able to assist in answering the question: Does the government want to support this policy objective, and is a tax expenditure the best way of achieving it?

In many countries, tax expenditures are reported as part of the annual budget. This has the advantage that the tax expenditure report is a regular element of the budget. This is currently the case in India, South Africa and Chile. However, a disadvantage of this timing is that it is difficult for civil society groups and parliamentarians to respond to the tax expenditure report by making proposals to change tax expenditures in the budget.

An alternative approach would require that a tax expenditure report be released in advance of the annual preparation of the national budget. This could assist in ensuring that consideration of the report can meaningfully inform consideration of revenue and spending measures, although it could also contribute to a lack of attention being paid to the tax expenditure report which is not a core part of the budget cycle.

It is suggested that, if country resources are available, key elements of successful tax expenditure management require the following:

1. Definition of the "benchmark tax law" for each tax and of a "tax expenditure"—the definition of the benchmark should be clearly stated and defended within the tax expenditure report.
2. Comprehensive identification of all types of tax expenditures—a tax expenditure report ought to comprehensively report upon all tax expenditures. At a minimum the tax expenditure report should identify the most expensive tax expenditures and report in detail on those tax expenditures.

3. Method for estimating revenue foregone (a credible measurement frame-work)—the method used for estimating individual tax expenditures should be clearly set out in the report. A significant factor affecting the usefulness of a tax expenditure statement is the accuracy with which the cost of a particular tax expenditure is determined. The degree to which each tax expenditure estimate is reliable ought to be clearly indicated.

4. Break outs in the reporting of aggregate tax expenditures
   a. Tax expenditures should be organized by government function (e.g., health, social security, environment, industry assistance) and the revenue foregone should be estimated individually, and in the aggregate, for each function. This shows what government functions or payments are being funded through tax expenditures, compared to direct spending.
   b. Time series data over a period of years (such as a 3- or 5-year period), briefly noting any variations to the tax law or benchmark in that time, should be presented.
   c. Tax expenditures should be defined for different taxes at different levels of government and also aggregated across all levels of government, if possible.

5. Information for each tax expenditure:
   a. The estimated cost of the tax expenditure, with an indication of the reliability of the estimate, including the quality of the data upon which the estimate is based.
   b. The source of the tax expenditure (is it a tax law provision, administrative practice, or tax treaty?).
   c. The duration of the tax expenditure (is it subject to a "sunset clause" or is it ongoing?).
   d. The type of tax expenditure (is it, for instance, a tax exemption, a tax credit, or a reduced tax rate?).
   e. Policy justification for each tax expenditure (what is the policy objective of the tax expenditure and why is the tax expenditure the best means of achieving that objective?).
   f. Distributional impact of major tax expenditures, to the extent that data is available.
   g. For the most significant tax expenditures, the report should explain when the government last reviewed the tax expenditure to determine if it is good tax policy (the relative significance of tax expenditures might be determined by cost or other criterion such as potential impact upon social justice).

3.4.3 TWO CHALLENGES

This last section briefly considers two challenges in tax expenditure reporting that have become important since Paul McDaniel began his significant work in this field. The first challenge has dominated scholarly debate about tax expenditures in the U.S. and other OECD countries: it is the definition of the benchmark and, hence, of the fundamental concept of a tax expenditure. The second challenge concerns estimating and reporting the distributional impact of defined tax expenditures. These two challenges are discussed here in light of the experience of India, Chile and South Africa in conducting tax expenditure reporting.

In respect of the first challenge, it seems that there has not been much debate about the definition of the tax expenditure benchmark in India or South Africa. In India, the tax expenditure statement may be critiqued for failing to provide a benchmark; in South Africa, a benchmark is defined but not significantly debated. The lack of debate or, even, of a definition of the benchmark (though desirable) does not, it is suggested, detract from the political value of those country's tax expenditure reports.

In contrast, during 2011, the Chilean Finance Ministry established a Commission of Experts to review the definition and assessment of the tax expenditures, analyzing both the estimated amounts and the items included. The tax expenditure report presented in 2011 includes the methodological recommendations made by the Commission, showing an historical sequence updated with the new methodology. For both the identification and measuring of the tax expenditures on the Income Tax, in Chile it has been assumed that it aims to tax "income." Nonetheless, the income tax has over time had various modifications, which aim to give tax relief on savings and investments, in such a way that it has become a hybrid income-consumption tax. That is, the tax base is in some cases income, in other cases consumption and, in general, an intermediate amount between income and consumption. Hence, it would be sound to assume that the intention of the lawmaker is either to tax consumption or only partially to tax income. This hybrid nature of the Chilean income tax raises the issue of how to define the tax expenditure benchmark. If it were considered that the taxing of consumption were the benchmark, some tax expenditures that are currently reported as such would cease to be so, most significantly, the deferral of personal tax from business income, which is the biggest amount item. There would also not be recognized as tax expenditures deductions of individual pension fund payments. As a counterpart, a negative tax expenditure should be recognized whenever income instead of consumption is taxed.

The debate about the tax expenditure benchmark currently underway in Chile could as easily occur in many other countries globally, which operate, in effect, hybrid income-consumption tax laws.[80] It points to the need for the government to identify explicitly a benchmark. Still, it remains possible for the tax expenditure report, having identified that benchmark, to report against it as previously, as a way of providing information to the legislature and public about taxes and expenditures, whichever benchmark is chosen. If governmental resources are available, it is

---

80. As has commonly happened in countries worldwide: see, e.g., H. Aaron, H. Galper & J. Pechman (eds.), *Uneasy Compromise: Problems of a Hybrid Income-Consumption Tax* (Washington, D.C.: Brookings Institution, 1988).

feasible for the government to estimate and report tax expenditures against two benchmarks—income and consumption. It is questionable, however, if this would significantly enhance the quality of public debate about the tax system. If resources are not available, the question becomes which benchmark is most useful in supporting the fundamental purpose of tax expenditure reporting, being the provision of information for political debate. It is suggested here that a comprehensive or "normal" income tax benchmark is likely to be more suitable in this regard, but this is a matter for the political and treasury decision-makers in Chile to determine.

More generally, the author shares the frustration expressed by Paul McDaniel himself, in his final work on tax expenditures published posthumously in 2011, in which he critiqued the US Congress Joint Committee on Taxation move away from defining the tax expenditure benchmark as a "normal" or Shanz-Haig-Simons income tax benchmark, towards some other "reference" approach, as a "change that makes no changes."[81] The debate about the benchmark is in a sense fundamental, but is also fundamentally distracting from the primary purpose of tax expenditure reporting.

The second challenge, that has received increasing attention—reflected in the most recent collection on tax expenditures—concerns the extent to which tax expenditure reports should attempt distributional analysis of tax expenditures.[82] Currently, there is no requirement in the IMF *Code* or OECD *Best Practices* for governments to report on how fiscal policy decisions impact different income groups or segments of the population. However, in the most recent version of the *Manual* that accompanies the IMF Code, the IMF acknowledges that fiscal discipline may involve political tradeoffs and distributional outcomes that ideally should be disclosed:

> Reforms aimed at reducing fiscal deficits and improving macro stability, or at enhancing efficiency, may affect different income and social groups differently, and may hurt or benefit vulnerable and low-income groups more than others. It is important for transparency that some assessment of these impacts be included in the budget documentation . . . Poverty and Social Impact Analysis refers to the analysis of the distributional impact of policies and policy reforms on the welfare of different groups, with a specific emphasis on the poor and vulnerable . . . Good practice would require that budget documentation include at least a simple analysis of the differential impacts of new policies and measures.[83]

---

81. P. McDaniel, "The Staff of the Joint Committee on Taxation Revision of Tax Expenditure Classification Methodology: What Is to Be Made of a Change that Makes No Changes?," in *Tax Expenditures: State of the Art*, ed. L. Philipps, N. Brook & J. Li (Canadian Tax Foundation, Toronto, Canada: 2011) and in Chapter 1 of this volume.

82. N Brooks, Jinyan Li and Lisa Philipps, "Tax Expenditure Analysis: State of the Art" in Phillips et al, *ibid.*, 1–25, p. 5; E Toder, B Harris and K Lim. "Distributional Effects of Tax Expenditures in the United States" in Philipps et al, *ibid.*, 4:1–35.

83. IMF, Manual, *supra* note 15, 44. The Manual goes on to briefly describe various methods that can be used to carry out a Poverty and Social Impact Analysis. *Ibid.*, 45.

This recommendation is not reflected in the IMF Code itself, possibly because of concerns that this type of information will increase the likelihood of political resistance to tough decisions about spending restraint or taxation, challenging the ability of governments to deliver on their promises of fiscal prudence and leading to "excessive politicization."[84]

Bird and Zolt have exhaustively explained how a fully credible and detailed distributional analysis of the incidence of taxes and benefits is very difficult.[85] Arguably, it may be even more difficult to ascertain the distributional impact of tax expenditures, when the estimates of revenue foregone do not take into account behavioral change, and even more so for countries with a low analytical capacity in government. Such difficulties also arise with respect to the all of the tasks of revenue estimating, forecasting, and the establishment of credible medium-term budget frameworks, which are recommended by the IMF and the OECD. Issues in measuring distributional effects include determining the benchmark, adjusting for timing effects, taking account of behavioural responses, determining price incidence of tax changes and determining how any extra revenue from eliminating a tax expenditure might be used.[86]

In spite of all of these difficulties, however, a key concern about tax expenditures, in addition to their effect on overall revenue collections, is their unequal impact. The "upside down" effect of providing tax deductions, instead of tax credits or direct spending, is well known. More generally, and unsurprisingly, civil society advocates involved with budget transparency have placed particular emphasis on distributional issues. The IBP's 2010 OBI questionnaire includes the following questions, among others, to be answered on a transparency scale of one to five:

> 55. Does the executive's budget or any supporting budget documentation present information on policies (both proposals and existing commitments) in at least the budget year that are intended to benefit directly the country's most impoverished populations? . . .
>
> . . .
>
> 57. Does the executive make available to the public an analysis of the distribution of the tax burden? . . . [87]

The Latin American survey of 2001 also highlighted the link between transparency and distributive justice, stating that "knowledge and analysis of the budget should be sufficient to make it possible for the external observers to verify whether the distribution of . . . resources and their application reflect social preferences and

---

84. D. Heald, "Fiscal Transparency: Concepts, Measurement and U.K. Practice," *Public Aadministration Review* 81 (2003): 723, 727.

85. R. Bird & E. Zolt, "Redistribution via Taxation: The Limited Role of the Personal Income Tax in Developing Countries," *UCLA Law Review* 52 (2005): 1627, 1639–1644.

86. Toder et al., *supra* note 82, p. 4:6.

87. OBI 2010 Survey Questionnaire, available from www.internationalbudget.org.

comply with the criteria of equality and justice."[88] A more recent study suggests that "[a]pplied budget analysis . . . makes it possible to evaluate who wins and who loses with the distribution of public resources."[89] Concern about the incidence of burdens and benefits is also evident in the South African study of 1999, which concluded that "analysis of tax incidence is lacking" in South Africa's budget documentation.[90]

General conclusions can be drawn from basic tax expenditure reports about which sectors, or classes, of taxpayer will benefit or not from particular tax expenditures. In spite of the technical difficulties, there may be scope to strengthen reporting of distributional aspects of tax expenditures in both developed and developing countries to illuminate the benefits received by different social groups and firms. For example:

- Income/wealth analysis: How do low income individuals or individuals with little wealth benefit from the tax expenditure compared to high income or wealth individuals?
- Gender analysis: Differential impact on women and men. For example, if only men work in the manufacturing industry in a particular country, a tax expenditure that reduces the tax burden on workers in manufacturing will benefit men more than women. An analysis of this expenditure may also identify policy reasons for the focus on manufacturing.
- Minority or regional analysis: a regional tax investment credit may have the goal of benefiting a minority group that lives in a particular region. The tax expenditure analysis may be able to identify if the credit is, in fact, benefiting that group.

The Chilean tax expenditure report does not carry out specific distributional analysis, in spite of the explicit requirement in the Constitution that taxing and spending must not discriminate, at least between regions and sectors. However, some basic distributional analysis is presented in the Indian *Statement of Revenue Foregone*, which includes a distributive analysis of corporate tax expenditures showing that the smallest firms were receiving the least benefits from these concessions. Overall, its corporate tax expenditure analysis reveals aspects of distributional effects of tax expenditures although it does not analyze these in depth. It demonstrates that tax expenditures preferring the corporate sector are significantly greater than tax expenditures in the noncorporate and individual sector and shows the unequal distribution across large and small enterprises and industry sectors through the use of effective tax rates.

---

88. IBP, *supra* note 37, p. 12.
89. Centro De Análisis E Investigación, *Latin American Index Of Budget Transparency 2005: A Comparison Of 8 Countries*, at 7 (2005), available at http://www.fundar.org.mx/indice2005/docs/Regional%20Transparency%CC20Report% 202005.pdf; see also *Latin American Index Of Budget Transparency 2003: A Comparison Of 10 Countries*, at 5 (2003), available at http://www.internationalbudget.org/themes/BudTrans/English.pdf.
90. IDASA. *supra* note 33, 21.

A recent analysis has also been done of the gender impact of an aspect of Indian personal income tax. The Indian income tax law contains a higher exemption for women (see Table 3.6 above). This is, formally, a positive tax discrimination in the income tax law, which is intended to assist gender equity. However, its effect in reality has been studied and found to be extremely small, because only a very tiny proportion of women pay income tax and so would benefit from this higher income tax exemption. More generally, tax expenditures in the income tax are an ineffective way to reduce poverty or assist low-income individuals in India. It is concluded that:

[T]the total number of individual taxpayers is about 27 million out of a total population of about 1 billion, so approximately 2.7 per cent of the population falls within the income tax net . . . Women likely constitute less than 3 per cent of this small number . . . tax-paying women are only about 0.00001 per cent of all women and 0.27 per cent of working-age women. In other words, the use of income tax as a means to further gender equality seems limited.[91]

The South African *Tax Expenditure Statement 2011* also makes some brief comments on the distributional impact of tax expenditures, but these seem generally to serve the government's interests in justifying its tax base, rather than having the general goal of increasing public understanding of distributional impact of tax expenditures. For example, it states in respect of the VAT exemption of food:

Estimates from the 2005/06 Income and Expenditure Survey by Statistics South Africa (StatsSA) suggest that the poorest 20 per cent of households accounted for about 7.9 per cent of total expenditure on food and non-alcoholic beverages, and the top 20 per cent of households accounted for 39.9 per cent. Assuming that the poorer households' share of expenditure that is VAT zero rated on the list of "basic food items" is slightly higher (about 10 per cent), the monetary benefit that accrued to them was about R1.4 billion (10 per cent of R13.9 billion) in 2008/09, while the upper 20 per cent of households received a benefit of R5 billion (about 36 per cent of R13.9 billion). This is not the most effective form of relief for the poor.[92]

In this statement, the government suggests that an exemption from VAT is not the most effective form of relief or subsidy for the poor. Alternatives, such as direct grants or transfer payments, or a reduction in other kinds of tax, may be more effective. Estimating the revenue foregone from this major tax exemption from VAT shows that the tax base is not, ultimately, as broad as it could be, but indicates some of the distributional (and political) tradeoffs in that policy decision.

---

91. P. Chakraborty, L. Chakraborty, K. Karmakar & S. Kapila, "Gender equality and taxation in India: An unequal burden?," International Development Research Centre (Canada), in *Taxation and Gender Equity: A Comparative Analysis of Direct and Indirect Taxes in Developing and Developed Countries*, ed. C. Grown & I. Valodia (2010: Routledge), 94–118, available as an open e-book from http://www.idrc.ca/openebooks/469-7/#page_94.
92. See Republic of South Africa, National Budget 2011, *Budget Review* Annexure C, p. 182, http://www.treasury.gov.za/documents/national%20budget/2011/review/Annexure%20c.pdf.

3.5   CONCLUSION

Since the leading work done by Paul McDaniel and Stanley Surrey on the concept of tax expenditures, it remains that the concept has a primarily political purpose, to draw legislators', and the public's attention to the many concessions, exemptions, and other incentives in the tax law and hence to the implicit "cost to revenue," or revenue foregone, as a result of these concessions. This is still its most valuable function, and it is thus best understood as a strategic intervention into the budget process that should enhance budget debate. If the budget is, as the OECD suggests, the most important policy document of a government, the question of who receives information and is empowered to participate is crucial for the legitimacy, fairness, and sustainability of budget decisions. A process of budgeting that provides information and space for analysis and political negotiation is always imperfect, but is nonetheless a worthy goal.

The IMF Manual for Fiscal Transparency acknowledges "citizens" as one part of the "public" audience for fiscal information but does not discuss how citizens might be empowered to participate in budget processes although they should be given "the information they need to hold their government accountable for its policy choices."[93] The OECD Best Practices also addresses the role of citizens, in particular, by requiring publication of reports and active promotion of citizens' and NGOs' understanding of the budget process.[94] The IMF and OECD both find that the most important way to achieve accountability to citizens is, unsurprisingly, through legislative review of an executive budget.[95] For such accountability to have any content, this approach implicitly requires a democratic legislature. It may not be surprising that the India, South Africa and Chile, which all have substantial and informative tax expenditure reports, also have functional and vibrant democracies (in spite of the many challenges that they face).

Work of NGOs on fiscal transparency is focused on empowering civil society groups to engage in the budget process. However, the "idea of promoting open budgets is one that can gather support from a wide range of actors, leading to a coalition not available on other issues"—including business interests, international organizations and civil society—so that, in the right circumstances, "governments find them hard to oppose."[96] So, it has been suggested that in Chile, fiscal reform requires the combined macroeconomic, managerial, and political role of budgets and the need, in the longer term, to establish a political consensus through increasing and strengthening the contributions of the Congress, in addition to a strong

---

93. IMF, Manual, *supra* note 15, p. 6.
94. *OECD Best Practices, supra* note 10, pp. 8, 14.
95. 2007 IMF CODE, *supra* note 14, §§ 2.1.1, 4.3.2; *OECD Best Practices, supra* note 9, at 14.
96. Int'l Budget P'ship, Transparency and Participation in the Budget Process: Why Focus on Budget Transparency and Participation, http://www.internationalbudget.org/themes/BudTrans/index.htm.

government leader and a strict fiscal rule.[97] It is not surprising, in this author's view, that it is the vibrant democratic states that have increasingly adopted tax expenditure reporting. Increasing knowledge about tax expenditures is one step in establishing more legitimate tax systems in many developing countries, as well as enhancing public knowledge about government finance in general, and thereby supporting democratic engagement in budget decisions. This is the lasting legacy of Paul McDaniel's comparative work on tax expenditures.

---

97. M. Marcel & M. Tokman, "Building a Consensus for Fiscal Reform: The Chilean Case," 2(3) *OECD Journal on Budgeting* 2(3) (2002), at 35, 37.

Chapter 4

Tax Reform and Tax Expenditures in Australia

Richard J. Vann[*]

4.1   INTRODUCTION

Paul McDaniel maintained his interest and passion for tax expenditures throughout his career, starting with his work with Stanley Surrey in the U.S. Treasury, through their joint publications in the area in the 1980s, his work with the OECD, right down to his final posthumous contribution to the topic.[1] The tax expenditure

---

[*]   Challis Professor of Law, University of Sydney.
1.   Paul's assistance was acknowledged in S. Surrey, *Pathways to Tax Reform* (Cambridge: Harvard University Press, 1973), ix, the first book-length study of the idea, and they worked together on two seminal books in the 1980s, S. Surrey & P. McDaniel, *Tax Expenditures* (Cambridge: Harvard University Press, 1985), Paul R. McDaniel & Stanley Surrey, *International Aspects of Tax Expenditures* (Deventer: Kluwer Law and Taxation Publishers, 1985). His last contribution was P. McDaniel, "The Staff of the Joint Committee on Taxation Revision of Tax Expenditure Classification Methodology: What Is to Be Made of a Change That Makes No Changes?," in *Tax Expenditures: State of the Art*, ed. L. Philipps, N. Brooks & J. Li (Toronto: Canadian Tax Foundation, 2011). The OECD work in which Paul was involved was *Tax Expenditures: A Review of Issues and Country Practices* (1984) and *Tax Expenditures: Recent Experiences* (1996). The OECD has recently returned to the topic, in *Tax Expenditures in OECD Countries* (2010).

Yariv Brauner & Martin James McMahon, Jr. (eds), *The Proper Tax Base: Structural Fairness from an International and Comparative Perspective—Essays in Honour of Paul McDaniel*, pp. 87–105.
© 2012 Kluwer Law International BV, The Netherlands.

concept rapidly spread beyond the United States, reaching Australia in 1980.[2] Although our main personal contact involved another of Paul's enduring interests, international taxation,[3] tax expenditure analysis is back in the news in many countries as they grapple with fiscal deficits. Australia recently completed a substantial review of its tax system—called Australia's Future Tax System (AFTS)—and although not as fiscally pressed as many other countries, is proceeding with some substantial changes to the tax system and contemplating others.[4] For the first time in thirty years, tax expenditure analysis was **not** at the heart of the process. Hence, this is an appropriate time from an Australian perspective to consider the strengths and weaknesses of the tax expenditure concept as a tax reform tool. It is noteworthy that Paul McDaniel did not consider tax reform the purpose of such analysis,[5] but many of its advocates do.

After setting the background about the new approach to tax reform in the AFTS report, the chapter turns to the impact of the current tax and AFTS's proposed tax system for labor income and then the deleterious effects both have on domestic saving. In the discussion, the AFTS approach is contrasted with the work of Apps and Rees, which provides an alternative view. Using that view, it is concluded that the taxation of income from capital is different to labor income. While the AFTS review agrees with the conclusion, it comes from a very different theoretical approach and identifies very different drivers for making taxation policy decisions. This is a significant policy division and raises concerns about current policy directions in taxing income from capital. Tax expenditure analysis makes little or no appearance in the AFTS report on these fundamental issues of the tax system, although the underlying idea of taxing income from different sources the same is influential at various points.

---

2. Tax expenditures began to be reported in Australia in the 1980–81 Budget as an Appendix to Statement No. 4 of Budget Paper No. 1 and have been the subject of a separate annual publication since 1986, see Treasury, *Tax Expenditures Statement* (1986) 2. Annual publication is now required by law under the *Charter of Budget Honesty Act 1998* and the latest version is *Tax Expenditures Statement 2010* (2011), www.treasury.gov.au/documents/1950/PDF/2010_TES_consolidated.pdf. Two reviews in the mid 1980s gave impetus to the fuller publication of information, Report from the House of Representatives Standing Committee on Expenditure, *Taxation Expenditures* (1982), Economic Planning Advisory Council, *Tax Expenditures in Australia* (1986). The first academic discussion of the concept in Australia seems to be R. Hamilton, "The Concept of a Tax Expenditure Budget" in *Taxation in Australia* 17(1982): 30 (written after spending time in Harvard and meeting Surrey). All websites referred to in this chapter were last viewed on Feb. 28, 2011.
3. Apart from a fleeting meeting in the early 1980s, we first spent time together on a panel which Paul chaired at the 1994 Toronto Congress of the International Fiscal Association on interest deductibility in an international context. That led to a series of invitations for me to teach tax treaties and co-teach with Paul international tax planning at the new International Tax Program of NYU Law School which Paul was then establishing.
4. Australia's Future Tax System, *Report to the Treasurer* (2009), Part One Overview, Part Two Detailed Analysis available (along with all other documents produced during the review) at: http://taxreview.treasury.gov.au/Content/Content.aspx?doc=html/home.htm.
5. McDaniel, The Staff of the Joint Committee (2011), *supra* note 1.

The chapter then turns to the most obvious intersection of labor and capital income in Australia, pension plans, and discusses the implications of a system where Australia is one of a few significant countries in which private saving and investment out of labor income is required by government mandate. While this policy means that concerns about the possible impact on saving by the taxation of labor income is to some extent offset, it raises new tax issues, especially about the proper way to tax this saving. Again, the AFTS report follows a very different line to tax expenditure analysis under an income tax by adopting an expenditure tax benchmark for pension plans and owner-occupied housing. The author suggests that while the treatment of housing may be justifiable, the unusual Australian tax treatment of savings through pension plans, which in broad outline the AFTS report would continue, is very difficult to justify like its proposed treatment of investment income more generally, other than on pragmatic political grounds.

4.2 THE APPROACH TO TAX REFORM

The AFTS review was a watershed in Australian tax reform in a number of ways. One that has been often emphasized in speeches by its chair is that the report is a blueprint for long-term tax reform rather than a detailed program for immediate action.[6] The Government's response to date has been in this vein—relatively few of the larger changes proposed have been tackled,[7] and of those that have, one has not surprisingly proved very difficult politically, the resource rent tax which was partly responsible for the downfall of Kevin Rudd as Prime Minister and his replacement by Julia Gillard in mid-2010. Public pressure for tax reform continues, and the new Prime Minister is pushing ahead with a modified version of the resource rent tax and plans to hold a public forum on tax reform in late 2011, though the AFTS long-term strategy signals that not too much can be expected to happen quickly. It is somewhat odd that the Government is criticized for not implementing a report which did not expect immediate implementation.

More importantly, the AFTS review for the first time in Australia has taken on board (some of) the modern economic approach to taxation, and this is already permeating the Australian Treasury thinking about tax more generally. This is

---

6. K. Henry, "A tax system for Australia in the global economy" and "Lessons from tax reform past," http://taxreview.treasury.gov.au/content/Content.aspx?doc=html/speeches.htm. Henry was at the time Secretary of the Treasury (meaning the senior civil servant in Treasury—senior civil servants are not politically appointed in Australia in the same way as in the U.S.). The committee consisted in addition of another head of a government department, Jeff Harmer, two academics Greg Smith and John Piggott (the first a former Treasury official) and Heather Ridout, head of an industry association.

7. The main elements of the initial government response were the introduction of a resource rent tax, a modest cut in the company tax rate, small business tax reform, and changes to the taxation of pension plans. The details and subsequent developments are available on the Australian Government's tax reform website http://www.futuretax.gov.au/pages/default.aspx.

probably the most important, and in the longer term, likely to be the most divisive aspect of the review.

Traditionally tax reform in Australia, as elsewhere, has been based on the idea that a comprehensive tax system is best—tax everything of the same kind (such as income or consumption) in the same way, and this will inevitably enhance economic efficiency as it brings about the famous "level playing field" and equity as it treats like taxpayers equally. Hence, in the broad, the two most recent comprehensive tax reforms in Australia fit this pattern: the Labor Government 1985 reform can be characterized as the application of this idea to the income tax (including the introduction of capital gains tax, fringe benefits tax, the foreign tax credit and the imputation system of company-shareholder taxation), and the Liberal National Government 1998 reform can be characterized as the application of this idea to consumption tax and further application to income tax (the introduction of a quite broad value added tax called the Goods and Services Tax (or "GST") in place of a narrow based wholesale sales tax on goods, more or less complete abolition of accelerated depreciation and fairly full accruals taxation of financial instruments). During much of this period the tax rate was essentially seen as a value judgment independent of the definition of the tax base stemming from society's preferences for the size of government and for redistribution of wealth through the tax and transfer system, though there was an underlying theme of lower tax rates on a broader tax base to produce equivalent revenue.

The Australian Treasury annual *Tax Expenditures Statement* was generally the first recourse in the tax reform process. Although its methodology has been the subject of some debate between various lobby groups and government and has moved over time, the issue has never attracted the attention that it has in the United States, including recent toing and froing of the Joint Committee on Taxation.[8]

Modern economic thought on taxation based on work in welfare economics starting in the 1970s differs in a number of critical ways from this traditional approach.[9] First, the idea that it is possible to tax all income or all expenditure (which the "comprehensive" tax base idea suggests) is rejected. Household production (work in the household by the members of the household) and much

---

8. McDaniel, The Staff of the Joint Committee (2011), *supra* note 1, J.C. Fleming & R. Peroni, "Can Tax Expenditure Analysis be Divorced from a Normative Tax Base? A Critique of the 'New Paradigm' and Its Denouement," *Virginia Tax Review* 30 2010) 135. The modern Australian version is based on the Schanz-Haig-Simons comprehensive definition of income subject to the proviso that, "The benchmark may incorporate *structural elements* of the tax system where there are difficulties adopting the standard treatment as the benchmark. Such elements could include integral design features; for example, the progressive income tax rate scale for individual taxpayers." See *Tax Expenditures Statement 2010, supra* note 2, 20–21, 201–206; the Australian Treasury justifications for the exercise, 14–16, are transparency in public policy-making, a more comprehensive assessment of government activity and contributing to tax system design.
9. This discussion is not intended to be comprehensive on the modern economics approach, but rather to highlight some of the differences from the traditional comprehensive tax base (and tax expenditure) approach.

household consumption (leisure such as lying on the beach) cannot be taxed for a variety of reasons, notably because they cannot be reliably observed or measured by the government. Hence individuals have important untaxed production and consumption (leisure) choices available to them, and all real world taxes inevitably lead to economic distortions. The level playing field is not possible, and tax rates matter to efficiency due to the untaxed alternatives available through an individual's choices.

Another assumption underlying the comprehensive tax base, that the size of the economic response to taxes is the same across different kinds of income or consumption, is nowadays also rejected. Economic distortions depend on how sensitive demand or supply is to taxation. Because the demand for necessities is typically found to be unresponsive to price changes, taxing them produces less economic distortion than taxing luxury goods. Our demand for food is less sensitive to tax than our demand for French perfume. While taxing food under the GST was ultimately rejected in Australia for equity (fairness) reasons, there are many other areas where this style of argument is critical to tax reform.

One important feature of the analysis is the rejection of another important underlying assumption of the comprehensive tax base—that the burden of particular taxes landed in the right spot. Ultimately all taxes are borne by individuals, even though most taxes are collected in the first instance from business entities. The traditional approach was that sales taxes ended up being borne by the firm's customers, taxes on payroll (including wage withholding) by the firm's employees, and the company tax by the firm's shareholders. The incidence of taxes has always been problematic, but recent literature suggests that taxes paid by firms may end being borne other than where intended. For example, an increase in corporate tax may be borne by employees over time through reduced increases in wages—it all depends on the forces of supply and demand.

Finally, the approach also means that taxation cannot be analyzed in isolation from the rest of the economic system. Most notably, the tax and transfer (social security) systems need to be viewed as a whole, and indeed it is often necessary to take into account other economic policies in evaluating the economic impacts of the system on individual choices (housing being one example highlighted in the AFTS review and further discussed below).

The welfare economics approach to taxation means that there are no longer any accepted absolutes in tax policy analysis like the comprehensive tax base. Analysis of tax reform thus requires sophisticated theoretical and empirical studies to substantiate claims made in relation to the economic efficiency and distributional consequences of proposed tax measures. This shift in thinking has significant implications for the lobbying that always accompanies tax reform. On one side, it means that proposals that would be characterized as "concessions" under the comprehensive tax base and likely to be rejected in the past for that reason may receive fuller consideration. On the other, lobbyists will be expected to provide supporting economic and empirical analysis for their proposals. The AFTS consultation document, in summarizing submissions prior to its release, often makes the comment that claims are "unsupported," meaning unsupported by this kind of

91

analysis.[10] This is not to say that the comprehensive tax base idea is now entirely discounted in Australia, rather it is no longer the gospel that it was as recently as the 1998 tax reform.

Australia is not alone or the first in adopting the modern economics approach to taxation in official discourse. The same influence is evident in the U.S. President's Advisory Panel on Tax Reform.[11] In the U.K. with typical eccentricity, major tax review seems now to be left to the private sector supported by government money, but the same trend is evident, the latest being the Mirrlees' review.[12]

Now that we have moved beyond the comprehensive tax base in official policy terms in Australia and elsewhere, not surprisingly the new thinking gets converted to slogans such as capital is mobile, labor is immobile (with the implication of taxing income from capital at lower rates or not at all, while applying full progressive rates to labor income or—to judge by real tax systems—an inverted U-shape pattern of rates with the highest tax rates on middle income earners). The very thinking underlying the modern approach means, however, that such slogans can never be trusted. It also explains why tax reform will never end. As circumstances change so does the analysis of tax changes needed to achieve desired economic efficiency and distributional outcomes, even if the desired outcomes remain the same. The lack of absolutes in the new approach means that conflicting slogans will be everywhere, yet the "proof" may be a long time coming and not comprehensible to the public or the politicians—which may be one reason why the comprehensive tax base idea maintained its grip on official policy rhetoric for a long period after the new economic thinking on taxation had taken hold. The discussion below suggests that a great deal of caution is required in basing significant policy changes on the new slogans, and that policy makers may for some time yet be better sticking with the devil they know.

Supporters of tax expenditure analysis (and the proponents of the underlying idea of the comprehensive tax base) have not, of course, been immune to these developments.[13] They recognize the measurement limitations in the comprehensive tax base, but tend to dismiss them as a marginal or *de minimis* problem. Similarly, they understand that some things are more responsive to taxation than others but retain as their starting point or basic assumption that responses are the same. To the extent that the underlying driver of the tax expenditure analysis is some deeper reason than the comprehensive tax base (such as ability to pay), the significance of the problem of incidence seems likewise to be addressed by assumption rather than analysis. Oddly, the issue about the tax and transfer system being viewed as a whole does not figure strongly in tax expenditure analysis—this is unusual because the very point of tax expenditure analysis is that the tax system

---

10. Australia's Future Tax System, *Consultation Paper* (2008).
11. President's Advisory Panel on Tax Reform, *Simple, Fair, and Pro-Growth, Proposals to Fix America's Tax System* (2005). The publications of the panel are available at http://govinfo. library.unt.edu/taxreformpanel/.
12. Institute for Fiscal Studies Mirrlees' Review, *Tax by Design* (Oxford University Press, 2011). The publications of the review are available at: http://www.ifs.org.uk/mirrleesReview.
13. Fleming & Peroni, *supra* note 8, is a good but not the only example of these points.

is being used as the equivalent of raising taxes and then spending the revenue on some particular purpose, and that the same scrutiny should occur in such a case as for normal expenditures.

4.3 TAXATION OF LABOR INCOME

Unfortunately, the specific recommendations of the AFTS review seem to have fallen prey to such slogans as its recommendations in relation to labor income largely continue the trend of recent decades. That trend in Australia has been to significantly shift tax burdens for labor income from upper income taxpayers to lower and middle-income taxpayers and to tax secondary earners (largely women) at significantly higher rates than primary income earners (largely men).

This form of critique of the AFTS recommendations is based on the work of Apps and Rees.[14] The shift of taxation to lower- and middle-income earners from upper-income earners has been effected by the so-called targeting of various welfare benefits which in the past were universal (or by introducing new forms of tax credits with similar attributes). The targeting takes the form of limiting the benefit to persons below a certain income and then withdrawing the benefits from such persons as their income increases. The withdrawal rate operates as an additional implicit tax on the additional income when the tax and transfer systems are viewed as a single system. The saving from limiting the previously universal benefit is then returned to all taxpayers in the form of a tax cut. Those above the limit for the targeting of the welfare-payment benefit from the tax cut while losing the benefit, whereas those below the limit keep the benefit and have a tax cut plus an additional implicit tax.

In a zero sum (revenue neutral) game there will be winners and losers from the change. Not surprisingly, the highest income taxpayers get more benefit from the tax cut (whose value is greater the higher the income) than they lose from forgoing the fixed amount of universal benefit—and if they gain, those below them must lose. In addition, such a change inevitably produces a crazy pattern of effective marginal tax rates. It is surprising that a simple sleight of hand with such effects has generally been favorably received as an improvement to the tax system in Australia and elsewhere. Perhaps this is because this kind of change has been repeated incrementally over many years so that individually each change does not seem all that significant.

To understand the effect of higher tax rates on secondary earners, it is necessary to introduce households of more than one adult person into the discussion. Australia has always used the individual as the taxable unit in the income tax system, but the withdrawal of the welfare benefits in the process of targeting

---

14. P. Apps & R. Rees, *Public Economics and the Household* (Cambridge University Press, 2009), P. Apps, "Why the Henry Review Fails on Family Tax Reform," and R. Rees, "A New Perspective on Capital Income Taxation," in *Australia's Future Tax System: The Prospects After Henry*, ed. C. Evans, R. Krever P. Mellor & J. Freebairn (Sydney: Thomson, 2010).

described above has been based on household (family), not individual income. Hence if an extra dollar of income comes from the second member of the household getting a job, the withdrawal mechanism for the benefit still operates and acts as an implicit tax on that income even though under the formal individual tax rate scale, there is a zero bracket for the first $6,000 of income. As men in general keep working and earning a similar level of income over many years, the withdrawal effect impacts primarily women as secondary earners who get taxed more than men earning similar incomes. The alternative for many women in such cases is to provide untaxed household production, particularly in the form of childcare.

There is a very significant economic inefficiency created by this higher effective tax on a group (women with children) whose labor supply is very responsive to tax because of the untaxed production choices available to them. All that the AFTS review recommendations do in this area is smooth some of the crazier patterns in tax rates—they do nothing to change the large scale shift in tax burdens that has occurred or the impact of the system on women, notwithstanding acknowledgement of the problems the tax system can create for secondary earners. Tax expenditure analysis likewise has very little to contribute to this debate. It says nothing meaningful on the taxable unit[15] nor, as noted above, on the impact of the tax system in driving choices between taxed market labor income and untaxed household production (especially in the form of childcare), even though it will be obvious to women with children at least that these are central issues in the personal tax system.

4.4   SAVING AND TAXATION OF INVESTMENT INCOME

The new economics approach to taxation has been much concerned with the taxation of saving. Part of the concern is the "problem" of the double taxation of saving under the income tax which in turn has been linked to low saving rates, and part is the "mobility" of savings. Commonly suggested solutions have been a progressive expenditure (consumption) tax or a lower rate of tax on income from capital.

The general impression from this new analysis is that most saving comes from the highest income earners, and that it is the high rates of tax on their investment income under a progressive income tax that are the cause of the low level of saving. Impressions can be deceiving in this area as Apps and Rees show.[16] The data in

15. McDaniel & Surrey, *supra* note 1, 50–51, and compare the very contrasting views on the taxable unit of two strong advocates of tax expenditure analysis, N. Brooks, "The Irrelevance of Conjugal Relationships in Assessing Tax Liability" and Michael McIntyre, "Marital Income Splitting in the Modern World: Lessons for Australia from the American Experience," in *Tax Units and the Tax Rate Scale*, ed. J. Head & R. Krever (Sydney: Australian Tax Research Foundation, 1996).
16. See, *supra* note 14. The discussion below under this heading draws generally on the work of Apps and Rees where it refers to empirical evidence and the optimal tax on investment income.

Australia on which such statements are based relate to family, not individual incomes. What they disguise is that most of the saving in volume terms is coming from two earner households with average incomes and that the amount of saving is closely related to the income of the secondary earner in the household. Hence it is the deleterious effect of the current tax system on the labor supply of women which is much more responsible for the (lack of the) amount of saving that occurs in Australia rather than anything to do with the taxation of investment income. Perhaps the "capital is mobile, labour is not" slogan should be revised to "labour of secondary earners, and with it the amount of saving, is highly mobile, but income from capital is not"—the end of the new slogan is elaborated in the discussion below.

In a time when there are constant reminders about the economic time-bomb caused by the aging of the population and the need for increased productivity and saving (including by the AFTS review), changing the current and AFTS recommended policy settings for labor income would produce a double benefit. Not only would there be higher saving but increased productivity for unfortunately the empirical evidence is also clear that the effects of the system in discouraging secondary earners from entering, or as fully participating as otherwise would occur, in the market workforce has persistent effects across the working life of secondary earners caused by the degradation of workplace skills (loss of human capital) from choosing household production over paid employment.

The same style of analysis also has implications for the taxation of income from capital. The current Australian system, with many notable exceptions (pension plans and family homes which are taken up below and capital gains), taxes this income like labor income on an individual unit basis at the same progressive tax rates and generally attributes the income to the person who owns the investment which produces the income. The modern economic theory of taxation (but only when it properly incorporates the household in the analysis) does not give clear guidance as to what the optimal tax rate is for such income.

Again the analysis focuses on the fact that most income is derived by households, that part of the "full" income of all households consists of household production and that there is implicit trade occurring in the household. To take a simple example, if one member of the household is employed full-time in the market economy and the other member is engaged full-time in what in times past was called home duties, the sharing of the market income within the household effectively means that the household production of one member of the household is being paid for by part of the market income of the other member.

The result is that saving out of the market income within the household cannot meaningfully be attributed to one member or another without an intrusive and detailed (and probably impossible) analysis of what is occurring within the household, which tax systems generally and sensibly avoid. Family law in most countries disregards actual ownership of assets and tries to divide them in divorce proceedings on the basis of respective contributions to the household including household production (and here the law does become intrusive in order to attempt a fair division of assets acquired from household saving with much attendant

95

controversy). The same problem of observing contributions of household members has significant ramifications for taxation of income of small businesses, which involves both capital and labor income but will not be pursued here.

The current Australian tax law intuitively reflects this ambiguity about taxing income from capital because it effectively allows the adults in a household to allocate the income between them as they wish. This can be achieved simply by gifts from one member of the household to another and buying investment assets in the name of the other, or by more elaborate means such as discretionary family investment trusts. The result is that investment income ends up being taxed at the marginal rate of one or other adult member of the household as the household members choose.[17]

Rather than proceed by this line of analysis, the AFTS review seems to reflect at least four policy drivers in its discussion of the taxation of investment income (putting aside pension plans and the family home which are taken up under the next heading): first, the simple slogan referred to above that capital is mobile, labor is not; second, discrimination against future consumption; third, the current unevenness of tax rates on different kinds of investment income; and fourth, the impact of inflation on the measurement of income from capital, the clearest example being the over-taxation on a real basis of bank account interest. The AFTS solution is a discount of 40% for a wide range of investment income similar to the current 50% CGT discount in Australia; that is net investment income, including capital gains, is reduced by 40% and then taxed at marginal rates. The AFTS analysis—which is shared in a broad sense by the Bush and Mirrlees' reviews in the U.S. and U.K.—does not really stand up to scrutiny.

So far as the mobility of capital is concerned, this is mainly a significant issue for certain forms of *foreign* capital (income from capital not taxed at normal rates in the residence country—pension and sovereign wealth funds etc.). Income from foreign capital is subject to special rules already under the international tax system and can be dealt with quite separately from income from capital generally, so mobility is not a general reason for relieving income from capital from tax. As noted above, labor, at least of secondary earners, is highly mobile in the sense that there is a choice between taxed market income and untaxed household production. It is much more sensitive to tax than a significant proportion of income from capital, which is why from time to time suggestions are made for lower rates of tax on labor income of particular groups (women, the aged). As also noted above, Australia (and the AFTS review) do the exact opposite and tax the most tax sensitive labor income at high, effectively penal, rates. So why there is such a concern for mobility of capital is mysterious. Moreover, as a very large amount of domestic saving goes into personal residences and other forms of domestic investment, the

---

17. In Australia, as in most countries, the analysis is more complicated as much income from capital is taxed at the corporate tax rate; however, that does not affect the main points being made in the text. Australia, like the U.S., has a "kiddie" tax, which does not permit splitting of investment income with young children, so the freedom only relates to the adult members of the household.

idea that domestic capital is highly mobile (in the sense of being influenced by the domestic tax rate as compared to foreign tax rates) is implausible.

There is a much broader economic argument often made for completely relieving income from capital from tax, which is that the income tax discriminates between current and future consumption through the "double" taxation of future consumption (represented by the taxation of interest earned on income saved for future consumption). Similar to the discussion of labor income above, this argument, which is a life cycle issue, ignores the empirical evidence about actual life cycles that consumption patterns are fairly invariant over the life cycle with household consumption highest in the child-rearing phase. Moreover, the argument, which is framed in terms of perfect markets, ignores a very significant market failure that capital markets do not allow most individuals to borrow at appropriate interest rates to finance current consumption to smooth the differences between income and consumption over the life cycle.

Not surprisingly, even the economists have generally retreated from this approach (which exempts income from capital from tax entirely). The AFTS, Bush, and Mirrlees reviews all agree that general exemption of income from capital from tax is not justified, even if half-heartedly. One particularly unattractive version of the consumption tax ideal of the economists that found much favor in the recent past is the progressive expenditure tax, which would measure individual consumption for tax purposes by annual income less annual savings (i.e., income would be decreased by the increase of saving during the year or increased by a decrease of saving during the year and then subjected to a progressive tax rate). In the framework of the family, in which most income is earned and where the actual contributions to saving cannot be measured, the effect would be that assets would be held by the higher income earner (usually the male), which would make the work of the divorce courts even harder and the distribution of ownership of assets even more unfair. Australia fortunately avoids this outcome and hopefully will continue to resist the various progressive consumption tax justifications.

The optimal tax rate for investment income is a black-hole in the framework of the modern economic analysis for reasons of this kind. There is no empirical or theoretical reason to think that the AFTS percentage inclusion, Nordic dual income tax system with a flat rate of tax on capital income, or consumption tax zero rate is the correct answer to the optimal tax rate for capital income.

The current unevenness of tax rates on capital income under the modern economic analysis may or may not be a problem, depending on responsiveness to tax rates. The issue again is one of the efficiency and distributional effects of the current situation and the proposed AFTS change. Very little analysis is offered for return to a more comprehensive tax base, and the need for even tax rates for most of capital income, especially given that the different treatment of pension plans and family homes is accepted as discussed in the next section. More importantly, the different and crazy pattern of tax rates for labor income is accepted by the AFTS review (though with some attempt at amelioration). It is clear that there is much more labor income in the economy than investment income and no convincing justification as to why investment income is more sensitive to variation in tax rates than labor income.

Finally, the effect of inflation is no justification for a simple 40% exclusion of investment income, although inflation is undoubtedly an issue in measurement of investment income. If investment income is being separately measured on a net basis as proposed by the AFTS review, then the simple solution for the inflation problem is to reduce the measured net income by the inflation rate. Using inflation as (part) justification for an arbitrary reduction in capital income tax rates is another reflection of the lack of hard analysis in the area by the AFTS review.

One gets the feeling that the recommended AFTS treatment for capital income is a mix of practical pragmatism, and a return to the broad base is good style of argument favored by tax expenditure analysis rather than the modern economics approach, though some of the trappings of that approach are on show. The pragmatism is reflected in the difficulty of taxing capital gains in particular at full individual tax rates and moving the taxation of other capital income in the direction of capital gains rather than vice versa, as well as using the arguments discussed above as a (disguised) way of introducing a schedular treatment of investment income to prevent erosion of the income tax on labor income.[18]

The AFTS report is clear that its proposal for capital income is fairly rough and ready. Although given some emphasis, the proposal does not deal directly with the issue of deferral though this is one of the major causes of the differences in effective tax rates on various types of capital income. In this sense, the (very limited) government response to this AFTS recommendation in the form of some relief of taxation on deposit account interest income more directly addresses the reasons for the particularly heavy tax on deposit interest—the lack of deferral and the impact of inflation, as well as targeting the average person who is most affected by the problem. The very rich avoid the heavy taxation simply by avoidance (until the financial crisis at least) of this form of income. By comparison, the much more general approach of the AFTS report is much less targeted at this particular problem.

As with the discussion of labor income above, tax expenditure analysis does not have a great deal to offer on the issues of the tax rate on capital income, its measurement in conditions of inflation, and to whom the income should be attributed. The default position on the first question is generally that the same progressive rate schedule should apply to investment income as to other income; the analysis seems to be generally indifferent as to whether income is measured in historic or real terms, and attribution is disputed.[19] The AFTS review has retreated

---

18. The United States passive activity and like rules produce a similar schedular outcome. Australia had such rules briefly from 1985 to 1987, but generally continues to allow investment tax losses generated in the main by interest deductions to be offset against labor income.

19. There are varying views on all these issues in the tax expenditure literature. See, e.g., McDaniel & Surrey, *supra* note 1, 48–49, Brooks and McIntyre, *supra* note 15, and Fleming and Peroni, *supra* note 8. However, the inability to come to a general agreement on many of them indicates to the author that the analysis does not provide a powerful tool for resolving the most appropriate treatment.

in part, at least, to one of the underpinnings of tax expenditure analysis—taxing investment income from different sources the same, a view which seems to be shared by much of the modern economic analysis though that very analysis makes clear that such an assumption needs to be tested in terms of its efficiency consequences and distributional effects. More broadly, the discussion here questions many of the conclusions in the modern economic literature—while the broad approach has much to recommend it, the arguments for departure from a general income tax have not yet been made in a convincing way. Indeed there are good reasons to suspect that the approach in much of the literature would make the tax system both less efficient and less fair, largely because of the major missing element in the analysis, the household.

4.5   PENSION PLANS AND THE FAMILY HOME

The tax treatment of pension plans is much more obviously an intersection of labor and capital income than the issues discussed under the previous heading. Here the AFTS report deploys two arguments in favor of (further development of) the current system rather than any drastic change. First, the alleged bias of the income tax against future or deferred consumption (i.e., saving) noted above is regarded as so important for long term saving like pension plans and housing to justify a shift from the income tax to the consumption tax approach by more or less effective exemption for the investment income component in the pension plan mix.[20] Second, the tax on contributions (which relates to the labor income element in the pension plans area) is viewed as a tax on deferred rather than current income and so justifies different and lower rates than other (current) labor income, reflecting the generally lower tax rates that apply to people in retirement because of their lower income.

Australia's pension plan arrangements in virtually every respect are out of line with international norms, and so it is necessary to describe them briefly to give context to the preceding and following discussion. Australia does not have a social security tax financing income related benefits in retirement but rather has a flat rate income tested old age pension set at around 25% of average earnings. Further, Australia requires that 9% of wages be contributed to private pension plans which then generate retirement benefits in the form or lump sums or pensions (and additional voluntary contributions get similar treatment subject to generous limits). Such contributions are not taxable to the employee, deductible to the employer, and taxed at 15% in the pension plan. Investment income of pension plans is also taxed

---

20. The progressive consumption tax approach can be achieved in two main ways: by providing a deduction for savings and taxing withdrawals (which, for example, is the treatment of pension plans in most countries though not Australia), or by exempting income from capital from tax (which, for example, is the internationally common tax treatment for the family home). Under certain assumptions such as unchanging tax rate scales over time, the two are equivalent. Australia uses the term "superannuation" to refer to its pension plan system, but the text refers to pension plans to avoid distraction for non-Australian readers.

at 15%. Until 2007, distributions from pension plans were taxable at progressive rates with a 15% tax credit which produced a similar outcome on a number of assumptions as the more common international model, where contributions and fund income are exempt from tax and distributions are taxable in full. In 2007, distributions from pension plans were made fully exempt from tax from age 60, partly to deal with complexity in the previous system for retirees and partly to keep the baby boomer generation working (revenue not then being a concern because of the resources boom which was filling Australian tax coffers with very large fiscal surpluses).

The main AFTS changes proposed in pension plan tax arrangements are shifting the tax on contributions from the fund to the contributor (i.e., taxing contributions along with other labor income), providing a capped 20% tax credit for contributions and reducing the tax rate on fund investment income to 7.5% without the CGT discount (or AFTS proposed 40% general investment income discount) and extended to investment income in the retirement phase which currently is exempt. The effects of these changes are less than immediately obvious, though fairly fully explained in the AFTS report which is much more detailed in its proposals in this area than in many others. First, there is an effective increase in the mandatory contribution level. The increase arises because of the shift of the contributions tax out of the fund to the contributor. Instead of the fund having 7.65% after the contributions tax, it would have 9%. The Government has gone further and by a different route through its announcement of a rise over time of mandatory contributions to 12%, while keeping the tax on contributions in the fund (meaning an effective 10.2% contribution after the contributions tax).

Second, the imposition of normal labor income tax rates with a capped tax offset would keep the effective tax rate on contributions for most workers at 15% (given the AFTS proposed 35% tax rate across a broad range of income and 20% capped offset), but would in a sense reintroduce the 15% surcharge on higher income earners which existed from 1996 until 2005 though at different rates and not imposed on the fund. The result is a progressive but quite different tax rate scale for labor income contributed to pension plans compared with other labor income. Third, there is an evening up of tax rates on investment income in pension plans but quite different treatment from investment income outside pension plans in both measurement and tax rate.

As noted above, the argument for an alleged bias against deferred consumption is highly debatable. Indeed the AFTS report itself quotes evidence that most people are quite careful to ensure that they have enough to live on in old age given the current construction of the Australian tax and transfer system. Further, as contributions to pension plans are compulsory to a level which the AFTS report insists is adequate for sufficient income in old age, there is no need for tax concessions to produce adequate saving for that purpose. By its own reasoning the tax incentives only produce saving above the level needed for adequacy and thus tend to benefit those households with higher incomes and higher capacity to save. The report itself notes the often expressed concern that tax incentives for this group may simply tend to change the form but not the level of saving. While the effective higher contribution tax on higher income earners is intended to redress the current bias in favor of higher income earners, clearly there is still a significant bias in the proposed system.

The effect of the current and proposed system is to produce yet further variation in the already crazy pattern of tax rates on labor income explained above. Under the current system, there is effectively a 15% rate on an amount which varies with the level of income of the individual (with regards to the compulsory component) and with saving choices (for the voluntary component), and the proposed system would do little to change these features. The argument that this is a separate and appropriate progressive tax system for effectively deferred income looks like an ex post (and very weak) justification for the 2007 changes to the Australian system. Before then, the tax on pensions produced an additional layer of tax on the labor income which still meant more variation in the effective tax rate on labor income contributed to pension plans but not the much lower rates under the post-2007 system and the proposed AFTS system. The argument for evening up tax rates on investment income of pension plans is again a return to tax-everything-the-same argument but in a context where the tax rates on labor income are wildly varied and the treatment of investment income outside pension plans (and the family home) is very different.

The argument about deferred consumption is also deployed in relation to the family home as a justification for keeping the current tax treatment, which is a form of progressive consumption tax treatment (the income which pays for the home is taxed but not the return on the investment). Very little is said on this topic compared to pension plans, and it is generally recognized throughout the AFTS report that the treatment of housing by the tax, transfer, and regulatory systems is a very complex matter that requires a lot more policy work.

Nonetheless, there is a strong recommendation to apply taxes at much higher rates to all land, including family homes.[21] The justification is that land gives rise to immobile rents, and one of the other messages of the modern economics literature that seems to have developed into a new tax policy slogan is to heavily tax immobile rents which means to heavily tax land. If additional taxes are imposed on land in a way which is related to the value of the land, this amounts in effect to an

---

21. Again this needs to be understood in the context of the current Australian tax system under which local rates (property taxes) are levied on land to finance local services based on the unimproved value of the land, but at about a fifth of the United States rate as services like police and education are provided at the state and federal, not the local, level. Land tax is a state tax that currently applies mainly to commercial land on an annual basis also using the unimproved value (i.e., it does not apply to residential or farm land). Moreover, Australia has very high taxes on land transfers, often at 5% of transfer value, and the recommendation on land tax is intended in part to replace this tax (the extent not being very clear in the AFTS report). To the extent that this is simply a shift of tax on land from conveyance duty to another form, the change may not have much impact overall. The land transfer tax can also be seen as in effect a consumption tax on residential land as the GST exempts rental residential land from tax given that it is impossible politically and practically to levy GST on owner-occupied homes. All of this confirms the AFTS view that the position of residential land is very complex even as a tax matter, putting aside other regulatory issues.

income tax on the return from the land. Indeed when Australia briefly taxed the imputed rent on owner occupied homes early last century under the income tax, it did so by means of a percentage of the capital value. Hence the maintenance of the current income tax treatment of owner occupied housing may be undercut by the proposal on land tax.

If the family home is regarded as a form of long-term saving for adequate provision in retirement, then one wonders why some of the prudential and regulatory concerns underlying the pension plan tax system are not thought about in the context of the family home. Australia, like most countries, has rules designed to prevent pension plan moneys from being used to make short-term bets on the stock exchange (or anything else) through highly leveraged strategies as opposed to long-term unleveraged investment. Yet there is little to prevent retired people from betting the family home on the stock market, which proved to be a significant problem in the recent stock market bubble in Australia. It is not intended here to discuss what, if anything, should be done about this issue, though action is occurring in Australia and overseas, but rather to note that long-term saving for adequacy in retirement involves a number of risks, including investment risk and longevity risk (not knowing how long we will live and therefore either saving too much or not enough for adequacy).

The large shift from defined benefit to defined contribution schemes in the pension plan area over recent decades in Australia as in other countries has moved both investment and longevity risk onto members of pension plans whereas in the government, old age pension area the risk is effectively with the government. The AFTS report spends some time considering what to do about these risks and proposes that government encouragement be given to developing products that can deal with them. In the process it is recognized that there is a substantial market failure in the insurance markets, which makes the problem very difficult to deal with—the market failure being common for insurance generally and having to do with moral hazard and asymmetry of information.

There is very little debate about how these issues are dealt with in nearly all other developed countries—through social security taxes designed to fund income related non-means-tested pensions in retirement. It is simply assumed that the current system of mixed public and private provision for retirement will remain, and indeed there is considerable resistance to the idea of the government assuming a greater share of risk in the area. Of course social security systems in other countries are not without their own long-term risks, but it is surprising that there has not been a serious debate on this issue in living memory in Australia.

Again, one suspects that the AFTS recommendations in the pension plan and family home area are an exercise in political pragmatism rather than the rigorous application of modern economic thinking. In relation to pension plans, the AFTS review was obliged by its terms of reference to retain the tax exemption of pension plan end benefits—left to its own devices and ignoring recent history the review may well have gone for the overseas consumption tax model of not taxing contributions and fund income and taxing end benefits as that would remove the many international problems that arise from Australia's being out of step with the rest of the world (though they do not seem to receive any mention). Within that constraint they probably would have preferred full taxation of contributions and fund income with exemption of end benefits—the alternative consumption tax model. As it is, Australia is in a different house to the rest of the world for pension plans, and would under AFTS recommendations remain there. With regard to family homes, it became evident during the AFTS review process that directly taxing the family home under the income tax/CGT was not on the table politically—and hence the significance of the land tax recommendations while retaining the principal residence CGT exemption.

As with labor income, there are other ways of thinking about pension plans and housing in modern economic terms. With respect to housing, it provides the main means of counteracting the substantial shift over recent decades around the world in ownership of wealth to the wealthiest as it forms the main source of wealth of average Australians (Australia having a high level of home ownership). In other words, it helps to preserve the progressivity of the tax and transfer system, and the claims about the economic inefficiencies of the tax system's failure to tax housing in the same way as other investments have not been demonstrated, given the complexity of the problem in tax and broader terms. It has also proved a much more stable form of wealth than financial assets. In the last 40 years, there has been only one significant bubble and correction in the Australian housing markets (1990), whereas in the last 25 years alone there have been five in the financial markets (global financial crisis 2007, tech bubble 2000, Asian financial crisis 1997, the recession of 1992 and the "greed is good" 1987 crash). Claims about the superior performance of financial assets compared to residential housing are hard to make out in an Australian setting.

By contrast, the pension plan tax system is significantly biased in favor of higher income earners and is largely concentrated in relatively risky financial assets. For average workers, there is not a great deal in the tax "incentives" given that the means test for the government pension has the effect that the pension from private plans to a large degree replaces the government pension many retirees would otherwise receive, and the pension plan tax rates are nowhere near as beneficial, if at all, in their case. They are forced into the system by its mandatory nature, whether or not it is what they would do if there were a choice. Major issues surrounding the system, such as public versus private provision and related issues of risk, receive little attention. Arguments in favor of the current Australian system (and the AFTS approach) in terms of a modern economic analysis based on efficiency and distributional consequences are yet to be made out.

The AFTS review commissioned research into the question whether the simple psychological makeup of *homo economicus* as an individual welfare maximizer that underlies most modern economics is sufficiently robust to justify tax policy making on the basis of such economic analysis alone.[22] Though it does not

---

22. A. Reeson & S. Dunstall, "Behavioural Economics and Complex Decision-Making: Implications for the Australian Tax and Transfer System" available at http://taxreview.treasury.gov.au/content/Content.aspx?doc=html/commissioned_work.htm.

seem to have had much of an impact on the AFTS report, the author suspects that at least in the case of housing and care in retirement (and food and childcare), there are much more fundamental human drives at work—the family and government are structured in most societies to provide basic human necessities of food, shelter and security including support for those who cannot provide for themselves (children, the disabled and the aged). In the current Australian context, people will buy houses and save for their retirement (including "investments" in children) whatever the tax system does. From an economists frame, this is often an argument for not giving any tax incentives for the behavior; indeed it suggests that heavier taxes than normal can be applied because the behavior will not be much affected by taxes (so that the taxes have lower efficiency costs). From a broader view, it may be thought a reason for the government to assist as much as it can in the behavior, given the societal—and broader human psychological—benefits that it produces.

The income tax treatment of pension plans and the family home are often recorded as two of the largest tax expenditures in the income tax system.[23] The conclusion is not infrequently drawn that the tax treatment of one or both should be aligned with the comprehensive tax base and in effect be taxed like labor income and/or other income from capital. While tax expenditure analysis provides clear direction in this case (compared with many of the issues discussed above), the previous discussion is intended to suggest that the slogan nature of many conclusions drawn from that analysis needs to be resisted. Equally, while the slogans derived from modern economic analysis of tax systems also need to be rejected, the general approach in that analysis (together with a broader understanding of the fundamental human drives at work) provide a way forward in thinking about saving for retirement and owner occupied housing.

4.6   CONCLUSION

Policy and political debate is understandable in such contested areas as the appropriate general tax treatment of labor and investment income, and for that reason alone, we cannot expect tax reform to one day magically be over, let alone the implications of the relativist approach to tax policy in modern public economics espoused but not entirely practised by the AFTS review in Australia. The author accepts that modern welfare economics is superior to tax expenditure analysis as an approach to tax reform, but considers the simplified slogans often derived from the economics analysis much less justifiable than slogans derived from tax expenditure analysis.

There are two main reasons for this view. First, the economics approach may be 40 years old, but it is still highly defective at the theoretical and empirical level (with some honorable exceptions) largely because of the failure to properly incorporate households into the analysis. While tax expenditure analysis suffers from

---

23. In Australia together they far exceed all other tax expenditures combined, *Tax Expenditure Statement 2010, supra* note 2, 4–7.

the same problem, it does not go anywhere nearly as wrong as the economics analysis as a result. Second, the economists draw extremely strong policy conclusions often based on highly questionable assumptions and without any regard for the empirical data on the very questions they are investigating. Tax expenditure analysis was invented by and is largely the domain of lawyers. Lawyers deal in facts (data) and are generally cautious about strong conclusions, preferring to treat each case on its merits on an intuitive basis. Each group has something to learn from the other.

Paul McDaniel combined the best of both worlds. He spent many years developing and refining tax expenditure analysis in the company of economists, but was reticent about claiming that it was the key to tax reform. It was and is an important tool of analysis in some, but by no means all, areas of the income tax. It also provides a form of rhetoric in tax debate that used judiciously is more likely to carry the day than some of the slogans derived from modern economics.

Chapter 5

Tax Reform Paul McDaniel Style: The Repeal of the Grantor Trust Rules

Laura E. Cunningham & Noël B. Cunningham[*]

5.1   INTRODUCTION

One of the many profound contributions that Paul McDaniel made to tax policy discourse was his insistence on the need to maintain a razor sharp distinction between tax expenditure analysis on the one hand, and tax policy analysis on the other. While tax expenditure analysis may be policy analysis, it is not *tax policy* analysis. The failure to distinguish between the two forms of analysis, Paul argued, has hampered efforts at tax and spending reform.[1]

Paul was emphatic that tax expenditure provisions should be analyzed as government spending programs, and can be justified only if they stand up to the scrutiny of spending analysis: are they wise, effective and efficient subsidies. The term "tax reform" is reserved for changes in the structural components of

---

[*]   Laura E. Cunningham, Professor of Law, Benjamin N. Cardozo School of Law, Yeshiva University. Noël B. Cunningham, Professor of Law, New York University School of Law. The authors would like to thank Caroline Waldner for her research assistance in preparing this chapter, and our friends and colleagues Len Schmolka and Stewart Sterk for their comments on an earlier draft.
1.   See generally, P. McDaniel, "Identification of the 'Tax' in 'Effective Tax Rates,' 'Tax Reform' and 'Tax Equity'," National Tax Journal 38. (1985): 273.

Yariv Brauner & Martin James McMahon, Jr. (eds), *The Proper Tax Base: Structural Fairness from an International and Comparative Perspective—Essays in Honour of Paul McDaniel*, pp. 107–117.
© 2012 Kluwer Law International BV, The Netherlands.

the tax system, including the appropriate tax rates, taxable unit, and accounting rules. It is only in analyzing these structural provisions that the traditional tools of tax policy analysis, including concepts of horizontal and vertical equity, play a meaningful role. Paul described the concept of tax equity, horizontal and vertical, as follows: "In the absence of problems in the technical tax structure, taxpayers with the same amounts of income will incur the same economic tax, and taxpayers with higher incomes will incur progressively greater economic tax liabilities than lower income taxpayers."[2] Structural provisions that violate those principles should be the target of tax reform. Yet once the taxpayer's economic tax is determined, offsetting reductions in the taxpayer's actual tax bill caused by subsidies in the form of tax expenditures must be justified under spending principles. While questions of equity no doubt arise in constructing spending programs, the concept of *tax equity* is not helpful in analyzing whether the spending program instituted through the tax expenditure is a good one.

To illustrate, consider section 121 of the Code, which excludes up to $250,000 ($500,000 in the case of a married couple) of gain from the sale of a principal residence. We could try to apply traditional tax policy criteria in evaluating a proposal to repeal § 121. Does it meet horizontal equity criteria, i.e., does it treat taxpayers with the same economic income equally? Clearly not, because a taxpayer who sells stock at a gain of $250,000 is fully taxed on that gain, and the seller of a principal residences goes untaxed. Does it satisfy vertical equity criteria, by treating low-income taxpayers fairly vis-à-vis high income taxpayers? Again no, because it is available only to taxpayers who can own a home. Is it economically neutral, i.e., does it have an impact on taxpayer's economic behavior? It is clearly not neutral, in that it favors investments in one type of asset (homes) over others by making those investments tax exempt. Yet has this tax policy inquiry told us anything about whether § 121 should be repealed? Not really, because § 121 is in the Code not because it is necessary to accurately measure income, but because of Congress' desire to encourage home ownership. It is clearly a tax expenditure, and a taxpayer who utilizes and excludes $250,000 is receiving a subsidy from the government. Her economic income clearly includes that $250,000 gain, thus her "economic tax" would include the tax on that gain. But the reduction in calculating her actual tax bill caused by the exclusion of the gain amounts to a subsidy payment to her by the government. The fact that this is all accomplished on a net basis through her income tax return is irrelevant. Tax policy criteria do not guide us in deciding whether this subsidy is wise or appropriate. Instead the provision must be analyzed as to whether it represents a good use of the government's money, i.e., is it a good spending program? While equity considerations should certainly come into play in evaluating it as a spending program, they are but one of the many considerations policy makers should weigh in deciding whether this is a good subsidy.

Paul believed that "tax reform" efforts that challenge specific tax expenditures on tax equity grounds are misguided, and the resulting confusion has

---

2. *Ibid.*, 277.

"contributed significantly to the failure of those 'tax reform' efforts."[3] Instead, Paul argued, that "action with respect to tax expenditures does not involve 'tax' reform at all; it involves 'spending' reform."[4]

This confusion is graphically illustrated in the current Congressional debate over "tax reform" and "spending reductions." While politicians call for drastic cuts in spending, they reject proposals to limit tax expenditures, calling those proposals "tax increases." Witness the wording of the "Taxpayer Protection Pledge" produced by the "Americans for Tax Reform, organization, to which 235 Congressmen and 41 Senators have subscribed:

I will:
ONE, oppose any and all efforts to increase the marginal income tax rates for individuals and/or businesses; and
TWO, oppose any net reduction or elimination of deductions and credits, unless matched dollar for dollar by further reducing tax rates.

Grover Norquist, president of Americans for Tax Reform, has stated that eliminating tax breaks to reduce the deficit is "just a dirty trick for raising taxes," and "tax increases are not an option."[5]

This insistence on viewing any reductions in tax expenditures as tax increases, rather than the spending reductions, is frightening. In this era of cost cutting, tax expenditures should be on the same chopping block with direct spending programs. Only then can the difficult decisions of what to cut and whom to impact be coherently made.

In the midst of the current frenzy over spending reductions, we believe that one significant opportunity for tax reform exists. We believe that repeal of the grantor trusts rules would represent real tax reform in the Paul McDaniel sense. The grantor trust rules are not tax expenditures; they are structural provisions of the Code that were enacted for vertical equity reasons, to preserve the progressivity of the income tax rate structure. We believe that not only do they no longer serve their original purpose, they actually defeat that purpose today.[6] They are being used by wealthy taxpayers to avoid transfer taxes. This not only creates equity problems within the transfer tax system, it has the ripple effect of reducing progressivity of the overall federal tax system. Repeal of these provisions would represent significant and important tax reform.[7]

---

3. *Ibid.*
4. *Ibid.*
5. B. Faler & H. Przybyla, "When a Tax is a Tax may be Pivotal Issue for U.S. Debt Panel," Bloomberg Business Week (Nov. 8, 2010), www.bloomberg.com/ . . . /when-a-tax-is-a-tax-may-be-pivotal-issue-for-u-s-deficit-reduction-panel.html.
6. Professor Len Schmolka once commented with respect to the grantor trust rules, "It is not a matter of the cure being worse than the disease. It is, rather, that the cure has become the disease." L. Schmolka, FLPs and GRATs: What To Do? 2000 Tax Notes Today, 49–105, para. 93.
7. In addition to Professor Schmolka (who advocated repeal), several other commentators have called for the repeal or substantial reform of the grantor trust rules. See most recently Mark L. Ascher, "The Grantor Trust Rules Should Be Repealed," Iowa L. Rev. 96 (2011): 885 and Jay A. Soled & Mitchell Gans, "Sales To Grantor Trusts: A Case Study of What the IRS and Congress

5.2　　　　　　　THE GRANTOR TRUST RULES

Since the adoption of the 16th Amendment, the rate structure of the U.S. income tax has been progressive to one degree or another. The policy justifications for a progressive rate structure have been widely discussed in the literature.[8] Paul McDaniel viewed the rate structure as one of the essential structural components of the income tax. The rate schedule at any given time represents Congress' view of the appropriate distribution of the tax burden among taxpayers with different income levels. Increases or decreases in the level of progressivity represent "tax reform" in that they are based on changes in Congress' view of that distribution.

The level of progressivity of the income tax rate schedule has varied widely over the history of the income tax. Although in 1913 the initial marginal rates were quite modest with the highest rate set at 7%, by 1918 with the advent of WWI the rate schedule became dramatically more progressive, with a top marginal rate of 77%. A steeply progressive rate structure creates an incentive for taxpayers to attempt to spread their income among as many taxpayers as possible. Since each person constituted a taxpayer, one of the earliest tax planning techniques was to split one's income among family members. Illustrative is the seminal case of *Lucas v. Earl*,[9] in which a taxpayer had assigned to his wife one-half of his salary and attorney's fees for 1920 and 1921 (when the top marginal rate was 73%). The question before the court was whether this assignment should be respected for purposes of Federal income taxes. The Supreme Court applied the famous "fruit and tree" metaphor and held that it should not. The Court stated that a taxpayer should not be able to escape taxation on his earnings "by anticipatory arrangements and contracts however skillfully devised. . . ."[10]

Because entities are taxpayers too, similar attempts were made to divert income by transferring investment assets to trusts.[11] Under the rules applied to

---

can do to Curb Aggressive Transfer Tax Techniques," Tenn. L. Rev. (2011, forthcoming). Those who have called for repeal include J. Dodge, "Simplifying Models for the Income Taxation of Trusts and Estates," American Journal of Tax Policy 14 (1997): 127; and S. Kamin, "A Proposal for the Income Taxation of Trusts and Estates, Their Grantors, and Their Beneficiaries," American Journal of Tax Policy 13 (1996): 215. Those who have called for substantial revision include J. Soled, "Reforming the Grantor Trust Rules," Notre Dame Law Review. 76 (2001): 76, R. Danforth, "A Proposal for Integrating the Income and Transfer Taxation of Trusts," Virginia Tax Review 18 (1999): 545; and J. Peschel, "The Impact of Fiduciary Standards on Federal Taxation of Grantor Trusts: Illusion and Inconsistency," Duke Law. Journal (1979): 709.

8. The classic article making the case against progressivity is W. Blum & H. Kalvin, Jr., "The Uneasy Case for Progressive Taxation," University of Chicago Law Review. 19 (1952): 417. For an excellent counterpoint, see J. Bankman & T. Griffith, "Social Welfare and the Rate Structure: A New Look at Progressive Taxation," California Law Review 75 (1987): 1905. See also T. Griffith, "Progressive Taxation and Happiness," Boston College. Law Review 45 (2004): 1363.

9. 281 U.S. 111 (1930).

10. *Ibid.*, 115.

11. For an excellent and concise history of the evolution of the grantor trust rules, see B. Bittker & L. Lokken, Federal Taxation of Income, Estates, and Gifts, 3rd ed. para. 80.1.1 (New York: Warren, Gorham &Lamont, 2003).

trusts at the time, either the trustee or the beneficiary was taxed on a trust's income, depending on whether the trust's income was distributed, regardless of the terms of the trust or the powers retained by the creator of the trust. So even if a trust could be revoked by the grantor at any time, it was respected as a taxpayer independent of the grantor. For this reason, the revocable trust became the entity of choice to split income. The obvious appeal of this technique was that it allowed wealthy taxpayers to maintain complete control over their wealth while enjoying substantial income tax savings. In response, in 1924 Congress enacted a statute that taxed the grantor of a revocable trust on the trust's income, whether or not the income was distributed.[12] The purpose of this provision was clear: it was a structural provision designed to preserve the integrity of the progressive rate structure. Although there were some flaws in the original legislation, most were eliminated and by 1934 revocable trusts could no longer be used for income splitting.

During the mid-1930s, when the highest marginal rate reached 79%, taxpayers began designing trusts that, while not revocable, still allowed the grantor to wield substantial control. These trusts included those that were irrevocable for a set period of time, during which the grantor retained no beneficial interest but did retain a variety of administrative powers that allowed him to continue to control the assets in the trust. A good illustration of this type of trust is found in case of *Helvering v. Clifford,*[13] in which the taxpayer established an irrevocable trust with a five-year term. During the term of the trust the income was payable, in the discretion of the trustee, to the taxpayer's wife. At the end of the five-year term, the trust terminated and the corpus reverted back to the taxpayer, and any undistributed income would pass to the wife. The taxpayer named himself trustee and retained broad discretionary powers over both the corpus and the income. The Service argued that although this transaction was not specifically covered by statute, the income from the trust still should be taxed to taxpayer/grantor, not his wife or the trust. Although the grantor had no current beneficial interest in the trust, as trustee he controlled the trust's investments, he determined whether the trust income would be distributed or accumulated, and the corpus would revert to the grantor in five years. The Supreme Court held for the government, finding that:

> [W]e cannot conclude as a matter of law that the respondent ceased to be the owner of the corpus after the trust was created. Rather the short duration of the trust, the fact that the wife was the beneficiary, and the retention of control over the corpus by respondent all lead irresistibly to the conclusion that respondent continued to be the owner for purposes of § 22(a) [the predecessor of § 61].[14]

While Court's opinion in Clifford made it perfectly clear that under certain circumstances the grantor of a trust would be taxed on its income if she maintained too

---

12. Revenue Act of 1924, Pub. L. No. 176, 43 Stat. 253, 277.
13. 309 U.S. 331 (1940).
14. *Ibid.,* 335.

much dominion and control over the trust, it gave very little guidance on exactly what quantum of dominion and control was too much. Since the use of trusts to split income was a widely used technique, the decision triggered "a tidal wave of litigation."[15] It was clear that additional structural rules were necessary for the administration of the tax laws and to protect the progressive rate structure. These rules were first supplied by Treasury in 1946 when it promulgated the so-called "*Clifford* regulations,"[16] In 1954 these regulations were codified and, in conjunction with early provisions relating to revocable trusts, became known collectively as the "grantor trust rules."[17] Under these rules, if the grantor retains a 5% reversionary interest or certain powers affecting the enjoyment or the management of the trust assets, the grantor "shall be treated as the owner" of the trust assets, and hence taxed on the income generated by the trust.[18]

The legislative purpose behind these rules was perfectly clear: it was thought that these rules were necessary to prevent taxpayers from splitting their income using trusts while maintaining certain powers, administrative or beneficial, over the trust. Enactment of these rules certainly fell into the category of "tax reform" as Paul McDaniel defined it: they were viewed as necessary to preserve the integrity of the rate structure. For several decades, during which time top marginal rates ranged from 70% to 91%, the grantor trust rules served their purpose; wealthy individuals were constrained from using trusts to both control their assets and shift the income from the assets to lower bracket taxpayers.

In the last 30 years, however, several aspects of the income tax have changed that have undercut the utility of the grantor trust rules. Indeed, we believe that the grantor trust rules are no longer necessary to protect the progressivity of the income tax and are in fact being used to undercut the overall progressivity of the U.S. tax system. First, reductions in maximum rates and flattening of the rate schedule have markedly reduced the incentives to split income among related taxpayers. Beginning in the early 1980s, the income tax rate structure has become markedly less progressive, and top marginal rates have dropped dramatically. Maximum rates went from 70% to 50% in the early years of the Reagan administration, and plummeted to 28% with the Tax Reform Act of 1986. While rates crept back up during the 1990s, they have not exceeded 40% since 1987. Second, in 1986 Congress enacted the so-called "kiddie tax," which generally taxes unearned income of children younger than 18 years of age at their parents' marginal rates.[19] Essentially this provision forecloses the utility of assigning investment income to one's children, either directly or through trusts. Finally, the income tax brackets for trusts have been telescoped and are not nearly as progressive as they once were. In 2010, for example, all taxable income of a trust over $11,200 is

---

15. Bittker & Lokken, *supra* note 12, at para. 80.1.1.
16. T.D. 5488, 1946-1 C.B. 19.
17. I.R.C. §§ 671–679.
18. I.R.C. 671.
19. I.R.C. § 1(g).

taxed at 35%.[20] This means that the maximum annual savings in income taxes that one can achieve by utilizing a trust is just over a $1000. Given the expenses of maintaining a trust, this savings does not provide a very strong incentive, if any, to use a trust for income shifting. It seems quite clear that the grantor trust rules are no longer necessary to safe-guard the progressive rate structure.

The fact that the grantor trust rules no longer serve their intended purpose doesn't necessarily lead to the conclusion that they should be repealed. Perhaps they just represent excess verbiage in the statute. But recent planning techniques have employed the rules in a manner that actually defeats their original purpose, by allowing significant avoidance of the federal transfer taxes. Transfer tax avoidance raises multiple tax policy concerns. First, any type of tax avoidance raises not only revenue problems but horizontal equity problems as well. Second, if you accept the notion that one of the principal roles of the transfer taxes is to backstop the income tax and to add a degree of progressivity to the federal tax system as a whole, then techniques that utilize the grantor trust rules of the income tax to evade the transfer taxes erode progressivity.

5.3   THE INTENTIONALLY DEFECTIVE GRANTOR TRUST

The technique employed is to create what are known as "Intentionally Defective Grantor Trusts" or "IDGT's."[21] The trusts exploit the inconsistency in the treatment of the following transaction under the income tax and the transfer taxes.

5.3.1   BASIC IDGT TRANSACTION

G transfers $10,000,000 to an irrevocable trust, naming her brother as trustee. Under the terms of the trust, during G's life the trustee in his sole discretion has the power to distribute (or not) the income and/or corpus of the trust among G's children and grandchildren. G retains the right to reacquire the corpus of the trust and substitute other property of equivalent value. Upon G's death, the trust property is to be divided equally among all G's grandchildren or their estates.

For purposes of the transfer taxes, G has made a completed gift, i.e., G has given up "dominion and control" over the property. The transfer of the corpus will be taxed as a gift at the time the trust is created. G has retained no powers over the trust that will cause it to be included in his estate when he dies. However, for income tax

---

20. Under current law, the maximum annual savings from fully utilizing the rate structure for a trust is $1,025.

21. For an excellent analysis of all of the issues related to intentionally defective grantor trusts, see D. Ricks, "I Dig It, But Congress Shouldn't Let Me: Closing the IDGT Loophole," ACTEC Journal 35 (2011); 641 [hereinafter Ricks]. For a practitioner's perspective, see T.R. Harris, "IDGT's—When Defective is Effective" (May 2006) (unpublished manuscript on file with authors) and T. Baird, "A Potpourri of Leveraged Transfers Using Defective Grantor Trusts," ALI-ABA Course Study Materials (July 2001).

purposes, because of the grantor trust rules, G is treated as the "owner" of the trust corpus for two reasons: first, the trustee, a nonadverse party, has the power to control the beneficial enjoyment of the trust's income and/or corpus,[22] and second, G can reacquire the corpus by substituting property of equivalent value.[23] The consequence of the inconsistent treatment is that G will continue to pay tax on the income generated by the trust, income that economically belongs to his children and grandchildren. And because that income tax liability is imposed upon G by the Code, rather than the actual beneficiaries of the income, when G pays the tax he is not viewed as making a transfer to the beneficiaries for transfer tax purposes.[24] To illustrate, in the above example, suppose that the trust earns 6% or $600,000 during its first year of existence. Although the full $600,000 inures to the benefit of the trust and its beneficiaries, as a result of the grantor trust rules, G is liable for the income tax on $600,000 ($210,000 at the maximum rate of 35%). Because the tax dollars come out of G's pocket, and not the income of the trust, G is in a very real sense making an additional transfer to the trust (and its beneficiaries) of $210,000. Yet that annual "gift" escapes the transfer tax entirely.

5.3.2 IDGT INSTALLMENT SALE TRANSACTION

The IDGT can be used in conjunction with the installment sale rules to compound the tax savings for wealthy individuals. To illustrate, consider the following transaction:

> T is 55 years old, married and very wealthy. At all times, T is in the 35% income tax bracket. Several years ago, she and her husband created a family limited partnership (FLP) which holds marketable securities, currently valued at $1 billion. In December of 2011, T creates an irrevocable trust (the Trust) for the benefit of her children and their descendants, to which she contributes marketable securities of $10,000,000. T appoints her brother as trustee to whom she gives the discretion to distribute (or not) trust income and/or corpus among the beneficiaries. T also reserves the right to reacquire the corpus by substituting property of equal value. On January 1, 2012, T sells a 15% interest in the FLP to the Trust for $100,000,000, the interest's appraised fair market value.[25] Under the terms of the sale, the Trust executes a secured

---

22. I.R.C. § 674(a) & (c).
23. I.R.C. § 675(4)(C).
24. Rev. Rul. 2004-64, 2004-4 C.B. 7.
25. A 33 1/3% discount in the value of the underlying assets is fairly conservative for an FLP under current practice. Recently the Tax Court blessed a 35% discount in Miller, v. Commisioner, T.C. Memo 2009-119 and a 30% discount in Pierre v. Commissionr, 133 T.C. 24 (2009). Both of these cases dealt with FLPs that held marketable securities and cash, and neither had sympathetic facts. For a discussion of these cases, see L. Cunningham, "FLPs, the Transfer Taxes, and the Income Tax," Tax Notes 127 (2010): 806. See generally, L. Cunningham, "Remember the Alamo: The IRS Needs Ammunition in its Fight Against the Family Limited Partnership," *Tax Notes* 86 (2000): 1461.

promissory note for the entire purchase price, which it agrees to pay in a balloon payment at maturity in 9 years.[26] The note bears interest at the current Federal mid-term rate of 3% annually.[27] In 2012, the FLP earns 10%,[28] or $100 million, and allocates and distributes to the Trust its 15% share, or $15 million. The Trust earns an additional $1 million in income on its initial corpus, for total income for the year of $16 million. At the end of 2012, the Trust pays T $3,000,000 in interest as required by the note. The Trust does not make any distributions and reinvests the balance of $13 million in additional securities.

On the creation of the trust, T and her husband have made a completed gift of the $10 million.[29] They will not current owe any gift tax, however, because of the unified credit under § 2505.[30] Furthermore, no distributions from the Trust will be subject to the generation skipping transfer tax, or GST.[31] However, for the same reasons outlined above,[32] T is treated as the owner of the trust for income tax purposes. This means that T is liable for all the income taxes imposed on the Trust. This also means that the installment sale is ignored for income tax purposes.[33] One cannot sell property to oneself. Not only is the sale not treated as a realization event, for income tax purposes the $3,000,000 interest payment is ignored. T is liable for the tax on the Trust's $16 million of income, or $5.6 million. At the end of

---

26. When planning these transactions, it is necessary that the installment sales contract bear adequate stated interest to prevent the transaction from being a below market loan under § 7872. The amount of interest that is adequate depends on the term of the note. If the term of the note is more than 3 years, but not over 9 years, the Federal mid-term rate is the minimum rate; if the term is longer than 9 years, the Federal long-term rate is the minimum rate. Because the Federal mid-term rate is significantly less than the long-term rate, nine years is very often the term of the notes used in this transaction.

27. For March 2011, the Federal mid-term rate was 2.44% compounded annually and the Federal long-term rate was 4.30% compounded annually. See Rev. Rul. 2011-6, 2011-11 I.R.B. 537.

28. We have used a 10% rate of return for ease of computation. Although this may seem rather high given the current economic conditions, historically it is not. From 1900 to 2003, the average nominal return on large, publically corporate stock was 11.7% and the real rate of return was 8.5%. See R. Brealey, S. Myers & F. Allen, *Principles of Corporate Finance*, 8th ed. (New York: McGraw-Hill/Irwin 2006), 149.

29. As a technical matter, they have given up sufficient "dominion and control" within the meaning of Treas. Reg. § 25.2511-2(b) for the gift to be complete.

30. I.R.C. § 2513.

31. For purposes of the GST, T and her husband are both treated as transferors. § 2652(a)(2). Each individual is permitted an exemption from the GST of $5 million, which she can allocate to transfers that she designates. I.R.C. §§ 2631(a) & (c) and 2632. On the assumption that T and her husband allocate their respective exemptions to the Trust, the applicable rate for all distributions from the Trust will be zero. I.R.C. §§ 2641 & 2642.

32. See I.R.C. §§ 674(a) and § 675(4)(C).

33. In Revenue Ruling 85-13, 1985-1 C.B. 184, the Service held that any exchange between a grantor and her grantor trust is not a realization event. On the facts of the ruling, the grantor gave to a trust his unsecured note, bearing adequate stated interest, for the sole asset of the trust. The Service viewed this as a borrowing of the Trust's assets and, under § 675(3), the Trust became a grantor trust. The Service refused to treat the transaction as a sale, refusing to follow Rothstein v. U.S., 735 F. 2d 704 (2nd Cir. 1984).

2012, in addition to the interest in the FLP, the corpus of the Trust has grown to $23,000,000.[34]

To see how this transaction plays out, let us assume that from 2013 through 2020, each year the FLP and the Trust earn 10% taxable income on all their investments, the FLP distributes to the Trust its share of that income, the Trust pays T $3,000,000 of interest on the note, the Trust makes no distributions, and on January 1, 2021, the Trust pays the principal balance on the note of $100,000,000. On these assumptions, on January 1, 2021, after the payment of the balance of the note, the trust will own the 15% interest (with an undiscounted value of $150 million) and, in addition, will own other assets worth over $76 million![35] Yet T has not paid one penny in transfer taxes![36]

Now let's get aggressive! Each year as the corpus of the Trust grows, it has the wherewithal to purchase additional interests in the FLP.[37] Indeed, each year it could purchase an additional 15% interest in the FLP. Let's assume that the Trust did in fact purchase an additional 15% for each of the following five years on the same terms as the original one. If it did so, in 15 years when T is 70 years old, the Trust will own 90% of the FLP (worth $900 million) and, in addition other assets worth over $585 million.[38] And still no transfer taxes paid!

5.4   THE ARGUMENT FOR REPEAL

While it hopefully is obvious at this point that the grantor trust rules should be repealed, let us make the point explicitly. First, recall Paul's description of horizontal and vertical equity in the income tax:

> In the absence of problems in the technical tax structure, taxpayers with the same amounts of income will incur the same economic tax, and taxpayers with higher incomes will incur progressively greater economic tax liabilities than lower income taxpayers.[39]

That's as good a working definition of horizontal and vertical equity as one is apt to find. As applied to the transfer taxes, one would want to see that taxpayers making the same amounts of transfers of wealth will incur the same economic transfer tax,

---

34. The increase in value is due to the $16 million in income less the $3,000,000 in interest paid to T.
35. At a 10% annual interest rate, the future value of an annual payment of $13 million for 9 years is equal to $176,533,200. After paying off the note of $100 million, the Trust will be left with $76,533,200.
36. It should be pointed out that if T dies during the term of the note, the principal amount of the note and any accrued interest would be includible in T's estate.
37. Many practitioners argue that the trust should have assets in an amount equal to at least 10% of the installment note before the installment sale to prevent the possible application of § 2036(a)(1). See Ricks, *supra* note 32.
38. At a 10% annual interest rate, the future value of an annual payment of $76 million for 6 years is equal to $586,386,000.
39. See *supra* note 3.

and taxpayers making larger transfers of wealth will incur progressively greater economic transfer tax liabilities than those making smaller transfers. The type of wholesale transfer tax avoidance that occurs through the use of the IDGT absolutely, clearly, and unequivocally violates these notions of equity in the transfer taxes, and leads us to the conclusion that the grantor trust rules should clearly be repealed.

There is an additional irony that, we believe, puts the nail in the coffin of the grantor trust rules. Multiple justifications have been offered for the transfer taxes, and one that we find particularly persuasive is that they serve to backstop the income tax, and preserve some measure of progressivity in the overall federal tax structure as the income tax becomes gradually less progressive over time.[40] To the extent that the transfer taxes are subject to the type of avoidance allowed by the IDGT, their role in preserving the progressivity is diminished, if not eliminated. The result is that a set of provisions that were designed in the name of progressivity have become a tool in the attack on progressivity, and that we find unacceptable.

5.5   CONCLUSION

The grantor trust rules were once an important structural provision of the income tax, preventing wealthy, high bracket taxpayers from retaining control of their assets while shifting the income from those assets to lower bracket trusts. Given the sharp reduction in maximum tax rates, and the flattening of the rate brackets applicable to trusts, the grantor trust rules no longer play a useful role in the income tax. They are being used, however, to avoid transfer taxes on enormous amounts of wealth. They are clearly not tax expenditures; they are structural provisions of the Code that must stand up to scrutiny on equity grounds. And that they clearly cannot do. They are therefore ripe for tax reform, Paul McDaniel style.

---

40. See M. Graetz, "To Praise the Estate Tax, Not to Bury It," Yale Law Journal 93 (1983): 259, 272.

Part II

The Fair Tax Base and International Tax Reform

Chapter 6

Horizontal Equity Revisited

James Repetti & Diane Ring[*]

6.1   INTRODUCTION

In a 1993 article,[1] Paul McDaniel and James Repetti reviewed a debate between
two economists, Richard Musgrave and Louis Kaplow, about whether "Horizontal
Equity" (HE) has any significance independent of "Vertical Equity" (VE) in
designing a tax system.[2] HE is defined to mean that equals should be treated
alike.[3] VE is defined to mean that an appropriate distinction should be made in
the treatment of people who are not alike.[4] Although disagreement exists, HE in

*   Diane Ring is a Professor of Law and Associate Dean of Academic Affairs at Boston College Law
     School. James Repetti is the William J. Kenealy, S.J. Professor of Law and Associate Dean of
     Academic Affairs at Boston College Law School. The authors thank participants in the tax policy
     seminar at the University of Indiana School of Law (Bloomington) for their helpful comments.
1.   P. McDaniel & J. Repetti, "Horizontal Equity and Vertical Equity: The Musgrave/Kaplow
     Exchange," *Florida Tax Review* 1 (1991): 607.
2.   L. Kaplow, "Horizontal Equity: Measures in Search of a Principle," *National Tax Journal* 42
     (1989): 139 [hereinafter Kaplow I]; Richard A. Musgrave, *The Theory of Public Finance:
     A Study in Public Economy* (McGraw-Hill 1959), 160 [hereinafter Musgrave I], R. Musgrave,
     "Horizontal Equity, Once More," *National Tax Journal* 43 (1990): 113 [hereinafter Musgrave
     II]; L. Kaplow, "A Note on Horizontal Equity," *Florida Tax Review* 1 (1992): 191 [hereinafter
     Kaplow II]; R. Musgrave, "Horizontal Equity: A Further Note," *Florida Tax Review Florida Tax
     Review* 1 (1993): 354 [hereinafter Musgrave III].
3.   Kaplow I, *supra* note 2, at 140–41; Musgrave I, *supra* note 2, at 113.
4.   Kaplow I, *supra* note 2, at 140–41; Musgrave I, *supra* note 2, at 113.

Yariv Brauner & Martin James McMahon, Jr. (eds), *The Proper Tax Base: Structural Fairness from
an International and Comparative Perspective—Essays in Honour of Paul McDaniel*, pp. 121–137.
© 2012 Kluwer Law International BV, The Netherlands.

our tax system has generally been thought to require that individuals with the same income should pay the same tax. VE has generally been thought to require a progressive rate structure that imposes progressively higher rates on individuals with higher incomes.

Kaplow argued in 1989 that HE is not a useful tool for tax policy because it has no normative content and no significance apart from VE.[5] Kaplow further asserted that the use of HE in tax policy analysis is harmful because "it will lead policy-makers astray when they are encouraged to sacrifice other values in the pursuit of HE."[6] Thirty years earlier, in 1959, Musgrave (Musgrave I) had also concluded that HE lacked normative content. He stated:

> The requirements of horizontal and vertical equity are but different sides of the same coin. If there is no specified reason for discriminating among unequals, how can there be a reason for avoiding discrimination among equals? Without a scheme of vertical equity, the requirement of horizontal equity at best becomes a safeguard against capricious discrimination—a safeguard which might be provided equally well by a requirement that taxes be distributed at random.[7]

Indeed, Musgrave's analysis went a step further. He argued in 1959 that *both* HE and VE were inadequate for formulating tax policy because both depended on a determination of some measure for distinguishing equals and unequals.[8] He reasoned, "An objective index of equality or inequality is needed to translate either principle into a specific tax system."[9] In other words, the notion that equals should be treated equally requires specification of the criteria used to determine who is equal and unequal, and that specification will in turn require appeal to some form of distributive justice.

However, in response to Kaplow's 1989 assertion, Musgrave reassessed his own views and decided that he had been wrong (Musgrave II). After surveying various forms of distributive justice, he concluded that HE has a normative basis that is firmer than VE, stating:

> [T]he requirement of HE remains essentially unchanged under the various formulations of distributive justice, ranging from Lockean entitlement over utilitarianism and fairness solutions. That of VE, on the contrary, undergoes

---

5. Kaplow I, *supra* note 2.
6. *Ibid.*, 140. See also D. Elkins, "Horizontal Equity as a Principal of Tax Theory," *Yale Law & Policy. Review*. 24 (2006): 43, 44–59 (arguing that it is possible to design a tax system that is both economically efficient and distributive but that "blatantly violates" HE.) For example, this might occur because some variations of HE require that the order in which taxpayers are ranked by income be preserved in a tax reform. As discussed, *infra* at notes 45 to 48, the forms of HE that require pre-tax ordinal rankings to be preserved are really applying VE, not HE. Thus, the tension created by such regimes is in fact a tension between efficiency and the distributive justice goals specified by the particular tax system.
7. Musgrave I, *supra* note 2, at 160.
8. *Ibid.*
9. *Ibid.*

drastic change under the various approaches. While HE is met by the various VE outcomes, this does not mean that HE is derived from VE. If anything, it suggests that HE is a stronger primary rule.[10]

In the 1993 article, McDaniel and Repetti (M–R) agreed with Musgrave I that both HE and VE lack independent significance. In this chapter, we reexamine the appropriate role of HE in tax policy and the debate that has occurred subsequent to the M–R paper. We agree with Musgrave I's original assessment and later determinations by Kaplow and M–R. HE does not serve a useful role in formulating tax policy. In addition, we agree with Musgrave I and M–R that VE also is not useful without appeal to a theory of distributive justice.

There are important reasons, however, why debate about the role of HE has continued. HE is not a useful substantive tool for tax policy *design*, but it may serve a useful role in: (1) establishing the *process* to be used to design tax policy; and (2) assessing the administration of the resulting rules. We agree with Musgrave I's suggestion that HE and VE are merely both sides of the same coin since starting an analysis by asking what the appropriate criteria is to determine which persons are not alike yields the same result as starting the analysis by asking what criteria should be used to determine whether persons are alike. But the accuracy of Musgrave I does not destroy the insight of Musgrave II. Equality is not important in formulating tax policy because taxation is an algorithm that will always tax equally those defined as equals.[11] Equality does, however, define the process for designing a tax system by requiring that the government justify its selection of criteria to measure who is equal (and not equal).[12] HE lingers in the tax debate because, by starting with the notion that all should be treated equally, HE requires a government to articulate the rationale for any tax policy that imposes "different" taxation. HE tells us that government should communicate the rationale for different treatment; it does not tell us what the treatment should be.

Moving on to implementation and administration of the tax system, some tax scholars have relied on HE to serve as a benchmark for assessing governmental administration of the tax law, the idea that enforcement should be fair. As Musgrave observed (somewhat negatively), "[i]n the absence of vertical equity norms, the case for horizontal equity is reduced to providing protection against malicious discrimination, an objective which might be met more simply by a tax lottery."[13] As considered more extensively below,[14] HE could be viewed as a safeguard against arbitrary enforcement of tax laws and, therefore it stays at the forefront

10. Musgrave II, *supra* note 2, at 116–117.
11. This result is not avoided by employing a different definition for HE that looks to see whether "similar" taxpayers (rather than the "same" taxpayers) are taxed in a similar way (rather than the "same" way). Whatever criteria are used to identify taxpayers who are "similar" will result in such taxpayers being taxed in a similar way.
12. K. Simons, "The Logic of Egalitarian Norms," *Boston University. Law Review* 80 (1990): 693, 714 and 748 (arguing that a right to equality requires a decision maker to provide a "rational explanation" for a difference in treatment").
13. R. Musgrave, "ET, OT and SBT," *Journal of Public Economics* 6 (1976): 3, 4.
14. See *infra* text accompanying notes 54–61.

of tax consciousness because arbitrary enforcement would be particularly pernicious in a system that does not usually[15] make public disclosures regarding each
taxpayer's liability for taxes. HE does not define the form of enforcement, but does
require the government to justify why enforcement is not uniform.

6.2   WHY HE AND VE LACK NORMATIVE CONTENT?

In their review of the Musgrave—Kaplow debate, M–R agreed with Musgrave
I that VE, the notion that an appropriate difference should be made among taxpayers that are different, lacks normative content because a theory of distributive
justice is required to determine the "appropriate" difference that should be made.
For example, VE, by itself, does not lead to the conclusion that we need a
progressive income tax. It is necessary to refer to an underlying theory of justice
and to make some key economic assumptions in order to conclude that a
progressive rate structure is desirable.[16] We might, for example, justify the imposition of progressive tax rates on income based on a theory of justice that believes
equal tax burdens should be imposed on all taxpayers and on a key assumption
about the rate at which the utility of income decreases as income increases.[17] If the
utility of income decreases at an accelerating rate as income increases, a
progressive rate structure is required to impose equal burdens on taxpayers.[18] It
is the reference to some outside normative theory and economic assumptions that
designs the tax system.

M–R also concluded, as had Kaplow and Musgrave I, that HE lacks
independent significance for two reasons. First, a theory of distributive justice
that treats different taxpayers differently will always require that equals be treated
equally. For example, a system that seeks to impose equal burdens on taxpayers
will require that identical burdens be imposed on taxpayers with what has been
determined to be equal income. Similarly, a system that imposes tax burdens based
on the taxpayers' abilities to pay will impose the same burden on taxpayers that
have the same ability to pay (i.e., that have the same income). HE adds nothing to
the design of the system and indeed may distract from the proper consideration of
the more fundamental issues of distributive justice that underlie the treatment of
taxpayers.[19] This is particularly true in a tax system, where liability is calculated by

---

15. Most tax returns are not publicly disclosed. Public charities, however, are required to publicly
    disclose their federal tax returns. I.R.C. § 6104(d).
16. McDaniel & Repetti, "Horizontal Equity and Vertical Equity," *supra* note 1, at 610.
17. *Ibid.*
18. Technically, the rate will be progressive, proportional or regressive, depending on whether the
    elasticity of the marginal utility of income with respect to income is, respectively, greater than,
    equal to, or less than one. R. Musgrave & P. Musgrave, *Public Finance in Theory and Practice*
    (New York: McGraw-Hill College, 1973): 200.
19. McDaniel & Repetti, "Horizontal Equity and Vertical Equity," *supra* note 1, at 620–621.
    See A. Infanti, "Tax Equity" *Buffalo Law Review* 55 (2008): 1191, 1195 (criticizing VE
    and HE as being concerned only with economic differences of taxpayers and consequently

mechanically applying an algorithm to the selected tax base. The focus should be on the selection of the tax base.

Second, and more broadly, the notion that equals should be treated equally requires specification of the criteria used to determine who is equal. Once the criteria for determining equality are selected, it follows that those with the same criteria should be treated the same.[20] But selection of the criteria to measure equality requires that we once again refer to distributive justice. For example, should equality be based upon equal incomes or equal amounts of consumption? Those concerned about persons with few resources may be troubled by the distributive effect of a consumption tax and, therefore, may favor an income tax. Regardless of whether one believes that the criteria must reflect the overall vision of distributive justice in society[21] or alternatively can be more tightly linked to the tax system,[22] selection of the criteria to measure equality will always lead back to distributive justice with the result that HE will always be subsumed within VE.

M–R concluded, as had Musgrave I, that the use of VE and HE in designing a tax system is a poor proxy for the actual theory of distributive justice that underpins the design of the tax system and that questions about tax design should be directed to the specific theory of distributive justice. Subsequently, Liam Murphy and

---

foreclosing "consideration of non-economic forms of difference (e.g., of race, ethnicity, gender, sexual orientation, or physical ability) when determining the appropriate allocation of societal burdens, even though these other forms of difference have served, and continue to serve, as the basis for invidious discrimination that already imposes heavy burdens on its victims."); L. Martinez, "The Trouble with Taxes: Fairness, Tax Policy, and the Constitution," *Hastings Constitutional. Law Quarterly* 31 (2004): 413, 422–424 (observing that application of VE and HE require appeal to underlying notions of fairness); T. Griffith, "Should Tax Norms be Abandoned: Rethinking Tax Policy Analysis and the Taxation of Personal Injury Recoveries," *Wisconsin. Law Review* 1993 (1993): 1115, 1156–1157. See also Elkins, *supra* note 6 at 86–87 (concluding that several possible justifications for horizontal equity can all be proved unsuccessful; and suggesting that justification of HE depends on "the moral entitlement of each individual to his free-market holdings."). Elkins' conclusions about the relationship between HE and the taxpayer's claim to keep the post-market/pre-tax holdings itself demonstrates that even this use of HE is predicated on a normative and distributive conclusion derived outside of HE.

20. In the related area of constitutional law, Peter Westen has argued that equality is a tautology because once the criteria for determining whether persons are the same, it follows that they will be treated similarly. Peter Westen, "The Empty Idea of Equality," *Harvard Law Review* 95 (1982): 537, 547–548. As in the tax area, this view has stirred significant debate. See, e.g., S. Burton, "Comment on 'Empty Ideas': Logical Positivist Analyses of Equality and Rules," *Yale Law Journal* 91 (1982): 1136; E. Chemerinsky, "In Defense of Equality: A Reply to Professor Westen," *Michigan Law Review* 81 (1983): 575; K. Greenawalt, "How Empty is the Idea of Equality?," *Colorado. Law Review* 83 (1983): 1167; K. Karst, "Why Equality Matters," *Georgia Law Review* 17 (1983): 245.

21. See, e.g., L. Murphy & T. Nagel, *The Myth of Ownership: Taxes and Justice* (New York: Oxford University Press, 2002), 15, 25, 30 (asserting the unbreakable link between tax fairness and overall justice).

22. See, e.g., K. Kordana & D. Tabachnick, review of *The Myth of Ownership: Taxes and Justice*, edited by L. Murphy & T. Nagel, *Virginia Law Review* 89 (2003): 647, 653–654 (challenging Murphy and Nagel's rejection of tax system derived "fairness"). See *infra* text accompanying notes 30–32.

Thomas Nagel took the analysis a step further and argued that forms of distributive justice frequently applied by tax theorists to design tax systems—the "benefit" and "equal sacrifice" doctrines—were *also* useless in designing a tax system that seeks to achieve justice.[23] They argued that identifying a just tax requires looking outside the tax system and focusing on the "broader principles of justice in government."[24] They reason that the starting point of a tax, such as each taxpayer's income, is itself the product of government policies. Evaluating an income tax based solely on the amount of taxes assessed ignores an important factor—the fairness of the pre-tax incomes earned by the taxpayers. Murphy and Nagel view the tax system as an instrument that helps achieve governmental objectives for justice. They assess the current state of tax policy analysis as inadequate, stating:

> [The] entire [current] approach is flawed in its foundations. If the distribution produced by the market is not presumptively just, then the correct criteria of distributive justice will make no reference whatever to that distribution, even as a baseline. Distributive justice is not a matter of applying some equitable-seeming function to a morally arbitrary initial distribution of welfare. Despite what many people implicitly assume, the justice of a tax scheme cannot simply be evaluated by checking that average tax rates increase fast enough with income.... [O]nce we reject the assumption that the distribution of welfare produced by the market is just, we can no longer offer principles of tax fairness apart from broader principles of justice in government.[25]

Again, even if one is not fully persuaded by their arguments that traditional tax theories, such as the benefit principle or the equal sacrifice principle, offer nothing to tax policy, their overarching point that tax system design *fundamentally turns on decisions about distributive justice and moral principles accurately underscores the hollowness of both VE and HE.*

---

23. Murphy & Nagel, *The Myth of* Ownership, *supra* note 21, at 16–19, 24–30.
24. *Ibid.*, 30.
25. *Ibid.* For an earlier argument that tax analysis needs to take into account the conditions that gave rise to the distribution of the tax base, see Patricia Apps, *A Theory of Inequality and Taxation* (Cambridge University Press, 1981), 4 ("[T]ax theory remains firmly grounded upon an innate or inherited endowments theory of inequality. The aim of the analysis here is to examine tax incidence and tax distortions taking account of the way in which institutional inequality is initiated and perpetuated."). Many others also have noted that economic wellbeing is the result of many factors, including the individual's initial starting point, the efforts of others, and merit. See, e.g., M. Graetz, "To Praise the Estate Tax, Not to Bury It," *Yale Law Journal.* 93 (1983): 259, 275–279 (questioning "those who simply assume that the market distributes rewards to people who deserve them and denies rewards to people who do not"); S. Leviner, "From Deontology to Practical Application: The Vision of a Good Society and Tax System," *Virginia Tax Review* 26 (2006): 405, 415–418 ("[D]ifficulty with the view of the market as neutral or providing just rewards is that, in the real world, people do not enter the market with equal resources including identical or otherwise equivalent talents, skills, or backgrounds."); A. Sen, "The Moral Standing of the Market," in *Ethics and Economics*, ed. E. Paul, et al. (1995), 1, 1–19.

6.3   EFFORTS TO SUSTAIN A DESIGN ROLE FOR HE

Before examining the process and administrative roles identified for HE in the tax system, this Part reviews arguments offered by scholars post-M–R to revive and support HE's place in shaping substantive tax policy. In 2003, Kevin A. Kordana and David H. Tabachnick suggested such a role for HE, but did not elaborate. They stated:

> While it is true that there can be no blanket rule requiring horizontal equity, it does not follow that issues of uniformity do not count at all. From what we have argued above with respect to the benefit principle and the equal sacrifice principle, it should be clear that issues of uniformity can be relevant, if subordinate, to distributive aims.[26]

It is not clear to us exactly what role Kordana and Tabachnick (K–T) contemplate for HE because their discussion of the benefit principle and equal sacrifice principle did not discuss HE. Indeed, we believe that there is little they could have said. The benefit principle "requires that taxpayers contribute, via taxation, in proportion to the benefit they derive from government."[27] The equal sacrifice theory states that taxation should reduce each taxpayer's welfare by an equal amount.[28] Since K–T do not focus on HE, they did not consider the arguments of Musgrave I and Kaplow that HE would contribute nothing to the design of a tax system.[29] To apply the benefit or equal sacrifice doctrine, it is first necessary to determine how benefits and sacrifice should be measured. For example, should the determination of the amounts of benefits received and the sacrifices made in paying taxes be based on an assumption that the utility of money declines as income increases?[30] To decide this issue reference must be made to theories of welfare economics and theories of declining marginal utility. Once those decisions are made, it follows that those obtaining the same utility from benefits received or losing the same utility from taxes paid should be treated the same.

In their discussion of the benefit and equal sacrifice principles, K–T examine Murphy and Nagel's argument that such theories have no role in achieving justice because justice needs to be measured by directly examining the theory of justice that is guiding *all* governmental functions—taxing and spending. K–T state:

> For Murphy and Nagel, the benefit principle is subject to the charge of "myopia"—it ignores government spending, that is, the provision of public

---

26. Kordana & Tabachnick, review of *The Myth of Ownership, supra* note 22, at 663.
27. *Ibid.*, 653.
28. *Ibid.*, 661.
29. HE collapses into VE because it is necessary to determine how benefits and sacrifice should be measured in circumstances where persons will have received different amounts of benefits and income. See, e.g., R. Musgrave & P. Musgrave, *Public Finance in Theory and Practice*, 3rd ed. (New York: McGraw-Hill College 1980): 229–242; J. Repetti, "Democracy and Opportunity: A New Paradigm in Tax Policy," *Vanderbilt Law Review* 61 (2008): 1130, 1137–1141.
30. See, e.g., Musgrave & Musgrave, *Public Finance in Theory and Practice, supra* note 29, at 239–42; Repetti, "Democracy and Opportunity," *supra* note 29, at 1137–1141.

goods and redistribution, and gives guidance only about how to raise tax revenue. Their basic idea, we think, is that if one is committed to a theory of distributive justice, the achievement of the aims of that theory may be hampered by any attempt to comply with the benefit principle. If the over-arching conception of distributive justice takes fairness into account but allows for justifiable inequalities, criticisms of resulting inequalities on the basis of fairness are ill motivated (because the inequalities are justified by the overarching conception of distributive justice). The conception of distributive justice determines fairness in taxation; therefore, a tax policy that at first glance appears inequitable might, all things considered, be justified.

For example, a tax structure that is consistent with Rawls's difference principle may allow for what would appear (under, for example, the benefit principle) to be inequities in tax policy. However, these inequities are, all things considered, justified if the inequities are necessary to maximize the position of the least well-off. Thus, the question of justice in taxation is not separable from the question of overall distributive justice. To the extent the benefit principle treats these two questions as separable and addresses only the issue of justice in taxation, it is, for Murphy and Nagel, objectionable.[31]

K–T respond to Murphy and Nagel in part by positing situations in which the government's "overall distributive justice" may leave unanswered specific issues pertaining to the design of the tax system. For those specific design issues, traditional notions of tax equity can be the tie-breaker. They state:

> If two or more economic schemes equally maximize the demands of the conception of distributive justice, and if one scheme contains a tax system that satisfies the benefit principle while the other(s) do not, one who held the benefit principle could invoke it to adjudicate between schemes. Doing so is not inconsistent with the maximizing conception of distributive justice.[32]

We agree with this insight, but we do not see how it makes the case for an independent role for HE in the design of the tax system. Satisfaction of the *benefit principle* (that the tax burden correspond to the level of benefits received) will automatically require that those with equal benefits be treated the same, assuming that this does not conflict with the governmental scheme of "overall distributive justice." Perhaps KT envision a similar but independent tie-breaker role for HE, where such equivalences occur.[33] However, this possible construction of K–T's defense of HE ultimately would not stand: (1) the tie breaker reasoning they explicitly used in defense of the benefit principle was in their own terms a "rarely" applicable role,[34] and (2) unlike the benefit principle which provides some of its own content, HE, even in this limited setting still has no independent principles to draw upon in breaking the tie (any principles it would recite would have already

---

31. Kordana & Tabachnick, review of *The Myth of Ownership*, *supra* note 22, at 653–654.
32. *Ibid.*, 654–655.
33. *Ibid.*
34. *Ibid.*, 665.

formed the basis of VE determinations of taxation). Thus, while K–T make the case for application of traditional theories of tax justice, such as the benefit theory, to the design of a tax system, their discussion of the benefit and equal sacrifice theories does not support a role for HE. In a subsequent portion of their article that discusses determination of the tax base, K–T do foreshadow an argument that has been employed by others (and examined below) to argue for the independence of HE on political process grounds. They assert that "uniform treatment is preferable . . . out of deference to a democratically made decision, or as a matter of equality or autonomy."[35] The next Part examines how others have further articulated what could be termed a "process" role for HE.

6.4   CRITIQUE OF THE ASSERTION THAT HE LACKS NORMATIVE CONTENT

6.4.1   HE as a Process Requirement

Despite the persuasive nature of the analysis that HE collapses into VE (and that VE requires the independent selection of norms and criteria grounded in distributive justice), assertions have persisted in the tax literature that HE should play an important role in the design of a tax system. As Jeffrey Kahn has observed, "Many persons do give weight to horizontal equity, and even those who do not frown on unequal treatment of the same item."[36] In an effort to discern and specify the undeniable appeal of HE, scholars have carved out a role, but one that is not on par with VE and does not make claims on substantive tax policy design. Brian Galle, in a 2008 paper, defends HE as independent of VE, primarily by constructing a role for HE that we contend is best understood as one grounded in the context of political process and political theory, and not as an independent policy role.[37] The core of his argument is that HE can be understood as standing for the position that the pre-tax allocation of income (specifically the pre-tax ordinal ranking of taxpayers with similar amounts of income[38]) should receive deference from tax writing legislators because that allocation was generated under existing rules (tax and nontax) approved by an earlier Congress:

> I want to defend here the notion that our accumulations of cash or contentedness, as they stand prior to being subjected to tax, should have some weight.

---

35. *Ibid.*, 667–668.
36. J. Kahn, "The Mirage of Equivalence and the Ethereal Principles of Parallelism and Horizontal Equity," *Hastings Law Journal* 57 (2006): 645, 652.
37. B. Galle, "Tax Fairness," *Washington & Lee Law Review* 65 (2008): 1323.
38. *Ibid.*, 1359–1361. The notion that HE requires the pretax ranking of taxpayers to be preserved is based on the idea that taxpayers who have "equal shares in the pre-tax distribution" should have "equal shares in the post-tax distribution." If the relative rankings of taxpayers changes after tax, that change may indicate that equal taxpayers are not being treated equally because they now have different shares. As discussed, *infra* at notes 45–47, the use of such rankings to measure HE is very controversial.

I begin with the idea that pre-tax distributions may be non-random, and, indeed, may be the deliberately chosen result of a perfectly just system of laws other than the tax laws. To disturb that distribution might then be an injustice, or, at a minimum, could imply that the moral judgment of the tax-law drafters is superior to the judgment of those who put in place the rest of society. HE, therefore, could represent the extent to which the tax system defers to explicit or implicit moral judgments made elsewhere in society or in government.

Put another way, suppose that we sit as lawmakers on a legislative committee with the authority to draft tax statutes, and we hold sufficient sway over our colleagues to obtain passage of whatever we enact. Let us posit that earlier this year, our colleagues enacted a farm subsidy bill whose distributive consequences we find appalling. Would it be legitimate or proper for us to enact a 100% tax on receipt of that subsidy? It is arguable, I claim, that the answer is no. If that intuition is correct, then it follows that there are constraints on tax legislation that do not arise purely out of distributive justice norms, but that instead depend on political theories, such as an obligation, again, to defer to the reasonable judgments of others. [Citations omitted].[39]

Galle's argument here is specifically about tax reform—not the first tax law written at the start of society, government and the economy, but the tax reform contemplated in the midst of an ongoing legal, economic and tax system. He makes this distinction to move beyond Murphy and Nagel's claim that government and market cannot exist without taxation, and all must be contemplated as a totality.[40] But why grant deference to a prior Congress? To support this position, Galle envisions the tax writing function as a tripartite role—in which one of the roles lends itself to deference to prior Congressional determinations:

Why would we want, or be obliged, to grant such deference? I suggest here two possible lines of thought. Both lines depend on one prior assumption. I assume that the Tax Code comprises not one, but in fact three distinct governmental systems or modes: raising revenue, redistributing wealth, and enacting other policy goals. Each of these modes might have its own set of rules or norms. My claims about HE for the most part are limited to tax's revenue function, although the absence of HE can signal to us that we need to justify our tax decision by resorting to one of the other two modes.

Turning, then, to the two possibilities, I argue that HE can be justified both by the unique purpose of the revenue function as well as on welfare grounds. In order for revenue-raising to serve its basic function, and to command widespread popular acceptance, it must be open to any reasonable view of good government. It follows, albeit along a twisty path, that the

---

39. *Ibid.*, 1327.
40. *Ibid.*, 1335.

principles underlying the revenue function should give significant weight to pre-existing distributions of societal goods.[41]

Essentially, Galle's core claim (elaborated in more detail) is that the revenue function of tax legislation drafting does not by its own terms incorporate any normative component, and when exercising that function legislators should give deference to the prior, democratically determined choices that resulted in the current pre-tax distribution of resources:

> In particular, I argue here that, because the sole purpose of revenue is to make possible a flourishing deliberative democracy, and because it is possible that allowing the revenue system [i.e. the revenue function of new tax legislation] to make its own policy judgments would interfere with deliberations elsewhere, the revenue process should simply accept as a given, any reasonably policy choice.[42]

Thus, in considering tax reform, legislators should be inclined to leave the pre-tax ordinal ranking of taxpayers by "income" undisturbed.[43] Galle recognizes one of the likely challenges to this articulation of an independent HE: that tax legislation is *not* exclusively a revenue function but includes redistribution and other policy goals on a regular basis and therefore this intertwined role provides no support for deference. In anticipation of this argument, Galle offers a separate justification for HE grounded in considerations of legislative efficiency:

> For those who find this form of deontological reasoning unpersuasive, I also roughly model the circumstances in which we can expect respect for HE to increase overall societal welfare. Taking as given the justice of existing arrangements can reduce the costs of deliberating about alternative rules, as well as the transaction costs and transition costs that attend the political process. At times, though, these gains may be swamped by the inefficiency of separating redistributive "corrections" from the revenue process itself.[44]

We think that these are valuable insights, raising interesting and important questions about political process, particularly the iterative dimension of legislative drafting, but they do not defend HE as in independent concept of "fairness." We reach this conclusion for several reasons. First, Galle's core claim of HE— that we should preserve the rank order of taxpayers—really constitutes a claim about VE. In their 1993 article, M–R reviewed Kaplow's critique of economists who argued that HE was violated (and thus had an independent function) when a tax law change altered the pre-tax rankings of taxpayers. Kaplow makes a key observation: the process of ranking and protecting ranking actually constitutes assessments of and determinations about those who are not equal—which is the

---

41. *Ibid.*, 1327–1328.
42. *Ibid.*, 1346.
43. *Ibid.*, 1359–1361 (noting that the pre-tax position of taxpayers reflects the "preferred ranking of individuals" by society reflected in prior legislation).
44. *Ibid.*, 1328.

domain of VE.[45] Further, Kaplow notes in his discussion of the economists on ranking (and Galle essentially agrees)—if HE only requires preservation of ranking, it would do very little. Why? Consider an abbreviated version of Kaplow's hypotheticals.[46] In World #1, A has 100 and B has 95 of income before tax. HE is violated if, after tax, A has 94 and B has 95. However, in World #2, A has 100 and B has 95 before tax, but after tax A has 147 and B has 51. In this case, HE is not violated although the disparity between the taxpayers' incomes has increased significantly. Thus, consistent with Kaplow I and M–R, we would conclude that a meaningful application of HE here is essentially VE, and in any event is literally only about those who are exactly equal under the existing concept of VE.

Second, the initial concept of the pre-tax ranking of taxpayers (which Galle argues HE guides us to protect) implies that we know what to count—what goods, services, and benefits are relevant for determining the ranking. But to have a ranking, we must already have in place a concept of VE to define what should be counted (i.e., to define the tax base). This observation alone is not inconsistent with Galle's argument, but explicitly acknowledging this point helps clarify precisely what Galle is claiming. In urging that tax reform be particularly attentive to existing rankings he envisions that in this moment before tax reform there are in place both rules implementing a concept of VE (which defines the tax base and tax burden) and some nontax legislation that together result in a "pre-tax reform" ordering of taxpayers.[47] It is really the net result (i.e., ordering of taxpayers by income) of the existing tax and nontax legislation combined that Galle urges be protected, given his attention is on tax reform. Thus, Galle's HE is an assertion that Congress should not change its VE over time, at least not to the extent it could alter taxpayer ranking.

Why not change VE? The answer to this leads to our third concern with this articulation of an independent HE. The HE argument relies on isolating and examining only the revenue raising function of Congress. However, in reality there are no such constraints on Congress—it is free to act in any and all capacities simultaneously—and it does so. Legislation regularly reflects a mixture of revenue, redistribution and nontax policy goals. Given this observation, an argument for HE grounded in only the revenue function provides no discernible guidance. Moreover, it begs the reverse question, "Is it undesirable for Congress to undo existing tax policy (rooted in its redistributed and other policy goals) through reforms outside the tax law?" Ultimately, the decisions of a later Congress on tax reform may be best understood as part of both the messy dynamics of the political process and the smoothing process of the republican form of government in which power shifts

---

45. Kaplow I, *supra* note 2, at 141.
46. Kaplow II, *supra* note 2, at 194.
47. Galle's use of the phrase "pre-tax" here can be a bit confusing. It is possible that the world as it looks before tax reform produces the following result: under the combination nontax law and existing tax law taken together, certain taxpayers receive $X, and others receive $X +1. We understand Galle to say that a problem then arises *if and when* Congress later seeks to implement *new* tax legislation that would change the net effect of what Congress had intended, to date, to be the ultimate rank order of taxpayers. See generally, Galle, "Tax Fairness," *supra* note 38, at 1346.

are meant to occur gradually through the different and overlapping electoral schedules of the President, Senate, and House of Representatives.

Finally, Galle's grounding of HE in an efficiency analysis—suggesting costs savings can be generated by assuming the fairness of existing distributions and not engaging in additional tax reform—joins an active dialogue regarding legislative process and efficiency. But as with other efforts described earlier to secure a distinct place for HE, we do not consider this an example of HE used to prescribe a self-contained notion of fairness for taxpayers. Rather, it is use of HE terminology in a different conversation about efficiency-based assessments of the legislative process. By introducing the concept of efficiency as a method to evaluate that process, Galle is appealing to a different form of distributive justice in order to add content to HE.

While we disagree with Galle's defense of HE, we think that he has insightfully pointed future debate about HE in the correct direction—one that connects the persistence of HE to the underlying theme of equality among citizens and the expectation that the government only make changes based on careful consideration and articulated reasoning. HE refuses to perish because it represents a presumption for equal treatment under the laws of an egalitarian society. In a related area, a debate about whether equality is an empty concept in the context of constitutional has occurred.[48] Surprising agreement exists between those who view equality as an empty concept and those who do not that the government should be required to act for appropriate reasons. That is, even those who argue that equality is an empty concept, agree that persons should be protected from government acting for the wrong reason.[49] For example, Christopher Peters has argued that the case of *Yick Wo v. Hopkins*,[50] in which the plaintiff was denied a laundry license because of his race, should not be viewed as requiring equality of treatment, but rather requiring that the government correctly apply a substantive rule that privileges should not be granted or denied based on race or ethnicity. Peters asserts that equality is empty because it requires one to look to an underlying substantive rule to define equalilty. Once the substantive rule is identified (race is irrelevant), the government must correctly apply such rule.[51] Similarly, Kenneth Simons, an advocate for equality having independent significance, argues that equality requires that the government explain why it is treating people differently.[52] He states that a "demand for reasons for inequality is one important type of equality right...."[53]

Thus, there is surprising unanimity for a justificatory role for equality in a different area of law. Perhaps, the lingering (languishing) loyalty to HE in the tax

---

48. See, e.g., Westen, "The Empty Idea of Equality," *supra* note 20 at 547–548; Burton, "Comment on "Empty Ideas," *supra* note 20; Chemerinsky, "In Defense of Equality," *supra* note 20; Greenawalt, "How Empty is the Idea of Equality?," *supra* note 20; Karst, "Why Equality Matters," *supra* note 20.
49. See, e.g., C. Peters, "Equality Revisited," *Harvard Law Review* 110 (1998): 1210, 1219–1220.
50. 118 U.S. 356 (1886).
51. Peters, "Equity Revisited," *supra* note 49.
52. Simons, "The Logic of Egalitarian Norms," *supra* note 12, at 714 and 748.
53. *Ibid.*, 748.

literature reflects this role. HE remains in our collective tax consciousness because in a democratic society we expect an explanation for why people are being treated differently. HE tells us that government should communicate the rationale for different treatment; it does not tell us what that different treatment should be.

6.4.2   HE as Even-Handed Enforcement

Up to this point the strongest articulation of an independent role for HE is a secondary one: ensuring that the government demonstrates it has carefully considered tax laws that produce different taxation (i.e., different tax bills), given the broad-based commitment to equal treatment in the legal system. Thus, HE here is not doing the work comparable to VE, which serves (albeit indirectly) as the vehicle for framing our views on the appropriate burden borne by each taxpayer. Rather, HE should be seen as addressing another part of the regime—not the design of the system, but the process of design.

A careful review of the proponents of HE, however, reveals that many supporters of HE draw upon a role for HE in the administration of the tax law. Joseph Dodge has argued that HE serves as a check on the application of utilitarian welfare to individuals. He states:

> Horizontal equity derives from the command that likes should be treated alike, which is a maxim of civil justice whose origins predate, and are independent from, welfare economics . . . . Of course, the horizontal equity norm in taxation is incomplete, because it leaves unspecified the index of comparison (for example, ability to pay, standard of living, income and so on) . . . . Theories of redistribution can be contractarian, utilitarian, or religion-based, but conventional welfare economics is utilitarian, since it inquires into the net social gains and losses from a given policy. It is characteristic (and perhaps a weakness) of utilitarian thinking that the welfare of the individual is readily subordinated to collective welfare. The ethical command that likes should be treated alike is similar to concepts of "rights" in imposing limits on the utilitarian approach.[54]

We interpret Professor Dodge's argument to mean that the right to equal treatment is not a principle of design but instead a principle of conduct that controls all governmental interaction with citizens. Indeed, in a subsequent article, Professor Dodge describes HE and VE as "formal norms" that "equally-situated persons should be treated equally" and "unequally-situated persons should be taxed differently to an appropriate degree."[55] He uses the term "formal norm" in the

---

54. J. Dodge, "A Combined Mark-To-Market and Pass-Through Corporate-Shareholder Integration Proposal," *Tax Law Review* 50 (1995): 265, 372, n. 42.
55. J. Dodge, "Theories of Tax Justice: Ruminations on the Benefit, Partnership, and Ability-to-Pay Principles," *Tax Law Review* 58 (2005): 399, 401.

Rawlsian sense of meaning the process by which laws are administered.[56] He goes on to observe that "substantive norms" then provide a standard to measure equality:

> The role of "substantive" tax fairness norms is to provide an index or standard of relevant equality and inequality. The most commonly cited substantive tax fairness norms include: (1) the equal-sacrifice norm; (2) the benefits-received-from government norm; (3) the "well-being" (or "standard-of-living") norm, and (4) the ability-to-pay norm.[57]

The notion that HE governs the arbitrary enforcement of tax law has also been championed by John A. Miller. He has observed:

> The conclusions offered by McDaniel and Repetti are sound in a narrow pedantic sense. My concern is that their analysis fails to allow for the more primitive and malevolent possibilities of human existence. They assume a societal rationality and rule mindedness that assures equality even without relying on the principle of equality. Belief in the importance of the principle of equality, on the other hand, assumes that humanity possesses a limitless propensity for persecution and arbitrariness. It is in the context of an irrational and discriminatory world that equality's meaning and utility stand out.[58]

The role for HE proposed by Miller is similar to that proposed by Dodge and Musgrave. He views HE as a check on arbitrary or even pernicious application of tax laws to taxpayers. We believe that the common thread running through all of these articulations of an administrative role for HE could be stated perhaps more bluntly and with particular force in the case of the income tax system. HE plays a distinct, separate and effectively *operational* role. As a general concept, which could be applicable to government rules and actions beyond the tax arena, HE holds that although the concept of VE can comprehensively account for equity concerns[59] in the design of our substantive tax law, something more is needed to address the operational concern that the law (crafted under a vision of VE) need be *implemented* by government actors in a manner consistent with the terms of the tax law. Essentially, HE steps in at this secondary stage to serve as an explicit warning that the law should be applied uniformly. Perhaps this could be taken as an implicit

---

56. *Ibid.*, 453 (stating, "This idea of fairness—which otherwise can be referred to as "formal justice" and (in its tax version) as horizontal equity—has considerable value in itself."). At the end of this sentence Professor Dodge cites to Rawls. *Ibid.*, 453, n. 222 (citing J. Rawls, *A Theory of Justice* (Cambridge: Harvard University Press, 1971), 58–60). In the pages referenced by Dodge, Rawls states, "If we think of justice as always expressing a kind of equality, then formal justice requires that in their administration laws and institutions should apply equally (that is, in the same way) to those belonging to the classes defined by them.... Formal justice is adherence to principle, or as some have said, obedience to system." J. Rawls, *A Theory of Justice* (Cambridge: Harvard University Press, 1971), 58.
57. Dodge, "A Combined Mark-To-Market," *supra* note 55, at 401.
58. J. Miller, "Equal Taxation: A Commentary," *Hofstra Law Review* 29 (2000): 529, 536.
59. Of course, as articulated above, VE lacks internal normative content and must draw upon some theory of distributive justice and morality.

expectation of any just and democratic government. But isolating this concern— particularly on behalf of individual members of society in their dealings with the arguably significant power of the State—can serve as a constant reminder to State actors that good laws are insufficient. Society demands good enforcement as well.

This secondary, administration-oriented role of HE may be singularly important in tax law. Although one could imagine a tax system with entirely transparent filings, audits and tax payments, that is not the U.S. system, nor is it common in other comparable tax systems. As a result, there is little opportunity to verify whether the tax law is being applied in a sufficiently consistent manner. Litigated cases can provide a limited window on tax enforcement, but they represent a small fraction of the many interactions between the government and taxpayers. Moreover, the primary facts available to the outsider are those the judge has chosen to include in the opinion. Thus, while case law can assist in understanding positions asserted by the government against taxpayers' interests (hence the litigation), it does little to quell the concern that the government may not be applying the law uniformly. The constant reminder regarding uniformity, framed in the compelling language of HE, implicitly elevates the standard for administration to the same level as the standard for substantive law design (VE). The prominence of HE promotes society's goals of norm building in the administrative State and constraining government actors with power and limited public scrutiny.

The difficulty with this analysis is that HE is not helpful in insuring even-handed enforcement. In a world of finite resources, not every taxpayer can be audited.[60] In deciding who should be audited, it is necessary to refer to something beyond HE. For example, such choices may seek to maximize utility—target the taxpayers from whom we can expect to obtain the greatest additional tax revenue (such as those engaged in cash businesses), or they may seek to reinforce progressivity—target high-income taxpayers to insure that they are bearing a progressively greater burden. HE does not guide us in selecting among these objectives. It is necessary to once again appeal to some other source to decide how to best accomplish enforcement.

6.5   CONCLUSION

In the years since M–R's 1993 article evaluating the intellectual landscape on HE, the question has continued to generate controversy and debate. Perhaps one way to encapsulate the question after all this time is to ask—if we started with HE as our motivating concept in setting tax policy and burdens where would we be? If HE says treat equals the same, what does our tax system look like? The answer is—we don't know because the term has no independent meaning for fairness and equality. We must turn to some theory of distributive justice to determine equality and to determine an appropriate tax burden. At this point HE collapses into one concept,

---

60. The IRS examined 1.11% of returns filed by individuals in 2009. IRS, *Internal Revenue Data Book* 26 Table 9b (2010).

which is generally referred to as VE. The crucial point is not that this single concept is VE, but that VE and HE are together a *single* concept which *lacks normative content* and is itself only a *proxy* for theories of distributive justice and morality. It is a detour in history that led us to frame the issues of equality and fairness in the tax system in the language of VE and HE—a path which has both masked the emptiness of the concepts and overemphasized the possibility of two, distinct fairness inquires. We have been sidetracked from our larger task of tackling our disagreements over the underlying questions of distributive justice and morality, but perhaps can return now with renewed vigor to these intractable questions.

For those who remain committed to a gut sense that HE means something, we would say, "yes, but a different something." Several of the post-1993 authors discussed above constructed a role for HE but it was not a role in determining tax burdens and tax equity. Instead, HE became the language for expressing ideas on process for determining tax policy and the administration of the tax system. Both constitute crucial facets of our system of government but they are not the same as the burden and equity questions. We question the usefulness of viewing HE this way because HE does not provide guidance as to how administration of the tax system should proceed. But another role for HE may be that it represents agreement that government should be required to articulate reasons for treating taxpayers differently. Perhaps the close link of tax policy to the process of tax policy creation and the administrative practice explains the unstated but visceral commitment to HE that has continued to spark debate over the past 20 years. We don't imagine the debate is over, but we look forward to a deepening inquiry into the driving questions of distributive justice and morality as pillars of our tax policy.

Chapter 7

What Is This Thing Called Source?*

*Lawrence Lokken***

7.1   INTRODUCTION

Under many income tax systems, including that of the United States, residents are taxed on worldwide income, regardless of source, and nonresidents are taxed on income from sources within the taxing country. This dual basis of taxation may result in double taxation because residents earning income abroad are often taxed on the income by both the source country and the residence country. Double tax relief is generally considered essential to the very existence of healthy international business and investment markets. By international consensus, the residence country has primary responsibility for providing double tax relief. The United States unilaterally provides double tax relief in the form of a credit for income taxes paid to other countries, but this credit may not exceed the U.S. tax, before credit, that is ratably allocable to taxable income from sources outside the United States.[1] In other countries, double tax relief may take the form of a credit or an exemption from tax, but the relief is limited to income originating outside the taxing jurisdiction (e.g., income attributable to permanent establishments located

---

*   Apologies to Cole Porter.
** Professor of Law Emeritus, University of Florida College of Law. Portions of this chapter are taken from a long-forgotten article, L. Lokken, "The Sources of Income from International Uses and Dispositions of Intellectual Property," 36 *Tax Law. Review* 36 (1981): 233.
1.   I.R.C. §§ 901, 904.

Yariv Brauner & Martin James McMahon, Jr. (eds), *The Proper Tax Base: Structural Fairness from an International and Comparative Perspective—Essays in Honour of Paul McDaniel*, pp. 139–148. © 2012 Kluwer Law International BV, The Netherlands.

outside the country).[2] The source of income is thus relevant to the taxation of both residents and nonresidents.

U.S. tax law contains an elaborate set of rules prescribing the sources of various types of income. Interest income is from U.S. sources if it is paid on an obligation of a domestic corporation or noncorporate resident, but is otherwise from sources outside the United States.[3] Generally, dividends are from U.S. sources only if received from a domestic corporation.[4] Income from the performance of personal services is from U.S. sources only if the services are performed in the United States.[5] Rents received under leases of tangible property located in the United States are from U.S. sources, and royalties are from U.S. sources if paid for the right to use licensed intangibles in the United States.[6] The rules governing the source of income and gain on sales and exchanges of property are themselves an elaborate body of law.[7]

A foreign corporation or nonresident alien individual engaged in a trade or business in the United States is subject to U.S. tax on income effectively connected with that trade or business.[8] Although not expressed as such, the statutory definition of income effectively connected with a U.S. trade or business is essentially a source rule because it identifies income with sufficient geographical connection with the United States to be taxable in this country.[9] Similarly, income tax treaties typically allow the United States to tax business profits of a resident of a country with which the United States has a treaty only to the extent that the profits are attributable to a permanent establishment that the taxpayer maintains in the United States.[10] The concept of income attributable to a permanent establishment is also a source rule, as that term is used in this chapter.

The U.S. source rules do not, individually or collectively, express a general concept of source. The lack of a general conception is problematic for at least two reasons. As a policy matter, the sufficiency of a particular rule cannot be evaluated without some standard against which it can be measured. Also, the lack of a general concept complicates the process of determining the source of types of income not addressed by the statutory rules. Courts agree that absent an applicable statutory rule, the source of an item of income should be determined by analogy to the rules

---

2. See H. Ault & B. Arnold, *Comparative Income Taxation: A Structural Analysis,* 2d ed. (New York: Aspen Publishers, 2004).
3. I.R.C. §§ 861(a)(1), 862(a)(1).
4. I.R.C. §§ 861(a)(2), 862(a)(2). Dividends from foreign corporations can be from U.S. sources, in whole or in part, if more than 25% of the corporation's income derives from U.S. trades or businesses, but foreign corporations typically avoid crossing this threshold. See B Bittker & L. Lokken, *Federal Taxation of Income, Estates and Gifts,* 3d ed. (New York: Warren, Gorham & Lamont, 1999), para. 73.3 (Bittker & Lokken).
5. I.R.C. §§ 861(a)(3), 862(a)(3).
6. I.R.C. § 861(a)(4).
7. I.R.C. §§ 861(a)(6), 862(a)(6), 863, 865. See Bittker & Lokken, *supra* note 4, at para. 73.6.
8. I.R.C. §§ 871(b), 882(a).
9. This definition is found in § 864(c).
10. See U.S. Model Income Tax Convention of Nov. 15, 2006, Art. 7(1); OECD Committee on Fiscal Affairs, Model Tax Convention on Income and on Capital Art. 7(1) (2010).

stated in the statutes,[11] but without an overall concept of source, it is difficult to say what is analogous and what is not.

This chapter undertakes to provide a conceptual framework for source determinations. It proposes a model for these determinations and applies the model to a few types of income. The model is developed most fully in its application to interest income and income related to interest.

7.2 THE MODEL

Source rules, in the broader sense of the term used here, are the core of the provisions defining the geographic boundaries of the tax jurisdiction claimed by an income tax law. A government's claim of tax jurisdiction may be based on benefits provided, ability to pay, or both. The benefit principle is that the taxes borne by a taxpayer should be related to the value of the governmental services and protections that the taxpayer enjoys. The ability to pay principle is that the aggregate tax burden should be allocated among taxpayers in ways that reflect their relative abilities to pay taxes.

Neither of these principles, standing alone, is helpful in formulating source rules. Most income taxes are progressive. Progressivity is justified by the ability to pay principle and is rarely defended on benefit grounds. Any aspect of an income tax law that is based on the benefit principle alone is therefore inconsistent with the theoretical basis of the law as a whole. Ability to pay, on the other hand, is unrelated to the geographic origins of taxpayers' incomes. An affluent subject of Monaco has a substantial ability to pay taxes, for example, but this ability provides no basis for a claim that his income is from U.S. sources.

A general principle can, however, be formulated by combining the benefit and ability to pay concepts. Because source rules cannot be derived directly from the ability to pay principle, benefit provided must be the theoretical foundation of jurisdiction to tax income on the basis of source. But, benefits received by individuals as consumers that do not directly assist in the production of income are not related to the issue of source. And, the benefit principle, as applied under a progressive income tax, must not be stated in a way that implies that each taxpayer's liability for tax approximates the value or costs of benefits provided to the taxpayer. These limitations are satisfied by a source principle that apportions a taxpayer's ability to pay among jurisdictions in a way that reflects the governmental services and protections available to the taxpayer in profit-seeking activities. Income originates wholly within a jurisdiction under this principle if services and protections of the government of that jurisdiction are the only governmental services and protections directly utilized in earning the income. If income is earned by processes that are directly aided by services and protections of two or more

---

11. For example, Bank of America v. United States, 680 F.2d 142 (Ct. Cl. 1982); Container Corp. v. Commissioner, 134 T.C. 122 (2010).

governments, the income assigned to each jurisdiction should be the income that derives from activities carried on and capital employed under its protection. Relationships between income producing processes and governmental services and protections should, in sum, be the basis of rules that identify the origin of income. A government should apply the ability to pay principle, consistently with its application of the principle generally in its law, in deciding whether income of foreign individuals and companies originating within the country should be taxed and, if so, in deciding on the rate of tax.

This approach is suggested by the Supreme Court's opinion in *National Paper & Type Co. v. Bowers.*[12] The taxpayer, a domestic corporation that purchased goods in the United States and sold them abroad, contended that it was deprived of due process of law by the imposition of U.S. tax on its income from these transactions because foreign corporations were are not taxed on income from similar transactions. The Court disagreed, holding that the United States may tax all income of a domestic corporation, regardless of source, because the corporation is supported by "the power of the United States to protect its interests and redress its wrongs in whatever part of the world its business may take it."[13] Foreign corporations, in contrast, are only taxed on income from U.S. sources because "only that income is earned under the protection of American laws."[14] Similarly, the predecessor of the Tax Court stated, "The basic rule is that the consideration for taxation is protection of life and property and that the income rightly to be levied upon to defray the burdens of the U.S. government is that income which is created by activities and property protected by this government."[15]

Because benefits provided are the jurisdictional foundation of source taxation, but is not the basis of decisions relating to rates of tax, the relative costs or values of governmental services and protections in various jurisdictions should not be relevant to issues of source. Reliable estimates of the amounts of income earned under the protections of various governments cannot be derived from the relative costs or values of governmental services and protections because profit levels tend not to vary directly with these costs or values. Profit rates tend to be lower in stable economic environments, where governmental services and protections are most valuable, than in places characterized by economic or political instability because investors will undertake the risks associated with instability only if they expect greater profits than those obtainable by less risky investments in stable environments. Tax revenues needed to finance programs that promote stability must therefore be provided by higher rates of tax, rather than expanded source claims.

---

12. National Paper & Type Co. v. Bowers, 266 U.S. 373 (1924).
13. National Paper & Type Co. v. Bowers, 266 U.S. 373, 376 (1924).
14. National Paper & Type Co. v. Bowers, 266 U.S. 373, 376 (1924). See also Barclay & Co. v. Edwards, 267 U.S. 442 (1924).
15. Piedras Negras Broadcasting Co. v. Commissioner, 43 B.T.A. 297, 309 (1941), quoting from R. Paul & J. Mertens, *Law of Federal Income Taxation,* Vol. 4 (Callaghan Co., 1934), 350.

7.3 APPLICATIONS OF THE MODEL

7.3.1 GENERALLY

Several of the U.S. source rules are readily explained by the model presented here. For example, the rules appropriately place income from services in the jurisdiction in which the services are performed because governmental services and protections of this jurisdiction are typically the only governmental services and protections utilized directly in earning this income. For the same reason, the model also justifies the rules for rents from leases of tangible property, which assign the rents to the jurisdiction in which the property is located during the lease term.

Other source rules are best seen as approximations. The rules for dividends— U.S. source if the corporation is domestic, and foreign source if the corporation is foreign—are an example.[16] Because dividends derive from the distributing corporation's business activities and investments, they benefit directly from all governmental services and protections that the corporation enjoys in these activities and investments.[17] If a corporation's activities and investments are located in two or more jurisdictions, the model argues for apportioning its dividends in proportion to the sources of the corporation's earnings. For example, if a foreign corporate group derives significant income from activities and investments in the United States, some portion of its dividend distributions might reasonably be characterized as U.S. source income to the shareholders.[18]

Such an apportionment is probably not practicable, however. Many U.S. persons hold shares in foreign companies whose books are not open to U.S. tax authorities. Even for foreign corporations whose financial statements are available

---

16. Another, less easily justified, approximation also underlies these rules: A corporation is considered domestic if it is organized under the laws of the United States, a U.S. state, or the District of Columbia, and is classified as foreign if it is organized under the laws of any other jurisdiction. I.R.C. §§ 7701(a)(4), (5). A corporation's place of incorporation may bear no relationship to the locations of its activities and investments. For example, before Congress enacted limiting legislation in 2004, several U.S. companies reincorporated in Bermuda, even though they derived no significant income from Bermuda. See Bittker & Lokken, *supra* note 4, at para. 66.2. This artificiality is, however, beyond the scope of this chapter.
17. For this purpose, a corporation's activities and investments include activities and investments of subsidiaries because earnings of subsidiaries may ultimately be distributed as dividends to shareholders of the parent corporation.
18. Under current law, dividends from a foreign corporation are apportioned between U.S. and foreign sources if at least 25% of the corporation's income is effectively connected with trades or businesses of the corporation in the United States. I.R.C. § 861(a)(2)(B). No portion of the dividends is from U.S. sources, in contrast, if the corporation carries on U.S. activities through subsidiary corporations, rather than directly, regardless of the proportion of the corporation's income that derives from U.S. subsidiaries. The source of dividends is not rationally related to whether a corporation carries on its activities directly or through subsidiary corporations. It is likely that most foreign corporations with significant U.S. operations organize their affairs to stay below the 25% threshold. The threshold rule is probably little more than one of the many reasons why foreign corporations generally operate in the United States through subsidiaries, rather than permanent establishments.

in the United States, an apportionment rule would require complex conversions from foreign financial accounting rules to U.S. tax accounting rules, which often could not be made without deeper access to the corporations' books.[19] Even for domestic corporations, an apportionment rule would raise many practical difficulties. Under an apportionment rule, for example, it might not be possible to determine the source of dividends distributed during a particular year until the corporation completed its accounting for the year.[20] Payors of U.S. source dividends to non-U.S. persons must know the source of the dividends when the dividends are paid in order to determine whether to withhold U.S. tax from the dividends.

In sum, the source rules for dividends probably express the model advanced here as well as is feasible.

7.3.2 INTEREST INCOME

Under the U.S. rules, interest is generally from U.S. sources if it accrues on "obligations of noncorporate residents or domestic corporations," and interest on obligations of other obligors is from foreign sources.[21] Under the model, interest originates where the borrower utilizes the borrowed funds because governmental services and protections at that location are central to the success of the borrower's venture, which generates the capacity to pay interest on the loan.

The premises underlying the U.S. international tax rules for apportioning deductions for interest expense are: (1) money is fungible and (2) borrowed funds therefore should usually be considered used ratably in all of a taxpayer's activities and investments. According to the regulations, the "fungibility approach recognizes that all activities and property require funds and that management has a great deal of flexibility as to the source and use of funds," and a borrowing for any purpose "generally" frees "other funds for other purposes"; it is therefore

---

19. The regulations prescribe a system for making this conversion, but this system requires access to a corporation's books in full detail and only applies to for foreign corporations controlled by U.S. shareholders. Treas. Reg. § 1.964-1.
20. This problem could be mitigated by basing the apportionment on the sources of a corporation's earnings for prior years. For example, the rule that sometimes treats dividends from a foreign corporation as U.S. source income, in whole or in part, is based on the corporation's gross income for the three years preceding the payment of the dividend. I.R.C. § 861(a)(2)(B). Dividends are, however, considered distributed first from current earnings and profits. I.R.C. § 316(a). A retrospective rule would thus weaken the case for making the apportionment—to better reflect the true sources of the distributed income.
21. I.R.C. §§ 861(a)(1), 862(a)(1). The few statutory exceptions from this rule are also consistent with the model. For example, interest on deposits with a foreign branch of a U.S. bank is from foreign sources, and as is interest from a foreign partnership that is—predominantly engaged in the active conduct of a trade or business outside the United States—if the interest is neither paid by a U.S. trade or business engaged of the partnership nor allocable to partnership income that is effectively connected (or treated as effectively connected) with a U.S. trade or business. The latter rule, enacted in 2004, was necessitated by long-standing regulations treating a partnership, whether domestic or foreign, as a U.S. resident for this purpose if it is engaged in a trade or business in the United States. Treas. Reg. § 1.861-2(a)(2).

"reasonable . . . to attribute part of the cost of borrowing to such other purposes."[22] Generally, for U.S. persons, the regulations apportion interest expense ratably by asset values.[23] Interest expense is traced to particular uses of borrowed funds only in unusual circumstances.[24]

The fungibility concept is sound in theory, and the rules spun out of this concept are generally administrable and not unduly burdensome for taxpayers.[25] In contrast, tracing rules that the regulations prescribe for use by noncorporate taxpayers, principally in domestic contexts, are highly artificial and easily manipulated.[26]

Several U.S. rules recognize that the characterization of interest income is simply the opposite side of the coin from the apportionment of interest expense. For example, for purposes of the foreign tax credit limitation, interest, rent, and royalties received from a controlled foreign corporation (CFC) are "passive category income—to the extent "properly allocable to passive category income of the" CFC, and an item of interest, rent, or royalty income is attributable to passive category income to the extent the CFC's deduction for the item is allocated or apportioned to passive category income of the CFC.[27] From this, it is reasonable to generalize that to the extent that interest expense is apportioned to particular activities or investments of the debtor, the creditor's interest income should be considered derived from income produced by those activities or investments.

Applying the fungibility concept under the model leads to the conclusion that interest income usually derives from all income-producing activities and investments of the obligor. As discussed above in connection with dividends, apportioning income received from an entity among the entity's activities and investments in various locations is not practical. The present source rule for interest, assigning all interest income to the country in which the obligor is resident, is probably the best available approximation. Most obligors, although certainly not all of them, locate their activities and investments predominantly in their home countries. Absent a feasible means of apportioning interest income among the sources of the obligor's income, placing interest income entirely in the residence country of the obligor is the best available approximation of the model.

---

22. Temp. Treas. Reg. 1.861-9T(a). For the rules and methods derived from the fungibility concept, see Bittker & Lokken, *supra* note 4, at paras. 73.10.2–73.10.4.
23. Temp. Treas. Reg. §§ 1.861-9T(f)(1), (g).
24. For example, interest on debt—specifically incurred for the purpose of purchasing, constructing, or improving real property may be allocated solely to income from that property if, among other things, the property secures the debt and the creditor has no other recourse against any the debtor or other property of the debtor. Temp. Treas. Reg. § 1.861-10T(b).
25. Complaints about the U.S. rules on apportioning interest expense are widespread in the business community, but these complaints generally do not question the appropriateness of the fungibility concept. See, e.g., S. Hannes & J. Riedy, "Time to Move to a Worldwide Group Approach for Apportioning Interest," *Tax Notes International* 22 (2001): 2897.
26. Temp. Treas. Reg. 1.163-8T, discussed in Bittker & Lokken, *supra* note 4, at para. 52.10.
27. I.R.C. § 904(d)(3)(C); Treas. Reg. §§ 1.904-5(c)(2), 1.904-5(c)(3).

7.3.3   INTEREST BY ANALOGY

Absent an applicable statutory rule, U.S. courts determine the source of an item of income by analogy to the rules stated in the statutes.[28] An unprovided for item thus takes its source characterization from the rule for interest income if it is more analogous to interest than to any other type of income for which there is a statutory rule. For example, the Court of Claims held that acceptance and confirmation commissions earned by a U.S. bank with respect to export letters of credit issued by foreign banks were most closely analogous to interest, not compensation for services, because the U.S. bank, in each such transaction, substituted its credit for that of the foreign issuing bank.[29]

The Tax Court, in contrast, held that fees received for guaranteeing debt of another person are most analogous to income from services, not interest, and that the fee income is thus not from U.S. sources if the recipient of the fees is not a U.S. person, even if the payor of the fees, and obligor of the guaranteed debt, is a U.S. person.[30] The taxpayer, a domestic corporation, issued notes to investors, and its parent, a Mexican company, guaranteed payment of the notes. The taxpayer paid guarantee fees to the parent but withheld no tax from the payments, taking the position that the fees were income to the parent company from sources outside the U.S. The IRS argued that tax should have been withheld because the fees were fixed or determinable annual or periodical (FDAP) income from U.S. sources.[31]

The parties to the case agreed that guarantee fees are FDAP income,[32] but they disagreed on the issue of source. Because the Code then contained no source rule explicitly applicable to guarantee fees, the court proceeded by analogy, determining the "source of income in terms of the business activities generating the income or . . . the place where the income was produced."[33] The IRS contended that the payments were most closely analogous to interest and were therefore from U.S. sources because they were an obligation of a domestic corporation. The court rejected this characterization, noting that a guaranty "lacks a principal characteristic of a loan because" a guarantor does "not extend funds to" the

---

28. For example, Bank of America v. U.S., 680 F.2d 142 (Ct. Cl. 1982); Container Corp. v. Commissioner, 134 T.C. 122 (2010); Howkins v. Commissioner, 49 T.C. 689 (1968).
29. Bank of America v. U.S., 680 F.2d 142 (Ct. Cl. 1982).
30. Container Corp. v. Commissioner, 134 T.C. 122 (2010). Compare General Electric Capital Canada Inc. v. Queen, 2009 T.C. 563 (Canada 2009) (holding that taxpayer correctly treated payments to parent for guaranteeing taxpayer's debt as interest for Canadian withholding tax purposes).
31. A foreign corporation receiving FDAP income from U.S. sources is subject to U.S. tax on this income at a flat rate of 30%, and a U.S. person paying the income to the foreign recipient is required to withhold this tax from the payment. I.R.C. §§ 881(a), 1442(a).
32. See Treas. Reg. § 1.1441-2(b) (generally defining FDAP income to include all income other than gains on sales of property).
33. Container Corp. v. Commissioner, 134 T.C. 122, 136 (2010). See Hunt v. Commissioner, 90 T.C. 1289, 1301 (1988) (the sourcing concept is concerned with the earning point of income or, more specifically, identifying when and where profits are earned).

borrower.[34] It found that services income is a better analogy: "Guaranties, like services, are produced by the obligee [guarantor] and so, like services, should be sourced to the location of the obligee."[35]

Congress promptly overturned the Tax Court's holding by adding provisions stating that an amount received "for the provision of a guarantee of any indebtedness" is income from U.S. sources if it is received from a domestic corporation or a noncorporate resident of the United States and is payment for guaranteeing indebtedness of that person.[36] This rule closely parallels the source rule for interest.[37] An amount received from a "foreign person for the provision of a guarantee of any indebtedness of such person" is also from U.S. sources if it is "connected with income" of the foreign person that "is effectively connected (or treated as effectively connected) with the conduct of a trade or business in the United States."[38] The latter rule means that a guarantee fee received from a foreign person may be from U.S. sources if the foreign person is engaged in a U.S. trade or business (or deemed to be so engaged) and is allowed a deduction for the fee in determining its income effectively connected with the U.S. trade or business.[39] A guarantee fee received from a foreign person in any other circumstance is income from foreign sources.[40]

Congress' solution is clearly better than the Tax Court's. Interest is often defined as "compensation for the use or forbearance of money."[41] For present purposes, it is useful to disaggregate interest into two components: a risk-free return on borrowed money and compensation for the risk of the borrower defaulting on the obligation to repay (risk premium). Perhaps, only the former is, in the strictest sense, compensation for the use or forbearance of money, but interest on

---

34. Container Corp. v. Commissioner, 134 T.C. 122, 139 (2010).
35. Container Corp. v. Commissioner, 134 T.C. 122, 141 (2010).
36. I.R.C. § 861(a)(9)(A). The statutory rules on guarantee fees apply to "guarantees issued after" Sep. 27, 2010. Pub. L. No. 111–240, § 2122, 124 Stat. 2504 (2010).
37. The parallel is not, however, exact. For example, a guarantee fee is U.S. source income only if received from a U.S. obligor for guaranteeing debt of that obligor. Interest on debt of a U.S. obligor is from U.S. sources, whether it is received from the obligor or another person. For example, if a foreign person, as guarantor of debt of a U.S. person, is required to pay interest on the debt, the interest is from U.S. sources. Treas. Reg. § 1.861-2(a)(5). Congress may have added the requirement that a guarantee fee be received from the U.S. obligor to avoid the conclusion that fees under credit default swaps are guarantee fees to which the rule applies. For credit default swaps, see L. Lokken, "Taxation of Credit Derivatives" (2010), available at http://papers.ssrn.com/sol3/papers.cfm?abstract_id=1509681).
38. I.R.C. "861(a)(9)(B).
39. Although the interest source rules contain nothing analogous to this rule, the branch interest rule of § 884(f) has the effect of treating interest as income from U.S. sources if it is deductible by a foreign obligor in determining its income effectively connected with a U.S. trade or business. See Bittker & Lokken, at para. 67.8.3.
40. I.R.C. § 862(a)(9).
41. Deputy v. Du Pont, 308 U.S. 488, 498 (1940). The Supreme Court has often cited this definition. For example, Commissioner v. Nat'l Alfalfa Dehydrating & Milling Co., 417 U.S. 134, 145 (1974); U.S. v. Midland-Ross Corp., 381 U.S. 54, 57 (1965). See I.R.C. "461(g)(1)—(charge for the use or forbearance of money).

credit between nongovernmental lenders and borrowers always includes a risk premium. If a borrower's debt is guaranteed by another person, the second element is reduced, but if the guarantor charges a fee for the guarantee, the borrower's total expense, including stated interest and the guarantee fee, is more or less the same.[42] The guarantee fee substitutes for some or all of the risk premium that the lender would otherwise charge. In a broader sense of the term, the risk premium is part of the "compensation for the use or forbearance of money" because the borrower must pay it to obtain the use of the money. Because the risk premium is interest when it is paid to the lender, it should be treated as analogous to interest when paid to a guarantor.

In terms of the model, interest income originates at the borrower's place of residence because the income derives from the borrower's use of the borrowed capital in activities and investments presumed located in the borrower's home country. Similarly, a guarantee fee originates in the borrower's country of residence because it derives from the borrower's use of the borrowed capital.

7.4　　　　CONCLUSION

The U.S. statutory source rules and their application could be improved by a statement of an overall conception underlying these rules. The goal of this short chapter is to provide such a conception.

---

42. Presumably, the total expense is less than it would be under an unguaranteed loan because the added bother of making two transactions, rather than one, is not otherwise justified. This difference is not relevant to the present discussion.

Chapter 8

Formula Based Transfer Pricing

Yariv Brauner[*]

8.1   INTRODUCTION

In the ongoing debate over the desirability of introducing formulary elements
into the international tax regime, my teacher, mentor, colleague and friend, Paul
McDaniel, took sides with the proponents of formulary apportionment. In 1994
he published "Formulary Taxation in the North American Free Trade Zone,"[1]
where he analyzed whether the NAFTA countries should adopt a formulary
system of taxation within their free trade zone, and concluded that doing so
could resolve many of the potential tax-induced distortions to free trade he
identified in the article. In numerous discussions of the transfer pricing rules
within international tax policy we have explored the merits of adopting an
exclusive formula-based regime. This chapter represents my own conclusions
from that debate, eventually supporting its adoption in replacement of the current
U.S. arm's length based transfer pricing regime. Such conclusions are made
independently of other reforms of the international tax regime that may be on
the agenda.

---

[*]   Professor of Law, University of Florida, Levin College of Law.
1.   P. McDaniel, "Formulary Taxation in the North American Free Trade Zone," *Tax Law Review*
     (1994): 691.

Yariv Brauner & Martin James McMahon, Jr. (eds), *The Proper Tax Base: Structural Fairness from
an International and Comparative Perspective—Essays in Honour of Paul McDaniel*, pp. 149–176.
© 2012 Kluwer Law International BV, The Netherlands.

The general discussion of the merits and disadvantages of formulary apportionment has recently heated and benefited from important contributions.[2] The heart of the debate is the question whether we (the world in general and the United States in particular) should replace the current international tax regime that grants tax jurisdiction to countries based on the "source" of the income at issue and the residence of that income's earner, with a regime that divides such jurisdiction between countries based on other attributes of the income as factored in a pre-agreed upon formula.

A critical part of the debate involves a controversy over the desirability of our current arm's length based transfer pricing rules and the universal difficulty of implementing them in a globalizing world. The current transfer pricing crisis is undoubtedly a serious challenge to the stability of the international tax regime and an important factor contributing to the recent calls for a formula based international tax reform, yet it is not the only, and maybe not even the most important reason for the recent policy debate's intensity.[3] Not often has a formula-based reform limited to the transfer pricing rules, replacing the current arm length-based regime, been separately discussed.[4] This is the focus and sole aim of this chapter.

The chapter discusses the choice between the current arm's length based transfer-pricing regime and a formula based transfer-pricing regime. It does not address the wider question of replacing our source based international tax regime for taxing business income with a formula based regime. It is important to distinguish between these two questions, since although a more comprehensive international tax reform to a formula based regime would logically necessitate also a similar reform of the transfer pricing rules, the opposite is not necessarily true. Even if such comprehensive reform is rejected for whatever reasons, it may still be possible, and, this chapter argues desirable, to implement the narrower formula based reform of the transfer pricing rules only. As demonstrated below, many of the objections to a formula based reform may be valid in the context of the more comprehensive reform of the business income tax rules, but not, or to a lesser extent, in the context of the narrower transfer pricing reform.[5]

---

2. See, e.g., R. Avi-Yonah & K. Clausing, "Reforming Corporate Taxation in a Global Economy: A Proposal to Adopt Formulary Apportionment," in *Path to Prosperity: Hamilton project Ideas on Income Security, Education and Taxes*, ed. J. Furman & J. Bordoff (Washington, D.C.: The Brookings Institution, 2008): 319, 327; S. Morse, "Revisiting Global Formulary Apportionment," *Virginia Tax Review.* (2010): 593; J. Roin, "Can the Income Tax Be Saved? The Promises and Pitfalls of Adopting Worldwide Formulary Apportionment," *Tax Law Review* 61 (2008): 169; W. Hellerstein, "International Income Allocation in the Twenty-first Century: The Case for Formulary Apportionment," *International Transfer Pricing Journal* 12 (2005): 103.
3. See E. Kleinbard, "Stateless Income," *Florida Tax Review* 9 (2011): 699.
4. Although, the debate did originate in a discussion of the desirability of the arm's length standard and its alternatives. See, e.g., S. Langbein, "The Unitary Method and the Myth of Arm's Length," *Tax Notes* 30 (1986): 77.
5. For somewhat similar criticism, although framed differently, see, J. Weiner, "Redirecting the Debate on Formulary Apportionment," *Tax Notes* 115 (2007): 1164.

Why do we need to reform our transfer-pricing regime? Well, first one should appreciate the importance of the transfer pricing rules at this time. With globalization, transfer pricing became a primary concern of both the taxpayers and the governments of the productive countries.[6] As multinational enterprises grow in importance and power, the transfer pricing rules that target abusive tax planning by these entities grow in importance. A very large, completely new industry has emerged in the last few years to address this legal area of growing importance and, additionally, the largest tax disputes in the United States have centered on these rules.[7] Most importantly, although in no way the only U.S. tax avoidance mechanism used by U.S. multinational enterprises, transfer pricing is one of the primary mechanisms used for this purpose, and clearly is the crudest and simplest among them. This is partly because the current regime, which leans exclusively on the implementation of the arm's length standard, is broken. It serves well the strongest taxpayers, yet dearly harms the United States and its economy, as well as that of all productive countries.[8] Both the U.S. government and the Organization for Economic Cooperation and Development (OECD) essentially admit the dire state of the current transfer-pricing regime, yet they concentrate their efforts on repeatedly fixing it without acknowledging the failure of their approach that exclusively relies on the arm's length standard.[9] The difficulty with this approach is that it adds further incoherence to an already complex and quite confused regime, and, more importantly, that it is difficult to legally implement. A good example of this difficulty can be found in reviewing recent cases in which U.S. courts could not understand this remedial approach to arm's length based transfer pricing, and refused to deviate from the traditional, literal application of the arm's length standard.[10]

The starting point for the discussion is the current debate over the desirability of formula based international tax reform. Section 2, therefore, sheds light on how the debate is currently framed, proceeding to demonstrate that some of the most controversial issues in this debate either do not interfere with an independent formula based transfer pricing reform, or are wrongly construed in that context.

---

6. See the Ernst & Young Annual Transfer Pricing Surveys, http://www.ey.com/GL/en/Services/Tax/2009-Global-Transfer-Pricing-survey.
7. See, e.g., M. Durst, "Congress: Fix Transfer Pricing and Protect U.S. Competitivenes," *Tax Notes* 128 (2010): 401, 403–404.
8. See, e.g., M. Sullivan, "Transfer Pricing Costs U.S. At Least $28 Billion," *Tax Notes* 126 (2010): 1439–1443. See also Y. Brauner, "Value in the Eye of the Beholder: The Valuation of Intangibles for Transfer Pricing Purposes," *Virginia. Tax Review* 28 (2008): 79.
9. See, e.g., transfer pricing guidelines 1979 OECD Report, para. 14; 1995 OECD Guidelines, paras. 3.58 to 3.74. For a similar observation, see Reuven Avi-Yonah and Ilan Benshalom, "Formulary Apportionment: Myths and Prospects—Promoting Better International Tax Policy and Utilizing the Misunderstood and Under-Theorized Formulary Alternative" (Oct. 16, 2010). U of Michigan Law & Econ, Empirical Legal Studies Center Paper No. 10–029; U of Michigan Public Law Working Paper No. 221., Available at SSRN: http://ssrn.com/abstract=1693105.
10. See, e.g., Y. Brauner, "Cost Sharing and the Acrobatics of Arm's Length Taxation," *Intertax* 38 (2010): 554.

Section 3 then proceeds to focus only on the transfer pricing rules. It discusses the rhetorical logic of our current transfer pricing regime and the evolving domination of the arm's length standard. It analyzes both the perceived advantages and critique of arm's length in theory and practice in order to explain the failing of the current regime.

Alternative reforms, based on formulary apportionment, or the acknowledgement that transfer prices, although necessary in the current international tax regime, are essentially arbitrary, are analyzed in section4. Design premises and concerns are explicitly discussed in order to steer the debate onto a practical path and away from the general slogans that so often characterize it. Although a concrete prescription is beyond the scope of this chapter, it wishes to redefine a discourse that perhaps will have just that as its explicit goal. Section 5 concludes.

8.2 THE CURRENT DEBATE OVER THE DESIRABILITY OF A FORMULA BASED INTERNATIONAL TAX REFORM

The intensity of globalization and the rise of the dominant multinational enterprises present serious challenges to the current international tax regime. Although successful, and some would argue "miraculously" successful, its roots are strongly grounded in the world and economic reality of the period in which it was created and started to blossom. It has been very successful in solving tax disputes, and particularly in alleviating the double taxation threat to international business throughout the twentieth century. Its success is manifested in that international tax rules are fairly harmonized worldwide with few fractions.[11] Yet, recent phenomena, including revolutionary changes in global communications and transportation often associated with what we call "Globalization," challenge the stable longevity of this regime in the twenty-first century. More specifically, the increasing role of cross-border services, intangibles, and multinational enterprises in international business has weakened the power of governments to regulate the global economy. At the same time economic power is being spread between more countries than in the past, the gap between rich and poor countries widens.[12]

These changes expose the weaknesses of the current regime. This regime is based on a simpler reality of cross-border business. It depends on the ability to relatively easily identify the location of income producing activities, such as the presence of flesh-and-blood persons providing services to others in close proximity, and the location of tangible goods crossing borders through physical, well-defined border controls. In that reality it was relatively simple to identify a "source" for each income item based on some reasonable, pseudo-economical rules that over time were accepted by all parties involved as "fair," and crystallized

---

11. See, e.g., Y. Brauner, "An International Tax Regime in Crystallization," *Tax Law Review* 56 (2003): 259.
12. See, e.g., the United Nations' Human Development Reports central site, http://hdr.undp.org/en/ humandev/.

into the regime we now know. The basic rules of this regime provide that income taxes, as personal taxes, may be levied by the country of residence of the relevant income earner since the primary economic allegiance of such taxpayer belongs to that country. Yet, the taxing rights of the country of residence were residual in nature, because at the same time it was universally considered fair to tax income in the location where it was generated—that is in the source country. The duality of acceptable taxing claims by both source and residence country was solved by supposedly giving primacy to the claim of the source country, yet such primacy was limited and confined to cases where it was considered fair. This is the basis of our current division of taxing rights between the countries of the world and the embedded solution to double taxation threats to international business.

The recent challenges to this regime have emerged simply because, increasingly, international business involves intangible assets, services, purely financial transactions, electronic commerce and complex, sophisticated business structures that are just impossible to fit into the current less complex, physical presence driven paradigm. Generally, countries and leading international organizations have attempted to adapt by tweaking those rules without throwing the baby out with the bathwater.

An alternative approach, promoted by academics and other experts in recent years, suggests that the current regime is irreparable and that paradigmatic reform is required.[13] The heart of this alternative approach is to eliminate the dependence on source and physical presence that has proven unworkable. It suggests a shift to formulaic taxation, i.e., to divide taxing claims based on a more sophisticated combination of factors that will be agreed upon by the countries involved rather than on a singular source rule.

This, of course, is not truly a paradigmatic shift since it still relies on some notion of allegiance between income and a country based on pseudo-economic factors and the same perceptions of fairness. Nonetheless, this approach proposes a better chance of dealing with the difficult cases presented by the modern global economy. Since all the involved, including the critics, were educated and produced by the current regime this is not surprising.[14] Similarly unsurprising was the fact that almost universally this reform discourse revolved around a familiar and already-in-place regime—that of the U.S.' states' formulary business (corporate) taxation that is based on a limited set of factors: the location of assets, employees and sales.[15] These reform proposals were never seriously considered, yet formulary elements were increasingly introduced into the current regime without

---

13. See, *supra* note 2.
14. See M. Graetz, "The David R. Tillinghast Lecture: Taxing International Income: Inadequate Principles, Outdated Concepts, and Unsatisfactory Policies," *Tax Law Review* 54 (2001): 261.
15. See, e.g., J. Weiner, "Using the Experience in the U.S. States to Evaluate Issues in Implementing Formula Apportionment at the International Level," *Tax Notes International* 23 (1996): 2113; W. Hellerstein & C. McClure, "The European Commission's Report on Company Income Taxation: What the EU can Learn from the Experience of the U.S. States," *International Tax & Public Finance* 11 (2004): 199.

explicit reform or admittance of such.[16] This section describes these formulaic reform proposals, and analyzes the main arguments in the debate.

8.2.1   FORMULAIC REFORM PROPOSALS

A comprehensive review of all formulary apportionment proposals is beyond the scope of this chapter, yet a short survey of some of them is helpful to understand the scope of the debate and the arguments made by this chapter.

One set of proposals attempted to elect the most advantageous single factor to be used by a formulaic regime. Professors Reuven Avi-Yonah and Kimberly Clausing proposed a reform that would be based on a sales-only formula.[17] This is effectively the trend among the U.S.' states due to the difficulty of valuing assets and the fear of manipulation of the payroll factor and the potential distortions that its inclusion may result in.

Professor Lawrence Lokken, although a critic of formulary apportionment, opined in the past that, if implemented, formulary apportionment should use an assets-only formula, primarily because assets are the least manipulable factor among the three and therefore is least vulnerable to taxpayers abuse. Finally, Professor Ilan Benshalom explained the importance of payroll to curb some firms from manipulating the formula.[18]

Another set of proposals introduce hybrid, practical, compromise-based solutions that purport to be more politically feasible and somewhat imitate the trend among governments and the OECD to de facto divorce themselves from an arm's length methodology, while keeping its rhetoric alive. Avi-Yonah and Benshalom proposed an adoption of formulary taxation only in the case of transactions in intangibles that present the most difficult valuation challenges.[19] The attraction of their proposal is the solution it proposes to the issue of which the current regime clearly has no solution, and that it does not completely dispose of arm's length methodology and the integrity of the existing regime. It further demonstrates that it is possible to adopt different solutions to different problems in lieu of the all-or-nothing rhetoric that typically opposes formulary taxation. Avi-Yonah, Clausing and Durst proposed an adoption of a universal formulary profit split method to replace the current source-based corporate taxation regime.[20] This proposal is similarly attractive because it imitates the de facto trends among governments and the OECD and because it is based on a familiar method, profit split, that is

---

16. In particular, the rise to glory of the Cost Plus Method and Profit Split transfer pricing methods, and that of Advanced Pricing Agreements. For a similar observation, focused on the use of formulaic profit split, see Avi-Yonah & Benshalom, *supra* note 9.
17. Avi-Yonah & Clausing, *supra* note 2, at 319.
18. I. Benshalom, "The Quest to Tax Financial Income in a Global Economy: Emerging to an Allocation Phase," *Virginia. Tax Review* 28 (2008): 165.
19. Avi-Yonah & Benshalom, *supra* note 9.
20. R. Avi-Yonah, K. Clausing & M. Durst, "Allocating Business Profits for Tax Purposes: A Proposal to Adopt a Formulary Profit Split," *Florida Tax Review* 9 (2009): 497.

currently permissible under our arm's length-based transfer-pricing rules, even if in a different format.

Another segment of discourse regarding formulaic taxation is focused on the European Union and the possibility of its Member States adopting formulaic taxation. The European context is somewhat different than the global issue because in Europe the Member States on one hand agreed not to harmonize direct income taxation, yet on the other hand subjected themselves to constitutional-like constraints that were interpreted by the European Court of Justice to require at least some harmonization of these rules. Being a smaller and maybe a more homogeneous group than all the countries of the world, they had, so went the argument, maybe a better chance of agreeing on a formula that would be fair to them all. An earlier initiative is commonly called "home state taxation."[21] The idea was that each European group would be taxed under the tax rules of the Member State where it resides.[22] All Member States would then mutually recognize each other's laws. A competing, more recent yet now dominant, initiative is the work on a Common Consolidated Corporate Tax Base (CCCTB) for European taxpayers.[23] Note, however, that technically this project attempts to reach agreement on tax base, and does not include a discussion of a method for division of this tax base or revenue from its taxation between Member States. Of course, having a single tax base would make an application of formulary taxation much easier, yet one does not necessarily depend on the other. Joann Weiner and others produced multiple assessments of potential adoption of formulary taxation among European Member States.[24]

8.2.2   The Main Arguments in the Debate

8.2.2.1   Economic Based *versus* Arbitrary Taxation

The first argument often made in any debate over formulary apportionment regards the fundamental basis of the discussed regime. Arm's length proponents emphasize its intention to follow a correct, and hence fair economic reality, while formulary apportionment is considered arbitrary. Opponents respond that in reality arm's length follows a fictional, legal reality that is economically distorted (and distorting), whereas formulary apportionment is true to its nature as a tax base division

---

21. S.O. Lodin & M. Gammie, *Home State Taxation* (Amsterdam: IBFD Publications BV, 2001).
22. Specifically, the proposal was for an election to be taxed where the parent had its headquarters.
23. The project has its own website where most of the relevant material is available. See: http://ec.europa.eu/taxation_customs/taxation/company_tax/common_tax_base/index_en.htm.
24. J. Martens Weiner, "Practical Aspects of Implementing Formulary Apportionment in the European Union," *Florida Tax Review* 8 (2007): 629; J. Martens Weiner, "Formulary Apportionment and Group Taxation in the European Union: Insights from the United States and Canada" (European Commission, Taxation and Customs Union, Working Paper No. 8, 2005); P. Weninger, *Formulary Apportionment in the EU* (Intersentia Publishers, 2009).

mechanism resulting from an admittedly arbitrary compromise between competing tax jurisdictions.

Even though this is supposedly the most principled argument in the debate, it is technically flawed, substantively weak and effectively unimportant at the policy-making level. It is effectively unimportant because it has been acknowledged for some time now that arm's length taxation and formulary apportionment are not really distinct on principle, but rather are different points, or more accurately ranges, on the same continuum.[25] The pragmatic policy question is therefore not which method to choose but rather closer to which method wants to be on such continuum. This is particularly true in the current environment where the major international tax players wish to maintain arm's length rhetoric, yet are willing to deviate from its ideals quite a bit in practice.

Both regimes are arbitrary, and most importantly it is not the case that arm's length reflects any economically sound principles that are relevant to its tasks. In many cases, and more so (maybe always) in the difficult cases, there are no adequate comparables and hence a weak basis to establish transfer prices based on other market transactions as the arm's length ideal envisions. Finally, much of the debate is technically flawed because it compares an idealistic arm's length transfer pricing regime with a globally harmonized formulaic international business tax regime. Although universal in the sense that many countries follow in principle the arm's length standard, transfer pricing regimes are primarily unilateral and domestic. Even tax treaties add little to the coordination of transfer prices— these inherently bilateral (or multilateral) concepts. Similarly, advanced pricing agreements that have become increasingly popular in recent years, and were viewed as a promising mechanism to coordinate transfer pricing between countries, are yet to serve in this role, being overwhelmingly unilateral in scope at present.[26]

Another dimension of flawed comparison is that between the current transfer pricing regime, which functions solely to measure income of the taxpayer—multinational enterprises that fall in a country's tax jurisdiction—and a formulaic regime that divides tax bases between competing jurisdictions. This latter function is performed in the current international tax regime by the source (and residence) rules and therefore they, and not arm's length methodology should be compared. Once the correct comparison is established, it is evident that if one views transfer pricing as effectively a tax base division rule, then it is a problematic rule as it uses a norm—arm's length—that deviates from the regular consensus division rule that is based on source and residence.[27] At the income measurement level the current arm's length based rules should be compared with an explicitly arbitrary formula

---

25. See R. Avi-Yonah, "The Rise and Fall of Arm's Length: A Study in the Evolution of U.S. International Taxation," *Virginia Tax Review* 15 (1995): 89; B. Arnold & M. McIntyre, *International Tax Primer*, 2nd ed. (Kluwer Law International, 2002), 80.

26. See, e.g., the recent 2009 report, Announcement and Report Concerning Advance Pricing Agreements, Mar. 29, 2010, http://www.irs.gov/pub/irs-utl/2009finalstatutoryreport.pdf.

27. Brauner, "Value," *supra* note 8.

based income measurement methodology. Standing alone, this comparison obviously does not result in any principled advantage of "realness" or economic correctness for arm's length in fulfilling the income measurement task.

Finally, Avi-Yonah and Benshalom have made the argument that formulary apportionment is in fact less arbitrary than arm's length from the revenue collection perspective "because they are less susceptible to manipulation by intra-MNE contractual arrangements."[28] This chapter does not subscribe to this observation although it is probably generally true, since it relies on the same flawed general comparison between formulary and arm's length based regimes. Opponents of formulary taxation could establish scenarios where this is not the case, and therefore it is sufficient for the purposes of this chapter that one understands that formulary taxation is not per se "more arbitrary" and hence inferior to the current source and arm's length based international tax regime.

8.2.2.2 The Three Factor Formula

Interestingly, the majority of the formulary apportionment debate surrounds not the substance but rather the form or design of suggested formulae. As already mentioned, most commentators limit themselves to the framework of U.S.' state tax systems, i.e., three factor formulae that includes sales, assets and payroll/employees. This focus was partly justifiable, as essentially all parties in the debate understood over the years that one cannot really compare arm's length with formulary apportionment solely in the abstract. In particular, if one proposes a fundamental reform of the current system, one must present a specific alternative and demonstrate that it is not only superior to the current regime, but also that its implementation is feasible. The U.S.' states taxation formulae provide that element of legitimacy to common formulaic proposals. Nonetheless, this dependence effectively eliminated a discussion of any alternatives beyond three factor formulae.

Often, and quite from the beginning of the debate, formula based solutions were rejected with the claim that they are not practical. Yet, this rejection targeted primarily the three factor formulae in general and the states' income tax systems in particular.

Essentially all of the states impose their income taxes, if any, on taxpayers with taxable presence (a business "nexus") within their territorial jurisdiction, yet only on the portion of their income that is allocated to the relevant state by its own unique formula that is based on one or more of the factors mentioned above. The experiences of the states serve, on one hand, the formulary apportionment proponents that use it as strong evidence that their system works, and quite successfully, and is not merely an academic whim. On the other hand, formulary apportionment opponents argue that there are many problems with the states' income tax systems, and particularly that those systems result in double taxation

---

28. Avi-Yonah & Benshalom, *supra* note 9 (response to Myth no. 1).

and double non (or under) taxation, and therefore is incompatible with the most fundamental goal of an international tax regime.[29]

The most powerful argument against formulary apportionment in this context has been that even the U.S.' states were unable to agree on a single formula to divide tax bases among themselves, and therefore it is unrealistic to expect all or most of the countries of the world to reach an agreement on a formula to divide business income tax bases between them.[30] The countries of the world are much less homogeneous, their political and economic interests diverge more than those of the states and they do not have even a benchmark for tax accounting that the individual countries can use. Although unilateral adoption of formulary apportionment is rarely discussed, one can imagine that under such a scenario countries will tend to adopt formulae that will fit their economic characteristics and give them an advantage in tax collection. The end result will again produce some double taxation and double nontaxation, or undesirable or unfair tax competition.

A separate discourse focused on the factors themselves. Hypothetical analyses of what countries will choose to do concentrated on the advantages that the various factors or combinations of factors may present to different countries. Yet, most of the attention was paid to pragmatic, and particularly to enforcement challenges. Productive assets were promoted as the least manipulable or movable factor and thus least exposed to abusive tax planning. Yet, it may not be realistic or desirable to exclude intangible assets that are easily movable and require the most complex and expensive valuation. Sales were also promoted as a less manipulable factor, yet realistically they could be shifted in costly and wasteful tax planning, and most importantly they present obvious imbalances between countries that are likely to raise unbridgeable fairness concerns. Similarly, payroll gives an advantage to richer countries and is likely to have very different results than competing formulae that use mere numbers of employees. This discourse seems to often result in a chronic impasse.

Yet, this impasse is not inevitable; it simply results from the pathological path dependence and conservative clinging to the familiar. Essentially all of the participants in the discourse assume that the best formula will be the one that is best justified economically (or pseudo-economically). Alternatively, a second best formula may also be acceptable if it presents a convincing administrability advantage. Yet, note that the whole idea of formulary apportionment was to free oneself from the attraction to pseudo-economic reasoning and to admit the arbitrary nature of transfer pricing. This leaves the pragmatic argument intact, and indeed administrability and costs (discussed more specifically below) are important, yet if this were the sole concern there is little reason to cling to the three factor formulae. The only justification possible to this course of action is that it is

---

29. See, e.g., W. Wilkins & K. Gideon, "Memorandum to Congress: You Wouldn't Like Worldwide Formula Apportionment," *Tax Notes* 65 (1994): 1259.
30. *Ibid.* See also E. Coffill & P. Willson Jr., "Federal Formulary Apportionment as an Alternative to Arm's Length Pricing: From the Frying Pan to the Fire?," *Tax Notes* 59 (1993): 1103.

politically perceived as more palatable. This may be the case, yet it needs to be researched further, separately and explicitly as such.

8.2.2.3 Unilateral *versus* Multilateral Solutions

An often mentioned argument against formulary apportionment is that it cannot be implemented unilaterally and is unlikely to be adopted worldwide.[31] This argument is related to the argument that formulary apportionment may only be possible if implemented based on a harmonized, comprehensive tax base agreed on by all participants. This chapter takes as an assumption that international agreement over a formula is unlikely to be achieved in the short term, and therefore the discussion of this solution, although potentially desirable, is beyond its scope. This section focuses on the possibility of adopting formulary apportionment gradually, in an agreement between a few countries, or even unilaterally by, for example, the United States. The basic argument against this solution is, as already mentioned above, that different jurisdictions will choose, out of justified self-interest, to use formulae that benefit them based on their economic characteristics and projections. Consequently, different trade partners are certain to have differing formulae, a situation that will result in over (double) or under taxation. Countries with labor intensive industries, for example, will emphasize the employee factor in their formula, countries with heavy industries might emphasize the assets factor, and rich countries will want to feature the sales factor in their formula. This could be solved only by a large multilateral agreement that is unlikely to be achieved, and therefore formulary apportionment is not implementable. This argument is supported by the fact that the current international tax regime, and maybe more than any of its components the arm's length based transfer pricing rules, already allegedly enjoy universal acceptance. Therefore, it supposedly enjoys a cost advantage, but also a certainty advantage that is particularly powerful in tax policy where conservatism is very strong and there exists genuine concern over the fragility of the current international tax regime. Finally, the most influential people in the international tax policy world have a personal stake in the preservation of the current regime.

Another version of this argument that is also partly about the costliness of formulary taxation is that it would require a messy renegotiation of all tax treaties and will destabilize the current international tax regime. This argument is quite weak because the lack of ability of the current regime to solve commonplace situations is clearly more threatening than a desirable reform of the current international tax regime. Second, as demonstrated by Avi-Yonah, it is not

---

31. J. Neighbour & J. Owens, "Transfer Pricing in the New Millennium: Will the Arm's Length Principle Survive?," *George Mason Law Review.* 10 (2002): 951; M. Markham, *The Transfer Pricing of Intangibles* (Kluwer Law International, 2005), 134; R. Culbertson, "Is There a Formula in Your Future? Formulary Apportionment, The Arm's-Length Principle, and the Future Role of Profit Splits," *Tax Management Transfer Pricing Report.* 5 (1997): 557. See also the OECD's *Transfer Pricing Guidelines for Multinational Enterprises and Tax Administrations,* e.g., para. 3.64.

necessarily difficult to reconcile the current rules with a formulary reform. The most relevant conflict for the purpose of this chapter is the reliance of the current rules on the arm's length standard which will have to change in any formulary reform. Well, first, the reliance on arm's length, although universal, does not rely on hard law, but is merely interpretative. Countries will have to agree on a new way of dividing their tax bases, yet they will do that anyway if they choose to engage in reform. An argument that reform is costly is misguided since it applies to any reform. There is no particular argument that indicates that formulary reform should be particularly costly, especially since countries engage in negotiation of the division of the tax base between them anyway under the current tax treaties based international tax regime.

Finally, note that Avi-Yonah and Benshalom, based on similar assumptions as are made in this chapter, took a somewhat different position, arguing that indeed this argument may be challenging to unitary taxation, yet it does not pose a challenge to their proposal to limit the formulary solution to problematic areas that the current regime cannot solve, such as in the area of the transfer of intangibles.[32] Although somewhat implicitly, they agree with the assertion of this chapter that formula taxation does not have to be an all encompassing solution based on an all-or-nothing approach. The next section similarly argues that formulary apportionment based transfer pricing reform does not necessarily require a universally harmonized tax base. This chapter accepts the solution of Avi-Yonah and Benshalom as independently desirable, yet argues that it should not be limited to intangibles and the reliance on arm's length in transfer pricing rules should be abandoned completely.

8.2.2.4 Costliness—Simplicity, Compliance and Enforcement

In reality, the heart of the formulary apportionment debate is not about principles, but rather about costs. Beyond the argument over the design of the desired formula and whether international consensus may be achieved over such design, most of the serious debate is over the question whether formulary apportionment is truly simpler, i.e., less costly than arm's length.[33] This debate started even before it was became obvious that the current regime is broken,[34] and a fundamental reform is a necessity, not just a desire. It has also been the initial powerful argument in the arsenal of formulary apportionment proponents faced with the always conservative and resistant to change tax policy crowd.

The argument is quite simple: instead of costly economic studies and documentation that the current regime requires and that are based on many problematic

---

32. Avi-Yonah & Benshalom, *supra* note 9 (response to Myth no. 2).
33. S. Christensen, "Formulary Apportionment: More Simple—On Balance Better?," *Law & Policy in International Business* 28 (1996–1997); 1133.
34. However, Brian Lebowitz has predicted that it would be the end of international taxation. See B. Lebowitz, "Transfer Pricing and the End of International Taxation," *Tax Notes* 84 (1999): 1527.

judgment calls and approximations that are difficult to establish and even more difficult to audit, taxpayers will simply apply a formula, using data that they already have or that is easily calculable, and derive a number that will be used as the income of the related parties when they transact among themselves. Opponents of formulary apportionment dismiss this argument as simply false. In particular, they note that if the "assets" factor is part of the formula, independent valuation, including the most problematic valuation of intangibles, is required, which effectively eliminates the alleged advantage of formulary apportionment over arm's length. Moreover, they argue that the basis for comparison and calculation will be difficult to establish at the multilateral level. Indeed, the attempt of the European Union to reach an agreement over a common consolidated corporate tax base demonstrates the difficulties of establishing this common benchmark for calculations. In response, formulary apportionment proponents should admit that in practice it would not be simple and the need to value intangibles introduces complexity and costs, yet the other parts of the formula will indeed be simpler and cheaper to calculate.

Even the valuation of intangibles should be less costly under formulary apportionment. First, because it is not necessarily the case that assets will be part of the formula. Second, because only the total value will need to be established. The division of that value between the competing jurisdictions should be simpler since it will be based on an explicitly arbitrary rule, not one that purports to reflect a nonexisting economic reality and hence needs to withstand challenges that the actual economic reality may prevent. Finally, since it is not necessarily the case that this reform will be multilateral, the base complexity may be phantom, and each country will base its calculations on its own tax accounting rules—exactly as it does under the current regime.

A serious challenge for a formulary solution is its lack of flexibility.[35] This argument is rarely made explicitly. Opponents of formulary apportionment argue that any formula chosen will present, on one hand, waste since it will inevitably cause changes in behavior of multinational enterprises, and on the other hand will provide multinational enterprises a roadmap for tax planning. This argument is weak since in this respect formulary apportionment is not different than the current arm's length based regime, and is even likely to be superior to it since it is likely to be based on less manipulable factors and it avoids the pretention of pseudo economic analysis and the administrative costs that it entails. Nonetheless, the lack of flexibility is unsatisfactory on its own. Take two countries that agree on a formula based on an equal flow of factors of production and equal cross investment. What would happen if after some years the balance changes? The consequences of the formula will affect the presumptive market based change. Treaty, and hence formula negotiations, are notoriously long and costly so it is unlikely, although not impossible to imagine, that constant renegotiations can solve this issue. Furthermore, developing countries may argue that formulae based on current state of affairs may hinder their quest to develop and equalize the economic

---

35. This is the only serious apolitical challenge in the view of this author.

conditions between them and developed countries. This may present a political challenge, in addition to the practical challenge mentioned above, and provide ammunition to opponents of formulary taxation that advocate conservatism and maintenance of the current regime as a default solution, despite its obvious inferiority. In response to that, more sophisticated solutions that take dynamism into account are required, yet for the purposes of this chapter it is sufficient to realize, as explained in the next section, that this concern belongs primarily to an overhaul of international business taxation and does not really concern a more modest transfer-pricing-only reform.

| 8.2.3 | DISTINGUISHING THE DEBATE OVER FORMULAIC INTERNATIONAL TAX REFORM FROM TRANSFER PRICING REFORM |

The formulary apportionment discourse focused, as already mentioned, on international tax reform and on assisting the international tax regime in facing the challenges discussed above. The corresponding reform in transfer pricing has been consistently embedded into this discourse, often with little attempt to distinguish between the two. Although the latter is a natural component of the former, they should be distinguished from each other. The debate over the proper taxation of corporations worldwide is naturally more complex and much more fundamental than the manner in which one measures the income of multinational enterprises. One may argue that the latter is still the heart of the whole debate. Although not solved here, what this chapter wishes to make clear is that transfer pricing reform may be achieved without a fundamental shuddering of the bases of the whole international tax regime. Moreover, some of the strongest arguments against formulary apportionment are less persuasive or are completely irrelevant in the context of a mere transfer pricing formulaic reform.[36]

First, the substantive argument against formula based transfer pricing is weak. It is indeed arbitrary, yet the current arm's length based rules do not themselves reflect economic realities; they simply camouflage their arbitrariness with analyses that uses economic terminology and methodology, yet in fact follow legal fiction rather than economic reality. This is particularly true where transactions involving intangibles are concerned, where arm's length was effectively abandoned even by the tax authorities of the United States.[37] Transactions involving intangibles are crucial to this policy debate because the ownership of intangibles is primary to multinational enterprises organizing as such,[38] and because the lion's share of potentially abusive transfer pricing based tax planning involves transactions

---

36. Related, yet not similarly focused criticism was expressed by Weiner against the Avi-Yonah & Clausing proposal mentioned above in "Redirecting the Debate on Formulary Apportionment," *Tax Notes* 115 (2007): 1164.
37. Applying, primarily, CPM and Profit Split analyses rather than the traditional arm's length methods.
38. See, e.g., R. Caves, *Multinational Enterprise and Economic Analysis* (Cambridge: Cambridge University Press, 1996), Chapter 7.

involving intangibles. Also, substantive arguments may matter when comprehensive international tax reform is discussed, yet they are less persuasive in the limited context of transfer pricing reform due to the recent effective collapse of our arm's length transfer pricing regime that makes reform imperative. Any reform proposal includes an introduction of formulary or arbitrary elements that pushes the regime further away from the literal arm's length ideal.

Second, in terms of design, a limited transfer pricing reform is necessarily more practical than a comprehensive international tax reform. In principle it must be easier to devise a formula that will measure income of parts of multinational enterprises than one that will divide tax bases between countries. More particularly, the attachment to the pseudo economic factors to justify tax bases belonging to one country or another is inevitably stronger than a reliance on them in the assignment of income of a multinational enterprise between two or more parts of that enterprise (that happened to be separate taxpayers in different countries— solely for legal purposes). Moreover, one could imagine that countries will consider division rules that are straightforward about their arbitrary condition, if agreed upon and perceived fair, in the particular context of transfer pricing, since all countries acknowledge the artificiality of dividing a single economic organism into fictional parts solely for legal purposes. Yet, doing so for the actual business income taxing rules may be more difficult since it is a longstanding practice to tax all types of business income uniformly. It would be difficult to introduce a system that applies only to income of multinational enterprises. This difficulty does not exist in the limited context of transfer pricing since these rules apply only to multinational enterprises and since the division norm in this area already deviates from the general income division rules by applying the arm's length standard and not source or residence-based norms.

Third, although seemingly unpopular and little discussed it must be the case that unilateral reform of the transfer pricing rules will be more likely to occur than a comprehensive reform of the general business income taxing rules. Most international trade and business is subject to rules that intend to eliminate or ameliorate double taxation, whether by treaty application or via unilateral relief provisions. This is not the case in the transfer pricing field. Even though arm's length as a standard is essentially universally adopted, its content varies significantly from one country to another. Tax treaties provide little coordination between countries, and even in cases where governments and taxpayers actually reach agreements or compromises with taxpayers, such agreements do not extend across borders. This means that economic double taxation is the norm rather than the exception in transfer pricing practice. Even worse, due to the flexibility and intellectual unsoundness of arm's length, double nontaxation or under taxation is even more prevalent than double taxation, and countries do little to cooperate to combat this phenomenon.[39] But, unilateral action is not necessarily the only

---

39. This phenomena is best demonstrated in the recent report by the Staff of the Joint Committee on Taxation, *Present Law and Background Related to Possible Income Shifting and Transfer Pricing* (JCX-37-10, Jul. 20, 2010).

option. The biggest losers of aggressive transfer pricing planning are likely to be the largest economies that are also major trading partners of each other. They could jumpstart reform of transfer pricing only to combat this tax avoidance, and they are much more homogeneous and have similar interests than all the countries of the world, so it is not unimaginable that they could agree on a common compromise formula, with or without an expectation to later convince other productive jurisdictions to join in at least on the debate over the design of the formula. Sitting on the fence is simply too costly.

Fourth, formula based transfer pricing should be less costly than the current arm's length based rules. Indeed, the particular design of the formula will dictate the extent of cost saving, yet all of the proposals on the table at this point appear to be much simpler and cheaper than the costs of compliance and enforcement of our arm's length based regime. The most obvious savings would be in the elimination of the need to search for comparables that are not easily available and often non-existent in the case of intangibles and hence require significant resources to extract available data and accommodate the fiction of comparables with scientifically-looking methodology. Some observations are due here: the more arbitrary and transparent the rules are the simpler and less costly it should be to administer them. Moreover, even if intangibles will require valuation, this valuation should be simpler and less costly than the one required under the current regime. This is because no pseudo attribution rules will be required to be implemented. At worst, the costs of the valuation of intangibles will be the same as is under the current regime. But, once valuation is just that, and not part of the division rules, it will inevitably be more accurate and informing. Taxpayers will be freed of the forced reliance on market based valuation, and will be able to use other approaches as deemed appropriate by their relative experts. Finally, as already mentioned above, assets will not necessarily be part of the formula.

In conclusion, the opposition to formulary apportionment is based on arguments that are either weak or are targeted at certain design details that may or may not be part of the eventual reform. Yet, even those arguments that have validity are weakened or disappear when only a limited transfer pricing reform is discussed rather than a fundamental formula based international tax reform.

Now that the focus on transfer pricing is established, the chapter proceeds, next, with a discussion of the conceptual basis of the current transfer pricing regime and its evolution into the global dominance it enjoys at present in order to, later, establish the parameters for its reform.

8.3 THE LOGIC OF OUR TRANSFER PRICING REGIME AND THE DOMINATION OF ARM'S LENGTH

The primary impetus for much of the formulary apportionment debate comes from frustration with our current transfer pricing rules. Although the current international tax regime has been struggling to adequately deal with several other issues, such as financial derivatives and intangibles in general, in transfer pricing the difficulty stemmed not from the fundamental basis of the international tax regime, but rather from the fictional basis for these rules, namely the arm's length standard, itself a deviation from the foundation of the international tax regime.[40] In addition, the increasing role of transfer pricing in aggressive tax planning has amplified the pressure on governments to focus on these rules.

8.3.1 ARM'S LENGTH IN THE UNITED STATES

The origins of the U.S.' transfer-pricing regime are found in a rule that intended to combat domestic corporate tax avoidance by groups of domestic corporations.[41] At a later stage this rule was effectively converted into the current transfer pricing rule that combats abuse by groups of corporations that transact across borders. Almost concurrently, arm's length was adopted as the dominant implementation standard for this rule; the benchmark for appropriate intercompany pricing, the deviation from which may trigger IRS action.[42] Nonetheless, in the absence of guidance on how to apply this standard the courts have resorted to reasonability in transfer pricing cases, and only in the 1960s began to focus on a literal arm's length analysis. In response, the government came out in 1968 with the first set of transfer pricing regulations which attempted to guide taxpayers on how to determine arm's length prices, using the originally prescribed methods. The courts welcomed the regulations, and since the 1970s have consistently applied the arm's length standard in transfer pricing cases, refusing all challenges to the regulations and the arm's length standard regardless of whether it was the government or taxpayers who initiated the challenges. What I call the literal arm's length analysis, i.e., the insistence on setting transfer prices based on prices charged in comparable market transactions without much thought about alternatives and with little sophistication in the comparability analysis, was very attractive to the courts and the Internal Revenue Service, since it presented the pretense of a principled, scientific, market analysis that required little discretion in a genuinely complex field. This period was described by Professor Reuven Avi-Yonah as the "rise" of the arm's length standard, to be followed by its gradual decline in the two decades to follow.[43] However, the recent *Xilinx* case demonstrates that at least the rhetoric of the courts, supporting a mandatory, literal application of the dominant standard, has not weakened to date.[44]

In the next twenty years the courts struggled to apply the arm's length standard, particularly in cases that involved intangibles.[45] They often resorted to formulaic solutions that were in essence closer to an application of the supposedly

---

40. See Brauner, "Value," *supra* note 8.
41. See, e.g., Avi-Yonah, "The Rise and Fall of Arm's Length," *supra* note 25.
42. See discussion *ibid*, at 97.
43. *Ibid.*
44. See analysis in Brauner, "Cost Sharing," *supra* note 10.
45. See Brauner, "Value," *supra* note 8, para. IV.B.

rejected reasonability standard than the literal arm's length standard.[46] The difficulty was so significant that Congress intervened in 1986 with the sole amendment to section 482 that added the "commensurate with income" requirement in the case of intangibles. This addition had not fit naturally with the literal arm's length rhetoric,[47] and, indeed, was effectively abandoned for a period of years. In 1994, though, the government introduced regulations that provided new methods of applying the arm's length standard. These methods were supposed to correct some of the deficiencies in the application of the 1968 methods, particularly in the case of intangibles. The new methods introduced in 1994 clearly departed from the literal arm's length standard, yet they have been applied in a manner that kept the rhetoric of arm's length possible.[48] Since then, these methods have dominated the practice of transfer pricing in the United States. In addition, an advance pricing agreement program that provides further protection from literal arm's length standard has developed and thrived for some taxpayers.[49] Finally, multinational enterprises increasingly used cost sharing, the single direct safe harbor from arm's length prescribed in the regulations, to export their most valuable intangible assets out of the U.S.' tax jurisdiction. Later, when the government challenged the scheme, the courts provided taxpayers protection based on the literal arm's length rhetoric.[50]

Despite the gradual substantive departure from the arm's length standard and the recent embarrassments, the government, and similarly the OECD, have repeatedly resisted all calls for reevaluation of the exclusive application of the arm's length standard.[51] The courts' position has evolved even less, and a recent decision has taken it to the extreme by declaring the arm's length standard the "purpose" of transfer pricing rules rather than a means to ending corporate abuse of the rules.[52]

8.3.2   THE UNIVERSALITY OF ARM'S LENGTH

Arm's length rhetoric extends beyond U.S. borders: the international tax regime, led by U.S. elements, has evolved to include arm's length as one of its principal

---

46. *Ibid.*
47. See, e.g., L. Sheppard, "Reflections on the Death of Transfer Pricing," *Tax Notes Today* (Sep. 17, 2008).
48. See, e.g., Brauner, "Value," *supra* note 8, para. IV.A.
49. See IRS site, http://www.irs.gov/businesses/corporations/article/0,id=96277,00.html, and the recent (2010) annual report, announcement 2011–22; 2011–16 IRB 672.
50. See report on recent cases in Brauner, "Cost Sharing," *supra* note 10.
51. In fact, the OECD Transfer Pricing Guidelines include increasingly voluminous language on the rejection of a formula based reform. See, e.g., section III.C. of the guidelines that is devoted in its whole to the rejection of global formulary apportionment.
52. Xilinx, Inc. v. Commissioner, 598 F.3d 1191 (9th Cir. 2010), reversing its now withdrawn opinion in Xilinx, Inc. v. Commissioner, 567 F.3d 482 (9th Cir. 2009), and affirming Xilinx Inc. v. Commissioner, 125 T.C. 37 (2005).

features.[53] This focus on arm's length began with the work of the League of Nations and extends to the more recent carrier of the torch, the OECD. The OECD has been even more reluctant to consider its reform. In the last thirty years, as transfer pricing has become more important, the OECD has stuck by the arm's length standard as the exclusive mechanism of transfer pricing enforcement. In more recent publications, the OECD even added language and strengthen the rhetoric in support of arm's length and rejection of the alternative formulaic approach to transfer pricing. Furthermore, it enforces discipline among its members and other states that abide by its model, not to depart from this standard.[54] Even the U.S.' reforms mentioned above were criticized as not sufficiently in adherence with arm's length.

The result of the work of these international organizations is that, inevitably, arm's length has evolved into the de facto universal standard for transfer pricing application. The power of the OECD supported this convergence process, and effectively forced it upon all countries. Again, the rhetoric was more important, and in hindsight also more effective, than the reality that it was not truly a seamless convergence of rules.[55] The most important function of this rhetoric has been its effectiveness in eliminating the development of alternative rules.[56]

Being a universal standard was also important since it became itself an important reason not to reform the current transfer-pricing regime.

8.3.3 DEFENSE OF ARM'S LENGTH

Despite the lack of comprehensive study of policy options during the evolution of arm's length to its dominant position today, its basic rationale was never positively established, partly because it has rarely been challenged until recently. The most fundamental justification for the use of this standard is probably that it provides a

---

53. A United Kingdom legislation (General Rule 7, Income Tax Act, 1918) adopted a similar provision to the United States transfer pricing rules back in 1918, yet the United States' influence resulted in a more frequent mention of its legislation as the "original" arm's length articulation. See H. Hamaekers, "Arm's Length—How Long?," in *International and Comparative Taxation, Essays in Honor of Klaus Vogel*, ed. K. Van Raad, et al. (Kluwer Law International, 2002): 20.

54. For example, Mexico abandoned its traditional formulary transfer pricing rules in favor of the OECD transfer pricing guidelines, to join the OECD. See R Avi-Yonah, "Commentary (to H. David Rosenbloom, "The David Tillinghast Lecture—International Tax Arbitrage and the "International Tax System," "Tax Law Review 53 (2000): 137), *Tax Law Review* (2000):167, 170, citing J. González-Béndiksen, "Mexico Amends Transfer Pricing Rules," *Tax Notes International* 90 (1997): 459.

55. S. Langbein, "The Unitary Method and the Myth of Arm's Length," *Tax Notes* 30(1986): 625.

56. Moreover, recently, the OECD has extended the "front" by mandating the use of the guidelines and arm's length pricing in the attribution of profits to permanent establishments. See, e.g., the central, relevant OECD site: http://www.oecd.org/department/0,3355,en_2649_37989746_1_1_1_1_1,00.html, and the final (2010) OECD report, available at: http://www.oecd.org/dataoecd/23/41/45689524.pdf.

market-based mechanism that allows the general international tax norms to apply equally and similarly to transactions between related and unrelated parties. The advantage of this approach is that it allows the system to be based on a unitary, over-arching set of rules that both make sense and are long and universally used. In addition, the reliance on the all-knowing, objective market is comforting to policymakers, even though it is clearly false as it is in this case. Consequently, arm's length provides an appealing promise of accuracy and correctness (primarily when presented in contrast to the arbitrariness of formulary apportionment). This promise plays well into the primary concern of the current international tax regime, namely the elimination of double taxation, since only an accurate, mathematical methodology can aspire to tax income once and only once.[57] This comfort, augmented by the universality of the arm's length standard made the resistance to change very powerful, despite the pressure created by the changing world economy and the globalization of markets.

At present, the universality of the standard and its centrality to our international tax regime are probably the main reasons articulated in support of the standard, regardless of the weak substantive case for its retention. Most of the contemporary discourse focuses on the comparison of various reform proposals, primarily those that are formula based, with arm's length. Unfortunately, more often than not reform proposals are compared to an idealized arm's length based transfer pricing regime rather than the one we have today. This diminishes the appeal of reform as any transition is naturally costly—economically and politically.

8.3.4   CRITIQUE OF ARM'S LENGTH

It is not difficult to understand that the support of arm's length is lacking in substance. Indeed, even the most avid proponents of arm's length—the OECD and the U.S.' government—consistently deviate from the core principles of arm's length. They have gone to great length to protect the façade of arm's length, while effectively abandoning it in substance in many instances.

The most basic critique of the arm's length standard is that it does not reflect economic reality while creating a false pretense that it does and that that is its strength. In particular, arm's length simply ignores the (economic) reasons behind the decision of firms to operate across-borders in a hierarchical form rather than contract with unrelated parties. Multinational enterprises face uniquely high costs when they choose to expand globally. They could typically save significant start up costs if they chose instead to contract with local, unrelated firms in the various locations of expansion since such firms would already have local expertise, ties, etc. Nonetheless, multinational enterprises choose not to do so and incur such expenses because they believe that it will eventually result in higher profits through

---

57. R. Avi-Yonah, "International Taxation of Electronic Commerce," *Tax Law Review* 52 (1997): 507.

internalization of many of the costs, and primarily through much higher expected profits from their proprietary intangibles.[58] Arm's length requires related parties to charge prices in transactions among themselves as if they were unrelated parties, ignoring these differences in risks, costs and expected returns. Note that arm's length does not just impose neutrality between transactions between related and unrelated parties; it forces market prices on nonmarket transactions in a one-sided equalization fiction. This weakness of arm's length is most apparent in the case of the so-called "internal comparables," when taxpayers transact with both related and unrelated parties.[59] In such cases taxpayers are enthusiastically required to use in the transactions with related parties the same prices that they charged in their transactions with unrelated parties. Yet, it is clear that if a firm chooses to contract with unrelated parties in some countries while establishing itself locally in others, it does so for a reason—an economic (inequivalent) reason. Still, governments love internal comparables because they seem to be easy to enforce and to justify. They do not need to worry about complex valuation issues triggered by differences in the subjects of the compared transactions because they are identical.

In fact, much of the current transfer pricing rules and practices are driven by ease of enforcement and practicality concerns, yet these difficulties are first and foremost the result of the insistence of the government to maintain the rhetoric of arm's length. Arm's length is very complex to administer and hence it is very costly to comply with and enforce. Much has been written on the notion of comparability—the most fundamental implementation device of the arm's length standard. To comply with arm's length, taxpayers are required to price (valuate) their own nonmarket transactions using market prices charged in other transactions. Naturally, with the very minor exception of internal comparables mentioned above, these other transactions differ from the subject transaction in many respects. The core practice of transfer pricing is to isolate transactions that are similar enough to the subject transaction, to identify the differences and to assess an appropriate value for these differences to be later reflected in adjustments from the comparable market prices to the established transfer price. This is very much like the art of general valuation based on the market approach. Yet, unlike general business valuation, experts are constrained. They are strongly cuffed by the market approach to valuation and specific procedures dictated by transfer pricing regulations and other IRS proclamations. Moreover, in general business valuation it is acknowledged that such valuation is an art that is designed to assist management (or other players) in making business decisions. In contrast, transfer pricing must result in a single, set dollar amount on which tax is calculated. The margin of error and manipulation in effect results in significant bias in favor of certain taxpayers

---

58. R. Vann, "Reflections on Business Profits and the Arm's Length Principle," in *The Taxation of Business Profits Under Tax Treaties*, ed. B. Arnold, J. Sasseville & E. Zolt (Toronto: Canadian Tax Foundation, 2006):133, 140–141.

59. These comparables are often considered the "best" from a government's position. See, e.g., S. Kamath, "Internal Comparables Trump External in Transfer Pricing TNMM, Delhi Tribunal Says," 2011 *Worldwide Tax Daily* 92–94, and U.S. Steel Corp. v. Commissioner, 617 F.2d 942 (2nd Cir. 1980).

(intangibles heavy multinational enterprises) and significant costs to all multinational enterprises. Moreover, the transfer pricing regime has created from scratch a large, economically wasteful industry which exists only to serve the need to supply these particular valuations.

8.4   THE DESIGN OF A FORMULA-BASED TRANSFER PRICING REGIME

As already mentioned, the framework for discussing the design of any potential formula based international tax regime, including its transfer pricing component, has always been based on the U.S.' states' formulary business taxation system. Essentially all (if not all) of the states tax corporate taxpayers based on the location of assets, employees and sales within their jurisdiction, so all reform proposals included an assessment of a formula based on one or more of these factors.

This is a logical result of a natural path-dependent behavior of tax scholars and professionals who operate within the framework of the current international tax regime that is, as explained above, "source" based. This means that income some-how naturally "belongs" to certain countries, and therefore such countries have a factual and economically natural first claim over the taxation of such income. Based on this, partly anachronistic, partly just false, logic, it seems reasonable for formulaic taxation to be based on factors that supposedly justify the assignment of income items to one or another of the potential taxing jurisdictions.

An obvious problem with this framework is that it ignores the fact that this pseudo-economic thinking is at least partly the cause for the current regime's failures that formulaic taxation attempts to correct. At the minimum, one must consider the alternatives to this system. First and foremost, there may be other factors, beyond assets, payroll/employees and sales that could be used in the same manner in the formula. More dramatic alternatives include negotiated income (also arbitrary in the sense that it is not based on particular economic or pseudo economic factor) or profit split regimes.

It is important to understand that there is not, and there cannot be, any economically correct manner to divide the income of a multinational enterprise that is economically unitary between its parts that were separated from each other arbitrarily by a legal fiction: the separate corporate personality. Alas, the income must be divided between taxing jurisdictions somehow, yet such split must be essentially arbitrary and we must free ourselves from the illusion that it is possible to do that in a completely nonarbitrary manner. Now, this does not mean that in some cases simple pseudo economic logic cannot be reasonable and acceptable by all. Indeed, the origin of the current regime came from that less complex world where cross-border issues included individuals sometimes performing straightforward services in multiple countries, and corporations manufacturing goods in one country and selling and marketing them in others. In such cases one may argue more successfully that, for example, the wages of a service provider should be split among the jurisdictions in which she physically performed the services, and that the profits of the above mentioned corporations should be divided among the home (manufacturing) and target jurisdictions based on costs incurred in each of them, for example. Although not free of difficulties, current norms may still work relatively well in these circumstances, yet they completely fail in cases where remote services, complex intangibles and financial transactions are involved. Since the latter transactions are increasingly more important components of international business, and are the very reason for firms to organize themselves as hierarchical, multinational enterprises, which are the targets of the transfer pricing rules.

The design choice strongly depends on the context of the reform contemplated. It is quite common in the literature to propose global reforms in a contextual vacuum, really based on an assumption that all or at least all the important countries will adopt it contemporaneously. The easiest, and indeed most common, critique of this approach is that it is not feasible that every state would agree to it, and little attention is paid to the differing interests of the countries that may be involved. This chapter takes a somewhat different path by commencing the analysis, next, with the possibility of the United States adopting formulaic transfer pricing, first unilaterally, and then as a part of various groups of countries.

8.4.1 UNILATERAL ADOPTION OF FORMULAIC TRANSFER PRICING

The starting point of any formulaic transfer pricing rule adopted unilaterally is of course assignment of the whole profit to the U.S.' taxpayer in our case. This means that the United States will apply its tax rules to the entire profit earned by a multinational group in transactions involving U.S. corporate taxpayers. Note that the transfer pricing rules serve only to measure the income of the relevant taxpayers and nothing beyond that. Therefore, the above does not mean that the United States will fully tax this entire profit, since, for example, foreign tax credits may be available to the U.S.' taxpayer for taxes that the competing jurisdiction will assess on the same income. It is likely that the competing jurisdiction will reciprocate with a similar rule that will measure its taxpayer's income as the entire income earned by the group. Another realistic response is for the other country to not reciprocate, but rather simply continue to apply its own arm's length based rules and tax the relevant taxpayers as it would have taxed them before the U.S. reform.

The first scenario is likely to often result in double taxation. First, because some taxpayers will incur tax liabilities on the same profits in competing jurisdictions, and many countries do not employ indirect tax credit mechanisms and when they do these are limited in scope.[60] Second, and relatedly, most countries use some formalistic source rules that follow residence norms that will dictate that the same income will be sourced domestically in both of the competing jurisdictions, denying potential foreign tax credits that are available (essentially universally) only with respect to foreign source income. The same latter point is also the reason why

---

60. Even the United States' rule, in section 902, is limited to 10% ownership and actual dividends.

unilateral double tax relief mechanisms would not work in these cases—foreign tax credits are not allowed against domestic source income, and exemption is similarly available only for foreign source income. Consequently, such a purely unilateral solution cannot work under these terms. Note that this is the case even in situations where tax treaties apply. Such treaties require relief of double taxation under Article 23 or its equivalents, and attempts to resolve dual residence issues under Article 4 or its equivalents, yet they do not generally deal with income assignment or its measurement directly. This is left entirely to domestic law and hence is not affected by tax treaties. Furthermore, most treaties do not deal with determining the source of income, which may assist in providing at least some relief of double taxation, again leaving it to the domestic laws of the parties. Finally, essentially all tax treaties include a version of Article 9 of the OECD Model that very weakly requires respect among the treaty partners to each other's transfer pricing adjustments, yet in our scenario these rules may not apply since such adjustments relate to two different taxpayers. More problematic is the fact that Article 9 has been universally and forcefully interpreted to implement the arm's length standard as the supreme norm for solving transfer pricing issues and the solution discussed here clearly deviates from this standard. This may be viewed as a violation of the treaty obligation or an extreme departure from the longstanding interpretation of this norm.

The second scenario may be more promising because the extent of double taxation found there should be more limited, and the lack of reciprocation may result in a more welcoming environment for compromise in cases where clear double taxation is apparent. Yet, this is merely a speculation and pragmatically cannot be guaranteed in advance. A particularly problematic issue would be the deviation from the arm's length standard by only one of the parties to a tax treaty.

Moreover, this scenario is very similar to a more comprehensive international tax reform proposal that has been promoted and considered seriously over the last half of a century in the United States, namely the repeal of deferral. Much has been written on the merits of repealing deferral, yet it has failed to become law due to political pressures by industry, using the recently popularized "competitiveness" argument. Additionally, it was argued that it would be difficult to enforce such a reform since it would be costly and sometimes impossible to obtain and accurately account for the information required from the various foreign subsidiaries behind the corporate and foreign veils. Repealing deferral, however, is not identical to the above scenario because it does not affect a transfer pricing issue where, for instance, the U.S. taxpayer involved is a subsidiary rather than a parent corporation and the parent corporation's country of residence does not repeal deferral itself. Nonetheless, one could argue that unilateral adoption of formulary apportionment of the variety described above could meet the same political resistance to repealing deferral because of the similar consequences of both reforms.

Consequently, it is unlikely that the United States would choose this maximal solution if it were to unilaterally adopt formulaic transfer pricing. The alternative to this rule would be to return to a formula based on factors that may seem reasonable or fair in their division of the contested income between the competing jurisdictions. It has been convenient for commentators to use the familiar states' factors in this context; yet, this line of thought had suppressed the debate because it was exposed to the response that the world countries will never agree on one formula. The conflicting interests of various countries matter differently; however, when a country such as the United States wishes to unilaterally implement a formula that will be based on such factors in order to measure income of its taxpayers who are multinational enterprises, is a powerful step in achieving global formulary apportionment. It was already demonstrated that a maximizing formula is unlikely to succeed, so the United States in this situation needs a formula that will be perceived as sufficiently fair or reasonable, yet still beneficial to it.

It follows therefore that such formula cannot be designed with only narrow enforcement effectiveness in mind. Some important contributions to the formulary apportionment policy literature attempted to support a supposedly practical approach, resulting in proposals to adopt an assets-only or sales-only formula which is unlikely to be tolerated by other countries in this specific scenario. A first step in this analysis should be to assess what factors benefit and what factors hurt the United States. Since this would be a unilateral and singular rule, the appropriate approach would be to examine the position of the United States *vis-à-vis* all of its trade partners.[61] Bilateral deviations are possible, and maybe even welcome, yet this will be discussed in the next section.

If what matters is to have a relatively simple formula that would work in all cases, and most importantly would be perceived as fair, a direct 1/3 sales, 1/3 payroll and 1/3 assets formula could be used as a starting point. This would have to be applied on a worldwide basis and use a line-drawn threshold for "looking through." Several basic adjustments and anti-abuse mechanisms must be established. First, the difficult case of intangibles must be solved because it is one of the primary mechanisms to shift income away from the United States and one of the easier to manipulate. The strength of the United States and one of its primary hopes for sustained growth depends on the strength of research done in the United States and management conducted from the United States. Therefore, a mechanism to account for it should be established. One example could be similar to the rule we already have for accounting for research and development expenses. This means that, for example, if a firm's research and development activity takes place primarily within the United States, the portion of its domestic intangible assets (one way to account for it would be total value minus the more easily valuated assets, including primarily tangible property) should be 50%, plus the domestic ratio of its sales. Other assets could be allocated by location if that information is sufficiently clear. This could be made a rebuttable presumption, left for taxpayers to demonstrate that a larger portion of their intangible assets duly belong to foreign members of their group. Similarly, management activity within the United States should be accounted for. Much debate surrounded a potential reform of the residence test for U.S. corporations to include a subjective element that would account for management activity in the United States. Regardless of the outcome of that debate, there is

---

61. For illustrative purposes we will take a static approach, yet a more sophisticated, dynamic analysis is more appropriate.

no question that much of the intangible value of multinationals is derived from their "minds"—their management teams that in the case of United States and U.S. related multinational enterprises all reside and operate within the United States with little willingness to relocate. This could be incorporated into the formula in a similar manner that research and development is. Finally, particular manipulations should be addressed by particular anti abuse rules or a general one, although the latter has historically been frowned upon in the United States.

This formula is superior to the single factor formulae because it should be easier to present as fair and transparently arbitrary. The last mentioned adjustments and any anti abuse rules that are indeed fair should be more palatable to our trade partners even if they chose not to cooperate with the United States and adopt formula based transfer pricing rules.

Another approach could be even more surgical, i.e., deal with particular types of income separately. This is quite similar to the proposal of Avi-Yonah and Benshalom to introduce formulary apportionment only in the area of intangibles and keep the traditional arm's length methods intact otherwise.[62] I have little quarrel with this pragmatic approach and I think that it works well within the framework of the discussion in this chapter. Similarly, recent voices out of the U.S. government and the OECD have been advocating an introduction of even more formulaic elements into the transfer pricing rules, and primarily encourage the use of profit splits. My only concern with these proposals is that keeping arm's length and the rhetoric in support of its literal version has proven very resistant to change, and I would be worried that unless a comprehensive and fundamental reform is implemented, the positive changes may remain hostage to such rhetoric as it has been to date.

A unilateral reform may or may not be designed to attract other trade partners to join in and adopt formulary apportionment. The biggest economies are the largest victims of transfer pricing abuse, so they all have a basic interest to cooperate. Yet, of course, political issues may prevent this course from materializing. Nonetheless, if the U.S. government predicts that others are likely to follow its lead and adopt formulary apportionment, more careful consideration of this possibility should be made in the design of the initial formula. If successful, a small group of important economies can be very influential in leading a larger, if slower and gradual, shift away from arm's length. The rise to domination of arm's length itself is probably the best historic precedent which demonstrates the feasibility of such an evolution.

8.4.2   A Bilateral Approach

A bilateral (or small scale multilateral) approach could be an extension of the unilateral approach discussed above. The biggest benefit of this approach is in its increased legitimacy and momentum. Technically, a bilateral approach would

---

62. Avi-Yonah & Benshalom, *supra* note 9.

be an easier method for cooperating countries to implement in overcoming the challenge that the introduction of formulary apportionment presents to existing tax treaties. They could simply agree that between themselves arm's length is not the overarching interpretation standard in cases of transfer pricing related disputes.

A different approach would be to stay within the boundaries of the current international tax regime and limit the difficulties presented by a unilateral approach only to cases involving nontreaty countries, while addressing relationships between treaty countries in a more collaborative manner. Practically, this would mean amending or even renegotiating the tax treaties since formulaic solutions do not sit well with the current treaty regime, and are possibly incompatible with current Article 9 of the OECD Model. Theoretically, a treaty partner may consent to the United States switching to a formulaic transfer pricing regime without reforming its own system, yet this seems problematic and unstable. Consequently, the parties should agree to adopt their own formula. Note that due to tax treaties' elective nature such treaty formulae should be backed by domestic rules that will make sure that the treaty solution is not effectively abandoned.

An interesting option would be to have a benchmark formula for domestic purposes and to negotiate a treaty formula or to find a compromise between the treaty partner's version of arm's length and the U.S.' formula, separately with countries willing to negotiate. At first glance this seems very "messy," and in most situations (those that involve more than two countries) over or under taxation may be prevalent in the beginning of the process. This risk, however, seems exaggerated to me since productive countries, and particularly countries in which multinational enterprises effectively reside, are all struggling already with massive under and over taxation under our supposedly harmonized arm's length based regime. The reason for their relative inaction is the stubborn resistance to change in the OECD, led by the United States.

8.4.3   A MULTILATERAL SOLUTION

This is where most of the discourse to date has taken place. The two primary questions are what formula should be adopted and how may such multilateral adoption be realized. This issue is beyond the scope of this chapter since my basic assumption is that it would be unlikely to expect such action in the short term. Yet, many commentators, including myself, have written about the necessity of some form of an international forum for cooperation and coordination of tax policies. The questions discussed in this chapter would be a natural content to be considered and acted upon by such forum and could be one of the initial areas where cooperation and coordination would make the most sense if a gradual approach is to be taken in a multilateral setting. Again, the evolution to dominance of arm's length methodology through the empowerment of the OECD in the current international tax regime serves as the best historical precedent for this eventuality of a formulary apportionment dominated regime to be realized.

8.5 CONCLUSION

This chapter discussed a potential reform of our arm's length based transfer pricing rules, replacing them with a formula based regime. It focused on this reform separately from a more comprehensive reform of the international business tax regime from our source based rules to a formula based regime. A key theme of this chapter is that much of the criticism of formulary apportionment proposals disappears or is weakened when we limit the debate in this manner. Moreover, a reform of our transfer pricing rules is more important and necessary in the short term. Absent a reform, changes are introduced in an ad hoc manner and are taken hostage to the rhetoric of the literal arm's length standard which is the fundamental problem with the current regime in the first place.

A prescriptive reform is beyond the scope of this chapter, and it is realistically too dependent on many political elements, domestic and international, to be realistic at this stage. Yet, this chapter discussed several scenarios under which such reform could take place. It attempted to demonstrate that some of the brakes put on such reform may be unjustifiable. In particular, it concludes that it is both advantageous and possible for the United States to introduce formula based transfer pricing rules unilaterally. The article discussed the manner in which this could be done and potential response by the U.S.' trade partners. It stressed the importance of a perceivably fair formula and of transparence for the success of such a move.

The benefits of any reasonable formula-based reform of our transfer pricing rules include simplification and significant reduction of both compliance and enforcement costs resulting from transfer pricing. This does not mean that elaborate rules and, particularly, anti-abuse mechanisms are not required, yet if these rules and mechanisms are reasonably targeted at actions that very few can justify as acceptable, they could be worked into the system with no significant increase in its administrative costs. The primary challenge of this reform is opposition of the largest corporate groups in the country and their advocates, yet this opposition will be apparent regardless of the content of an international tax reform. At present, the U.S. government is starving for revenue and is facing a multi-trillion dollar deficit while these American corporate groups "sit" on an estimated over 2 trillion dollars of cash in Ireland, a large portion of which was generated by simple transfer pricing manipulation. Reform, therefore, is imminent and a thoughtful, balanced and honest reform should take into account the points made by this chapter and any additional research and commentary that shall follow.

Part III
A Comparative Perspective

Chapter 9

The EU proposed CCCTB—Some Tax Treaty Issues[*]

Kees van Raad[1]

9.1 INTRODUCTION

Companies that engage in cross-border business activities within the European Union (EU) will frequently be subject to corporate income taxation in more than one EU Member State (MSs). This typically happens when a multinational company operates in different countries through subsidiaries or branches (permanent establishments). If the territory of all EU Member States combined were a single tax jurisdiction, the income of a corporate group and its individual member companies operating within the EU would be subject to the same tax rules. And, if under those rules it would be permitted to file a consolidated return for the group companies combined, things would even be still easier. The current reality, however, is quite different. In each EU MS where a group has tax presence in the form of one or more subsidiaries or branches, a tax return must be filed. That involves the application of different tax rules, discussions with different tax administrations, appeals to different administrative organs and courts, etc. Further, transactions among the group companies may raise transfer pricing issues and

---

[*] This contribution was completed in February 2011.
[1] Professor of international tax law, University of Leiden. Chairman, International Tax Center Leiden.

Yariv Brauner & Martin James McMahon, Jr. (eds), *The Proper Tax Base: Structural Fairness from an International and Comparative Perspective—Essays in Honour of Paul McDaniel*, pp. 179–186.
© 2012 Kluwer Law International BV, The Netherlands.

reorganizations within the group may result in (capital gains) taxation for the companies and/or shareholders involved, whereas similar transactions and reorganizations within the same tax jurisdiction will often not give rise to transfer pricing issues respectively will qualify for deferral of capital gains taxation. And, moreover, losses of one group company can, as a rule, not be used by group companies in another country.

One of the economic aims of the European Union is to create a level playing field for companies operating across national boundaries within the EU. The 2009 Treaty on the Functioning of the European Union (TFEU) and its predecessors (the latest one being the European Community Treaty) have granted the EU Member States a high degree of autonomy with respect to income taxation. Apart from the few Directives that have been issued in the area of company taxation, the tax sovereignty of EU Member States is effectively restricted only by the freedom of movement rules of the TFEU. While these rules have been interpreted quite broadly by the Court of Justice of the EU (ECJ), they only apply to cross-border income. If a multinational company operates in a large number of EU Member States through individual subsidiaries, many tax issues that may arise will concern domestic issues of these subsidiaries and will therefore be beyond the reach of the fundamental freedom provisions of the TFEU. At the same time it is obvious that a company that operates in different EU Member States through a host of subsidiaries encounters an overall administrative burden that will greatly exceed the burden faced by a similar company operating with the same number of subsidiary companies in a large single country.

Since the very beginning of the EU and its predecessors various attempts have been made to harmonize corporation taxation within the EU. In the early years efforts were made to harmonize the taxation in respect of corporate distributions: the 1963 Neumark Report (split-rate system: different tax treatment and distributed and retained earnings), the 1970 Van den Tempel Report (classical system), and the 1975 European Commission proposal for a partial imputation system with a corporation income tax rate band of 45%–55%. After the failure of these various attempts, the European Commission came up in 1988 with a draft Proposed Directive for harmonization of the tax base of the corporation income tax, but also this initiative met a similar fate. Rather than proposing harmonization, the 1992 Ruding Report suggested an "approximation" of the tax base (and a rate band of 30%–40%). After also this attempt failed, the European Commission called in 2001 for, in the longer term, a consolidated corporate tax base for EU-wide activities of multinational enterprises. Within that perspective four options were examined: Home State Taxation (HST), Common Consolidated Base Taxation (CCBT), European Corporate Income Tax (EUCIT) and compulsory harmonization of existing corporate tax bases.

Various political organs within the EU supported different options (e.g., the European Parliament: HST, the Council of Ministers (ECOSOC): a compulsory harmonized base). Also a discussion emerged whether the International Financial Reporting Standards ("IFRS," adopted by the International Accounting Standards Board and based on a 2001 predecessor: the International Accounting Standards (IAS)) could be used as a starting point for a common tax base. In 2003 the conclusion was reached that a Common Consolidated Corporate Base Taxation (CCCBT) was the only balanced way forward and in 2004 the Council of Ministers agreed to establish a CCCTB Working Party.

With ups and downs and occasional pauses this Working Group has been operating since. A Commission-proposed CCCTB Directive was scheduled to be released in 2008. After various delays, a proposal will be released in March 2011 (i.e., before the publication of this Festschrift but after the submission of this contribution to it). It is not unlikely that some of the details that are discussed below, will come out differently in the proposed Directive.

9.2   A VERY BRIEF OUTLINE OF THE PROPOSED
           CCCTB RULES

The proposed CCCTB will in the first place be available on an optional basis for multinational enterprises (MNEs) that are based within the EU.[2] Such enterprises will have the choice to apply the rules of the EU CCCTB regime or to continue to be subject to the national corporation income tax systems of the individual EU MSs. In the CCCTB regime EU-rules will apply to compute the tax base that comprises the EU-wide income of these MNEs. These rules apply to opting CCCTB group members: the EU parent company together with its $50+\%$ subsidiaries and its permanent establishments (PEs). Where a group company is controlled (in terms of voting rights) for at least 75%, its profits and losses (along with the profits and losses of group PEs) are included in a consolidated base. This base (the balance of the individual profits and losses of all of the group's companies and permanent establishments) is divided among the MSs of these companies and PEs on the basis of a formula (cf. the apportionment key used in the United States to allocate to the individual U.S. States for state tax purposes the income of U.S. companies that operate in more than a single state within the U.S.). Individual EU Member States will retain the unrestricted right to set the tax rate to be applied to the income share of the group's consolidated income attributed to that state.

To avoid a veto from the EU Member States that are strongly opposed to the introduction of a CCCTB (such as the U.K. and Ireland), on the basis of a particular rule of the TFEU it will be probably be proposed that individual EU MSs are not obliged to endorse the CCCTB system for companies and PEs within their territory; they may choose to continue to exclusively apply their own corporation tax system. It is hoped, however, that after the CCCTB has made a start with a (pilot) group of EU MSs (CCCTB-MSs) and its advantages have been demonstrated, other MSs will follow.

---

2. The CCCTB regime is also available for group companies and PEs that are controlled by a non-EU parent but only to the extent these companies and PEs are within the EU MSs that have opted for applying the CCCTB regime.

9.3 SOME ISSUES UNDER TAX TREATIES

9.3.1 INTRODUCTION

Under the proposed rules the consolidated tax base will be divided among the CCCTB States on the basis of a formula. As an apportionment of that base among the individual group companies will likely come out differently from a division based on the arm's length rule laid down in tax treaties, an issue arises in cases where with regard to an EU company with income from a non-EU country that has a tax treaty with the residence state of the EU company concerned, that residence state's CCCTB-share of the foreign income exceeds the amount thereof determined at an arm's length basis as laid down in that treaty. By taxing its CCCTB-share the EU residence country will tax a larger amount that the (arm's length) amount it is permitted to tax under the tax treaty. Where such an issue arises among participating CCCTB MSs, these countries are required under the TFEU treaty rules to adjust their tax treaty provisions to accommodate the allocation under the CCCTB rules. This is different where companies belonging to a CCCTB-group derive income from outside the EU. It is also different where companies from outside the EU derive income from a company that is a member of a CCCTB-group.

To illustrate these issues, the case will be analyzed of a CCCTB group that derives income through companies in two EU MSs that have joined the CCCTB system: MS-C1 with resident company C1-Corp and MS-C2 with resident company C2-Corp. One of these companies is assumed to receive income (e.g., business income, interest income) from outside the EU. Also the reverse case will be considered: O-Corp is residing in State O outside the EU (and is outside the scope of the CCCTB system) and is assumed to receive an interest payment from one of these two CCCTB companies.

9.3.2 A CCCTB COMPANY RECEIVES INTEREST INCOME FROM OUTSIDE THE EU

This case involves in the first place taxation of the interest income by non-EU State O and the restriction imposed on that taxation by the treaty between State O and MS-C1. Further, there is an issue regarding the double taxation relief to be granted by MS-C1 (and perhaps also by MS-C2).

9.3.2.1 Double Taxation

To begin with the double taxation relief issue: in early draft CCCTB-proposals of the European Commission it was suggested that the CCCTB regime apply a water's edge approach. In that approach, all foreign income would be eliminated from the CCCTB and thereby would not give rise to any issues. In the worldwide income taxation approach that was later taken, however, the CCCTB regime has no such restriction anymore and need to include rules that provide for (juridical) double taxation relief.

In the most recent proposal it is indicated that for foreign *passive income* (juridical) double taxation relief will be provided in the form of a foreign tax credit. With regard to foreign *active income*, an exemption method is proposed. It is not fully clear whether this exemption will be an "income exemption" or a "tax exemption."[3] In an *income exemption* approach both profits and losses are eliminated from the CCCTB. Alternatively, if a *tax exemption* is applied (like The Netherlands does in its treaties and unilateral relief rules) foreign losses are taken into account (with later recapture) as this type of exemption is effected by "exempting" from tax collection the amount of tax that is (proportionally) attributable to the foreign income.

If the choice is made for an income exemption relief system, companies that now operate under treaties that allow for either a foreign tax credit or a tax exemption will be worse off as foreign losses will not (temporarily) be taken into account anymore. If the relief will take the form of a tax exemption another issue arises: in the (later) year in which the recapture takes place the apportionment factors will be different from those of the year in which the loss was suffered, with the result of a distortion among the CCCTB countries with regard to, on the one hand, the revenue loss suffered from their share in the foreign loss deducted in the year the loss occurs and, on the other hand, the benefit they later derive from the income addition when the loss is recaptured.

9.3.2.2   Treaty Application by the Third-Country State O

If State O has concluded tax treaties with both MS-C1 and MS-C2, income that C1-Corp receives from State O will be taxed by that state on the basis of its tax treaty with MS-C1. The fact that MS-C1 and MS-C2 have shared and redistributed the amounts of income the group derived from those countries will be no reason for State O to change in any way its application of the tax treaty it has concluded with MS-C1.

9.3.2.3   Treaty Application by CCCTB States MS C1 and MS C2

The issue here is that, while MS-C1 is the residence state of the legal recipient of, e.g., interest income derived from State O, the income is shared among C1-Corp and C2-Corp. The question therefore arises whether for purposes of the tax treaties that State O has concluded with MS-C1 and MS-C2, the amount of income attributed to C2-Corp under the CCCTB-rules as applied by the latter two states, should be recognized as income of indeed C2-Corp (and not of C1-Corp). This issue has a

---

3. In international literature often no strict distinction is made between the two types of exemption. The two distinctive features (foreign losses, effect of graduated tax rates) are often viewed as possible "add-ons" to an (income) exemption system. In the Commission papers reference is made to "exemption" without further qualification.

certain similarity with the divergence in income attribution of income of hybrid partnerships and the question arises whether a solution should be found along the lines developed in the 1999 OECD Partnership Report.

9.3.3   THIRD-COUNTRY COMPANY CORPORATION O DERIVES INCOME FROM CCCTB STATES MS-C1 AND MS-C2

Next, issues will be examined that arise when Corp O receives income from CCCTB states. As will be shown below, such income may or may not give rise to CCCTB issues, depending on the circumstances.

9.3.3.1   No Issue in Case of Income from Single Business Activity

When Corp O is active in CCCTB area only through a single business activity (a PE-operation or a subsidiary) for which it is taxable there, no CCCTB tax issue arises as there is no income shared with another CCCTB company or PE and redistributed among them.

9.3.3.2   Multiple Active Income Items

If Corp O, in addition to deriving e.g., PE-income from MS-C1, derives PE-income from MS-C2 or has a subsidiary resident in MS-C2, it will be subject to the CCCTB regime. Various issues arise.[4]

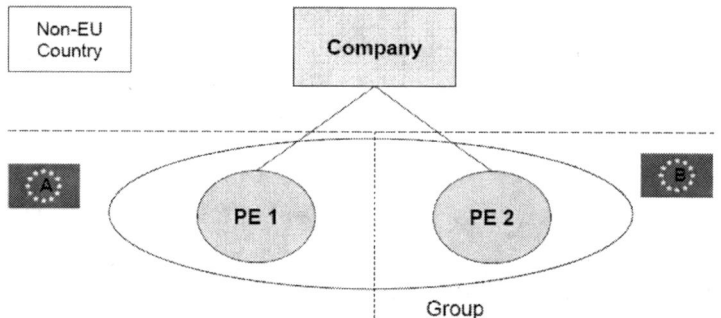

Let us assume that the income attributable under the arm's length rule of the tax treaties that State O has concluded with MS-C1 and MS-C2 amount to e.g., 40 and 60. Under the CCCTB formula application, however, of the total of 100 e.g., 80 is attributed to the MS-C1 PE and 20 to the MS-C2 PE. MS-C1 will violate Article 7

---

4. The picture below is taken from section 88 of paper European Commission paper CCCTB/ WP/057.

of its treaty with State O if it consequently taxes 80 (instead of 40). It appears unlikely that the position (taken by the European Commission in its document WP 26, pt. 34) that the formula income allocation is recognized by Article 7(4) (indirect method) of the 2008 OECD Model,[5] can be accepted.

The same issue arises if one of the PEs is replaced by a subsidiary:

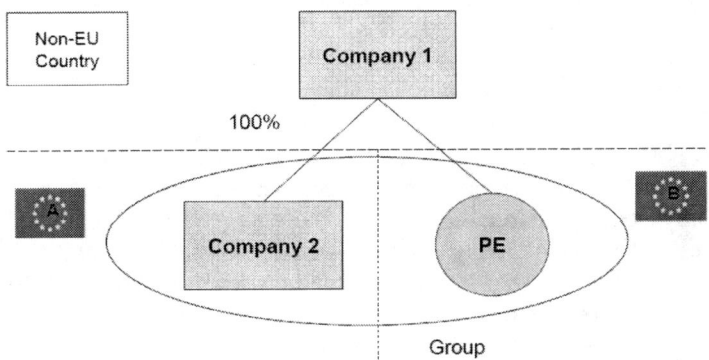

Here, in respect of the subsidiary, Article 9 OECD Model will have the same effect as Article 7 has for the PE, and the issue outlined above arises here in a comparable setting.

Similar issues arise when in the first of the two cases above, through one of the PEs a loss is suffered (e.g., 40 vis-à-vis +60 income in the other CCCTB state). If the loss-state as a result of the formula application is attributed a profit, State O will claim a violation of Article 7.2.

9.3.3.3   Passive income

We assume that O Corp receives an interest payment from C1-Corp. As C1-Corp and C2-Corp are CCCTB group companies, should the interest be treated as paid on the basis of the apportionment (e.g., 40–60) by each of the two companies? If yes:

(a) is source country taxation of the interest nevertheless controlled exclusively by the (CCCTB-harmonized) domestic law (regarding tax liability of nonresident companies) of MS-C1 as residence state of payor C1-Corp and MS-C1's tax treaty with State O? *or*

(b) is it controlled for only 40% by the treaty rules of MS-C1 and for the remaining 60% by the treaty rules of MS-C2?

---

5. Interestingly, in the overhaul of Art. 7 in the 2010 update of the OECD Model, para. 4 was deleted.

In case *b*, what if the treaty rules result in a tax amount that is larger than the amount that would arise under the domestic and treaty rules of MS-C1 (e.g., treaty withholding rate in MS-C1's treaty with State O is lower than that rate in MS-C2's treaty with State O, or treaty rates in both states are the same (e.g., 10%) but MS-C1 does not tax outgoing interest whereas State MS-C2does)?

It could perhaps be argued that State O may claim under its treaty with MS-C1 that only MS-C1's rules be applied, and that the above scenario does not apply.

9.4 CONCLUSION

The analysis above highlights some of the tax treaty issues that may arise in the application of the CCCTB regime in cases where income is earned by a group company from a source outside the EU and where a non-EU company earns income from within the CCCTB area. Creativity on the side of the EU and flexibility on the side of non-EU states are required to overcome these difficulties. It is important that these cross-border issues are solved as their solution will control whether CCCTB has a future. And CCCTB needs to have a future as the alternative systems for reducing the current tax burdens and drawbacks of cross-border business operations within the EU pose political challenges that may be even greater to overcome.

Chapter 10

Shared Legal Orders: Some Thoughts about the Influence of EU Case Law on International Tax Law Rules of the EU Member States

*Irene J.J. Burgers**

10.1   INTRODUCTION

Paul McDaniel and I shared a mutual interest in differences in legal culture and international tax law. Several times we discussed what would be best— exemption or credit, arm's length or formulary apportionment. Paul spent a year of his life in the Netherlands where he did research in amongst others the international tax law of the Netherlands. In a speech held in Groningen on Legal Culture and International Tax in 2008 he stressed the differences between the tax culture of the United States and that of the Netherlands, which is reflected amongst others in the choices for methods to prevent double taxation. The Netherlands applies the exemption method for the avoidance of double taxation in respect of active income, as this method does not disturb the choice of companies whether to invest in or outside their country of residence.

*   Professor of International and European Tax Law, Faculty of Law and Professor of Economics of Taxation, Faculty of Economics and Business, University of Groningen, the Netherlands.

Yariv Brauner & Martin James McMahon, Jr. (eds), *The Proper Tax Base: Structural Fairness from an International and Comparative Perspective—Essays in Honour of Paul McDaniel*, pp. 187–209.
© 2012 Kluwer Law International BV, The Netherlands.

The United States favors the credit method amongst others because this method prevents tax avoidance through investments in low tax countries. Paul also reflected on the differences in tax culture in respect of transfer pricing. The Netherlands is a small country with an open economy and a legal culture that considers the most important aim of a legal system is to provide equality. This is the reason why it values open norms. In respect of transfer pricing the general view is that this aim can best be achieved by applying the arm's length principle. Paul, being an advocate of formulary apportionment, explained that for larger states having a legal culture that highly values legal certainty and prevention of tax avoidance formulary apportionment may be the better choice.

In this chapter I will focus on the topics of our mutual interests—methods to prevent double taxation and transfer pricing legislation—from the perspective of shared legal orders—domestic law, international tax law and EU tax law. I do not intend though to elaborate on the issues I discussed with Paul regarding whether the exemption method or the credit method should be preferred.[1] Nor do I intend to discuss the merits or demerits of the arm's length method and formulary apportionment.[2] The aim of this chapter is to explore how the case law of the European Court of Justice (ECJ) concerning the application of the exemption method, as well as concerning transfer pricing, influences the power of the Member States to fill in the details of both exemption and transfer pricing in their domestic and international tax law and to reflect on the question whether it might be recommended to apply the rules developed by the ECJ in these cases not only in an EU context but also beyond. In respect of the exemption method only the case law concerning the application of this method to business income will be discussed.

---

1. For a discussion of capital import neutrality versus capital export neutrality see, e.g., R. Griffith, J. Hines & P.B. Sørensen, "International Capital Taxation," prepared for the Report of a Commission on Reforming the U.K. Tax system for the 21st Century, chaired by Sir James Mirrlees, ifs.org.uk/mirrleesreview and W. Schön, "International Tax Coordination for a Second-Best World (Part I)," *World Tax Journal* (October 2009): 79–82. For a discussion of proposals to introduce the exemption method in the United States see J.C. Fleming & R.J. Peroni, "Exploring the Contours of a Proposed U.S. Exemption (Territorial Tax System)," *Tax Notes International*, 41 (2006): 217–240. For a discussion whether within the European Market the exemption method or the credit method should be preferred see C. Bardini, "The Ability to Pay in the European Market: An Impossible Sudoku for the ECJ," *Intertax* 38, no. 1 (2010): 8–9. This author argues that the exemption method is to be preferred as it better ensures neutrality of taxation with regard to personal and business decisions, though the credit method has as advantage that it is more suitable for overcoming disparities, dislocations and double dipping.
2. Numerous articles have been published on this issue. See for recent publications on this issue from an OECD perspective, e.g., R.S. Avi-Yonah, "Between formulary apportionment and the OECD Guidelines: a proposal for reconciliation," *World Tax Journal* 2, no. 1 (2010): 3–18 and for some reflections on arm's length versus formulary apportionment in the light of the U.S. cost sharing regime Y. Brauner, "Cost Sharing and the Acrobatics of Arm's Length Taxation," *Intertax* (2010): 554 et. seq. Paul McDaniel elaborated on "NAFTA and Formulary Apportionment: An exploration of the Issues," in *Essays on International Taxation*, ed. H. Alpert & K. Van Raad (Deventer, the Netherlands: Kluwer Law International, 1993), also published in *Intertax* 1994/3.

Before focusing on specific case law concerning exemption and credit in section 2, the standards, principles, and tests concerning the powers of the Member States to develop rules, both in their domestic legislation as in a bilateral or multilateral context, will be summarized. These standards, principles and tests underlie the decisions described in sections 3 and 4.

In section 3, the ECJ *Lidl Belgium* and *Krankenheim* cases, decided in 2008, and two cases of the German Federal Finance Court (the Bundesfinanzhof (BFH)) decided in 2010, will be discussed concerning the question whether the exemption method as applied by Germany to a permanent establishment income derived in another Member State in the tax year in question restricted the freedom of establishment in the light of TFEU Article 49 (TEC Article 43) providing for freedom of establishment.[3] Moreover the *Stahlwerk Ergste Westig GmbH* case concerning the application of the exemption method in case of a permanent establishment of a German limited liability company situated in the United States will be presented. As the permanent establishment in this case was situated in a non-EU Member State the freedom of establishment could not be invoked in this case. Therefore this case dealt with the question whether the German rule restricted the free movement of capital (TEC Articles 56–58 (TFEU Articles 63–65)). The scope of the provisions concerning free movement of capital is broader in that in principle all restrictions to the free movement of capital and payments are abolished not only between Member States, but also between Member States and third States.

Section 4 reflects on transfer pricing. Tax treaties generally require arm's length treatment. This principle often, but not always, is codified in domestic legislation. Some states, such as Belgium, provide for specific anti-abuse rules in their domestic legislation. In the *SGI* case the ECJ ruled on the question under which circumstances such rules are in conflict with the EU treaty.

---

3. On Dec. 1, 2009 the Treaty of Lisbon entered in force. It amends the EU's core treaties:

   – The Treaty of Rome signed on 25 March 1957, as amended by several later treaties (the Treaty establishing the European Community (TEC)). Since the entering into force of the Lisbon Treaty this treaty is renamed the Treaty on the Functioning of the European Union;
   – The Treaty of Maastricht signed on 7 February 1992, as amended by the treaties of Amsterdam and of Nice (the Treaty on European Union (TEU)). This treaty extended the scope of cooperation between the Member States introducing new forms of co-operation between the Member States besides economic and social cooperation. Between 1993 and 1 December 2009 the European Union legally consisted of three pillars:
     o The European Community having legal personality dealing with economic, social and environmental policies
     o Common Foreign and Security Policy handling foreign policy and military matters
     o Police and Judicial Co-operation in Criminal Matters dealing with amongst others immigration and law enforcement.

   With the Treaty of Lisbon entering into force, both treaties have the same legal rank. The European Union moreover acquired legal personality and the pillar structure has been removed.

   For more information and the text of these treaties, see http://www.citizensinformation.ie/en/government_in_ireland/european_government/eu_law/lisbon_treaty/structure_of_the_treaties_governing_the_eu.html.

Each of the cases shows that Member States may provide for specific rules in their domestic legislation, but only if certain conditions are fulfilled. Section 5 contains a wrap up of the standards, principles and tests that follow from the case law described in this chapter. Section 6 contains some thoughts on transplanting these ECJ standards, principles, and tests in the OECD Commentary. Section 7 contains the conclusion.

10.2   STANDARDS DEVELOPED BY THE ECJ CONCERNING
            THE POWERS OF THE MEMBER STATES

EU legislation restricts the freedom of the Member States to develop rules both in their domestic legislation as in a bilateral or multilateral context. In several cases the ECJ clarified that:

(i) Member States retain the freedom to determine the basis of assessment and rate of tax applied to company profits. However, that power is not without limits. The Member States must exercise their powers in the field of direct taxation in accordance with Community law.[4]

(ii) Member States are in the absence of unifying or harmonizing measures adopted in the Community competent to determine:
– the criteria for taxation of income and wealth with a view to eliminating double taxation by means, *inter alia*, of international agreements and at liberty, in the framework of bilateral agreements concluded in order to prevent double taxation;
– the connecting factors for the purposes of allocating powers of taxation as between themselves;[5]

(iii) Nevertheless, the Member States as far as the exercise of the power of taxation so allocated is concerned, may not disregard Community rules.[6] The rules may not discriminate towards nationality or restrict the free movement of people, goods, services and capital, nor the freedom of establishment. Foreign nationals and companies must be treated in the host Member State in the same way as nationals of that State and the Member State of origin may not hinder the establishment in another Member State of one of its nationals or of a company incorporated under its legislation. However discrimination or a restriction may be justified by overriding reasons in the public interest provided its application is appropriate to ensuring the attainment of the objective in question and does not go beyond what is necessary to attain it.

---

4. See, e.g., CLT-UFA SA, C-253/02, Apr. 14, 2005, paras. 6–8.
5. See, e.g., Gilly, C-336/96, May 12, 1998, paras. 24 and 30.
6. See, e.g., Saint-Gobain, C-307/97, Sep. 21, 1999.

10.3   THE EXEMPTION WITH PROGRESSION METHOD
             AND EU LAW: THE GERMAN EXPERIENCE

10.3.1   INTRODUCTION

Until 1999 section 2a, paragraph 3 EStG jo. Section 32(b)(1) and (2) EStG (the German income tax law) provided for the "recapture method." The state of residence includes the income to be exempted in the taxable base, but gives up that part of the total tax on worldwide income that is related to the foreign income thus giving material effect to the exemption. In case a p.e.-loss is included in the residence states' tax base the loss will be recaptured in the year that profits arise in the p.e.-state.

The German legislature included this provision in its income tax as it considered:

- the exemption method does not fit in with the principle of residence as this method may result in an overall tax that is higher than the tax that would be levied if the total income would have been derived in Germany;[7] and
- the ruling of the BFH I R 90/79 that due to the exemption method provided for in tax treaties concluded by Germany—that not only applies for positive income but also for negative income—taxpayers were treated less beneficial in cases where a tax treaty applies in comparison to the situation where unilateral rules would be applicable.[8]

In 1999 Germany changed its domestic rules regarding the application of the exemption method thus that since that year p.e.-losses only have consequences for the progressive income tax rate of individuals. This rate is determined on the basis of worldwide income. But the foreign losses no longer are taken into account in calculating the taxable base (section 2a, paragraph 1 EStG).

10.3.2   CASE LAW OF THE ECJ

The ECJ cases described below concern the application of the exemption method to permanent establishment profits in the taxable years 1999 (*Lidl Belgium*) and 1990 (*Krankenheim*). The BFH cases concern the taxable years 1999 (BFH, February 3, 2010, I R 23/09) and 2000/2001 (2.4.2 BFH, June 9, 2010, I R 23/09). The BFH cases further refined the "*Krankenheim*-standard."

Lidl Belgium concerns the question whether the state of residence should include permanent establishment losses in the taxable base. The ECJ decision in *Krankenheim* further clarifies the standards the ECJ applies on permanent

---

7. H. Schaumburg, *Internationales Steuerrecht* 610 (Köln: Verlag Dr. Otto Schmidt, 1998).
8. L. Schmidt, *EstG Einkommensteuergesetz Kommentar*, 29th Auflage 58 (München:Verlag C.H. Beck, 2010).

establishment losses. This case concerned the application of the "always-somewhere principle." Permanent establishment state Austria disallowed loss compensation because under the recapture method the loss had been taken into account in Germany. The BFH had to decide whether this would imply that Germany cannot make use of the recapture.

Under pressure from the European Commission[9]—supported by the judgment of the ECJ of March 29, 2007 in Case C-347/04 (*Rewe Zentralfinanz*[10])—Germany changed section 2a EstG extensively in 2009. This ECJ case and the subsequent change in legislation will not be discussed as they do not concern p.e.-income but a loss incurred due to a write-off. The change in legislation mainly concerns the application of the credit method in nontreaty situations.[11] In the evaluation (section 10.3.5) the standards of EU law developed or applied by the courts in these cases and the way these standards restrict the freedom of Member States to apply the exemption method will be reflected on.

10.3.2.1   *Lidl Belgium*

On May 14, 2008, the ECJ delivered its ruling in *Lidl Belgium*.[12] Lidl Belgium is part of the Lidl and Schwarzgroup having its headquarters in Germany and owning more than 9000 supermarket and department stores throughout Europe.[13] Lidl Belgium carries on business as a distributor of goods, originally on the Belgium market, later on also on the Luxembourg market. Lidl Belgium is a limited partnership with its registered office in Germany. Both the limited partner and the general partner reside in Germany.

The case concerned the taxable year 1999, in which year the Luxembourg permanent establishment incurred a loss. This loss could not be taken into account

---

9.   European Commission Press Release, Oct. 18, 2007. The request takes the form of a "reasoned opinion" (second step of the infringement procedure provided for in Art. 226 of the EC Treaty (hereafter TEC)). If the attacked provisions are not amended in order to comply with the reasoned opinion, the Commission may decide to refer the matter to the European Court of Justice. The European Commission argued that section 2 of the German Income Tax Act as it read before 2009 created a disadvantage and hence an obstacle to establishment in another EU state and the free movement of capital. If the relevant national legislations are not amended in order to comply with the reasoned opinion, the Commission may decide to refer the matter to the European Court of Justice. http://europa.eu/rapid/pressReleasesAction.do?reference=IP/07/1547&format=HTML &aged=0&language=en&guiLanguage=en.

10. This case concerned the preclusion by section 2a EstG of the setting off for tax purposes of losses incurred by a parent company resident in Germany stemming from write-downs to the book value of shareholdings in subsidiaries established in the Netherlands.

11. Since 1999 section 2a, para. 1 EStG provided for limitations regarding the offset and deduction of amongst others permanent establishment losses. For an explanation of these changes see, e.g., F. Haase, *Internationales und Europäisches Steuerrecht* (Heidelberg: C.F. Muller, 2009); and L. Schmidt, *EstG Einkommensteuergesetz Kommentar*, 29th Auflage (München:Verlag C.H. Beck, 2010).

12. ECJ C-414/06.

13. rfkb.retailforward.com/companyprofile.aspx?cid=1086.

in Germany. The Bundesfinanzhof (the German Federal Finance Court) referred the following question to the Court for a preliminary ruling:

> Is it compatible with Articles 43 TEC and 56 TEC for a German company with income from industrial or commercial activities to be precluded, when calculating its income, from deducting losses from a permanent establishment in another Member State (in this case, the Grand Duchy of Luxembourg) on the ground that, according to [the Convention], the corresponding income from such a permanent establishment is not subject to taxation in Germany?[14]

The ECJ ruled that the German exemption with progression method as applicable in 1999 restricts the freedom of establishment:

> [T]he provisions of the EC Treaty concerning freedom of establishment are directed to ensuring that foreign nationals and companies are treated in the host Member State in the same way as nationals of that State . . . [but] they also prohibit the Member State of origin from hindering the establishment in another Member State of one of its nationals or of a company incorporated under its legislation.[15]

The tax situation of a company that has its registered office in Germany and its permanent establishment in another Member State is less favorable than it would be if the latter were to be established in Germany. Thus, a German company could be discouraged from carrying on its business through a permanent establishment situated in another Member State. However, a restriction on the freedom of establishment may be justified by overriding reasons in the public interest, provided its application is appropriate to ensuring the attainment of the objective in question and does not go beyond what is necessary to attain it.[16]

One of the overriding reasons formulated by the ECJ in earlier cases is the safeguarding of symmetry between the right to tax profits and the right to deduct losses.[17] Another reason accepted by the ECJ is the danger that losses might be taken into account twice.[18] In *Lidl* the ECJ accepted both reasons as justifications. The ECJ stated that:

> [T]he objective of preserving the allocation of the power to impose taxes between the two Member States concerned which is reflected in the provisions of the Convention, is capable of justifying the tax regime at issue in the main proceedings, since it safeguards symmetry between the right to tax profits and the right to deduct losses.[19]

---

14. Article 43 TEC concerns the freedom of establishment and Art. 56 TEC the free movement of capital.
15. Paragraph 19.
16. Paragraph 27.
17. Oy AA, Jul. 18, 2007, C-231/05.
18. Marks & Spencer, Dec. 13, 2005, case C-445/03.
19. Paragraph 33.

In circumstances such as those of the main proceedings to accept that the losses of a non-resident permanent establishment might be deducted from the taxable income of the principal company would result in allowing that company to choose freely the Member State in which those losses could be deducted.[20]

[T]he Member State must be able to prevent such a danger (see Marks & Spencer). . . . [21]

It is possible that a company might deduct, in the Member State in which its seat is situated, losses incurred by a permanent establishment belonging to it and situated in another Member State and that, despite such offsetting, the same losses might be taken into account subsequently in the Member State in which the permanent establishment is situated, when that establishment generates profits, thereby preventing the Member State in which the principal company has its seat from taxing that profit.[22]

Next the ECJ held that it is not in dispute that the tax regime of Germany is appropriate for ensuring the attainment of the objectives pursued by it. Moreover the regime does not go beyond what is necessary to attain it as the loss is not final: Luxembourg tax legislation provided for the possibility of deducting a taxpayer's losses in future tax years for the purposes of calculating the tax base.[23]

10.3.2.2   *Krankenheim*

The *Krankenheim* case[24] concerned the German exemption method as it read before 1999, thus including the recapture.

Krankenheim Ruhesitz am Wannsee-Seniorenheimstatt GmbH is a limited liability company operating a nursing home for elderly people with a psychiatric illness. The company had a permanent establishment in Austria from 1982 to 1994. The case concerns the permanent establishment loss for the taxable year 1990. As this loss had been offset in Germany in 1990, Austria disallowed the offsetting of the loss in Austria in respect of the years 1992 and 1993. In these years the permanent establishment realized profits. Germany recaptured the foreign loss and thus did not provide exemption in the respective years. The ECJ ruled the German legislation subjected resident companies with permanent establishments in Austria to less favorable treatment than that enjoyed by resident companies with

---

20. Paragraph 34.
21. Paragraph 35.
22. Paragraph 36.
23. Paragraphs 43–51. For critical remarks on this decision see amongst others "Opinion Statement of the Task Force on ECJ Cases of the Confederation Fiscale Européene on the Judgement," *European Taxation*, no. 11: 590–596.
24. ECJ Oct. 23, 2008, C-157/07.

permanent establishments situated in Germany.[25] The rules thus are incompatible with Article 31 of the EEA Agreement[26] which article contains similar provisions on freedom of establishment as the EC Treaty. However, the restriction is justified by the need to guarantee the coherence of the German tax system. Moreover, the tax regime is symmetrical, appropriate and entirely proportionate: permanent establishment losses are recaptured only up to the amount of permanent establishment profits in the taxable year. The Court decided:

> [T]he freedom of establishment cannot be understood as meaning that a Member State is required to draw up its tax rules on the basis of these in another Member State in order to ensure, in all circumstances, taxation which removes any disparities arising from national tax rules, given that the decisions made by a company as to the establishment of commercial structures abroad may be to the company's advantage or not, according to the circumstances.[27]

The restriction arises from the allocation of tax competences under the tax treaty in force and is due to the Austrian loss-provisions.

10.3.3   CASE LAW OF THE GERMAN FEDERAL FINANCE COURT (BFH) CONCERNING THE EXEMPTION METHOD AS APPLIED BY GERMANY

The *Krankenheim* standard was refined by the BFH in February 3, 2010, I R 23/09, concerning the taxable year 1995, and BFH, June 9, 2010, I R 23/09, concerning the taxable years 2000 and 2001. In both cases, the permanent establishment state provided for a loss carry-forward for a limited period. In the second case the permanent establishment was liquidated in 2001.

10.3.3.1   BFH, February 3, 2010, I R 23/09

The case concerned a GmbH that was a partner of a Luxembourg partnership. This partnership generated losses in the years 1986 to 1989. Beginning in 1995 the partnership generated profits. The permanent establishment losses could not be off-set in Luxembourg because carry forward of losses was limited to five years.

---

25. This author subscribes to the doubts of Meussen whether the ECJ fully understood the German tax regime applicable in the taxable year in question, 1999. The regime not only provided for the recapture method, but also provided for carry forward of losses in calculating the taxable base. Thus, companies with foreign permanent establishments are not treated less favorably than resident companies not having any foreign permanent establishment. See "The ECJ's Judgement in Krankenheim—The Last Piece in the Cross-Border Loss Relief Puzzle?," *European Taxation*, 49, no. 7 (2009).
26. The EEA Agreement entered into force on Jan. 1, 1994. Austria was a member of the EEA as from that date. Aim of the European Economic Area is to guarantee the free movement of persons, goods, services and capital; to provide equal conditions of competition and to abolish discrimination on grounds of nationality. The ECJ ensures the respect of the Agreement by the EU Member States and organs. Austria joined the EU on Jan. 1, 1995.
27. Paragraph 50.

The taxpayer argued that Germany in such case would breach the freedom of establishment provided by EU law if it would recapture the losses deducted in the years they occurred. The BFH argued against the taxpayer in its decision of June 9, 2010, I R 107/09, as the restrictive provision is needed to ensure the cohesion of the tax system of which it forms part.[28] The restriction is the result of the tax provisions in the permanent establishment state as the Member States remain competent to determine the criteria for taxation of income and wealth with a view to eliminating double taxation by means, *inter alia*, of international agreements in the absence of unifying or harmonizing measures adopted in the Community.[29]

10.3.3.2   BFH, June 9, 2010, I R 23/09

In this case a German resident GmbH had a permanent establishment in France. The case concerned the taxable years 2000 and 2001. In these years France allowed an indefinite carry forward of losses being the result of depreciation and for all other losses limited to five years. Difference with the previous case is that the permanent establishment in this case was liquidated in 2001. The BFH held that:

– the ECJ ruled that it is not incompatible with the freedoms provided in the EC Treaty for a Member State to preclude a company, when calculating its taxable profits, from deducting losses from a permanent establishment in another Member State if these losses can be taken into account in the permanent establishment state in future accounting periods;[30]
– the ECJ held that in the absence of unifying or harmonizing measures adopted in the Community the Member States remain competent to determine the criteria for taxation of income and wealth with a view to eliminating double taxation by means, *inter alia*, of international agreements;[31] and
– the ECJ does not require a Member State to draw up its tax rules on the basis of these in another Member State in order to ensure, in all circumstances, taxation which removes any disparities arising from national tax rules.[32]

However, in this case the permanent establishment has been liquidated, reason why the taxpayer could not take the losses into account in the permanent establishment state in future accounting periods. The BFH referred to the ruling of the ECJ ruled in the case *Marks and Spencer*,[33] concerning refusal by the U.K. tax authorities of Marks and Spencer's claim to offset losses incurred by its Belgian, German, and French subsidiaries in the U.K. (a state allowing group relief). The ECJ ruled in this

---

28. Paragraph 20.
29. Paragraph 21.
30. ECJ May 15, 2008, C-414/06 Case Lidl Belgium.
31. ECJ Sep. 21, 1999, C-307/97, Case Saint Gobain, para. 56 and ECJ Oct. 23, 2008, C-157/07, Krankenheim, para. 48.
32. ECJ Oct. 23, 2008, C-157/07, Case Krankenheim, para. 48.
33. ECJ Dec. 13, 2005, C-446/03.

case "a restrictive measure goes beyond what is necessary to attain the essential part of the objectives pursued" if:

- The nonresident subsidiary has exhausted the possibilities available in its State of residence of having the losses taken into account for the accounting period concerned by the claim for relief and also for previous accounting periods, if necessary by transferring those losses to a third party or by offsetting the losses against the profits made by the subsidiary in previous periods.
- There is no possibility for the foreign subsidiary's losses to be taken into account in its State of residence for future periods whether by the subsidiary itself or by a third party, in particular where the subsidiary has been sold to that third party.[34]

For the case in question this implies that although the tax treaty is symmetrical Germany must allow the p.e.-losses to be deducted in Germany. Other than in *Krankenheim* and in BFH, February 3, 2010, I R 23/09, the restriction is not the result of the provisions of the permanent establishment state, but of the liquidation of the permanent establishment. The losses must be deductible somewhere. Terra and Wattel[35] refer to this principle as the "Always-Somewhere principle." These authors assume the reasoning underlying this principle is that in an internal market it is unacceptable that a taxpayer, solely because of the fact he has used his treaty rights to cross an internal border, loses tax relief which would have been available to him had he not crossed the border.

---

34. Paragraph 55.
35. B. Terra & P.J. Wattel, *European Tax Law*, 5th ed. (Deventer: Kluwer Law International, 2008), 350. These authors refer to the following other cases where the state of residence was obliged to take into account negative items of income allocated by the tax treaty to the other jurisdiction:

    - ECJ Dec. 12, 2002, Case De Groot, C-385/00: the state of residence, the Netherlands, must ensure that the taxpayer will for the full 100% benefit from personal allowances, even though part of the income is allocated to the source state: in this case the exemption with progression as applied by the Netherlands at the time resulted in a 66% disallowance of personal allowances in the Netherlands as 66% of the income was allocated to Germany.
    - ECJ Sep. 18, 2003, Case Bosal Holding, C-168/01: this case concerned the question whether the state of residence of the parent company should allow deduction of financing costs of a nonresident subsidiary which was not subject to tax in the Netherlands if that state provided for a participation exemption and thus does not tax distributions of profits by the subsidiary to the parent company. The ECJ ruled that although Art. 4(2) of the Parent-Subsidiary Directive allows the Member States to disallow such cost deduction, this may not breach the freedom of establishment. The disallowance of cost deduction restricts companies in setting up subsidiaries in other Member States.
    - ECJ Sep. 7, 2006, C-470/04, Case N, C-470/04: the ECJ allowed the Netherlands to levy an exit tax on nonrealized profits from substantial shareholdings by means of a conservatory assessment (no current payment was required, but tax was due at the time the shares were sold to a third party) although in principle such a measure restricts the freedom of establishment as the measure protects the public interest. However, the Netherlands should accept post-emigrational capital losses, even though at the time these losses occur it does not exert any taxing power. Moreover the Netherlands was not allowed to ask for security for the later payment.

Thus, permanent establishment losses must be taken into account in the state of residence of the taxpayer in case of liquidation of the permanent establishment. The BFH moreover mentions two other circumstances, not at stake in the case in question, where permanent establishment losses should be taken into account:

- incorporation of a permanent establishment;
- transfer of the permanent establishment to a third party.[36]

10.3.4   CASE LAW OF THE ECJ REGARDING THIRD COUNTRIES: STAHLWERK ERGSTE WESTIG GMBH[37]

This case, concerning the taxable year 1999, is to a great extent similar to the case *Lidl*. The only difference is that the permanent establishment is located in the United States. Stahlwerk argued that the German exemption with progression method breaches the free movement of capital (Articles 56 and 58 EC = Articles 63 and 65 TFEU). The ECJ ruled that the German exemption with progression method as applied in 1999 restricts the freedom of establishment but not the free movement of capital. Thus the cases described above are of relevance only for internal EU-situations.

10.3.5   EVALUATION

Thus, it is the "Always-Somewhere" principle that restricts the freedom of EU-Member States to develop provisions on prevention of double taxation that is available in international tax law.

The case law shows that Member States applying the exemption method must apply it in such a way that:

- it safeguards symmetry between the right to tax profits and the right to deduct losses and/or prevents losses being taken into account;
- the method is applied in an appropriate and entirely proportionate way.

The principle of freedom of establishment implies that the losses should be deductible "Always-Somewhere" even though the tax system of the state of residence is symmetrical.[38] Thus, permanent establishment losses must be taken into account in the state of residence of the taxpayer in case of:

- liquidation of the permanent establishment;
- incorporation of a permanent establishment;
- sale of the permanent establishment to a third party.

---

36. Paragraph 19.
37. ECJ Nov. 6, 2007, C-415/06.
38. Some states, such as Denmark and France, apply cross-border group treatment.

The rulings of the ECJ in, amongst others, the *Lidl Belgium* and *Krankenheim* cases clearly show that the principle of freedom of establishment as laid down in the EU Treaty does not require the state of origin to treat a foreign permanent establishment similar to a foreign subsidiary (to which the participation exemption may apply): the ECJ does not require the Member States to abolish the recapture method. To this extent the ECJ case law does not restrict the choice of the Member States for a particular variant of the methods to prevent double taxation recommended by OECD and generally applied in tax treaties and unilateral rules for the prevention of double taxation.

However, the "Always-Somewhere principle" does restrict Member States choices. Member States that intend to change their system may limit the application of this principle to permanent establishment losses derived in other Member States. However, they may also feel that the principle should be applied to permanent establishment losses in general, as recent proposals of the Netherlands Secretary of State for Finance and the Study Committee Van Weeghel show.

10.3.6   CHANGE IN DUTCH EXEMPTION METHOD AS FROM JANUARY 1, 2012

Up till January 1, 2012, the Netherlands applied the recapture method for both unilateral and tax treaty purposes. In 2009 for several reasons the Secretary of State for Finance of the Netherlands proposed to replace the recapture method by full exemption, which would imply a major change in the Dutch tax policy. The Secretary of State for Finance justified this major change with the argument that the tax system should not make a distinction towards legal form. Besides that he raised other arguments for the replacement. He referred to the amount of administrative work for both the tax administration and the taxpayers related to the recapture method. Further anti-avoidance rules that proved to be necessary to prevent avoidance could be abolished. Moreover he raised the fundamental argument that it may not be appropriate to take foreign permanent establishment losses into account in the state of residence: the new rules should reflect a "territorial approach" of foreign permanent establishment losses.[39] The replacement of the recapture method by full exemption was supported by the Study-Committee Van Weeghel, a Committee installed by the Minister of Finance of the Netherlands on October 22, 2009 with the task to conduct a preparatory study for a fundamental reform of the income tax system of the Netherlands. In its report published on April 7, 2010 the Committee argued that a shift towards full exemption would prevent tax avoidance and would take away the distinction in treatment of permanent establishment and subsidiary. Moreover the Committee recommended such a shift may result in more tax revenue from which funding required for other changes in the income tax as recommended by the Committee can be financed.

---

39.   Brief Winstbelasting Multinationals 5 December 2009 Vergaderjaar 2009–2010, Kamerstuk 31369 (Letter on Taxes on business profits of Multinationals, December 5, 2009),

Both the Secretary of State for Finance and the Study-Committee Van Wee-ghel mentioned that the shift towards full exemption should not imply that liquidation-losses no longer can be taken into account, as the legislation would be EU-proof. Apparently they did not realize the "Always-Somewhere" principle developed by the ECJ requires an exemption to the full exemption method also in case of incorporation of the permanent establishment or its sale to a third party.

The proposal for replacement of the recapture method was included in the Tax Plan 2012 and is effective as of January 1, 2012. In the Memorandum of Explanation only two of the four arguments used by the Secretary of State for Finance are referred to: taking away a difference in tax treatment of permanent establishments and subsidiaries and the argument that less anti-avoidance legislation is needed.

Contrary to the proposals, the exemption method is changed into full exemption for legal bodies (paying corporate income tax) only. The new legislation is included in Articles 15e–15j Corporate Income Tax Act 1969 (hereafter CIT 1969), whereas the recapture method was and is—for other taxpayers than legal bodies[40]—included in the Decree for the Avoidance of Double Taxation 2001 (the unilateral rule, hereafter Dadt 2001). It contains in total 2239 words, whereas the legislator needed only 776 words for the recapture method (Articles 10–12 Dadt 2001) and 645 words for the anti-avoidance rule laid down in Article 13c CIT 1969.

The legislator realized that more exceptions to the full exemption method would be needed than those proposed by the Secretary of State for Finance and the Study-Committee Van Weeghel: the new legislation is fully in line with the "Always-Somewhere" principle. An exception to the full exemption method is made for losses derived at the time the taxpayer stops to derive profits from the other state (Article 15iCIT 1969). These losses—including liquidation losses, losses derived upon the sale of the permanent establishment to a third party and losses derived upon incorporation of the permanent establishment—will be taken into account in the Netherlands if this is the state of residence. The proposed Article 15i not only applies to permanent establishments in EU-Member States, but to all foreign permanent establishments of taxpayers resident in the Netherlands.

Amongst others Pijl[41] and Bender[42] criticized the proposed legislation, as it is too long and complex, there are technical errors and the underlying aim of the proposed changes could just as well have been achieved by an obligatory recapture e.g., five years after having taken into account the loss in worldwide income.

---

40. Articles 10–12 Dadt 2001 will remain in force for individual taxpayers.
41. H. Pijl, Enkele kanttekeningen bij de objectvrijselling in het Bleastingplan 2012, NTFR 2011/2223.
42. T. Bender, Objectvrijstelling voor buitenlandse winst—waarom eigenlijk?, NTFR 2011/2484.

10.4   TRANSFER PRICING RULES AND EU LAW:
         THE BELGIAN EXPERIENCE

10.4.1   INTRODUCTION

The question whether EU-Member States are restricted by EU law to fill in the details of their domestic transfer pricing legislation was at stake in the SG I case. For allocation purposes most tax treaties contain provisions reading similar to Article 9 of the OECD Model. Several states also included provisions requiring the arm's length principle to be used in their domestic (corporate) income tax legislation. For instance in Germany section 1 AuBensteuregesetz and in the Netherlands Article 8b Vpb "69 require the application of the arm's length principle. In Belgium Article 185 Wetboek van de inkomstenbelastingen 1992 (WIB 92: the Belgian income tax law) contains the codification of the arm's length principle of Article 9 OECD. Moreover, specific anti-avoidance provisions concerning transfer pricing are included in the WIB. One of these anti-avoidance measures is section 26 WIB 92. concerning unusual advantages (*abnormale voordelen*) and gratuitous advantages (*goedgunstige voordelen*). This section defines an unusual advantage as a gain that considering the present economical circumstances and the economic situations of the parties breaches the normal course of things and the principles or customs of business. A gratuitous advantage is defined as an advantage provided without any obligations or other equivalent value. Such unusual and gratuitous advantages provided without any obligations or other equivalent value. Such gains and advantages should be added to the income of the person providing the advantage, unless these advantages would be taken into account in the taxable income of the beneficial. This article to my knowledge was the first transfer pricing article on which the ECJ ruled whether such provision breaches the freedom of establishment in case it is restricted to nonresident tax-payers. In its ruling in the *SGI* case,[43] the ECJ not only upheld this restriction on the EU freedom of establishment. It also held that the EU Arbitration Convention cannot be invoked as justification.

10.4.2   *SGI*[44]

The *SGI* case concerns the tax years 2000 and 2001. The Belgian tax authorities argued that due to section 26 of the Wetboek van de inkomstenbelastingen 1992 (hereafter WIB 92) a company resident in Belgium, SGI, should include amongst others a fictitious interest of 5% on an interest free loan provided to its subsidiary in its taxable base. The Belgian tax administration was of the opinion that the company had provided its subsidiary an unusual advantage (*abnormaal voordeel*) or a gratuitous advantage (*goedgunstig voordeel*).

---

43.   ECJ Jan. 21, 2010, C-311/08.
44.   ECJ Jan. 21, 2010, C-311/08.

The tax administration moreover found management fees paid to SGI's parent company to be unreasonably high and not in proportion to the economic benefit provided by the Luxembourg resident parent for its managing activities, reason why the fees were considered not to be deductible on the basis of the same section. The taxpayer argued section 26 WIB 92 to be in conflict with the freedom of establishment provided in Article 43 EC. The ECJ held that the rule in question restricted the freedom of establishment as the advantages are added to the profits of the resident taxpayer only in case the beneficial company is a resident of another state. However, the restriction could be justified on the basis of two grounds: (1) a balanced allocation between Member States of the power to tax; (2) the prevention of tax avoidance.

The ECJ referred to its rulings in *Marks and Spencer* and *Lidl Belgium* that to give companies the right to elect to have their losses or profits taken into account in the Member State in which they are established or in another Member State could seriously undermine a balanced allocation of the power to impose taxes between the Member States (paragraph 61). It went on to state:

> In the present case, it must be held that to permit resident companies to transfer their profits in the form of unusual or gratuitous advantages to companies with which they have a relationship of interdependence that are established in other Member States may well undermine the balanced allocation of the power to impose taxes between the Member States. It would be liable to undermine the very system of the allocation of the power to impose taxes between the Member States because, according to the choice made by companies having relationships of interdependence, the Member State of the company granting unusual or gratuitous advantages would be forced to renounce its right, in its capacity as the State of residence of that company, to tax its income in favour, possibly, of the Member State in which the recipient company has its establishment . . . .[45]

> By providing that the resident company is to be taxed in respect of an unusual or gratuitous advantage which it has granted to a company established in another Member State, the legislation at issue in the main proceedings permits the Belgian State to exercise its tax jurisdiction in relation to activities carried out in its territory.[46]

In respect of the justification ground of tax avoidance the ECJ referred to its decision in amongst others *Marks and Spencer* (paragraph 57) that national measures restricting the freedom of establishment may be justified:

- where these measures specifically target wholly artificial arrangements designed to circumvent the legislation of the Member State concerned; or
- if the rule has no such specific target it may be justified by the objective of preventing tax avoidance, taken together with that of preserving the

---

45. Paragraph 63.
46. Paragraph 64.

balanced allocation of the power to impose taxes between the Member States if the rule has no such specific target.

The Court concluded that in light of the need to maintain the balanced allocation of the power to tax between the Member States and to prevent tax avoidance, taken together, it must be held that legislation such as that at issue in the main proceedings pursues legitimate objectives which are compatible with the Treaty and constitute overriding reasons in the public interest and appropriate for ensuring the attainment of those objectives.

Finally the ECJ elaborated on the question under which circumstances legislation does not go beyond what is necessary to attain the objectives pursued, taken together. The ECJ stipulated that this is the case if:

1. there is a suspicion that a transaction goes beyond what the companies concerned would have agreed under fully competitive conditions; and

2. the taxpayer is given an opportunity, without being subject to undue administrative constraints to provide evidence of any commercial justification that there may have been for that transaction.[47]

In case the measure goes beyond what the companies concerned would have agreed under fully competitive conditions, the corrective tax measure must be confined to the part which exceeds what would have been agreed if the companies did not have a relationship of interdependence.

The ECJ considered that Belgian tax law offers the taxpayer the opportunity to provide evidence of any commercial justification that there may have been for the transaction in question and that when the authorities persist in their intention of issuing a revised assessment the taxpayer may challenge the assessment to tax before the national courts. In those circumstances the referring court should examine whether there are any administrative constraints, or any commercial justification that there may have been for the transaction.[48]

The justification put forward by the Belgian government that the EC Arbitration Convention strongly diminishes the risk of double taxation was rejected by the ECJ. In order to invoke such procedure requires an extra administrative and economical effort of the taxpayer, whereas the procedure may take years, and thus requires the company to initially finance the extra tax burden. Moreover "decisive influence" as referred to in section 26 WIB 92 may have a broader scope than "associated enterprises" as referred to in the Arbitration Convention. Amongst others a dependent position in respect of raw materials or in the field of technical cooperation and the provision of security also falls under the scope of "decisive influence."

---

47. The ECJ refers to Test Claimants in the Thin Cap Group Litigation, para. 82.
48. Paragraphs 73 and 74. Philip Baker points out that this is not the case in for example the United Kingdom and that this detail on the burden of proof may end up being one of the particularly significant aspects of the case. P. Baker, "Transfer Pricing and Community Law: The SGI Case," *Intertax*, Volume 38, no. 4 (2010): 196.

10.4.3   EVALUATION

Most Member States included transfer-pricing rules in their domestic law. Research by Boone, Casley, van de Gucht and Chatar[49] shows that of the fifteen Member States researched[50] only three Member States do not have specific transfer pricing legislation.[51] Of the other States the level of sophistication differs. SGI will have an impact only on the national provisions of Austria, Germany, Italy and Slovenia.

Nevertheless the ruling is important for other Member States than Belgium as well as it provides some valuable insights on the justification ground that the national measure restricting the freedom of establishment targets wholly artificial arrangements designed to circumvent the legislation of the Member State concerned:

- The need to prevent tax avoidance is a mandatory requirement of public interest under the Court's rule of reason.
- The ECJ defines what are to be considered artificial arrangements: devoid of economic reality, created with the aim of escaping the tax normally due on the profits generate by activities carried out on national territory (paragraph 66).
- The ECJ explains that the justification ground of tax avoidance can be invoked both where the national legislation is specifically designed to exclude from the tax advantage it confers such purely artificial arrangements and where this is not the case. It is sufficient that the legislation at issue is able to prevent such practices.
- It may not be made excessively difficult to enjoy the EC Treaty rights. The taxpayer is allowed to provide evidence of any commercial justification without undue administrative constraints and should be provided with certainty on his tax position in a reasonable time.
- The ECJ sets the standards for determining whether national legislation which provides for a consideration of objective and verifiable elements in order to determine whether a transaction represents an artificial arrangement, entered into for tax reasons goes beyond what is necessary to attain the objectives relating to the need to maintain the balanced allocation of the power to tax between the Member States and to prevent tax avoidance: the commercial justification test.

---

49. P. Boone, A.J. Casley, J. van de Gucht & M. Chatar, "SGI Case: The Impact of the Decision of the European Court of Justice from a European Perspective," *International Transfer Pricing Journal* no. 3 (2010): 183.
50. Austria, Czech Republic, Denmark, Finland, France, Germany, Hungary, Ireland, Italy, Luxembourg, the Netherlands, Poland, Slovenia, Spain and Sweden.
51. Low impact in Austria and Luxembourg. Moderate impact in Chzech Republic, France, Italy and Sweden, high impact in the other countries.

– The ECJ rules the Arbitration Convention cannot be invoked as justification ground as it does not fulfill principles of timeliness, cost efficiency for the taxpayer as well as effectiveness.

10.5	WRAP UP OF ECJ STANDARDS, PRINCIPLES AND TESTS

The case law shows us that Member States are to a great extent free to formulate domestic legislation providing for rules that are applied in an international context. They may even restrict the free movement of taxpayers provided:

– there is an overriding reason in the public interest;
– of which the application is appropriate to ensuring the attainment of the objective in question; and
– it does not go beyond what is necessary to attain it.

Overriding reasons in the public interest in this context are:

– the objective of preserving a balanced allocation of the power to impose taxes since it safeguards symmetry between the right to tax profits and the right to deduct losses;
– the need to preserve the coherence of the tax system; and
– the need to prevent that taxpayers choose freely the Member State in which those losses could be deducted. Member States must be able to prevent such a danger.

A measure does not go beyond what is necessary to attain the objective pursued by it if:

– the "Always-Somewhere" principle is fulfilled;
– there is a suspicion that a transaction goes beyond what companies concerned would have agreed under fully competitive conditions;
– taxpayers are given an opportunity without being subject to undue administrative constraints to provide evidence of any commercial justification"; and
– taxpayers are provided with timely certainty on their tax position.

10.6	SOME THOUGHTS ON TRANSPLANTING THE ECJ STANDARDS, PRINCIPLES AND TESTS IN THE OECD COMMENTARY

10.6.1 INTRODUCTION

Now that the question of what standards, principles, and tests the ECJ developed in its cases concerning the exemption method and concerning transfer pricing rules has been developed, the next question is whether it is recommendable to apply these standards, principles and/or tests in a broader context. An example of such wider application is the full exemption legislation introduced in the Dutch Corporate Income Tax per January 1, 2012. The exception to this method for liquidation losses, losses derived upon the sale of the permanent establishment to a third party and losses derived upon incorporation of the permanent establishment is not confined to EU Member States.

The past decades have shown that international tax law and European tax law influence each other. European tax law uses concepts developed in international tax law, such as permanent establishment, exemption method, and credit method. International tax law incorporated arbitration that proved to be a powerful tool in a European context. The ECJ referred to principles developed in international tax law, more specifically in the OECD Model, in a number of cases. Shared legal orders thus learn from each other.

What may international tax law learn from the *Lidl, Krankenheim, Stahlwerk*, and *SGI* cases, as well as from the cases of the BFH that further refined the ECJ standards?

In my view it may learn from the "Always-Somewhere approach" and from the standards the ECJ developed concerning the commercial justification test and the burden of proof when applying that test.

10.6.2   THE "ALWAYS-SOMEWHERE PRINCIPLE"

Both in international tax law and European tax law states are free to choose which methods will be applied to prevent double taxation. Many states give preference for their resident taxpayers to the worldwide approach, as thus it is possible to take into account the ability to pay, another important principle of tax law. The ability to pay principle has a long history. Adam Smith introduced the principle in his famous book *An Inquiry into the Nature and Causes of the Wealth of Nations* in 1776.[52] He measured the ability to pay by referring to a person's income: positive and negative. The notion that personal circumstances also influence a person's ability to pay was recognized in later literature. Thus, it is submitted, foreign losses should be taken into account by a residence state adhering the ability to pay principle, as the losses influence a person's ability to pay. Both the credit method and the recapture method do so.[53] Full exemption fits in with a territorial approach.

---

52. Grapperhaus in his inaugural lecture held at Leiden University, the Netherlands, referred to even older sources. He mentioned that the oldest literature he had traced dates from 1070: the principle was used in respect of a tax for the delivery of pigs. F.H.M. Grapperhaus, *De pelgrimstocht naar het draagkrachtbeginsel* (Zutphen, The Netherlands: Walburg Pers, 1993), 63.
53. The credit method adheres to capital export neutrality: the total tax levied in both residence state and source state is equal to the tax that would be levied if the full amount of income would have been derived in the residence state. The recapture method adheres to capital import neutrality: income derived by a foreign taxpayer in a certain jurisdiction is taxed up to the same amount as when that income would have been derived by a resident taxpayer.

The exemption with progression method that only takes into account the source income for applying the tax rate (the German method used as from 1999) does not fully fit in with either the worldwide approach or with the territorial approach. States applying this method do take into account the ability to pay principle, but only in respect of the positive side of it from the state's perspective. For the negative side, these states apply the source principle. Taking into account final losses derived in the state of source in the tax base of the state of residence is an alternative that finds its roots in the example provided for in the OECD Model. The OECD mentions in Article 14 of the Commentary to Article 23 A and B of the OECD Model that states may chose between full exemption and exemption with progression, the latter being defined as the method in which the income which may be taxed in the source state is not taxed in the state of residence but the state of residence retains the right to take the source income into consideration when determining the tax to be imposed on the rest of the income. In the example of exemption with progression provided for in paragraph 20 of the Commentary to Article 23 A and B of the OECD Model, the OECD Model only takes into account the foreign income in determining the tax rate. It is submitted it would improve the quality of the OECD Commentary if the OECD would explain that the "Always-Somewhere" principle should be adhered to which may be done by taking into account permanent establishment losses as soon as they occur or no sooner than when they are final. This has a cash-flow disadvantage for taxpayers compared to the recapture method and may have progressivity effects, but the ability to pay principle is respected.

10.6.3   THE COMMERCIAL JUSTIFICATION TEST AND THE BURDEN
           OF PROOF

The commercial justification formulated by the ECJ test resembles the commercial rational behavior test the OECD formulate in its Business Restructuring report[54] which has been incorporated in the Chapter IX of the 2010 Transfer Pricing Guidelines:

> 9.171 The second circumstance in paragraph 1.65 explicitly refers to the situation where the arrangements adopted by the associated enterprises "differ from those which would have been adopted by independent enterprises behaving in a commercially rational manner...." Consistent with paragraph 9.163, tax administrations should not ordinarily interfere with the business decisions of a taxpayer as to how to structure its business arrangements. A determination that a controlled transaction is not commercially rational must therefore be made with great caution, and only in exceptional

---

54. For a critical analysis of this report see A.J. Bakker & G. Cottani, "Fourth Issues Note: Sting in the Tail," *International Transfer Pricing Journal* no. 2 (2009): 81.

circumstances lead to the non recognition of the associated enterprise arrangements.

9.172 Where reliable data show that comparable uncontrolled transactions exist, it cannot be argued that such transactions between associated enterprises would lack commercial rationality. The existence of comparable data evidencing arm's length pricing for an associated enterprise arrangement demonstrates that it is commercially rational for independent enterprises in comparable circumstances. On the other hand, however, the mere fact that an associated enterprise arrangement is not seen between independent enterprises does not in itself mean that it is not arm's length nor commercially rational.

The OECD refers to arrangements adopted by the associated enterprises differing from those which would have been adopted by independent enterprises behaving in a commercially rational manner, whereas the ECJ refers to artificial arrangements for which there is no commercial justification. Neither OECD nor ECJ provide for a definition of commercially rational manner or of commercial justification. Admittedly it may be too cumbersome to provide an exact definition. In case for instance the definition would be that there is a commercial reason, taxpayers may be tempted to take care that there is a commercial reason for an arrangement that is intended as tax avoidance. In that respect the SGI-case does not provide new insights for international tax law. In respect of the burden of proof the SGI-case may though, as the ECJ stresses the need for protecting the taxpayer's rights in that he is given an opportunity to provide evidence of any commercial justification without being subject to undue administrative constraints. The OECD remains silent on the burden of proof in the Business Restructuring Report. It only stresses that the taxpayer must have an adequate documentation:

9.47 It is a good practice for taxpayers to set up a process to establish, monitor and review their transfer prices, taking into account the size of the transactions, their complexity, the level of risk involved, and whether they are performed in a stable or changing environment (see paragraphs 3.80–3.83). The process of assessing the consistency with the arm's length principle of a taxpayer's risk allocations can be burdensome and costly. It would be reasonable to expect that the extent and depth of the analysis will depend:

– On the materiality of the risk and in particular on whether it has a significant profit potential attached to it, and
– On whether significant changes in the risk allocation have occurred, *e.g.* following a significant change of risk profile as a result of a restructuring.

The reference to the notion of options realistically available is not intended to create a requirement for taxpayers to document all possible hypothetical options realistically available. As noted at paragraph 3.81, when undertaking a comparability analysis, there is no requirement for an exhaustive search of all possible relevant sources of information. Rather, the intention is to provide an indication that, if there is a realistically available option that is clearly more attractive, it should be considered in the analysis of the conditions of the restructuring.

Though it is not so strange that the OECD did not develop thoughts about the burden of proof in the Business Restructuring Report, as it explicitly left domestic anti-abuse rules out of the scope of the Report as the burden of proof generally is ruled on in domestic legislation, it would have made the report more in balance if at least a few remarks would have been made on this issue, such as the considerations of the ECJ in SGI that states should guarantee the possibility of counterproof to the taxpayer and that the taxpayer will not be exposed to undue administrative constraints. To that extent a transplant of the ECJ's standards to those of the OECD is recommendable.

10.7   CONCLUSION

This discussion brings us to a conclusion in respect of the question of how the case law of the ECJ concerning the application of the exemption method and transfer pricing influences the power of the Member States to fill in the details of both exemption and transfer pricing in their domestic and international tax law, and allows us to reflect on the question whether it might be recommendable to apply the rules developed by the ECJ in these cases not only in an EU context but also beyond. Though at first sight EU Treaty law and international tax law clash, as the EU Treaty prohibits different tax treatment of the cross-border situation and a similar domestic situation, whereas international tax law treats resident and nonresident taxpayers different, both areas of law may learn from each other. International tax law may learn from the ECJ cases discussed above that the ability to pay principle requires an "Always-Somewhere approach." Moreover the principle of proportionality requires that taxpayers should not be exposed to undue administrative constraints, a principle applied in EU tax law that, it is submitted should be applied in international tax law as well.

Chapter 11

Intra Group Loans—A Swedish Perspective

Bertil Wiman[*]

11.1   INTRODUCTION

In an article honoring Paul McDaniel, it seems appropriate to address transfer pricing issues. I remember being in New York many years ago, when Paul took me out for a long lunch. We discussed the arm's length principle, a topic close to me as I had written my doctoral thesis on the U.S. transfer-pricing provision in section 482 of the Internal Revenue Code. Paul concluded that the arm's length principle had played out its role and was too hard to apply fairly on cross-border transactions. As I recall, he believed that it was no longer suitable because today multinationals operate in a way that is very different from when the arm's length standard was determined to be the correct way to allocate income among different jurisdictions.

Perhaps he would be pleased to read this note on recent developments in Swedish case law. I will analyze a case on intra-group loans rendered from a Swedish parent company to its Swedish subsidiary. In RÅ 2010 ref. 67, the so called *Diligentia* case, the Supreme Administrative Court decided a case on the tax treatment of the interest on a loan rendered by a Swedish parent to its Swedish

---

[*]   Professor of Tax Law, Uppsala University. This contribution is based on a study for a legal opinion presented in a pending Swedish tax case.

Yariv Brauner & Martin James McMahon, Jr. (eds), *The Proper Tax Base: Structural Fairness from an International and Comparative Perspective—Essays in Honour of Paul McDaniel*, pp. 211–221.

subsidiary. The decision has been quite discussed and has given rise to a number of questions. The issue whether the decision in this purely domestic case can be applied on cross-border transactions under Chapter 14, section 19 of the Swedish Income Tax Act (ITA), the Swedish arm's length provision, is in focus in my contribution.

11.2   RÅ 2010 REF. 67

In this case, Diligentia, a real estate company, had been acquired by an insurance company, Skandia Liv. At the time when it became a subsidiary of Skandia Liv, its real estate investments were financed through three external bank loans running at 4.5% interest. These external loans were replaced by two loans from the parent company, Skandia Liv, which loans were not mortgaged and had a fixed interest at 9.5%. The National Tax Agency concluded that the charged interest rate was above market rate and constituted a concealed dividend. Consequently, deductions for the excessive interest were denied. In the Supreme Administrative Court the question was whether the interest could be deducted under the general provisions on deductibility for necessary business costs, following Chapter 16, section 1 ITA. The lower court had found the interest to be excessive. At the Supreme Administrative Court level the company stated that the lower court had compared the interest rate on the loan with interest levels that applied for mortgaged loans, despite the fact that the intra group loan was not mortgaged. Thus, the issue at the Supreme Administrative Court circled around the importance of collateral for the loans when assessing the interest.

The Supreme Administrative Court made the following statements:

> Of vital importance when pricing loans is the risk that the borrower cannot fulfill his payments and the need for collateral that might exist. To some extent other conditions apply to a parent company that provides a loan to a subsidiary than what applies to an external lender. While the parent controls the subsidiary, the external lender typically only has limited insight into the subsidiary. The external lender might also be unsure as to the intentions of the parent company, for example concerning its willingness to support the subsidiary financially and in other ways if needs arise.

> This illustrates that loans from parent companies to subsidiaries have characteristics that affect the credit risk and thus the interest and that are missing when the lender and the borrower are independent of each other. Therefore, given the same conditions in other respects, the acceptable interest for tax purposes cannot outright be determined to what would have been considered market price had the lender been external.

> The Supreme Administrative Court finds that the credit risk in this case would have been lower than if the loan agreements would have been concluded between independent parties. Considering also the facts that have been

presented in the case about the terms of interest and other conditions that existed at the time, there is no reason to admit deductions with an amount higher than corresponding to an interest rate of 6, 5 per cent.[1]

The Supreme Administrative Court in this case emphasized, among other things, that Skandia Liv, as parent company, controlled Diligentia and had greater insight than external lenders. The discussion that has been conducted in Swedish tax journals has concerned to what extent the outcome of the *Diligentia* case will impact other cases of intra-group loans when a parent company has control over and insight in a subsidiary.

The National Tax Agency has in a statement, also cited in its Handledning för internationell beskattning (Guide to international taxation), claimed that the above quoted statements by the Supreme Administrative Court on the importance of a parent company's control over a subsidiary on the interest rate can also be applied to similar loans between related parties resident in different states, i.e., on cross-border intra-group loans.[2] I will in the next part deal with the question of pricing of cross-border loans between related enterprises. Doing so, I will especially focus on the significance that the loan is rendered by a parent company.

11.3   PRICING OF CROSS-BORDER LOANS

By way of introduction, it can be noted that there may exist competition between the Swedish arm's length provision in Chapter 14, section 19 ITA and other provisions in the ITA that concern pricing between related companies.[3] In RÅ 2004 ref. 13, one of the questions was whether an alleged excessive pricing when a Swedish company's acquired inventory from a foreign related company should be assessed according to the general provision on deductibility of necessary business expenses or the arm's length rule. The Supreme Administrative Court expressed its opinion that the arm's length rule is *lex specialis* for international transactions that takes precedence over general provisions when determining the taxable income of an enterprise.[4] The Supreme Administrative Court has reiterated this standpoint in RÅ 2006 ref. 37. Normally, therefore, a pricing issue between a Swedish company and a foreign related company should be assessed according to the arm's length

---

1. The Supreme Administrative Court decision in RÅ 2010 ref. 67. Unofficial translation by the author.
2. See Skatteverkets statement 2010-09-28, dnr 131 632628-10/111, in which the National Tax Agency states that the case can be applied on cross-border loans. But see another opinion expressed by K. Moran & R. Persson Österman, "Diligentia—vilken betydelse får målet vid tillämpning av korrigeringsregeln" *Skattenytt* 2010: 718–721; and M. Emanuelsson & A. Bernath, "Ägande lika med ställande av säkerhet," *Svensk Skattetidning* (2010): 772–783. See also *Handledning för taxering* (Stockholm: National Tax Agency, 2011), 354.
3. This issue is dealt with in the dissertation, S. Aldén, *Regelkonkurrens inom inkomstskatterätten* (Stockholm: Nerenius & Santérus Förlag, 1998). The cases from 2004 and 2006 are of course not discussed in this book.
4. See also M. Dahlberg, *Internationell beskattning*, 2d ed. (Lund: Studentlitteratur, 2007), 123.

provision.[5] Even though much more can be said on that issue, I will continue this contribution on the assumption that the arm's length rule takes precedence on a cross-border loan.

The following part of Chapter 14, section 19 is of importance:

> If the income of an enterprise is lower because conditions have been agreed that deviate from what would have been agreed between unrelated parties, the income shall be determined as if those conditions would not have been in place.[6]

Hence, in order for a reassessment of the taxable income it is necessary that the Swedish enterprise reach an agreement with the foreign related enterprise on conditions that deviate from what would have been agreed between unrelated parties. This means that a comparison must be made between the conditions that independent parties could have agreed upon. This is apparent from the wording.[7] Accordingly, a comparable price must be found.

How to determine a comparable loan and price is, however, not clear from the provision, nor is there much guidance to be found in the legislative history.[8] On the other hand, a great deal of work has been carried out within the OECD on the transfer pricing area. This work has been done against the background, among other things, of the fact that in OECD Model Tax Treaty there is a transfer pricing provision in Article 9. In relevant parts it states the following:

> [Where] conditions are made or imposed between the two (associated) enterprises in their commercial or financial relations which differ from those that would have been made between independent enterprises, then any profits which would, but for those conditions, have accrued to one of the enterprises, but by reason of those conditions, have not so accrued, may be included in the profits of that enterprise and taxed accordingly.

The wording entails a concrete reference to a comparison with that which two independent companies would have agreed upon. In the commentary to OECD Model Tax Treaty, Article 9.1, it is nevertheless not outlined how to conduct this comparison. Instead, it points to the OECD Transfer Pricing Guidelines for Multinational Enterprises and Tax Administrations (OECD Guidelines).[9] These came in 1995, and have continually been updated since, last time year 2010. These guidelines are the result of a work that has been in progress for a long time. It has resulted in several reports, of which the first came in 1979, titled Transfer Pricing and Multinational Enterprises.

---

5. For a general discussion on the relation between provisions for deducting costs and the arm's length provision, se L. Jernkrok, "16 kap. 1 § eller 14 kap. 19 § inkomstskattelagen—en fråga om regelkonkurrens," *Svensk Skattetidning* (2011): 228–249.
6. Unofficial translation by the author.
7. For this criterion, see, e.g., R. Arvidsson, *Dolda vinstöverföringar* (Stockholm: Juristförlaget, 1990), 111.
8. See proposition 1965:126 and SOU 1964:29.
9. OECD Model Tax Treaty, Commentary to Article 9.1, para. 1.

I will soon deal with those parts of the contents of the OECD Guidelines that are relevant for the issue of the significance of the fact that a parent company through its holding of shares has specific insight and control over its subsidiary. But first it can be observed that the OECD Guidelines also are relevant when assessing what the acceptable market price is when applying the Swedish arm's length rule. In RÅ 1991 ref. 101, which was a big case involving the Shell oil company, the Supreme Administrative Court indicated that:

> [A]lthough the guidelines that are presented in the OECD report are not binding for the Swedish tax authorities, the report, which is not in conflict with the Swedish arm's length provision, gives a good and well-balanced elucidation of the problems at hand. Thus, the statements provided in the report can, where applicable, serve as a guide concerning the application of aforementioned provision.[10]

It can be assumed that the significance that the 1979 report had for the assessment of the arm's length price in the Shell case normally would be attributed also to the OECD Transfer Pricing Guidelines, which came after the 1979 OECD report. The discussion of the arm's length principle that takes place in the Guidelines, and its recommendations, therefore are of great importance when interpreting Chapter 14, section 19 ITA. But it is important to point out, that naturally one is bound to the framework that the provision constitutes. It has to be a question of establishing the conditions that independent parties would have agreed. This means, for example, that an application of the so-called transactional profit methods, the transactional net margin method (TNMM), and the transactional profit split method (PSM), which are mentioned in the OECD Guidelines is not feasible if it leads to a result that deviates from what independent enterprises would have agreed.

The OECD Council has recommended to its Member States OECD that their tax administrations follow the OECD Guidelines when assessing transactions between related enterprises.[11] Of course, this presupposes that the laws of a member state contain the legislative tools to be able to consider the OECD Guidelines. The OECD Guidelines do not constitute supranational law, and therefore, there needs to be some way to interpret the domestic arm's length provision to contain a reference to the OECD Guidelines. Within the limits set by the criteria in Chapter 14, section 19 ITA, the contents of the OECD Guidelines are to be considered in the way that the Supreme Administrative Court has ruled.

It is in this manner that the OECD Guidelines are relevant in the Swedish context. Nevertheless, the OECD Guidelines are not designed as regular tax provisions, but, as the name implies, as guidelines. That means that to a certain extent

---

10. Supreme Administrative Court decision in RÅ 1991 ref. 101. Unofficial translation by the author.
11. OECD, Recommendation of the Council on the Determination of the Transfer Pricing Between Associated Enterprises C(95)126/Final).

they are standards of reasoning so as to be well suited for conveying in which way, or ways, intra-group transactions should be assessed.

I will now briefly go through the parts of the contents and methods of the OECD Guidelines that are mostly relevant to pricing of loans. The purpose is to establish to what degree the OECD Guidelines allow one to consider that a parent company has control and insight of a subsidiary when determining the arm's length price.

An important starting point for the arm's length principle is that all companies in the multinational group are treated as independent units, rather than inseparable parts of a single company.[12] It is the foundation for this principle purporting to allocate income between different countries. This also distinguishes it from the method that has been expressed in, among others, the proposed directive from the European Commission on the Common Consolidated Corporate Tax Base, CCCTB. That proposal entails a formulary apportionment of the consolidated group income between the jurisdictions involved. In order to support the effectiveness of the arm's length principle, the OECD Guidelines provides various methods. They in part contain the so called traditional transactional methods, and in part the transactional profit methods. The traditional transactional methods are the comparable price method, the resale price method, and the cost plus method. These methods were outlined already in the 1979 OECD report, but in the part concerning goods. In the OECD Guidelines, they are described as general methods, which, provided that various conditions are met, can be applied also to other types of transactions than goods.

Among the new methods in the OECD Guidelines, the two transactional profit methods appear, TNMM and PSM. In the general choice between a traditional transactional method and a transactional profit method, the OECD Guidelines state that a traditional method is preferable when one determines whether the terms and conditions between related enterprises are at arm's length.[13] And when it comes to the choice between the different traditional transactional methods, the comparable uncontrolled price method is designated as "the most direct and reliable way to apply the arm's length principle."[14] Accordingly, the comparable uncontrolled price method provides the best evidence of the price that independent parties might have agreed upon.

In order to find the market price, one looks for a comparable transaction. It is important to find the comparable that most resembles the controlled transaction. Here one distinguishes between an internal and an external comparable, i.e., between on the one hand independent transactions where one of the parties also has been part of the transaction that is being assessed, and on the other hand transactions between unrelated enterprises.[15] It is assumed that internal comparables can be more reliable, since they have a closer and more direct relation to the

---

12. OECD Guidelines, para. 1.6.
13. See e.g., OECD Guidelines, para. 2.3.
14. OECD Guidelines, para. 2.14.
15. OECD Guidelines, para. 3.27.

controlled transaction.[16] However, it is important that the transaction that one has found between independent parties really be comparable with the controlled transaction. It requires either that the comparable has taken place under the same terms as the controlled transaction, or that the differences that exist between the two transactions are quantifiable, so that the comparable price can safely be adjusted in order for these differences to be taken into account.[17] One conducts a comparability analysis, purporting to ascertain whether the controlled and the uncontrolled transaction are similar, and if not, what relevant differences there may be.

In OECD Guidelines five relevant important factors are enumerated as especially important in the comparability analysis.[18] They are:

- characteristics of property and services;[19]
- functional analysis (including assets used and risks assumed by each party);[20]
- contractual terms;[21]
- economic circumstances;[22] and
- business strategies.[23]

The comparability analysis must start in determining the facts of the controlled transaction in order to be able to find an uncontrolled transaction that is sufficiently similar to the controlled transaction. The comparability factors listed above have been determined to be the most important in that operation.

When it comes to pricing of loans it is normally possible to apply the comparable uncontrolled price method.[24] It thus should be applied because it provides the most reliable result. It is then necessary to find a loan arrangement between two uncontrolled parties that is either directly comparable with the loan at question or where the differences are of such a nature that they can be measured and taken into account when setting the arm's length interest rate. The five comparability factors must then be applied to loan transactions. To find a comparable loan one has to study the controlled transaction with respect to these comparability factors.[25]

---

16. OECD Guidelines, para. 3.27.
17. OECD Guidelines, para. 3.47.
18. OECD Guidelines, paras. 1.36, 1.38 et seq. see also Swedish National Tax Agency, *Handledning för internationell beskattning* (Stockholm: National Tax Agency, 2011), 262.
19. OECD Guidelines, paras. 1.39–1.41.
20. OECD Guidelines, paras. 1.42–1.51.
21. OECD Guidelines, paras. 1.52–1.54.
22. OECD Guidelines, paras. 1.55–1.58.
23. OECD Guidelines, paras. 1.59–1.63.
24. van der Breggen goes even further and claims that in practice it is only the comparable uncontrolled price method that can be used, as sufficient information for applying any of the other methods is lacking., see M. van der Breggen, "Intercompany Loans: Observations from a Transfer Pricing Objective," *International Transfer Pricing Journal* 13 (2006): 295, 297 [hereinafter van der Breggen, "Intercompany Loans"].
25. OECD Guidelines, paras. 3.1, 3.20.

However, no part of the OECD Guidelines directly applies these five compa-rability factors to intra-group loans.[26] The most common comparability factors for loans should be the amount of the credit, the length of the loan and whether and to what extent the interest is fixed, whether there is a mortgage or other collateral for the loan, the creditworthiness of the borrower, if the loan is subordinated other loans, the currency in which it is issued and the country of the debtor.[27] With respect to the facts in RÅ 2010 ref. 67, the issues of collateral and whether the loan is subordinated other creditors' rights and thus the creditworthiness of the loan are important. These factors are important to determine the risk premium an independent lender would have demanded.

In this context, considering the facts of RÅ 2010 ref.67, one must ask whether in a cross-border intra-group loan from a parent company to its subsidiary, for the comparability analysis as such one should at all consider that a parent company in its ownership capacity may possess specific knowledge about its subsidiary?

There are several aspects that are relevant in answering that question. To start with, to what extent do OECD Guidelines at all take into account the fact that there is a group relation when determining the arm's length price? There is only very limited support that for such a proposition. Much more support can be found for the opposite, namely that the OECD Guidelines disregards the group relation when determining the arm's length price. The whole basis for the arm's length principle is the "separate entity approach"[28] where each enterprise in the group is regarded as an independent, unrelated company[29] and where the comparison between con-trolled and uncontrolled transaction is "at the heart of the application of the arm's length principle."[30] It is not a perfect way to allocate income, but it puts members of a multinational enterprise and independent enterprises "on a broad parity."[31]

To disregard that the two related parties belong to the same group when determining the arm's length price means that the arm's length principle as a way of allocating income between different states is not perfect. In my doctoral thesis I have argued that the arm's length principle does not consider that the multinational group can be more efficient and more profitable than if the group members had been independent enterprises. It is precisely so because the method to allocate the income is done by reference to the pricing of unrelated parties, and that pricing does not contain any consideration to circumstances of a group of compa-nies as such circumstances does not exist between unrelated enterprises. This is also a fact that is recognized by and specifically highlighted in the OECD Guide-lines as a basis for the arm's length principle.

---

26. See e.g., van der Breggen, "Intercompany Loans," *supra* note 24 at 295, where the author considers this fact to be remarkable.
27. See, e.g., B. Wiman, Prissättning *inom multinationella koncerner* (Uppsala, Iustus Förlag, 1987), 212, and van der Breggen, "Intercompany Loans," *supra* note 24; Handledning för internationell beskattning (Stockholm: National Tax Agency, 2011), 351, et seq.
28. OECD Guidelines, Preface, para. 6.
29. OECD Guidelines, para. 1.3.
30. OECD Guidelines, para. 1.6.
31. OECD Guidelines, para. 1.8.

In addition to these basic methodological starting points that I have described, that one should disregard the fact that one company belongs to a group of companies is expressed also in Chapter VII of the OECD Guidelines on intra-group services. It is this chapter that most closest relates to intra-group loans, even if it focuses primarily on other types of intra-group services. The initial issue is whether a service has been rendered to another group member at all.[32] This is relevant for the following reason. Can the insight and control a parent company has over a subsidiary in any respect be a service for which the parent should charge the subsidiary? If not, then one may question why this insight and control should be a factor to consider when adjusting a comparable interest rate on a loan.

The question whether a service is at hand at all is not easy to answer. If an unrelated party would have been prepared to engage in the activity it is probably a service for which one should charge a fee within the group.[33] Regarding insight and control, for natural reasons no market exist. The control exercised by a parent company is based on the ownership as such.

It can be noted that costs for a so called "shareholder activity" may not be charged to the subsidiaries.[34] This is in accordance with the arm's length principle, to treat each entity in the group as independent. But the fact that insight and control exist when rendering and pricing a loan cannot be labeled a shareholder activity. It is more accurate is to say that insight and control flow from the existence of a group of companies as such. In OECD Guidelines it is stated that if a member of a group obtains incidental benefits attributable solely to it being part of a larger concern, it has not received an intra-group service. For instance, if a group member has a higher credit rating because it is affiliated with the group, it should not be charged by the parent company for the benefit of the higher credit rating. One might say that it is a question of an "implicit parent guarantee." For such one group member is not entitled to charge another group member a fee.[35] Conversely, one group member should not have to give a discount on a charged interest solely because the subsidiary is a member of the same group. Thus, it seems clear that being affiliated with a group of companies is not a factor that can motivate a charge from the parent company. For a charge, it has to be a more concrete service. Probably, what is needed is an explicit guarantee from the parent or a specific letter of support.[36]

What then is the relevance of the fact that one group member cannot charge another group member just for being a group member in determining the comparable price following the comparable uncontrolled price method? To start with, the question concerns a loan from a parent to its subsidiary. One shall disregard that the parent company controls the subsidiary. To provide a loan does, however, constitute a service. It then follows from the Guidelines that one shall compare the

---

32. OECD paras. 7.6–7.18.
33. OECD Guidelines, para. 7.6.
34. OECD Guidelines, paras. 7.9–7.10.
35. OECD para. 7.13. See also, e.g., van der Breggen, "Intercompany Loans," *supra* note 24 at 297–298, applying the same interpretation.
36. See L. Gäfvert, *Skatteplanering och kapitaliseringsfrågor* (Uppsala: Uppsala University, 1998), 78 et seq.

interest on the related loan with what independent parties would have charged under comparable circumstances.[37] As regards pricing of loans, there are normally a number of loans between unrelated enterprises with which to make a comparison. However, these unrelated loans may differ from the controlled transaction in various ways. Here, as always when applying the arm's length principle, an adjustment shall be made to take into account any relevant and material differences. I have, as described above, not been able to find any support in the discussion in the OECD Guidelines concerning important comparability factors that connects to such insight and control over a subsidiary that was expressed by the Supreme Administrative Court in RÅ 2010 ref. 67.

If the insight and control over a subsidiary that a parent company has would have been material in the comparability analysis, this should have been clearly expressed in the OECD Guidelines. In addition, it is not only when pricing loans that insight and control would be a factor in the comparability analysis. But these factors also are not mentioned as one of the relevant comparability factors to adjust for when applying comparable uncontrolled price method for goods.[38]

It can be discussed what the Supreme Administrative Court purported to say in the *Diligentia* case. The Court's statements probably were not intended to be so far reaching as it is sometimes asserted. But even if one would say that the Court considered insight and control to be relevant in this domestic loan case, that view cannot be transferred to a cross-border loan. Here, one is bound by the wording of Chapter 14, section 19 ITA, and consequently to the parts of the OECD Guidelines dealt with in this contribution. In my view, it follows from the OECD Guidelines that when applying the arm's length principle one shall disregard the fact that the parent company is the owner of the subsidiary, and thus disregard the insight and control it has. RÅ 2010 ref. 67 concerned loans between Swedish enterprises, and not between a Swedish enterprise and a foreign enterprise. The reasoning of the Court does not contain any reference to Chapter 14, section 19 ITA, or to OECD Guidelines. Accordingly, one cannot infer that the case will be decisive for international loans.

The reasoning by the Supreme Administrative Court may be interpreted in the light of the particular facts of the case. RÅ 2010 ref. 67 concerned a loan between a Swedish parent company and its Swedish subsidiary between which no right to give contributions existed.[39] The subsidiary had neither mortgaged the real estate to its parent company nor to any external lenders. In other words, there were no other loans for which the value of the real estate could be lost to the parent company. In my view, the statements by the Supreme Administrative Court should be understood against that background. When the Court makes statements about insight and control, it probably focuses on the fact that the parent company knows

---

37. OECD Guidelines, para. 7.19.
38. See OECD Guidelines, para. 2.18.
39. The Swedish group contribution system has the effect of allowing two companies in a group to offset losses and profits among each other, achieving similar effects for tax purposes as if they would have consolidated their accounts.

that the real estate is not mortgaged at all and that parent company, because it has control, can make sure that the subsidiary does not mortgage the real estate for external loans and thus cause the loans from the parent to lose their credit standing. This might have been one of these characteristic features the Court said exists for loan from a parent company and its subsidiary. One can make a comparison with a potential external lender being ready to give a loan to the same subsidiary having real estate that is not mortgaged and where the real estate will not be mortgaged to the external lender. This external lender will not, absent any contract to the contrary, have the same insight and the same control of what the subsidiary will do with the real estate as the parent company has. As I perceive the reasoning by the Supreme Administrative Court, it is against this background the Court found the credit risk was lower than if the loan had been rendered by an unrelated lender.

11.4   CONCLUSIONS

The decision in the *Diligentia* case should be interpreted narrowly and should be applied only to loans between related Swedish parties. Even then it should be applied only in cases with a similar fact pattern. It cannot be applied on cross-border loans, because for such loans the Swedish arm's length provision governs, and the wording of that provision, interpreted in light of the discussion in the OECD Transfer Pricing Guidelines, gives no support for considering the insight and control a parent company has over its subsidiary in applying the comparability analysis.

Chapter 12

European VAT and Jurisdiction to Tax

*Antonio Vázquez del Rey**

12.1   PLACE OF SUPPLY: RELEVANCE AND
UNDERLYING PRINCIPLES

Consumption has been traditionally taxed indirectly, i.e., through production or
sales taxes levied on the producer or the supplier who actually shifted the tax
burden to the customer. The European Valued Added Tax, which is first and
foremost a general tax on consumption, basically fits in this approach—any
supplies of goods and services made for consideration by a taxable person are
subject to tax.[1] Unlike personal taxes, VAT requires connecting factors other
than residence and nationality in order to ascertain where a transaction is taxable.
In other words, the territoriality principle implies that only those taxable events
which take place within the territory of the State are subject to taxation—a supply
of goods or services, an import, etc. remains outside its scope where this territorial
element is missing.

    The relevance of the place of supply particularly arises when more than a tax
jurisdiction is involved, e.g., where goods are produced in one State but consumed
in another. In order to determine which jurisdiction is entitled to tax, the
specialized literature has traditionally relied on the principles of origin country

---

*   Law Faculty, University of Navarra, Spain.
1.   Notwithstanding the VAT structure also includes a levy on imports for tax neutrality purposes.

Yariv Brauner & Martin James McMahon, Jr. (eds), *The Proper Tax Base: Structural Fairness from
an International and Comparative Perspective—Essays in Honour of Paul McDaniel*, pp. 223–257.
© 2012 Kluwer Law International BV, The Netherlands.

and destination country.[2] The destination country principle implies that goods and services are taxed where they are actually consumed, regardless of the jurisdiction where they have been produced or manufactured or the supplier is established. From this derives taxation upon imported goods while exports benefit from a tax refund. By contrast, the origin country principle implies that goods and services are taxed in the jurisdiction where they have been produced or the supplier is established, regardless of the place where they are to be consumed. As a result, imports are not subject to tax while exports remain taxed—the exporter does not benefit from a tax refund. The primary characterization of VAT as a tax on consumption justifies that, when dealing with international trade, the legal structure greatly relies on the destination country principle.

Each principle entails its own advantages and drawbacks which must be carefully weighed up. Obviously, when the principle of origin country applies, simplicity is a major advantage as all the supplies are subject to tax in the same country, i.e., where the goods have been produced or the supplier is established. Taxable persons do not have to split their turnover among different tax jurisdictions nor to apply different domestic regulations. Unfortunately, this leads to situations which are not consistent with the primary purpose of VAT which is levying a tax on domestic consumption. Moreover, tax neutrality at the destination country is at risk as goods may carry a different tax burden depending on whether they have been imported or domestically produced. Foreign customers also face a tax deterrent when deciding whether or not to acquire goods from national suppliers (not only will they be paying the local VAT but may find themselves exposed to double taxation). By contrast, where the destination principle applies, tax neutrality among local customers is basically guaranteed at the jurisdiction where goods are to be consumed, however, the supplier needs to split his turnover in order to fulfill the fiscal duties in every tax jurisdiction in which he carries out his activity. This extra administrative burden—and the costs it normally involves—may become a burdensome obstacle, particularly for small and medium enterprises. Besides, from the perspective of the Tax Administration, the fact that the taxable person is a foreign supplier involves an additional risk with regards to collection. To minimize these drawbacks, a reverse charge mechanism usually applies but only to a limited extent.

The place of supply is particularly relevant to European VAT. Although VAT is usually regarded as a single tax within the EU, there are as many different taxes as EU Member States. Those taxes are harmonized according to the EU VAT directives but they are levied by the national tax authorities according to their domestic rules, which differ from state to state. Obviously, the greater the harmonization of the place of supply provisions, the less the risks of double taxation or

---

2. A consistent and uniform application of the aforementioned principles obviously helps to avoid double taxation and nontaxation. It is important to highlight that both principles are only relevant when more than a tax jurisdiction is involved (regarding the place of supply of services, see Case 51/88 *Hamann*, paragraphs 17 and 18 and Case 155/01 *Cookies World*, paragraphs 47).

nontaxation.[3] In other words, the provisions on the place of supply constitute rules of conflict that determines the place of taxation and, consequently, delimit the powers of the States. Moreover, they allow a distribution of the amount collected among the EU Member States according to uniform rules.

Council Directive 2006/112/EC addresses the place of supply in Title V, however, as regards the place of supply of services, the original provisions have been amended by Directive 2008/8/EC of the Council, of February 12, 2008, which is part of the VAT Package. This is probably the most important change in VAT since 1992, when the intra-Community acquisition of goods was introduced as the disappearance of borders between EU Member States required new solutions in order to prevent any serious distortions in the European national markets. Moreover, the Council implementing Regulation (EU) No. 282/2011 of March 15, 2011 has been recently adopted in order to ensure a uniform application of the current VAT system in the different EU States. This regulation includes a number of definitions and other aspects relevant to the purpose of the place of supply.[4]

12.2   THE PLACE OF SUPPLY OF GOODS

12.2.1   OVERVIEW

The place of supply of goods is, in general, the place where the goods are either at the moment of the supply or at the beginning of the transport or dispatch. This criterion is provided in order to ensure that VAT taxes any domestic consumption of goods originally situated in the country. However, where goods are dispatched or transported to another tax jurisdiction, i.e., exports, intra-Community supplies, an exemption with the right of deduction (substantially similar to zero-rating) normally applies.[5] Accordingly, the place of supply of goods does not necessarily involve taxation in the jurisdiction where the supply is deemed to be made.

---

3. The objective pursued by those provisions within the context of the general scheme of the Sixth Directive, as the seventh recital in the preamble implies, is designed to secure the rational delimitation of the respective areas covered by national VAT rules by determining in a uniform manner the place where supplies of goods and supplies of services are deemed to be provided for tax purposes. The aim is also to avoid conflicts of jurisdiction which may result in double taxation or nontaxation (see, by analogy, Case 168/84 *Berkholz*, para. 14; Case 452/03 *RAL (Channel Islands) and Others*, para. 23; and Case 58/04 *Köhler*, para. 22). Actually, the determination of the place where taxable transactions are effected "is necessary in order to avoid conflicts concerning jurisdiction as between Member States." Therefore, as the ECJ has stated, "the object of these provisions is to avoid, first, conflicts of jurisdiction, which may result in double taxation, and, secondly, non-taxation" (Case 327/94 *Dudda*, para. 20 and Case 116/96 *Reisebüro Binder*, para. 12).
4. Since EU regulations are binding and directly applicable in all EU Member States, uniformity of application is best ensured this way. This Regulation (EU) No. 282/2011 of Mar. 15, 2011, which repeals the previous (EC) No 1777/2005, applies from Jul. 1, 2011.
5. Only exceptionally is the place of supply shifted to the destination country, e.g., supply of goods to be installed or assembled, supply of gas and electricity.

However, in order to be taxed, a supply of goods needs to be deemed supplied within the territory of the EU Member State claiming the VAT.

The destination country principle has been traditionally based on the "border tax adjustments." Until recently, international trade was mostly in goods—not services—which can be subject to a physical control by the customs authorities when they cross the border. At that moment the exporter—origin—country basically refunds any indirect tax on those goods, while the importer—destination—country levies a compensatory tax in order to guarantee tax neutrality within the domestic market. Despite this, certain customs regimes allow delaying the moment or even changing the place in which the import takes place. This is an option rarely found domestically but is common in international trade. The entry of goods through an EU Member State is a taxable import in another EU Member State some months later, nearer to the time and place of consumption, thus avoiding any prior taxation.

As mentioned, the destination country principle has traditionally relied on the existence of national borders; however, since 1993 there are no internal borders within the EU territory. From that time, intra-Community trade has been basically governed by a transitional hybrid regime which combines both the origin and the destination country principles. The elimination of fiscal barriers between EU Member States resulted, first of all, in the abolition of taxes on imports with regards to intra-Community trade. Second, the maintenance of the aforementioned rules on the place of supply of goods initially leads to a regime based on the origin country principle, as intra-community supplies are taxed at the jurisdiction where the goods are when the dispatch or transport starts, regardless of the European tax jurisdiction where they are to be consumed.[6] However, in order to avoid any significant distortions this may cause within the European national markets some specific regimes were introduced—distance sales, intra-Community acquisitions of goods. As a matter of fact, under the current circumstances the general rules on the place of supply of goods only provide a residual solution for intra-Community trade of goods which is mainly taxed at the EU jurisdiction where goods are to be consumed. Therefore, the intra-Community trade of goods is substantially governed by the destination country principle based, by obvious reasons, in techniques other than border tax adjustments.[7]

12.2.2   GENERAL RULES

The Directive basically contains two general rules, one for the supply of goods without transport (Article 31 EC VAT Directive) and another for the supply of goods with transport (Article 32 EC VAT Directive).

---

6. To these purposes, the Sixth Directive makes no distinction between "intra-Community" supplies and "internal" supplies (Case 245/04 *EMAG Handel Eder*, para. 46).
7. The solution coincides to a great extent with the one that has traditionally governed the supply of services.

The place of *supply of goods without transport* is deemed the place where the goods are when the supply takes place. This provision not only applies to immovable property but also to movable tangible goods which are supplied with no previous transport or dispatch, e.g., goods which are put at the disposal in the store or warehouse. The rule applies even when the supply takes place by means of securities or under any other means.

The place of *supply of goods with transport* is the place where the goods are at the time when dispatch or transport to the customer begins. Obviously, this provision is the most relevant when dealing with the international trade, regardless of the special rules examined below.

12.2.3 SPECIAL RULES

12.2.3.1 Generically Applicable to International Trade

The general rules are completed by a number of special provisions which intend either to simplify or to address some specific issues that the general rules fail to solve. Some of these provisions apply regardless of whether the transport of goods takes place between an EU jurisdiction and a third country or between two European countries. That is the case of the rules that apply to supplies of goods to be installed or assembled and supplies of gas and electricity through distribution systems. Both provisions are governed by the destination country principle:

(a) The place of *supply of goods* dispatched or transported by the supplier, by the customer or by a third party, *to be installed or assembled*, with or without verification that they work, is deemed to be the place where the goods are installed or assembled (Article 36 EC VAT Directive).[8] The object of the supply is the goods installed or assembled, not just a set of parts. As a matter of fact, although it fails to provide a definition of installation or assembly, the EC VAT Directive seems to refer to transactions of a certain material and financial relevance in which the installation or the assembly needs to be carried out prior to the delivery of goods.

The rationale of this provision has traditionally been found in the need to prevent the supplier from splitting the total value of complex

---

8. The supply and laying of a fabric-optic cable linking two EU Member States is considered a supply of goods for the purposes of Art. 8(1)(a) of the Sixth Directive. Although a rule of conflict of laws must allow for attribution of tax jurisdiction in order to make a transaction subject to VAT in only one of the Member States involved, in this situation the right to tax is held by each Member State pro rata according to the length of cable in its territory with regard both to the price of the cable itself and the rest of the materials and to the cost of the services relating to the laying of the cable (Case 111/05 *Aktiebolaget NN*, para. 50). That transaction is not subject to EU VAT for that part of the transaction which is carried out in the exclusive economic zone, on the continental shelf and at sea.

transactions with the purpose of reducing taxation at the EU destination country.[9] However, this issue is not that obvious once the Directive 8/2008/EC has introduced a new general rule on the place of supply which locates services provided to taxable persons in the jurisdiction where the recipient has his business established or a fixed establishment to which the services are provided (see Article 44 EC VAT Directive). At the other end, where the installation or assembly is carried out in a EU Member State other than that of the supplier, that State where the goods are to be installed or assembled must avoid double taxation (Article 36 EC VAT Directive). This provision not only requires an adequate coordination with the regime that applies both to distance sales and intra-Community acquisitions of goods but also with the related services. As regards imports of goods, the EC VAT Directive is not so demanding as it only provides that EU Member States may adapt national provisions so as to prevent double taxation (see Article 145(2) EC VAT Directive).

(b) The supply of *natural gas and electricity* through distribution systems (see Articles 38 et seq. EC VAT Directive) qualify as supplies of goods, however, the difficulties of a physical control favor a provision which locates the place of supply in the tax jurisdiction where those goods are to be consumed. The connecting factor varies depending on who the acquirer is. If the customer is a taxable dealer, i.e., a reseller, the place of supply is deemed to be the place where that person has established his business, has a fixed establishment to which the goods are supplied and, in their absence, his permanent address or the place where he usually resides. In any other situation—e.g., final consumers, taxable persons who are not resellers—the place of supply is deemed to be the place where the customer effectively uses or consumes the goods.

12.2.3.2 Specifically Applicable to Intra-Community Trade

A specific set of provisions only apply within the context of intra-Community trade. That is the case of distance sales (see Article 33 EC VAT Directive) and supplies of goods to passengers on board during intra-Community transport (Article 37 EC VAT Directive):

(1) In general, any supply of goods with transport is located in the jurisdiction where goods are at the beginning of the transport or dispatch of the goods. In this context, EU customers would find a tax incentive to buy goods from those EU Member States with lower tax rates so *distance sales* suppliers would be attracted to those jurisdictions. In order to avoid this, the place of supply is shifted to the jurisdiction where the dispatch

---

9. According to the general rule originally provided by Art. 9(1) of the Sixth Directive, the place of supply of the related services would be at the jurisdiction where the foreign supplier is established. Therefore, VAT would only be levied on the actual cost of the goods to be installed or assembled upon importation while services would escape taxation.

or the transport of the goods ends. Consequently, the turnover has to be split into the different tax jurisdictions and the supplier will have to fulfill his fiscal duties in every EU Member State in which he operates.[10]

This regime applies to distance sales of any items except the following: (a) new means of transport, (b) goods to be installed or assembled and (c) goods taxed under the special arrangements for second-hand goods, works of art, antiques and collectors' items. The exclusion is basically due to coordination reasons as those supplies are already covered by other specific provisions under VAT.[11] A further exception applies to supplies of goods which are subject to excise duties (alcohol, tobacco, hydrocarbons, etc.).[12]

The solution for intra-Community distance sales is driven by the destination country principle as far as the following requirements are met (see Articles 33 et seq. EC VAT Directive):

(a) Goods need to be dispatched or transported by or on behalf of the supplier from an EU Member State other than that of arrival, as is usual in mail-order sales. Obviously this requirement is missing where the intra-Community transportation or dispatch is arranged by the customer himself. When dealing with imported goods, the EU Member State of origin is deemed to be that in which the goods are imported. It could be argued otherwise that those supplies are not subject to VAT as the transport or dispatch started in a third country.

(b) The acquirers may only be public bodies, farmers subject to the VAT flat-rate special scheme, taxable persons without the right of deduction and, in general, nontaxable persons. Where the acquirer is a regular taxable person, the transaction normally qualifies as an intra-Community acquisition of goods, which is also taxed at the EU Member State of destination but through a different technique.[13]

(c) The purpose of the intra-Community distance sales regime is basically to avoid any serious distortions within the European national markets. From this derives that taxation in the EU Member State of destination is only triggered when sales to that jurisdiction rise to a significant amount, which is a total value of EUR 100,000—however, EU Member States may limit this threshold to EUR 35,000 or the equivalent national currency. This threshold refers to the amount supplied by the

---

10. To avoid this, which can turn into a major drawback particularly for small and medium enterprises, the EU Commission is considering the possibility of a one-stop mechanism for intra-Community distance sales.

11. Under the exceptions a) and b), VAT is levied in the EU Member State of arrival or installation while letter c) implies taxation in the EU Member State of origin.

12. The place of supply is always deemed to be the EU Member State where those goods arrive. The amount of such supplies is not included for the purposes of the threshold that applies to the distance sales.

13. The person liable to payment in an intra-Community acquisition of goods is the same that the person liable when the reverse charge applies, while the only taxable person under the distance sales regime is the supplier.

taxable person in the previous calendar year or the year in progress and once the threshold is exceeded, the supplier has to register in the EU Member State of destination where he is considered as the person subject to payment.[14] It must be emphasized that EU Member States may modify the limit between EUR 35,000 and EUR 100,000 which raises the issue as to whether the modification of the threshold by an EU Member State may alter the place of supply. In any case, the EU Member State must take the measures necessary to inform the tax authorities in the EU Member State in which the dispatch or transport of the goods begins.

Up to the limit, supplies of goods carry the VAT of the EU Member State of departure.[15] However, the supplier may opt to have all the transactions taxed in the EU Member State of destination, thus avoiding any concern about the moment when the shift takes place. The option may be exercised in different ways depending on each EU Member State and it must cover at least a two-year period. Presumably, the option will always be exercised whenever the EU Member States of destination apply lower rates. In any case, taxation in the EU Member State of destination has to be proved to the tax authorities of the EU Member State of origin.

(2) The place of the supply of goods to *passengers* made on board ships, aircraft or trains during the part of a *transport carried out within the Community* is deemed to be at the point of departure of the passenger transport operation (see Article 37 EC VAT Directive). Otherwise, the general rule on supplies of goods without transport would lead to a complex situation as each supply would be subject to the VAT applicable in the jurisdiction where the goods are at the time when the supply takes place. According to the ECJ, "the result is a simplified scheme of taxation which avoids, throughout the intra-Community journey, the successive application of the national VAT systems of the Member States through which the journey is made and, therefore, conflicts concerning tax jurisdiction between Member States" (Case 231/94 *Faaborg-Gelting Linien,*

---

14. VAT is not included for the estimation of that limit and the relative amount must be considered separately for each EU Member State.
15. The EC VAT implementing Regulation has clarified how the aforementioned threshold works. Where in the course of a calendar year the aforementioned threshold is exceeded, Art. 33 of the Directive 2006/112/EC does not modify the place of supplies of goods other than products subject to excise duty carried out in the course of the same calendar year which are made before the threshold applied by the Member State for the calendar year then current is exceeded provided that the supplier has not exercised the option and the value of his supplies of goods did not exceed the threshold in the course of the preceding calendar year. However, Art. 33 will modify the place of the following supplies: (a) the supply of goods by which the threshold applied by the Member State for the calendar year then current was exceeded in the course of the same calendar year; (b) any subsequent supplies of goods within that Member State in that calendar year; (c) supplies of goods within that Member State in the calendar year following the calendar year in which the event referred to in point (a) occurred.

and Case 58/04 *Köhler*, paragraph 22). For purposes of simplification, all the supplies of goods made to passengers are subject to tax at the jurisdiction of departure. In the case of a return journey, the return leg is considered to be a separate transport.

For this provision to apply, the following definitions must be taken into account. First of all, the "section of a passenger transport operation effected within the Community" is the section of the operation effected, without a stopover outside the Community, between the point of departure and the point of arrival of the passenger transport operation. The provision does not apply therefore to those sections of transport including a stop outside the EU territory.[16] Then, the "point of departure" is the first scheduled point of passenger embarkation within the Community, where applicable after a stopover outside the Community. And finally, the "point of arrival" is the last scheduled point of disembarkation within the Community of passengers who embarked in the Community, where applicable before a stopover outside the Community.

12.2.3.3   Chain Transactions

Chain transactions basically involve two or more supplies which usually only give rise to one transport or dispatch of goods between two different tax jurisdictions. Typically, there is a transaction between the original supplier and the intermediary and another between the intermediary and the customer, combined with a direct transport of goods from the first supplier to the customer. Where the transport or dispatch of goods starts in a third country, the general rule on the place of supply of goods with transport leads to no taxation. The importer and any subsequent acquirer before the importation takes place would claim the supply is not subject to VAT as the transport started outside the EU, while the importer, provided he is a taxable person, would claim for a tax refund of the VAT paid upon importation. In other words, goods would be VAT-free although they are to be consumed in a EU jurisdiction. In order to avoid this, the place of the supply by the importer or by any subsequent acquirers before the importation is deemed to be at the EU Member State of importation of the goods (see Article 33 (2) EC VAT Directive). Therefore, the importer—and any subsequent suppliers—must charge VAT on the supply while deducting the VAT levied on the import—or any acquisitions made at a previous stage. The same criterion applies when the importation is followed by an

---

16.   The ECJ has ruled that "any supply of goods effected on a ship during a stop in a third territory is deemed to be made outside the scope of the Sixth Directive, the tax treatment of the supply of goods falling, in that case, within the tax jurisdiction of the State in which the stop is made." To these purposes, stops made by a ship in the ports of a third country during which passengers may leave the ship, even for a short period, are "stops in a third territory" (Case 58/04 *Köhler*, para. 26). Art. 15 EC VAT implementing Regulation also states that the section of a passenger transport operation effected within the Community is determined by the journey of the means of transport and not by the journey completed by each of the passengers.

intra-Community supply of goods. The place of that intra-Community supply is deemed to be the place of importation.

12.3 THE PLACE OF INTRA-COMMUNITY ACQUISITIONS OF GOODS

12.3.1 OVERVIEW

The removal of the EU internal borders in 1993 brought a new taxable transaction into the VAT structure: the intra-Community acquisitions of goods.[17] In order to guarantee tax neutrality within the European national markets, any supply of goods to taxable persons and certain supplies to nontaxable persons are subject to VAT at the EU destination country. In this context, the person liable to payment is no longer the supplier but the acquirer of the goods in order to relieve the former from fulfilling the tax obligations in a State other than that in which he is established. For monitoring purposes, that intra-Community acquisition of goods is mirrored by an intra-Community supply at the EU origin country, according to the general rule on the place of supply of goods with transport (see Article 32 EC VAT Directive).[18] Notwithstanding this supply is exempted, it entails the obligation to file a tax return for the supplier.

The place of intra-Community acquisitions of goods is deemed to be the place where dispatch or transport of the goods to the person acquiring them ends. This raises some difficulties, particularly when the purchaser is not established in that jurisdiction. In order to prevent them, a secondary connecting factor has been introduced. The place of the intra-Community acquisition is deemed to be within the territory of the EU Member State which issued the VAT identification number under which the person acquiring the goods has made the acquisition, unless that person establishes that VAT has been applied in the jurisdiction where the transport ends (see Article 41 EC VAT Directive). This criterion applies only to those intra-Community acquisitions regarded in Article 2(1)(b)(i) EC VAT Directive[19] and, although it guarantees taxation of the intra-Community trade, tax neutrality can only be achieved to a certain extent as goods can be subject to VAT in a jurisdiction other than the one where they will be consumed. Besides, a further issue arises as

---

17. According to Art. 28a(3)(1) of the Sixth Directive, an intra-Community acquisition of goods is the "acquisition of the right to dispose as owner of movable tangible property dispatched or transported to the person acquiring the goods by or on behalf of the vendor or the person acquiring the goods to a Member State other than that from which the goods are dispatched or transported."

18. Basically the same transaction unfolds in two different taxable events relevant to each one of the jurisdictions involved. See also Case 245/04 *EMAG Handel Eder*, para. 46.

19. Only intra-Community acquisitions by a taxable person acting as such, or a nontaxable legal person, where the vendor is a taxable person acting as such who is not eligible for the exemption for small enterprises (see Arts 282 to 292 EC VAT Directive). The criterion does not apply, however, to intra-Community acquisitions of new means of transport nor products subject to excise duties.

this secondary criterion may reduce the effectiveness of the primary rule inasmuch as taxable persons achieve an immediate deduction in the State which has issued the VAT number. In order to prevent this, the ECJ has held that such intra-Community acquisitions cannot benefit from the general regime of deduction in that State.[20]

Leaving this aside, in order to co-ordinate both criteria, Article 41 provides that if VAT is applied first in the jurisdiction which has issued the VAT number and then in the place where the dispatch or transport of the goods ends, the taxable amount is reduced accordingly in the EU Member State which issued the VAT number under which the acquisition of goods were made. Finally, it must be pointed out that the right of the Member State in which the dispatch or transport ends remains unaffected regardless of the VAT treatment applied to the transaction in the Member State in which the dispatch or transport began. If the supplier originally charged the VAT, then he will have to correct this situation. Any request by a supplier of goods for a correction in the VAT invoiced and reported by him to the Member State where the dispatch or transport of the goods began will be treated by that Member State in accordance with its own domestic rules (see Article 16 EC VAT implementing Regulation).

12.3.2   CHAIN TRANSACTIONS

Intra-Community chain transactions raise their own issues as they involve two or more supplies which only give rise to one transportation or dispatch of goods between two EU tax jurisdictions. In a basic two-transactions scheme, only one intra-Community transaction takes place while the other transaction must be regarded as a domestic supply.[21] If the first of the two successive supplies is the supply that involves the intra-Community dispatch or transport, then the second supply is deemed to occur in that jurisdiction where the intra-Community acquisition has taken place. Conversely, if the supply that involves the intra-Community dispatch or transport of goods is the second of two successive supplies, then the first supply, which necessarily occurred before the goods were dispatched or transported, is deemed to take place in the Member State of the departure. Therefore, ultimately it all depends on which of the successive supplies the intra-Community transport or dispatch is attached to.

VAT triangulation takes place where those persons involved in an intra-Community chain transaction—e.g., A, B and C—are established in different EU jurisdictions and the first supplier (A) delivers the goods directly to the final customer (C). Apparently, where the intra-Community transport is linked to the

---

20. See Cases 536/08 and 539/08 *X and fiscale eenheid Facet-Facet Trading.*
21. The ECJ has held that where two successive supplies of the same goods, effected for consideration between taxable persons acting as such, gives rise to a single intra-Community dispatch or a single intra-Community transport of those goods, that dispatch or transport can be ascribed to only one of the two supplies (Case 245/04 *EMAG Handel Eder*, para. 45).

first supply, not only the intermediary will have to register and pay VAT on the intra-Community acquisition of goods in the EU jurisdiction where the dispatch or transport ends but also to charge the local VAT to the final customer. In order to simplify, Article 141 EC VAT Directive states that each Member State must take specific measures to ensure that VAT is not charged on the intra-Community acquisition of goods within its territory where the following conditions are met:

- the (first) acquisition is made by a taxable person (intermediary) who is not established in the member State concerned but is identified for VAT purposes in another Member State;
- the acquisition of goods is made for the purposes of the subsequent supply of those goods, in the State concerned, by the taxable person previously referred;
- the goods are directly dispatched or transported, from a Member State other than that in which the intermediary is identified for VAT purposes, to the person for whom he is to carry out the subsequent supply;
- the person to whom the subsequent supply is to be made is another taxable person, or a nontaxable person, who is identified for VAT purposes in the Member State concerned; and finally,
- this person has been designated as liable for payment of the VAT due on the supply carried out by the taxable person who is not established in the EU Member State in which the tax is due (see Article 197 EC VAT Directive).

Basically, the intermediary is relieved from any fiscal duties in the EU country where the transport of the goods ends while the acquirer, being a taxable person or a legal nontaxable person, is regarded as the person liable to payment in that jurisdiction (a reverse charge applies). Finally, the VAT identification number criterion—regarding the intermediary—does not apply to these triangular operations inasmuch as certain conditions are met. More specifically it is required that (i) the person acquiring the goods (the intermediary) establishes that he has made the intra-Community acquisition for the purposes of a subsequent supply within the territory of the Member State where the dispatch or transport ends (see Article 40 EC VAT Directive), for which the person to whom the supply is made has been designated as liable for payment of VAT (Article 197 EC VAT Directive); and (ii) the person acquiring the goods has submitted the recapitulative statement laid down in Article 265 EC VAT Directive.[22]

---

22. The recapitulative statement must include: (i) the VAT identification number of the intermediary under which he made the acquisition and subsequent supply of goods; (ii) the VAT identification number, in the State in which dispatch or transport ended, of the person to whom the subsequent supply was made by the taxable person; and (iii) for each person to whom the subsequent supply was made, the total value, exclusive of VAT, of the supplies made by the taxable person in the Member State in which dispatch or transport of the goods ended.

12.4   THE PLACE OF SUPPLY OF SERVICES

12.4.1   Overview

Traditionally, services have not played a role as significant as goods for the purposes of indirect taxes. Besides, international trade has been mainly focused on goods while services used to be supplied in an environment of geographical proximity. This explains why VAT has usually taxed the supply of services in the jurisdiction where the provider had his business established.[23] In general, the place of establishment of the service supplier can be considered a good proxy for consumption, however, when it comes to international supplies the result basically coincides with the origin country principle as the "export" of services remains taxable—i.e., no refund applies—while the "import" is not subject to tax.[24]

This scenario has changed dramatically inasmuch as the importance of the international supplies of services has grown over the years, particularly in the context of transactions between taxable persons. Originally, the 1977 VAT Sixth Directive only contained some exceptions to the general rule,—e.g., intangible services, services related to immovable property, etc.—however, the number of those provisions has increased greatly since 1993.[25] It is important to highlight that, unlike in the international trade of goods, taxation of services in the destination country relies exclusively on the place of supply provisions.[26] That involves a simpler but also a more imperfect solution than the two-step process that applies to the cross-border supplies of goods (de-taxation in the origin country plus taxation in the destination country).

Currently the EC VAT Directive provides two general rules on the place of supply of services, as well as a number of special rules. In order to determine the place of supply, special provisions take precedence over the general rules, which only apply subsidiarily—therefore, they should be better regarded as fall back rules.[27] These provisions are usually based on connecting factors that reflect

---

23. Until recently, this was the one and only general rule on the place of supply of services.
24. There are two aspects that must be clarified in these preliminary remarks. First of all, the fact that, unlike other tax systems, for the European VAT the legal concepts of import and export only refer to goods. Strictly speaking those concepts are of no relevance within the context of supplies of services; however, bearing in mind the tax consequences that derive from the rules on the place of supply, it might be helpful to rely on a usual meaning of "imports" and "exports" in order to highlight the regime applicable to international supplies. On the other hand, those concepts are used only as regards to services that may be taxed separately, i.e., they do not include any ancillary or connected services which are already regarded for tax base purposes within the context of supplies of goods or imports.
25. The origin of those provisions goes back to Art. 6(3) of the Second VAT Directive.
26. Border tax adjustments do not apply within this context as the intangible nature of services does not permit a physical control similar to the one that applies to goods.
27. B. Terra, *The Place of Supply in European VAT* (Kluwer, 1998), 57. Regarding the Sixth Directive on VAT, the ECJ has held that Art. 9(2) sets out a number of specific instances of places where certain services are deemed to be supplied, whereas Art. 9(1) lays down the

more accurately the place where services are to be consumed—e.g., the place where the customer is established, the place where the service is physically supplied, etc. As regards specifically intra-Community trade, although the definitive regime should be based on the origin country principle, the increasing number of specific provisions inspired by the destination country principle logically involves a progressive departure from the solution originally intended.

These considerations help to one understand the greater complexity that characterizes these provisions when compared to those applying to the supply of goods. Such complexity is mainly due to the diversity of conditions that need to be taken into account. Actually, the supplier needs to determine: (i) the content of the service; (ii) the status of the customer; and (iii) the place where the customer is established.[28] These conditions are needed in order to determine the tax jurisdiction where the service is deemed to be supplied and, eventually, who the taxable person is—under certain circumstances, the reverse charge applies. For the application of the rules governing the place of supply of services, only those circumstances existing at the time of the chargeable event are taken into account. Any subsequent changes to the use of the service received does not affect the determination of the place of supply provided there is no abusive practice (see Article 25 EC VAT implementing Regulation).

The supplier of services must keep evidence of all the aforementioned aspects in order to prove to the tax administration that he acted in good faith, particularly as regards those supplies in which he did not charge VAT. To the purposes of proving the content of the service, the supplier may have a contract, an invoice or other documents. Nevertheless, in practice it can be very difficult for the supplier to determine both the status and capacity in which the customer is acting.

The determination of the acquirer status—i.e., whether he is a taxable person or not—is needed not only for the purposes of the general rules but also for some particular provisions on the place of supply. To that purpose it is necessary to turn to the definition of taxable person included in Tit. III EC VAT Directive (see Articles 9 to 13). Besides, Article 43 EC VAT Directive specifically includes within the category of taxable person the following situations:

- A taxable person who also carries on activities or transactions which are not considered to be taxable supplies of goods or services subject to tax in accordance with Article 2(1) is regarded as a taxable person in respect of

---

general rule on the matter. When Art. 9 is interpreted, Art. 9(1) in no way takes precedence over Art. 9(2). In every situation the question which arises is whether it is covered by one of the instances mentioned in Art. 9(2); if not, it falls within the scope of Art. 9(1) (Case 327/94 *Dudda*, paras. 20 and 21). See also Case 68/03 *Lipjes*, paras. 16 and 17). For instance, as the principal and habitual activities of a veterinary surgeon do not fall within any of the special rules, Art. 9(1) of the Sixth Directive applied in Case 167/95 *Linthorst, Pouwels en Scheres*. Therefore, those supplies were deemed to have been provided not in the jurisdiction where the customer had his business established but in the supplier's.
28. Moreover, those services which are ancillary to a supply of goods or an import are not taxed separately but regarded as a component of the tax base.

all services rendered to him for the place of supply purposes.[29] Therefore, the place of supply is deemed to be in the EU Member State of destination, not only when the input services are related to the taxable or exempted activity but also when they relate to nontaxable transactions.

- A nontaxable legal person who is identified for the purposes of VAT is regarded as a taxable person for the purposes of the place of supply of services. The purpose of this provision is to take advantage of those legal entities which are already registered or are required to be registered—because of their intra-Community acquisitions of goods subject to VAT or because they have exercised the option of making those operations subject to VAT.[30] However, by no means does this provision intend nontaxable legal entities to be regarded as taxable persons only because they are recipients of taxable services.

In our view, these provisions not only intend to guarantee tax neutrality, as well as collection in the destination country, but also to reduce the administrative burden on the nonestablished supplier as the reverse charge normally applies to these situations.[31] By contrast, for the purposes of the general rules on the place of supply of services (see Articles 44 and 45 EC VAT Directive), a taxable person—or a nontaxable person deemed to be a taxable person—who receives services exclusively for private use, including use by his staff, must be regarded as a nontaxable person.

The EC VAT implementing Regulation provides with a greater legal certainty in order to determine whether or not the recipient is a taxable person. When dealing with EU acquirers the main reference is the VAT identification number. Actually, unless the supplier has information to the contrary, the supplier may regard a customer established within the Community as a taxable person where the customer has communicated his individual VAT identification number and the supplier obtains confirmation of the validity of that number and of the associated name and address (to this purposes see Article 31 of Council Regulation (EC) No. 904/ 2010 of October 7, 2010).[32] By contrast, the supplier may regard a customer

---

29. The ECJ had previously held this opinion with regard to Art. 9(2)(e) of the Sixth Directive (Case 291/07 *Kollektivavtalsstiftelsen TRR Trygghetsrådet*). Basically, the Court considered that in the absence of any express provision in the sense that the services supplied must be used for the purposes of the customer's economic activity, it must be concluded that the fact that the customer used those services for activities which fell outside the scope of the Sixth Directive did not preclude the application of that provision.
30. See Art. 214 (1)(b) of Directive 2006/112/EC.
31. The reverse charge usually applies when the provider is not established in the destination country nor has a fixed establishment therein from which services are provided and the acquirer is a taxable person or a nontaxable legal person.
32. Subsidiarily, the supplier may still regard the customer established within the Community as a taxable person where the customer has not yet received an individual VAT identification number, but informs the supplier that he has applied for it and the supplier obtains any other proof which demonstrates that the customer is a taxable person or a nontaxable legal person required to be identified for VAT purposes and carries out a reasonable level of verification of

established within the Community as a nontaxable person when he can demonstrate that the customer has not communicated his individual VAT identification number to him. On the other hand, when the customer is established outside the Community, the supplier may regard him as a taxable person, unless he has information to the contrary, if he obtains from the customer a certificate issued by the customer's competent authorities as confirmation that the customer is engaged in economic activities in order to enable him to obtain a refund of VAT.[33] Subsidiarily, the customer may still be regarded as a taxable person if the supplier has the VAT number, or a similar number attributed to the customer by the country of establishment and used to identify businesses or any other proof which demonstrates that the customer is a taxable person and if the supplier carries out a reasonable level of verification of the accuracy of the information provided by the customer, by normal commercial security measures such as those relating to identity or payment checks.

A further issue arises as regards the capacity in which the customer has acquired the service. Again, it can be certainly difficult for the supplier to determine the intended use by the customer. Unless he has information to the contrary, such as information on the nature of the services provided, the supplier may consider that the services are for the customer's business use if, for that transaction, the customer has communicated his individual VAT identification number. This rule seems to be addressed only to European customers as taxable persons established outside the Community have to provide the supplier primarily with a certificate issued by the foreign tax administration—only subsidiarily by communicating a non-EU VAT number. When services are intended for both private use and business use, double taxation may arise depending on which jurisdiction intends to levy the tax. To avoid this, that supply is covered exclusively by the general rule on the supply of services to taxable persons, provided there is no abusive practice. The wording of Article 19 EC VAT implementing Regulation suggests this rule only applies to those supplies which fall under the general rules.

12.4.2   GENERAL RULES

The 1977 Sixth Directive on VAT originally established a general rule on the place of supply according to which services were deemed to be supplied at the place where the provider was established. The European Commission and the EU Member States have recently considered, however, that the correct functioning of the internal market required an amendment of the EC VAT Directive which, according

---

the accuracy of the information provided by the customer, by normal commercial security measures such as those relating to identity or payment checks.

33. Council Directive 86/560/EEC of Nov. 17, 1986 on the harmonization of the laws of the Member States relating to turnover taxes—Arrangements for the refund of value added tax to taxable persons not established in the Community territory.

to the preamble of Directive 2008/8/EC, is "aimed at the modernization and simplification of the functioning of the common system of VAT." The Directive states
that the new provisions are designed according the following principle: "in all
supplies of services the place of taxation must in principle be that of consumption."
This approach implies a significant change in the philosophy of the EU VAT as
taxation at the place of establishment of the supplier is expressly abandoned as the
one and only general rule. A new general rule applies to services supplied to
taxable persons (business-to-business or "B2B"), which are subject to VAT in
the country where the customer is established, while the scope of the original
provision is limited to those services provided to nontaxable persons (business-
to-consumer or "B2C").

Not only the general rules share a similar structure but they also rely upon the
same concepts, no matter their connecting factors are essentially different: the
place of supply is deemed to be the place of the business establishment, unless
a fixed establishment located in a tax jurisdiction other comes into play. In their
absence, the place of supply is determined by the permanent address or the usual
residence.

- The place of business establishment is the place where the functions of the
  business's central administration are carried out (see Article 10 EC VAT
  implementing Regulation). In order to determine this place, account must
  be taken of the place where essential decisions concerning the general
  management of the business are taken, the place where the registered office
  of the business is located and the place where management meets. Where
  the aforementioned criteria do not allow the place of establishment to
  be determined with certainty, precedence must be given to the place
  where essential decisions concerning the general management. By contrast,
  the mere presence of a postal address does not qualify as the place of
  establishment of a business of a taxable person.
- The place of supply of services is determined by the place of business
  establishment unless the service is provided to or from a fixed establishment
  located in a place other. The concept of fixed establishment is only relevant
  for the purposes of the place of supply of services. As a matter of fact, a
  fixed establishment does not imply the existence of a different taxable
  person[34] but a different tax jurisdiction where the taxable person is liable
  under VAT. Obviously, this raises a number of issues as not only is
  necessary to determine when a particular situation can be regarded as a
  fixed establishment but also when a service is deemed to be supplied
  from or to such fixed establishment. With regard to the first aspect, Article 11 EC VAT implementing Regulation states that a fixed establishment is
  any establishment other than the place of establishment of a business, which
  is characterized by a sufficient degree of permanence and a suitable

---

34. See Case 210/04 *FCE Bank*.

structure in terms of human and technical resources.[35] Nevertheless, the fact of having a VAT identification number by itself is not sufficient to consider that a taxable person has a fixed establishment. The second issue is only partially addressed under the general rule on services supplied to taxable persons.

– The permanent address of a natural person, whether or not a taxable person, is the address entered in the population or similar register or the address indicated by that person to the relevant tax authorities, unless there is evidence that this address does not reflect reality. The place where a natural person usually resides, whether or not a taxable person, is the place where that person usually lives as a result of personal and occupational ties. However, where the occupational ties are in a country different from that of the personal ties, or where no occupational ties exist, the place of usual residence will be determined by personal ties which show close links between the natural person and a place where he is living.

Finally, the general rules on the place of supply expressly apply to the following situations: (i) the supply of services made in the framework of organizing a funeral, in so far as they constitute a single service; (ii) the supply of services of translations of texts, except for those services provided to nontaxable persons established outside the Community (see Articles 28 and 29 EC VAT implementing Regulation). Except for this latter reference, which implies that those services are not subject to EU VAT, no special rules apply.

12.4.2.1 Supply of Services to Taxable Persons

The general rule on the place of supply of services to taxable persons is governed by the destination country principle. The place of supply is deemed to be at the jurisdiction where the recipient has established his business (see Article 44 EC VAT Directive). Therefore, the "export" of services from EU providers is not

---

35. This criterion can be traced in Case 190/95 *ARO Lease*, in which the ECJ stated that "... in order to be treated, by way of derogation from the primary criterion of the main place of business, as the place where a taxable person provides services, an establishment must possess a sufficient degree of permanence and a structure adequate, in terms of human and technical resources, to supply the services in question on an independent basis." In any circumstances, "... when a leasing company does not possess in a Member State either its own staff or a structure which has a sufficient degree of permanence to provide a framework in which agreements may be drawn up or management decision taken and thus to enable the services in question to be supplied on an independent basis, it cannot be regarded as having a fixed establishment in that State." Similarly, "an undertaking established in one Member State which hires out or leases a number of vehicles to clients established in another Member State does not possess a fixed establishment in that other State merely by engaging in that hiring out or leasing" (Case 390/96 *Lease Plan Luxembourg*, paras. 28 and 29). Neither the physical placing of vehicles at customer's disposal under leasing agreements nor the place at which they are used can be regarded as a clear, simple and practical criterion, in accordance with the spirit of the Sixth Directive, on which to base the existence of a fixed establishment. See also Case 155/01 *Cookies World*, with regard to the place of supply of services concerning the leasing of vehicles.

subject to VAT while the "import" is taxed on a regular basis, which is not only consistent with the purpose of VAT but also: (i) prevents any distortions among local taxable persons,[36] and (ii) removes an obstacle for third countries' taxable persons wishing to acquire services from EU providers.[37]

This provision basically relies upon the place of establishment of the business customer; however, when services are supplied to a fixed establishment located in a tax jurisdiction other, then the place of supply is governed by the location of the fixed establishment. For the purposes of this provision, a fixed establishment is characterized not only by a sufficient degree of permanence but also by a suitable structure—in terms of human and technical resources—to enable it to receive and use the services supplied to it for its own needs (see Article 11(1) EC VAT implementing Regulation). In the absence of such a place of establishment or a fixed establishment, the place of supply is deemed to be where the recipient has his permanent address or usually resides.[38] It must be emphasized that if the recipient does not identify himself properly as a taxable person, then the supplier will normally apply the VAT of the EU Member State of origin.

The determination of the place where the customer is established may raise some difficulties to the supplier. According to Article 20 EC VAT implementing Regulation, he has to establish that place based on information from the customer and verify it by normal commercial security measures such as those relating to identity or payment checks. The information may include the VAT identification number attributed by the Member State where the customer is established. In our view, the main concern for the supplier must be whether the customer is established in the same tax jurisdiction than he is; otherwise, he will be usually relieved from levying a VAT other than the one that applies in the jurisdiction where he is established (a reverse charge will normally apply).

A further issue arises where services are provided to a taxable person established in more than one place, e.g., has a fixed establishment in a jurisdiction other

---

36. The concept of taxable persons includes SICAVs, i.e., collective investment vehicles (Case 8/03 *BBL*).
37. Regarding the scope of this provision, in order to create greater legal certainty, Arts 26 and 27 EC VAT implementing Regulation specifically include within the scope of this general rule the following supplies of services: (i) a transaction whereby a body assigns television broadcasting rights in respect of football matches to taxable persons; and (ii) the supply of services which consist in applying for or receiving refunds of VAT under Council Directive 2008/9/CE of Feb. 12, 2008 to taxable persons not established in the Member State of refund but established in another Member State.
38. Where that taxable person—the acquirer—is established in a single country or, in the absence of a place of establishment of a business or a fixed establishment, has his permanent address and usually resides in a single country, that supply of services is taxable in that country. The supplier must establish that place based on information from the customer, and verify that information by normal commercial security measures such as those relating to identity or payment checks. The information may include the VAT identification number attributed by the Member State where the customer is established. On the other hand, where the taxable person is established in more than one country, the supply will be taxable in the country where the taxable person has established his business.

or a number of them in different jurisdictions. In this context, rules are needed in order to help the supplier to identify the customer's fixed establishment to which the service is provided. To that purpose, the supplier has to examine the nature and use of the service. Where the nature and use of the service do not enable him to identify the fixed establishment to which the service is provided, then the supplier must pay particular attention to whether the contract, the order form and the VAT identification number attributed by the Member State of the customer and communicated to him by the customer identify the fixed establishment as the customer of the service and whether the fixed establishment is the entity paying for the service. Subsidiarily, where the customer's fixed establishment to which the service is provided cannot be determined in accordance to the aforementioned criteria or where services covered by the general rule are supplied to a taxable person under a contract covering one or more services used in an unidentifiable and nonquantifiable manner, the supplier may legitimately consider that the services have been supplied at the place where the customer has established his business.

The general rule on the place of supply of services to taxable persons has simplified considerably the number and diversity of provisions on the place of supply, making also irrelevant, to a certain extent, the existing ECJ case law. The current solution does not involve any extra administrative burden to local suppliers who render their services in other EU tax jurisdictions, as the reverse charge applies.[39] However, in order to monitor a proper self-assessment by the acquirer, those suppliers identified for VAT purposes must submit a recapitulative statement of taxable persons and legal persons which are not taxable persons, identified for the purposes of VAT, to which they have provided not-exempt services in the EU Member State where the transaction is taxable, and for which the recipient is liable to pay the tax.[40] Basically, the same control mechanism that already applied to intra-Community acquisitions of goods is now extended to services. Unfortunately, the exclusion of the not-exempt services not only requires knowing the exemptions that apply in the EU Member State of destination but also adds a new element of risk given the insufficient harmonization of internal exemptions and the possible existence of domestic limitations or requirements of which the supplier may be unaware. No similar duty exists where the taxable person is a non-EU supplier.

---

39. According to Art. 196 EC VAT Directive, VAT is payable by any taxable person, or nontaxable legal person identified for VAT purposes, to whom the services referred in Art. 44 are supplied if the services are supplied by a taxable person not established within the territory of the EU Member State. To that purpose, a taxable person who has a fixed establishment in the territory where the VAT is due must be regarded as a nonestablished supplier if the fixed establishment is not involved in the transaction. For control reasons, European suppliers must submit a recapitulative statement to the EU Member State where they are registered.

40. The statement must include the VAT identification number of both the supplier and the recipient of services in an EU Member State other than that in which the statement is to be submitted, and the total value of the supplies of services carried out by the taxable person in respect of each recipient of services.

12.4.2.2 Supply of Services to Nontaxable Persons

The general rule on the place of supply of services to nontaxable persons continues to be governed by the origin country principle. According to Article 45 EC VAT Directive, the place of supply is deemed to be the place in which the supplier has his place of business. Therefore, the "import" of services for final customers is not subject to VAT while the "export" is taxed on a regular basis.[41]

Although the provision basically relies upon the place of supply of the provider, when services are provided from a fixed establishment located in another jurisdiction, then the place of supply is the place where that fixed establishment is located. In order to qualify as a fixed establishment not only is it necessary a sufficient degree of permanence but also a suitable structure—in terms of human and technical resources—to enable it to provide the services which it supplies (see Article 11(2) EC VAT implementing Regulation). In the absence of such a place, the place of supply is the place where the supplier has his permanent address or usually resides with the aforementioned consequences.

Leaving aside the special provisions, the ECJ has traditionally supported the location of the service at the jurisdiction where the supplier had established his business.[42] Particularly, the original general rule on the 1977 VAT Sixth Directive has been interpreted in the following terms (Case 168/84 *Berkholz, para.* 17): "the place where the supplier has established his business is a primary point of reference inasmuch as regard is to be had to another establishment from which the services are supplied only if the reference of the place where the supplier has established his business does not lead to a rational result for tax purposes or creates a conflict with another Member State." From this approach it derives the following consequences: (i) the mere existence of a fixed establishment does not necessarily imply that the place of supply of the service is deemed to be at the jurisdiction where the establishment which supplies the services is located; (ii) a narrow interpretation of the concept of fixed establishment, which has been tempered over time.[43]

---

41. Therefore, suppliers from non-EU tax jurisdictions do not have to worry about any administrative burdens in the EU Member State where services are to be consumed. Moreover, EU suppliers do not have to split their turnover in the different jurisdictions where they operate.
42. Not only simplicity is a major advantage but also rationality and uniformity of the result.
43. The ECJ has ruled that "services cannot be deemed to be supplied at an establishment other than the place where the supplier has established his business unless that establishment is of a certain minimum size and both the human and technical resources necessary for the provision of particular services are permanently present" (Case 168/84 *Berkholz*, para. 8). From this perspective, "it does not appear that the installation on board a sea-going ship of gaming machines, which are maintained permanently, is capable of constituting such an establishment, especially if tax may appropriately be charged at the place where the operator of machines has his permanent business establishment." As a result, "an installation for carrying on a commercial activity, such as the operation of gaming machines, on board a ship sailing on the high seas outside the national territory may be regarded as a fixed establishment within the meaning of that provision only if the establishment entails the permanent presence of both the human and technical resources necessary for the provision of those services and it is not appropriate to deem those services to have been provided at the place where the supplier has

Furthermore, a strict interpretation of the special provisions on the place of supply has occasionally contributed to a greater application of the general rule.[44]

12.4.3 SPECIAL RULES

The VAT Directive contains a number of particular provisions which take precedence over the general rules on the place of supply. Most of these special rules rely upon the place where those services are physically supplied in order to guarantee they are effectively taxed in the jurisdiction where they are to be consumed. Some of them (general exceptions) depend exclusively on the nature of the services, regardless they have been provided B2B or B2C, while others (particular exceptions) only affect to certain services insofar as they are provided to final customers.

The ECJ usually tries to avoid special provisions to be regarded as exceptions to the general rules in order to avoid a narrow interpretation (See Case 108/00 *SPI*, paragraph 17). However, leaving this aside, they obviously derogate or depart from the general rules as other connecting factors seem to be more appropriate according to the nature of the services.[45]

---

established his business." According to this pattern, the Court has also held that the concept of fixed establishment "does not seem to apply to a place supplying restaurant services on a ship, especially where, as in this case, the permanent establishment of the operator of the ship affords an appropriate point of reference for the purposes of taxation" (Case 231/94 *Faaborg-Gelting Linien*). In our view, this approach has been tempered since Case 190/95, *ARO Lease*.

44. For the purposes of Art. 9(2)(e) of the Sixth Directive, the ECJ has held that neither the services of an arbitrator (Case 145/96 *Von Hoffmann*) nor those of executing a will (Case 401/06 *Commission/Germany*) can be regarded as services similar to a lawyer's. Likewise, the Court has held that a composite supply of services relating to waste collection—including collection, sorting, transport, storage, treatment, recycling and actual disposal of waste—is not ruled by the specific provision that applies to works on movable tangible property (Case 429/97 *Commission/France*). Therefore, although the main service, that is, the actual disposal of the waste, was specifically carried out in France, the place of supply of the composite service was deemed to be at the place where the supplier had the business established. According to the ECJ, "in view of the composite nature of that supply, the effect of applying such a connecting factor would be to create uncertainty as the rate of VAT at which the main contractor must invoice his customers whenever any of the operations comprising the composite supply takes in a Member State other than that in which the main contractor is established (para. 46). For the same reason, the application of that connecting factor would be liable to create conflicts of jurisdiction between Member States, which would run counter to the objectives of Art. 9 of the Sixth Directive (para. 47). It follows that such supply cannot be governed by the specific provision, regardless of whether the actual disposal of the waste constitutes work on movable tangible property within the meaning of that provision (para. 48). On the other hand, the general rule set forth in Art. 9(1) of the Sixth Directive lays down a definite, simple and practical criterion for the connection of that type of supply, which is that of the place where the supplier has established his business or has a fixed establishment from which the service is supplied. That provision is such as to ensure the rational and uniform taxation of the composite supply taken as a whole and to avoid conflicts of jurisdiction between Member States (para. 49)."
45. According to the ECJ, "it was necessary to make an exception to the general rule laid down in Art. 9(1) because a transporter's place of business is not an appropriate reference for

12.4.3.1   General Exceptions

The place of supply of the general exceptions is deemed to be the EU Member State in which services are materially carried out or provided, with some minor exceptions. Initially this requires the supplier to register for VAT purposes in the jurisdiction where he is to be regarded as the person liable to payment, however, when the recipient is a taxable person or a nontaxable legal person the reverse charge normally applies—therefore, the nonestablished supplier does not have to face any fiscal duties in the EU Member State of destination. However, that is not the case where the recipient is a final customer and that may have an important deterrent effect on suppliers from other EU Member States or third countries who are willing to carry out an economic activity within that State.

Basically, the general exceptions apply to services related to immovable property, passenger transport, restaurant and catering services and short-term hiring of means of transport and (until January 1, 2011) cultural services, commercial fairs and exhibitions. Each of them will be further analyzed in detail:

(a) *Immovable property* exerts an indisputable "force of attraction" over the place of supply of the related services. According to Article 47 EC VAT Directive, the place of supply of services connected to immovable property—including services provided by experts and estate agents, the provision of accommodation in the hotel sector or in sectors with a similar function, i.e. holiday camps or sites developed for use as camping site, the granting of rights to use immovable property and services for the preparation or co-ordination of construction works, i.e. services provided by architects, firms that provide on-site supervision—is the place in which the immovable property is located. The ECJ has stated that for this provision to apply, a "sufficiently direct connection" is required between the services supplied and the immovable property concerned, on the grounds that it would be contrary to the general scheme of that provision to place within the scope of that special rule every supply of services provided that it has a connection, even a very tenuous one, with immovable property, since a large number of services are connected in one way or another with immovable property.[46] However, there are

establishing territorial jurisdiction for tax purposes. The very nature of the performance of the specific nature constituted by transport, which is liable to be effected on the territory of more than one Member State, requires a different criterion, which essentially must make it possible to determine the jurisdiction of each of the States involved for tax purposes" (Case 283/84 *Trans Tirreno Express*, para. 17). See also Case 30/89 *Commission/France*, para. 14.

46. In this context the ECJ has held that the transmission of the right to fish by means of a transfer of fishing permits for valuable consideration constitutes a supply of services connected with immovable property (Case 166/05 *Heger*). Likewise, the place where services are supplied by an association whose business consists in organizing the exchange between its members of their timeshare usage rights in holiday accommodation, in return for which that association receives from its members enrolment, annual subscription and exchange fees, is the place where the property in respect of which the member concerned holds timeshare usage rights is situated

situations in which an adequate monitoring will be hard, e.g., mediation in the letting of immovable property between nonestablished parties. This provision does not apply, however, to the services provided by an intermediary acting in the name and on behalf of another person who takes part in the provision of accommodation in the hotel sector (see Article 46 EC VAT implementing Regulation).

(b) The place of supply of *passenger transport*—persons and their luggage—is deemed to be the place in which the transport is physically carried out, proportionate to the distances covered (Article 48 EC VAT Directive).[47] The provision is only relevant for international passenger transport by road (coach, taxi) or train as international transport by sea or air is exempted from VAT. The coach, taxi or train company must charge the VAT of each EU Member State it crosses, splitting the tax base according to the distances covered.[48] Obviously, not only is the provision difficult to apply but monitoring seems almost impossible.

(c) Another important exception regards the supply of services and ancillary services relating to *cultural, artistic, sporting, scientific, educational, entertainment* or *similar* activities, i.e. fairs, exhibitions, including the services provided by the organizers.[49] Those services are deemed to be supplied in the place where they are physically carried out (see Articles 53

(Case 37/08 *RCI Europe*). Obviously, if the general rule laid down in Art. 9(1) of the Sixth Directive applied, it would be easy for an economic operator such as RCI Europe completely to avoid VAT on its supply of services by establishing its registered office outside the area where the EU VAT applies. Leaving this aside, this specific criterion may involve some difficulties as regards the allocation of enrolment and annual subscriptions to timeshare properties located in different tax jurisdictions.

47. See Case 283/84 *Trans Tirreno Express*. The transport of goods is subject to a different regime which basically depends on whether the recipient is a taxable or a nontaxable person.

48. From this special provision also derives the need to allocate, in the case of the supply of cross-frontier passenger transport on an all-inclusive basis, the total consideration on a pro rata basis having regard the distances covered in each of the Member States concerned (Case 116/96 *Reisebüro Binder*).

49. The ECJ has held that the reference to "similar activities" in Art. 9(2)(c) of the Sixth Directive included services provided by an organizer to exhibitors at a fair or in an exhibition hall (Case 114/05 *Gillan Beach*). In this context, the Court pointed out a number of characteristics common to those activities mentioned in Art. 9(2)(c): a) complex nature of the services provided; b) number of different recipients; c) the fact that services are usually provided for specific events, and; d) the place where they are provided is easy to identify. Actually, the Court has disregarded the application of this provision to services consisting of research and development work relating to the environment and technology as they were not supplied to a number of different recipients but to a single taxable person (Case 222/09 *Kronospan Mielec*, para. 25). The ECJ also held that entertainment or similar activities do not require artistic input by the supplier of the services. Actually, an activity in respect of which the principal objective pursued by the supplier of services is the entertainment of its customers constitutes entertainment or similar activities to these purposes. In this context, enabling the public to use, for consideration, slot gaming machines installed in amusement arcades is regarded as constituting entertainment or similar activities (Case 452/03 *RAL (Channel Islands) and others*). Finally, the provision of sound-engineering, inasmuch as it is a prerequisite for the performance of an artistic or

et seq. EC VAT Directive). However, it must be noted that from January 1, 2011 the scope of this provision is considerably limited for services provided B2B, as only those services related to admission to those events—e.g., sale of tickets[50]—and ancillary services related to the admission remain taxable under this provision.[51] Any other supply of services falls under the general rule on the place of supply of services B2B. Regarding those services provided to nontaxable persons, the place of supply remains at the jurisdiction where they are physically carried out.

(d) The same general criterion basically rules the place of supply of *restaurant and catering services*.[52] Those services are deemed to be supplied in the jurisdiction where they are physically carried out (see Article 55 EC VAT Directive).[53] However, a particular provision applies to those services carried out on board ships, aircraft or trains during a section of a passenger transport operation effected within the Community. The place of supply of those services is at the point of departure of the passenger transport operation.[54] In these circumstances, the place of physical supply cedes because of the complexity that it involves. Likewise, the general rules on the place of supply of services should not apply in order to avoid

---

entertainment event, must be considered as an ancillary service for the purposes of Art. 9(2)(c) of the Sixth Directive (Case 327/94 *Dudda*, para. 31).

50. That reference includes the supply of services of which the essential characteristics are the granting of the right of admission to an event in exchange for a ticket of payment, including payment in the form of a subscription, a season ticket or a periodic fee. In particular this applies to the right of admission to: (i) shows, theatrical performances, circus performances, fairs amusement parks, concerts, exhibitions and other similar cultural events; (ii) sporting events such as matches or competitions; (iii) educational and scientific events such as conferences and seminars. However, this provision does not cover the use of facilities such as gymnastics halls and suchlike (see Art. 32 EC VAT implementing Regulation).

51. The provision applies to those services directly related to the aforementioned which are supplied separately for a consideration to a person attending an event (see Art. 33 EC VAT implementing Regulation), in particular the use of cloakrooms or sanitary facilities. The concept does not include, however, the mere intermediary services relating to the sale of tickets.

52. Article 6 EC VAT implementing Regulation states that restaurant and catering services mean "services consisting of the supply of prepared or unprepared food or beverages or both, for human consumption, accompanied sufficient support services allowing for the immediate consumption thereof." The provision of food or beverages or both is only one component of the whole in which services predominate. Restaurant services are the supply of such services on the premises of the supplier, and catering services are the supply of services off the premises of the supplier. On the contrary, the concept does not include the supply of prepared or unprepared food or beverages or both, whether or not including transport but without any support services.

53. Originally restaurant transactions fell within the general rule on the place of supply of services. Therefore, they were deemed to be provided at the place where the supplier had established his business (Case 231/94 *Faaborg-Gelting Linien*).

54. Basically we are dealing with the same connecting factor that applies to the supply of goods to passengers in such intra-Community transports (see Art. 37 EC VAT Directive). Actually, both provisions rely on the same concepts, i.e., "section of a passenger transport effected within the Community" and "point of departure of a passenger transport operation" and "point of arrival of a passenger transport operation." In cases of return journeys, the return leg is also considered a separate journey.

distortions and competitive advantages that would favor non-EU companies. A major drawback of this provision, as already mentioned, is that suppliers of restaurant and catering services need to register and fulfill any tax obligations in each EU Member State from which the transports departs.

Where restaurant services and catering services are supplied outside such a section but on the territory of a Member State or a third country or third territory, they are deemed to be supplied in the jurisdiction where they are physically carried out (see Article 36(2) EC VAT implementing Regulation). However, where those services are carried out within the Community partly during a section of a passenger transport operation effected within the Community, and partly outside such a section but on the territory of an EU Member State, then the place of supply is governed in its entirety according to the rules for determining the place of supply applicable at the beginning of the supply of the restaurant or catering service. Unfortunately, all these provisions raise obvious monitoring issues.

(e) The place of supply of *short-term hiring of means of transport* is the place where the means of transport is actually put at the disposal of the customer (see Article 56 EC VAT Directive). This obviously implies that rent-a-car companies must register in each European tax jurisdiction where they have vehicles for short-term hiring at the disposal of their customers.[55]

The expression "short-term" applies to the holding or the continuous possession of the means of transport for an uninterrupted period not exceeding thirty days and, in the case of vessels, no more than ninety days. To these purposes, the duration of the continuous possession or use will be determined on the basis of the contract between the parties involved. However, the contract only serves as a presumption which may be rebutted by any means in fact or law in order to establish the actual duration of the continuous possession or use (see Article 39 EC VAT implementing Regulation). The fact that the contractual period of short-term hiring is exceeded on grounds of force majeure has no bearing on the determination of the duration of the continuous possession or use of the means of transport.[56]

---

55. Originally Art. 9(1) of the Sixth Directive applied to these services for reasons of control. Since forms of transport may easily cross frontiers, it is difficult, if not impossible, to determine the place of their utilization (Case 190/95 *ARO Lease*, para. 14). Therefore, for the hiring out of all forms of transport, the Sixth Directive provided that the service was deemed to be supplied not at the place where the goods were used but, with a view of simplification and in conformity with the general rule, at the place where the supplier had established his business (Case 51/88 *Hamann*, paras. 17 and 18).

56. For the long-term hiring of vehicles, the general rules apply. Obviously, this raises an issue as parties may split a long-term hiring in multiple short-term hiring contracts. In order to avoid this, where hiring of one and the same means of transport is covered by consecutive contracts between the same parties, the duration is that of the continuous possession or use of the means of transport provided for under the contracts as a whole. To these purposes, a contract and its extensions will be regarded as consecutive contracts. Notwithstanding, the duration of a

The place where the means of transport is actually put at the disposal of the customer is the place where the customer or a third party acting on his behalf takes physical possession of it (see Articles 38(2) and 40 EC VAT implementing Regulation). On the other hand, the definition of "means of transport" includes vehicles, whether motorized or not, and other equipment and devices designed to transport persons or objects from one place to another, which might be pulled down or pushed by vehicles and which are normally designed to be used and actually capable of being used for transport.[57] It does not include, however, vehicles which are permanently immobilized nor containers.

Finally, as already mentioned, the general rules on the place of supply apply to long-term hiring of vehicles. However, from January 1, 2013 the place of supply to nontaxable persons will be, not the country where the supplier is established or has a fixed establishment, but the tax jurisdiction where the customer is established, has his permanent address or usually resides (see Article 56 EC VAT Directive).

12.4.3.2 Particular Exceptions

There are a number of special provisions which only apply to services provided to nontaxable persons. Some of them reject any application of the general rule while others only regard a particular situation—therefore, both the general rule and these provisions need to be taken into account in order to draw the complete picture regarding the place of supply of those services:

(1) No application of the general rule on the place of supply of services to nontaxable persons is allowed with regards to intermediation services, transport of goods and valuation of movable property and works on those goods.

(a) The place of supply of services to a nontaxable person by an *intermediary* acting in the name and on behalf of another person (disclosed agents) is the place in which the underlying operation is deemed to have been supplied (see Article 46 EC VAT Directive).[58]

---

short-term hire contract or contracts preceding a contract which is regarded as long-term will not be called into question provided there is no abusive practice. Similarly, unless there is abusive practice, consecutive contracts between the same parties for different means of transport are not considered to be consecutive contracts.

57. According to Art. 38(2) EC VAT implementing Regulation, the definition includes in particular the following vehicles: (a) land vehicles, such as cars, motor cycles, bicycles, tricycles and caravans; (b) trailers and semi-trailers; (c) railway wagons; (d) vessels; (e) aircraft; (f) vehicles specifically designed for the transport of sick or injured persons; (g) agricultural tractors and other agricultural vehicles; (h) mechanically or electronically propelled invalid carriages.

58. The ECJ had previously held that the place of supply of intermediary services rendered in connection with intra-Community acquisitions was ruled by Art. 28b(E)(3) of the Sixth Directive, regardless they were provided to a taxable or a nontaxable person (Case 68/03 *Lipjes*). From this perspective, intermediary services are deemed to be supplied in the jurisdiction in which the principal transaction takes place, no matter that supply fell within the scope of VAT or qualified as a nontaxable transaction. It must be noted that some parties in the aforementioned

This provision applies to the services of intermediaries acting in the name and on behalf of the recipient of the service procured and the services performed by intermediaries acting in the name and on behalf of the provider of the services procured (see Article 30 EC VAT implementing Regulation). On the other hand, as already mentioned, services to non taxable persons are deemed to be supplied in the jurisdiction where the supplier is established, therefore the mediator will have to register in that jurisdiction or, should any of the particular provisions apply, in the place where the main supply is deemed to be carried out, e.g. where the service is physically rendered out. In other words, intermediary services are treated as if they were ancillary to the underlying supply. However, if the underlying operation is supplied in an EU Member State which is neither that of the mediator nor that of the consumer, the transaction will be practically impossible to monitor.

This provision also applies to the intermediation in the provision of accommodation in the hotel sector or in sectors having a similar function when supplied to a nontaxable person (Article 31 (b) EC VAT implementing Regulation). However, the general rule on services B2B applies whenever those services are provided to a taxable person acting as such or a nontaxable legal person deemed to be a taxable person.

(b) The place of supply of the *transport of goods* to nontaxable persons, other than intra-Community transport, is the place where the transport actually takes place, proportionate to the distances covered (see Article 49 EC VAT Directive). As already mentioned, the same criterion applies to passenger transport (see Article 48 EC VAT Directive) in order to ensure that each EU Member State taxes transport services in respect of the parts of the journey completed in its territory.[59]

---

case argued that the special provision only applied when the underlying transaction was within the scope of VAT, while the general rule should apply to intermediary services where the main transaction was concluded between individuals.

59. See Case 30/89 *Commission/France*, para. 18 and Case 331/94 *Commission/Greece*. The Court has also held that this provision does not prohibit a Member State from applying its value added tax legislation to a transport operation effected between two points within its national territory, even where a part of that journey is completed outside its national territory, provided that it does not encroach on the tax jurisdiction of other States. Art. 9(2)(b) of the Sixth Directive in no way restricts the freedom of the Member States to extend the scope of their tax legislation beyond their normal territorial limits, so long as they do not encroach on the jurisdiction of other States (Case 283/84 *Trans Tirreno Express*). It cannot be inferred from this, however, that the Sixth Directive requires EU Member States to subject to VAT transport operations carried out within their territory in respect of that part of the journey occurring in or above international waters (C-30/89 *Commission/France*, para. 18). Not only the aforementioned approach seems inappropriate inasmuch as VAT is a territorial tax on consumption but also involves an obvious risk

As regards the intra-Community transport of goods, the place of supply to nontaxable persons involves a simpler solution. Those services are deemed to be supplied in the place of departure of the transport (see Articles 50 et seq. EC VAT Directive). To this purpose, "intra-Community transport of goods" means any transport of goods where the place of departure and that of arrival are located in the territory of two different EU Member States. Likewise, the "place of departure" is the place where the transport of the goods actually begins, regardless of the distances covered in order to reach the place where the goods are located; and, finally, the "place of arrival" is the place where the transport of the goods actually ends.

The EC VAT Directive allows the EU Member States to exclude the part of the intra-Community transport of goods which takes place in waters that do not form part of the Community territory. That exclusion applies mandatorily in international transport from or to a point outside the EU, and even in domestic transport, but for intra-Community transport it depends on the choice of each state.

The place of supply of ancillary transport activities, such as loading, unloading, handling and other similar services, to nontaxable persons is the place where those services are physically supplied.

(c) The place of supply of *valuations of/works on movable tangible property* is also the place where those services are physically carried out (see Article 54 EC VAT Directive).[60] This provision covers services to a nontaxable person consisting only of the assembly by a taxable person of the various parts of a machine, all of which are provided to him by his customer (see Article 34 of the EU VAT implementing Regulation), except where the goods being assembled become part of immovable property.

(2) Some special provisions address the "import" and "export" situations while the "intra-Community" supplies remain under the general rule on the place of supply. Basically, the EU VAT intends to tax the "import" of electronic services while excluding from taxation the "export" of intangible services. These provisions rely upon the permanent address or residence of the recipient.[61]

---

of double taxation. By contrast, the ECJ has recently held (Case 111/05 *Aktiebolaget NN)* that the supply and laying out of a fibre-optic cable between two EU Member States is not subject to VAT for that part of the transaction which is carried out in the exclusive economic zone, on the continental shelf and at sea.

60. See Case 429/97 *Commission/France*. The ECJ has excluded from this category those services principally and habitually carried out by a veterinary surgeon (Case 167/95 *Linthorst, Pouwels en Scheres*).

61. In general, it is not easy for taxable persons to determine such place so they usually have to rely on what the customer—a nontaxable person—says or what appears in public records.

(a) On a general basis, the "import" of services B2C is not subject to EU VAT. The increasing importance of e-commerce and services electronically rendered puts at risk the tax neutrality within the European Internal Market. To avoid this, the place of supply of *electronic services* B2C, particularly those listed in Annex II of the Directive, provided by a nonestablished supplier is deemed to be the jurisdiction where the nontaxable person has his permanent address or usually resides, that is, in the destination country.[62]

As mentioned, tax neutrality demands those services to be taxed at the place where the final customer is established whenever they are provided by taxable persons who have established their business outside the EU—or have a fixed establishment from which the service is supplied or who, in the absence of such a place of business or fixed establishment, have a permanent address or usually reside outside the Community. Where the supplier is established in a EU Member State, according to the general rule that applies to services provided B2C, the place of supply is the place where the supplier has established his business or where the fixed establishment from which the services are provided is located (see Article 45 EC VAT Directive).

Initially non-EU suppliers need to register in every EU Member State to which they supply their electronic services. However, in order to simplify this situation, a voluntary one-stop-shop mechanism has been introduced under Title XII Chapter 6 EC VAT Directive.

(b) On the contrary, services "exported" to nontaxable persons usually carry the VAT of the EU Member State where the supplier has established his business. Not only this is inconsistent with the condition of VAT as a tax on domestic consumption but it also turns into a major drawback for EU companies which sell services in a global market in competition with non-EU suppliers. In order to avoid this, the place of supply of the so called *intangible services* to a nontaxable person who is established, has his permanent address or usually resides outside the Community is the place in which that person is established or has his permanent address or usually resides (see Article 59 EC VAT Directive).

Article 59 EC VAT Directive has succeeded Article 9(2)(e) of the Sixth VAT Directive, which also applied to taxable persons established in a different EU tax jurisdiction. Obviously, this latter reference is no longer necessary inasmuch as the general rule on the place of supply of services to taxable persons already leads to the intended result—services are subject to VAT in the EU

The Directive does not state to what extent suppliers have to investigate those circumstances but it should never go beyond the requirements of the principle of good faith.

62. Where the supplier of the service and the receiver communicate by e-mail this does not by itself mean that the service is an electronically supplied service.

jurisdiction where the acquirer is established. Besides, Article 9(2)(e) relied on a series of EU Law concepts which must be interpreted uniformly in order to avoid instances of double taxation or nontaxation. To a certain extent, the new general rule has made irrelevant a number of the statements the ECJ had previously held with regards to Article 9(2) of the Sixth Directive.[63]

Regarding the current Article 59 EC VAT Directive, the "export" of the following services B2C is not subject to the EU VAT:

- Transfers and assignments of copyrights, patents, licenses, trademarks and other similar rights.
- Advertising services.[64]

---

63. Among others, see Case 377/08 *EGN* and Case 242/08 *Swiss Re Germany Holding*.
64. According to the ECJ with regards to Art. 9(2)(e) of the Sixth Directive, "the concept of advertising necessarily entails the dissemination of a message intended to inform consumers of the existence and the qualities of a product or service, with a view to increasing sales. Although that message is usually spread, by means of spoken or printed words and/or pictures, by the press, radio and/or television, this can also be done by the partial or exclusive use of other means" (Case 68/92 *Commission/France*, para. 16). In order to determine whether a given operation can be characterized as an advertising service, it is necessary in each case to take account of all the circumstances surrounding the service in question—e.g., where the means have been procured by an advertising agency—, bearing in mind that an operation may be characterized as a supply of advertising services even where it is not carried out by a supplier engaged in business as an advertising agency. From this derives that the provision covers:

A) Promotional activities as: (i) the sale by an advertising agency to its customer of articles intended to be handed out to consumers, services provided by an advertising agency in connection with various events such as recreational functions, cocktail parties, etc., as well as the production of advertising aids (Case 68/92 *Commission/France*, para. 20); (ii) the sale of movable tangible property in the context of an advertising campaign and services provided in connection with a variety of public-relations events, such as press conferences, seminars, cocktail parties and recreational functions . . . (Case 69/92 *Commission/Luxembourg*, para. 21); (iii) the provision of hotel services or recreational activities such as the supply of food or meals, the organization of shows, games, competitions, parties or any similar events (Case 73/92 *Commission/Spain*).
B) Advertising services the cost of which is included in the price of the advertiser's goods and which were originally supplied not by the party with whom the advertiser contracts but by another supplier who is in a contractual relationship with that party. Therefore, the previous Art. 9(2)(e) of the Sixth Directive not only applied to advertising services supplied directly and invoiced by the supplier to a taxable advertiser but also to services supplied indirectly to the advertiser and invoiced to a third party who in turn invoices them to the advertiser (Case 108/00 *SPI*). The fact that the advertiser does not produce goods or services in the price of which the cost of the advertising services may be included is not relevant for the purpose of determining the place where the services are supplied to the intermediate customer (Case 438/01 *Design Concept*). Moreover, the place of supply is, as a rule, according to Art. 9(2)(e) of the Sixth Directive, defined as the place where the recipient has his principal place of business and it is unnecessary for account to be taken of the fact that that recipient is not necessarily the final advertiser (Case 1/08 *Athesia Druck*, para. 27).

- Services of consultants,[65] engineers,[66] consultancy firms, lawyers, accountants and other similar services,[67] as well as data processing and the provision of information. This provision also applies to translation services according to Article 41 EC VAT implementing Regulation.
- Obligations not to carry on, totally or partially, a business activity or a right referred to in this paragraph.
- Banking, financial and insurance operations, including those of re-insurance, with the exception of the hiring of safes.[68]
- Supply of staff.
- Hiring out of movable tangible property, with the exception of means of transport.
- Provision of access to distribution systems for natural gas and electricity and of transport or transmission by way of the same, and the provision of other directly related services.
- Telecommunication services.
- Radio and television broadcasting services.
- Electronically supplied services, in particular those mentioned in Annex II EC VAT Directive. It must be noted that where the supplier of the service and the receiver communicate by e-mail this does not by itself mean that the service provided is a service provided electronically.

The previous list seems unnecessarily long and detailed, as a number of the references above make sense in the context of services provided to taxable persons.[69] Inasmuch as Article 59 EC VAT

---

65. The ECJ has excluded from the category of "services of consultants" those services principally and habitually carried out by a veterinary surgeon (Case 167/95 *Linthorst, Pouwels en Scheres*).
66. According to ECJ (Case 222/09 *Kronospan Mielec*), services consisting of research and development work relating to the environment and technology, carried out by engineers established in one Member State on a contract basis for the benefit of a recipient established in another Member State, must be classified as services of engineers. The Court has also held that an U.S. undertaking that customized software for a Dutch taxable person fell within the scope of this reference (Case 41/04 *Levob Verzekeringen and OV Bank*). Interestingly enough, the services consisted merely in transposing the program into Dutch and modifying it as required by the fact that in the Netherlands, agents are involved in such insurance contracts.
67. According to the ECJ, a service must be regarded as similar to those of one of the activities mentioned in Art. 9(2)(e), third indent, of the Sixth Directive when they both serve to the same purpose (Case 145/96 *Von Hoffmann*). From this perspective, neither an executor's services (Case 401/06 *Commission/Germany*) nor the services of an arbitrator (Case 145/96 Von Hoffmann) can be regarded as similar to a lawyer's services. The provision does not cover either those services principally and habitually carried out by a veterinary surgeon (Case 167/95 *Linthorst, Pouwels en Scheres*).
68. Apparently, the hiring of safes is governed by Art. 47 EC VAT Directive which rules the supply of services connected with immovable property, although no explicit reference is made in this provision.
69. The references contained in (i), (ii), (iv), (v)—as regards re-insurance—and (vi) are a clear example of this.

Directive only applies to nontaxable persons, the practical interest of those indents reduces at best to nontaxable legal persons.

12.4.4   FORTHCOMING MODIFICATIONS

The place of supply of *long-term hiring of means of transport* is currently governed by the general provisions. However, as mentioned, from January 1, 2013 the place of supply of those services to a nontaxable person will be the place where the customer is established, has his permanent his permanent address or usually resides. In the particular case of pleasure boats, the place of supply is where the boat is actually put at the disposal of the customer, where this service is actually provided by the supplier from his place of business or from a fixed establishment in that place. This provision applies to any hiring of means of transport B2C throughout a period that exceeds thirty days—ninety days in the case of vessels.

From January 1, 2015, the current rules on the supply of services of *telecommunication, radio and television broadcasting and electronics services* to nontaxable persons will be replaced by a new set of provisions. According to those provisions, the "import" will be taxed at the EU tax jurisdiction where the customer is established—this already applies under Article 58 EC VAT Directive but only with regard to electronic services—while the "export" will not be subject to the EU VAT—as already derives from Article 59 (i), (j) and (k) EC VAT Directive. In any case, the EU Member States will be able to resort to the use and enjoyment rule in order to avoid any undesirable effects (e.g., double taxation, nontaxation or distortion of competition). By December 31, 2014 the European Commission must present a report on the feasibility of applying efficiently the rules for the supply of telecommunications, radio or television broadcasting and electronic services to nontaxable persons and on the question whether these rules are still in line with the general policy as regards the place of supply of services.

12.4.5   USE AND ENJOYMENT RULE

One of the most difficult provisions regarding the place of supply is the "use and enjoyment" rule which is now contained in Article 59a EC VAT Directive. This provision, although conceived as an exception, entitles EU Member States to alter the harmonized structure so carefully assembled. According to this provision, in order to prevent double taxation, nontaxation or distortion of competition, EU Member States may deem, with regard to services the place of which is governed by Articles 44 (general rule B2B), 45 (general rule B2C), 56 (short-term hiring of means of transport) and 59 (intangible services B2C "exported" with no VAT), that:

(a) The place of supply of any or all of those services, if situated within their territory—e.g., inbound services B2B, outbound services B2C—is located outside the Community if the effective use and enjoyment of the services takes place outside the Community.

(b) The place of supply of any or all of those services, if situated outside the Community—e.g., outbound services B2B, inbound services B2C on a general basis, services B2C "exported" with no VAT—is located within their territory if the effective use and enjoyment of the services takes place in their territory (recapture rule).

The VAT Directive authorizes the EU Member States to lay down rules other than the harmonized connecting factors, even to a greater extent that they were previously authorized under the Sixth Directive. Obviously, a number of issues arise. First of all, the Directive does not provide a definition of "use and enjoyment" which may lead to significant differences among the EU countries. Moreover, the use and enjoyment depends on the nature of the service so, for instance, with regard to advertising services the ECJ has held that the place of use and enjoyment is the country from which the advertising material is disseminated (Case 1/08 *Athesia Druck, para.* 29) regardless the recipients may be located throughout the world. The connecting factors may also be different in order to locate the use of services inside EU Member States or outside the EU. Moreover, EU Member States may only introduce rules to recapture VAT on those services initially supplied outside the EU while they are not obliged to do so in order to waive taxation. The criterion also puts the supplier into a difficult position as he is required to know where the services are actually being used in a way this can be proven to the tax authorities. Besides, the VAT Directive does not specify the consequences when the customer changes his mind once the service has been supplied (i.e., a service which was planned to be used outside the EU is finally used inside or in both places).[70]

Regarding the scope of application, the provision does not apply to electronic services where they are provided to nontaxable persons not established in the Community. On the other hand, according to Article 59b EC VAT Directive, the EU Member States must apply this rule to telecommunications and radio and television broadcasting services to nontaxable persons who are established, have their permanent address or usually reside in a EU Member State, by a taxable person who is established outside the Community or who has a fixed establishment outside from which the service is supplied, or who, in the absence of those has his permanent address or usually resides outside the Community. Therefore, all telecommunications and broadcasting services provided by non-EU suppliers to private individuals residing in the EU are subject to VAT.

12.5 THE PLACE OF IMPORTATION OF GOODS

The place of importation of goods is the EU Member State within whose territory the goods are located when they enter the Community (see Article 60 EC VAT

---

70. However, according to Art. 25 EC VAT implementing Regulation, any subsequent changes to the use of the service received should not affect the determination of the place of supply, provided there is no abusive practice.

Directive). However, where, upon entry, goods which are not in free circulation are placed under one of the arrangements or situations referred to in Article 156 EC VAT Directive,[71] or under temporary importation arrangements with total exemption from import duty, or under external transit arrangements, the place of importation is the EU Member State within whose territory the goods cease to be covered by those arrangements or situations.[72] Similarly, where, on entry into the Community, goods from third territories, which are in free circulation, are placed under one of the arrangements or situations referred to in Articles 276 and 277 (basically, under a number of procedures equivalent to those applicable to imports of goods from third countries according to Article 156 EC VAT Directive, under a temporary importation arrangement with full exemption from import duties or the internal Community transit procedure), the place of importation is the EU Member State within whose territory the goods cease to be covered by those arrangements or situations.

---

71. Article 156 EC VAT Directive makes reference to those supplies of goods which are intended to be: a) presented to customs and, where applicable, placed in temporary storage; b) placed in a free zone or in a free warehouse; c) placed under customs warehousing arrangements or inward processing arrangements; d) admitted into territorial waters in order to be incorporated into drilling or production platforms, for purposes of the construction, repair, maintenance, alteration or fitting-out of such platforms, or to link such drilling or production platforms to the mainland; e) admitted into territorial waters for the fuelling and provisioning of drilling or production platforms.
72. According to the ECJ (Case 371/99 *Liberexim*), where goods transported by road under the external Community transit arrangements are placed in the Community market after a number of irregularities have been committed in respect of those goods in various Member States, the goods cease to be covered by those arrangements within the meaning of Art. 7(3) of the Sixth Directive 77/388/EEC, where the first operation which can be regarded as a removal of the goods from customs supervision was carried out.

SERIES ON INTERNATIONAL TAXATION

1. Alberto Xavier, *The Taxation of Foreign Investment in Brazil*, 1980 (ISBN 90-200-0582-0).
2. Hugh J. Ault & Albert J. Rädler, *The German Corporation Tax Law with 1980 Amendments*, 1981 (ISBN 90-200-0642-8).
3. Paul R. McDaniel & Hugh J. Ault, *Introduction to United States International Taxation*, 1981 (ISBN 90-6544-004-6).
4. Albert J. Rädler, *German Transfer Pricing/Prix de Transfer en Allemagne*, 1984 (ISBN 90-6544-143-3).
5. Paul R. McDaniel & Stanley S. Surrey, *International Aspects of Tax Expenditures: A Comparative Study*, 1985 (ISBN 90-654-4163-8).
6. Kees van Raad, *Nondiscrimination in International Tax Law*, 1986 (ISBN 90-6544-266-9).
7. Sijbren Cnossen (ed.), *Tax Coordination in the European Community*, 1987 (ISBN 90-6544-272-3).
8. Ben Terra, *Sales Taxation. The Case of Value Added Tax in the European Community*, 1989 (ISBN 90-6544-381-9).
9. Rutsel S.J. Martha, *The Jurisdiction to Tax in International Law: Theory and Practice of Legislative Fiscal Jurisdiction*, 1989 (ISBN 90-654-4416-5).
10. Paul R. McDaniel & Hugh J. Ault, *Introduction to United States International Taxation* (3rd revised edition), 1989 (ISBN 90-6544-423-8).
11. Manuel Pires, *International Juridicial Double Taxation of Income*, 1989 (ISBN 90-6544-426-2).
12. A.H.M. Daniels, *Issues in International Partnership Taxation*, 1991 (ISBN 90-654-4577-3).
13. Arvid A. Skaar, *Permanent Establishment: Erosion of a Tax Treaty Principle*, 1992 (ISBN 90-6544-594-3).
14. Cyrille David & Geerten Michielse (eds), *Tax Treatment of Financial Instruments*, 1996 (ISBN 90-654-4666-4).
15. Herbert H. Alpert & Kees van Raad (eds), *Essays on International Taxation*, 1993 (ISBN 90-654-4781-4).
16. Wolfgang Gassner, Michael Lang & Eduard Lechner (eds), *Tax Treaties and EC Law*, 1997 (ISBN 90-411-0680-4).
17. Glória Teixeira, *Taxing Corporate Profits in the EU*, 1997 (ISBN 90-411-0703-7).
18. Michael Lang et al. (eds), *Multilateral Tax Treaties*, 1998 (ISBN 90-411-0704-5).
19. Stef van Weeghel, *The Improper Use of Tax Treaties*, 1998 (ISBN 90-411-0737-1).
20. Klaus Vogel (ed.), *Interpretation of Tax Law and Treaties and Transfer Pricing in Japan and Germany*, 1998 (ISBN 90-411-9655-2).
21. Bertil Wiman (ed.), *International Studies in Taxation: Law and Economics; Liber Amicorum Leif Mutén*, 1999 (ISBN 90-411-9692-7).

22. Alfonso J. Martín Jiménez, *Towards Corporate Tax Harmonization in the European Community*, 1999 (ISBN 90-411-9690-0).
23. Ramon J. Jeffery, *The Impact of State Sovereignty on Global Trade and International Taxation*, 1999 (ISBN 90-411-9703-6).
24. A.J. Easson, *Taxation of Foreign Direct Investment*, 1999 (ISBN 90-411-9741-9).
25. Marjaana Helminen, *The Dividend Concept in International Tax Law: Dividend Payments Between Corporate Entities*, 1999 (ISBN 90-411-9765-6).
26. Paul Kirchhof, Moris Lehner, Kees van Raad, Arndt Raupach & Michael-Rodi (eds), *International and Comparative Taxation: Essays in Honour of Klaus Vogel*, 2002 (ISBN 90-411-9841-5).
27. Krister Andersson, Peter Melz & Christer Silfverberg (eds), *Liber Amicorum Sven-Olof Lodin*, 2001 (ISBN 90-411-9850-4).
28. Juan Martín Jovanovich, *Customs Valuation and Transfer Pricing: Is It Possible to Harmonize Customs and Tax Rules?*, 2002 (ISBN 90-411-9888-1).
29. Stefano Simontacchi, *Taxation of Capital Gains under the OECD Model Convention: With Special Regard to Immovable Property*, 2007 (ISBN 978-90-411-2549-1).
30. Michael Lang, Josef Schuch, & Claus Staringer (eds), *Tax Treaty Law and EC Law*, 2007 (ISBN 978-90-411-2629-0).
31. Duncan Bentley, *Taxpayers' Rights: Theory Origin and Implementation*, 2007 (ISBN 978-90-411-2650-4).
32. Sergio André Rocha, *Interpretation of Double Taxation Conventions: General Theory and Brazilian Perspective*, 2008 (ISBN 978-90-411-2822-5).
33. Robert F. van Brederode, *Systems of General Sales Taxation: Theory, Policy and Practice*, 2009 (ISBN 978-90-411-2832-4).
34. John G. Head & Richard Krever (eds), *Tax Reform in the 21st Century: A Volume in Memory of Richard Musgrave*, 2009 (ISBN 978-90-411-2829-4).
35. Jens Wittendorff, *Transfer Pricing and the Arm's Length Principle in International Tax Law*, 2010 (ISBN 978-90-411-3270-3).
36. Marjaana Helminen, *The International Tax Law Concept of Dividend*, 2010 (ISBN 978-90-411-3206-2).
37. Robert F. van Brederode (ed.), *Immovable Property under VAT: A Comparative Global Analysis*, 2011 (ISBN 978-90-411-3126-3).
38. Dennis Weber & Stef van Weeghel, *The 2010 OECD Updates: Model Tax Convention & Transfer Pricing Guidelines – A Critical Review*, 2011 (ISBN 978-90-411-3812-5).
39. Yariv Brauner & Martin James Mcmahon, Jr. (eds), *The Proper Tax Base: Structural Fairness from an International and Comparative Perspective— Essays in Honour of Paul McDaniel*, 2012 (ISBN 978-90-411-3286-4).